GRADUATE PROGRAMS IN
HUMAN RESOURCE
MANAGEMENT
2ND EDITION

SOCIETY FOR
HUMAN
RESOURCE
MANAGEMENT

SHRM FOUNDATION
SOCIETY FOR HUMAN RESOURCE MANAGEMENT

Acknowledgments

The SHRM Foundation thanks the following members of the Advisory Committee for their advice and expertise in developing the first national directory of HR master's degree programs.

Bruce J. Avolio, Ph.D.

Janet Barnes-Farrell, Ph.D.

Talya Bauer, Ph.D.

John Boudreau, Ph.D.

Daniel Cable, Ph.D.

Rosana Canton, SPHR

Angelo DeNisi, Ph.D.

Christy DeVader, Ph.D., SPHR

Louis R. Forbringer, Ph.D., SPHR

Robert Heneman, Ph.D.

Mark A. Huselid, Ph.D.

Steven Jacobs, SPHR

K. Michele Kacmar, Ph.D.

Tom Lee, Ph.D.

Beth McFarland, CAE

William Murry, Ph.D.

Dane Partridge, Ph.D.

Sara Rynes, Ph.D.

Susan Sands

Dale Scharinger, Ph.D., SPHR

Jerry Schoenfeld, Ph.D.

The SHRM Foundation is pleased to dedicate this directory to all human resource students and professionals pursuing a master's degree.

The data included in this directory is self-reported by colleges and universities. All content is for informational purposes only and is not to be construed as an endorsement of any college, university or degree program profiled in this publication. The Society for Human Resource Management and the SHRM Foundation make no warranties, claims or guarantees in regard to accuracy, completeness or currency of information and cannot accept responsibility for any errors or omissions or any liability resulting from the use or misuse of any such information.

The Society for Human Resource Management (SHRM) is the world's largest association devoted to human resource management. Representing more than 165,000 individual members, the Society serves the needs of HR professionals by providing the most essential and comprehensive set of resources available. As an influential voice, SHRM is committed to advancing the human resource profession to ensure that HR is an essential and effective partner in developing and executing organizational strategy. Founded in 1948, SHRM currently has more than 500 affiliated chapters within the United States and members in more than 120 countries. Visit SHRM Online at www.shrm.org.

The SHRM Foundation is a 501(c)(3) charitable organization affiliated with SHRM. The Foundation sponsors leading edge research and education to advance the HR profession.

For more information, contact: SHRM Foundation, 1800 Duke Street, Alexandria, VA 22314 Phone: (703) 548-3440 Fax: (703) 535-6473 www.shrm.org/foundation

Library of Congress Cataloging-in-Publication Data

Graduate programs in human resource management : a guide for students, faculty & employers / edited by Beth M. McFarland.— 2nd ed.
        p. cm.
Rev. ed. of : Directory of graduate programs in human resource management. 2000.
Includes bibliographical references and index.
ISBN 1-58644-026-8
1. Personnel management—Study and teaching (Graduate)—United States—Directories.
2. Universities and colleges—United States—Graduate work—Directories. I. McFarland, Beth M., 1963- II.
Society for Human Resource Management (U.S.) III. Directory of graduate programs in human resource management.
 HF5549.15 G73 2002
 658.3'0071'173—dc21

                                                                           2002006920

Contents

Appendixes

Indexes

Introduction

"The window of opportunity for HR to provide leadership in their organizations has never been greater."

Charles F. Nielson
Principal, Cabot Advisory Group

The SHRM Foundation is pleased to present this second edition *Graduate Programs in Human Resource Management*. To assist you in selecting the right degree program, this updated, comprehensive directory includes detailed profiles on 114 HR-related master's programs, two quick-reference tables (listing institutions by state and by degree offered), supplementary articles and a list of additional resources. This information provides both a useful overview of the various degree options and specific details on each program listed.

As the role of human resources continues to evolve, many HR practitioners find that they need to enhance their skills to become true strategic leaders. Earning a master's degree can prepare you to meet new challenges, take the next step in your career and increase your value to your organization.

The future of the human resource management profession is bright, because more companies understand that their workforce is, in fact, their most valuable asset. Employees already provide their organizations with a competitive advantage, and they will be even more important in the coming decade. Here's why:

- **We live and work in a knowledge-based economy.** Because knowledge resides with the individual, people are a company's key resource for innovation and growth in the 21st century.

- **Successful organizations are distinguished by their highly competent and motivated workforce.** Performance management and talent management programs, particularly recruiting, employee development and the retention of knowledge workers, will be essential for organizational success.

- **Mergers and acquisitions will continue to represent the fastest way for companies to grow.** Change management for newly formed, expanded or consolidated organizations and their employees will take on even greater significance. Individuals, teams and organizations will need to become more innovative and agile in responding to the rapid changes occurring in the global marketplace.

These critical "people" issues place human resources at the center of an organization's strategy for success. Consequently, HR professionals have an unprecedented opportunity to provide strategic leadership to their organizations. This will require us to adopt a different mind-set and acquire new skills. Specifically:

- HR leaders must understand how a business operates and have a thorough grasp of both HR and business fundamentals. This knowledge must then be applied to manage organizational culture and maximize employee contributions.

- HR leaders need to act as entrepreneurs. That means being proactive, "thinking outside the box," aligning the HR strategy with the larger organizational direction and having the courage and communication skills needed to lead their organizations successfully.

To enhance the effectiveness of HR professionals and the value of the human resource management profession, the SHRM Foundation engages in the following initiatives:

- **Leading-edge research.** Current and recent projects have explored topics such as HR measurement, linking human capital to bottom-line results, the impact of technology on the HR function, globalization and the changing role of the HR professional.

- **Thought Leaders retreat.** This annual gathering brings together HR leaders and practitioners to discuss critical issues on the horizon. The insight generated by these retreats is then disseminated to the HR community.

- *Making Mergers Work: The Strategic Importance of People.* Produced with Towers Perrin, this highly acclaimed business book is an excellent resource for understanding how HR can add value in every stage of the merger and acquisition process.

Many Foundation volunteers and staff have worked hard to compile *Graduate Programs in Human Resource Management*, and their names are listed in the acknowledgments section of this book. However, two individuals deserve special recognition. This publication would not have been created if not for the vision and dedication of Bruce Avolio, Ph.D., past SHRM Foundation president. Dr. Avolio identified the need for this product, led the development process, generated support and made it happen.

I would also like to thank Beth McFarland, CAE, manager of special projects for the SHRM Foundation, for her outstanding work in putting together this expanded second edition. As former manager of the SHRM student program, she has a unique understanding of the needs and concerns of both traditional-age and adult HR students.

Finally, I want to thank each one of you for your commitment to lifelong learning. The SHRM Foundation is proud to be your partner in the pursuit of HR excellence.

Samuel J. Bresler, SPHR, CCP
President
2002 SHRM Foundation Board of Directors

How to Use the Directory

Graduate Programs in Human Resource Management is a centralized source of information on HR-related master's programs in the United States. This data can be used in a number of ways: Students and professionals selecting a master's degree program will find a broad range of information and a good overview of the various degree options together in one place. College recruiters deciding which campuses to target can use this publication to locate master's programs with an emphasis on the skills most needed by their organizations, such as labor relations or global business. College or university professors and administrators who are creating a new HR master's program or modifying an existing degree program will consult this directory to benchmark and learn about other programs.

The directory presents detailed information on 114 master's degree programs. The data contained in this publication is self-reported by the universities via a 13-page survey completed during the 2001–2002 academic year. It is for informational purposes only. Any college or university with an HR-related master's degree program was eligible for inclusion in this directory and the universities were not charged a fee to participate. Inclusion in this publication should not be construed as an endorsement by the Society for Human Resource Management (SHRM) or SHRM Foundation of any college, university or degree program. Participation is voluntary, and it can therefore not be assumed that a degree program not included in this publication is of any lesser quality than those listed here.

For ease of use, the survey data has been organized into the sections listed below. The following information explains the meaning of the data in each category, how it was compiled and how the information can best be used.

Location; School/Department
After the name of the institution, each profile lists the city and state where the college or university is physically located. Since many programs offer online courses and distance learning, do not assume that a program is inaccessible because it is located far away. A list of programs offering these learning options can be found in the Index. After the school's location, a specific college or department may be listed. If provided by the institution, this information tells you where the specific degree program is located within the college or university. This information gives you an important clue to the program's focus. If the program is part of the business school, it will likely be taught from a business perspective; if the program is located in the school of psychology, you can expect a greater focus on understanding individual behavior in the context of scientific and research data.

Degree
HR-related master's degree programs vary widely in their scope, required courses and focus. If you are seeking a broad-based business degree, then an MBA might be right for you.

If you want only in-depth HR knowledge, then an MS-HRM degree is probably the answer. This book profiles many different types of degrees. For more information on the various HR degrees available, see the section titled "Which Degree Is Right for You?" on page 9. To view a list of colleges and universities by degree type, see the table titled "Programs by Degree Type" on page 21. Since the content of degree programs varies widely from school to school, be sure to look closely at the required and popular elective courses listed for each program to get a better idea of each program's emphasis.

University Overview/Program Description

This section provides a quick overview or snapshot of each college and university. When reviewing programs, this information can help you get a big picture view of the institution.

Degree Requirements

Use the information here to find out how many credits must be completed to earn a degree, whether transfer credits are accepted and the average and maximum amount of time it takes to complete the master's program. Full-time programs can generally be completed in as little as one year or as long as four years. Part-time programs can take from one and one-half years to four years or longer to finish. Some programs require as few as 10 courses to complete the degree (three credit hours per course, on average); some (often MBA programs) require as many as 25 courses. Most programs will consider the transfer of a limited number of graduate credits from other accredited institutions.

Tuition

Tuition figures are presented in two ways: per year and per credit hour. Information may be listed in one or both of these formats depending on what the institution supplied. Both in-state and out-of-state tuition rates are listed for institutions that provided this information. While researching universities, you will consider whether you would prefer a large research institution or a smaller private school. Tuition costs for out-of-state students at public, state-funded institutions can be triple the cost for in-state students. However, some graduate programs offer in-state tuition for graduate students. Private institutions generally have higher tuition rates, but charge the same fees for in-state and out-of-state students.

Program Delivery

The term "traditional day program" means a majority of master's students are enrolled full-time and attend day classes on a traditional college schedule. A "nontraditional program" provides more flexibility in when and how students attend class. To accommodate working students, classes may be held in the evening, on weekends or even online. Most of the students in a non-traditional program attend part-time, and they tend to be working adults juggling multiple work/family commitments. Other program formats, including study abroad, distance learning and executive education, are also noted in this section. See the index at the back of this publication for lists of universities by program delivery type.

Faculty

The number of faculty in the degree program is a good indication of the size of the program and the breadth of perspective you will be exposed to. Full-time faculty are more likely to be involved in ongoing research while part-time faculty are more likely to be working or consulting outside the university. The faculty to student ratio can give you an indication of how much personal attention you can expect to receive in the program, and the primary teaching methods will give you an idea of what the classes are like. "Faculty involvement" refers to faculty members being actively involved in outside academic and professional organizations. This involvement helps them to maintain a big picture perspective of the field and to stay current on the latest research and business issues. The "top 5 faculty publications" section refers to articles written by faculty members that have been published in academic journals or other publications. If you have a specific area of interest, you may want to look for faculty members who specialize in this area and involve students in their research or consulting work.

Students

"Total enrollment" should refer to enrollment in the degree program only. However, some institutions may include the total enrollment for the college or department in this number, so it is best to verify this with the university itself. The full-time enrollment number, the number of students working full time and the average age of the students tells you whether the program is primarily a traditional day program or a non-traditional program for working adults. The demographic information gives you a good picture of the diversity of the student body. The minimum admission requirements and average student profile, where supplied, offer you a benchmark to help you determine your competitiveness as an applicant to that program.

Institutions use many criteria in the decision to admit graduate students. Undergraduate grade point averages (UGPA's) and entrance exams are very important; however, they do not give the whole picture. Letters of recommendation, personal statements, work experience and even personal interviews often influence the decision. Communicating with admissions directors will help you understand how to make yourself a more attractive candidate to the degree programs. *Do not assume you are not qualified for a program based on the minimums presented here.* Be sure to verify this information by speaking to an admissions representative at any university you would like to attend.

Program Resources

This section gives you an overview of the additional resources available to supplement a degree program. At some universities you are now required to have your own computer to complete assignments or access information. Some non-traditional programs may offer access to online library facilities but have no physical library. More programs now offer assistance in preparing for professional certification in human resource management. See the section in this directory on "HRCI Certification: Your Professional Edge" for information on HR certification. For a complete list of programs that offer certification preparation, see the Index.

Many programs have SHRM student chapters or affiliations with local professional SHRM chapters. Appendix D lists the location of more than 370 SHRM student chapters in the United States, Puerto Rico and Guam. These chapters will help you to develop your HR professional networks, and they also encourage preparation for professional certification through the Human Resource Certification Institute (HRCI).

While researching programs, you should investigate financial aid opportunities such as fellowships, scholarships, assistantships and loan packages. Fellowships are awards based on academic merit and sometimes include tuition and fee waivers. These packages range in value between $4,000 and $20,000 annually and are generally available only to full-time students.

Scholarship awards come from many sources and generally do not include tuition packages. They may be awarded to full-time or part-time students and can be based on many factors (including academic merit and community service). Scholarship awards can range from $500 to $5,000 per academic year.

Assistantships are generally of two types, research and teaching. They are usually half-time appointments (20 hours of work per week) and almost always include tuition and fee waivers. These are generally available to full-time students, and their value can range from $6,000 to $22,000.

The SHRM Foundation funds two scholarships for HR graduate students. Visit the Foundation's web page (**www.shrm.org/foundation**) and click on "Education Grants & Scholarships" for application information. Scholarship applicants must be national student members of SHRM.

Curriculum

Both required and popular elective courses are listed in this section. Reviewing the list of courses that make up the degree provides a good overview of what you will learn in the program. Your career aspirations should determine whether you will look for a well-rounded generalist curriculum or a more specialized program. While some programs have very structured curriculum requirements with few electives, others have only a few required courses and offer a broad range of electives to allow you to tailor the degree to your needs. Where available, career tracks and concentrations within the degree program are listed. If an internship is required as part of the program, that is noted as well. For more details on specific program requirements, visit the university web sites listed in the "Contact Information" section of each profile.

Career Services

Since traditional students go to school full time and have less work experience, traditional day programs tend to emphasize internship and job placement services. An active career services office will work with anywhere from 10 to 100 college recruiters annually who conduct campus information sessions and recruiting activities. Approximately 75% of the students in these programs compete for jobs in the national labor market, while the remaining students compete in international or local labor markets. Most traditional day programs collect placement data that include placement percentages and salary information. Your research on such programs should include a list of companies that recruit and other placement statistics.

Since nontraditional programs are designed for the working professional, they are less focused on job placement and rarely collect placement and salary data. Most of the nontraditional programs surveyed did offer some type of career services activities to their students. These opportunities include alumni networks, resume services, interview training, mentoring and online job posting (which are also available in most traditional programs). It is important to point out that the placement information for schools offering the MBA with HR concentration degree includes all MBA graduates in the class. That means the average starting MBA salary will also include those specializing in finance, marketing, computer science and other management areas. Starting salaries for MBA/HRM graduates might be lower than the figures listed here, so we recommend that you verify these salary numbers with the universities.

Points of Excellence

This section provides an opportunity for each university to highlight something unique or special about its program. Highlights could include faculty research, curriculum content, teaching format, career services or other program activities.

Contact Information

Faculty and administrative contact information is included to assist you in contacting a college or university.

Admission Deadlines

This section lists the deadlines for admission. For programs you are interested in, we encourage you to verify this information directly with the university. Many programs now offer online admissions packages. If a program offers an online application, that is noted here as well.

In conclusion, this directory represents a valuable first step in identifying HR master's degree program options. However, it should not be relied upon as your sole source of research. Since degree programs constantly change, we encourage you to consult university web sites and contact admissions offices for the most current information. See the "Additional Resources" section in the back of this book for a list of other helpful web sites to visit. If you are planning to begin a graduate degree, we wish you well on your experience. We welcome your feedback and comments on this publication. Please use the Feedback Form located in the back of the book to provide us with your suggestions. Thank you for using this directory.

The Value of a Graduate Degree in HRM

By Rosana Canton, MA/IR

More than ever, human resource professionals are being challenged to build a competitive advantage for their employers through effective HR delivery systems. This requires practitioners to move beyond the traditional human resource focus of compliance, administration and policy management. Today's practitioners must expand their competencies in project management, strategic development and leadership.

Continuous professional development will be required to establish credibility and create value in the fast-changing global business environment. Obtaining a graduate degree in human resource management is one way to prepare for a higher-level career in strategic HRM. A graduate degree can supplement existing HR knowledge while providing a solid foundation in the more strategic aspects of human capital management.

What to Expect in Graduate School

HR graduate programs go beyond the basic concepts taught in undergraduate courses and professional certification programs. A master's degree helps you to develop the knowledge and skills necessary to design effective strategies for selecting, rewarding, motivating and leading employees. In graduate school, you'll work with diverse professionals—including program alumni, academics and peers—to analyze and synthesize opportunities to add value while operating under internal and external constraints.

Benefits for Traditional-Age Students

For traditional full-time day students, the value of an advanced degree in an HR-related subject is immediately tangible: An HR professional with a master's degree has a starting salary of up to twice the starting salary of someone with a bachelor's degree. A master's degree also affords graduates greater opportunity to compete in a global labor market where their careers will have few boundaries.

Your master's degree will lead to more challenging work assignments and greater opportunities for advancement. You will be expected to contribute to your organization in a more strategic way. In addition, your graduate school experience will link you with a mutually beneficial network of HR professionals, alumni and colleagues.

Benefits for Working Professionals

For working HR professionals, obtaining a master's degree can enhance your credibility and open doors to new career opportunities. It can help you understand how business decisions are made and how the HR function affects an organization's bottom line. Many human resource professionals realize at some point in their career that the jobs they aspire to require an advanced degree. Obtaining your master's degree can help you move beyond basic HR administration into a more exciting strategic role. Advanced education can provide new insights into the origins of employment practices and the theory and research behind them. Employers often reinforce the importance of a graduate degree by recognizing new competencies and promoting graduates into strategic positions where they are able to create greater value for their organizations. At any stage in your career, whether you are a junior-, mid-, or senior-level professional, a graduate degree in HR can benefit both you and your employer.

Conclusion

Obtaining a master's degree is an effective way for students or working professionals to upgrade their knowledge and broaden their future career options. Whether you decide to pursue a master's degree full time or part time, you and your organization will benefit immensely from your increased knowledge and competencies. You will develop yourself and enhance your value as a strategic HR professional in today's rapidly changing and competitive global business environment where "knowledge is power."

The Future of Human Resource Management

By Dave Patel, Manager, Workplace Trends and Forecasting
Abridged and reprinted from the SHRM Workplace Visions *newsletter, Issue 6, 2001*

"HR will no doubt continue to shrink in size, as have all staff functions in business. But it will most certainly become more important than it was this past generation."

Peter Cappelli,
George W. Taylor Professor of Management,
The Wharton School, University of Pennsylvania

The future of human resource management encompasses many things: outsourcing of administrative tasks, using technology to make HR transactions available directly to employees, effectively managing talent by designing flexibility and speed into policy architecture, developing business/financial literacy and creating unique corporate cultures through organizational development. All of these practices may require many changes to business as usual, and those changes may have to come with unprecedented speed. Earning an advanced degree can help HR professionals to actively lead and participate in these workplace changes.

Societal and economic changes in demographics, science and technology, globalization, and politics will play a significant role in the future course of human resources. An aging but healthy population may have vastly different expectations from younger people just graduating from school. The changing nature of work and the move toward a service economy may also affect how and where work gets done. Technology will continue to reshape the work of HR practitioners, just as it has revolutionized the way all employees do their jobs. And the inexorable move toward a global, interdependent economy, through all its fits and starts, may present many unique challenges and opportunities. Taken together, these forces may substantially accelerate the pace of change, and businesses that can master change may be at a distinct competitive advantage.

"The ultimate goal...is to have an HR team that is able to help their organizations adapt to the environment faster than the competition, thereby increasing the probability of business survival." *Steve Miranda, Vice President, Human Resources, Lucent Technologies Worldwide Services*

Demographics
Workplace demographics will change considerably over the next ten years as the U.S. population diversifies along age, gender and ethnic lines.

The U.S. Census Bureau estimates that by 2010, there will be about 67 million people 65 years of age or older living in the United States. The population age 85 and above is currently the fastest growing segment of the older population. But the older people of tomorrow may be much different in some respects than older people in the past, as advances in medicine, cultural shifts in lifestyles and financial worries radically change traditional notions of retirement. The aging population may provide employers with a great source of labor, but may also present huge challenges for health and elder care costs, and training with emerging technologies.

Women are asserting themselves into the workforce as never before. They outnumber men in earning bachelor's and law degrees, and account for 40 percent of doctorates. Still, societal norms about child rearing continue to play a significant part in women's careers. Members of Generation Y, the most technology-adept generation to come along, may question fundamental concepts of work because their ideas about work may fit with contingent work rather than traditional notions of work, leading to wholesale changes in how we work, and may also entail the redesign of compensation and benefits policies. The Census Bureau estimates that the nation's foreign-born population in 2000 was 28.4 million, about 1 in 10 U.S. residents, and the Population Reference Bureau forecasts that by the year 2030, the United States may be 24 percent Hispanic and 12 percent Asian.

The Role of Technology
From automated robots on factory floors to personal communications devices for knowledge workers, the use of technology has created a 24/7 economy ever bent on increasing productivity. Technology enables workers access to more information, including where to find that next job and how much of a salary increase to ask for, as well as providing employers with electronic monitoring capability.

Technology is also changing the nature of work, as project-based work done by virtual teams, sometimes based around the world, challenges age-old concepts of 9-to-5 work and two weeks of vacation. Technology may also spawn a generation of contingent workers, the so-called "free agents," whose interest and loyalty lie primarily with the type of work rather than with a particular employer.

In addition, labor forces may increasingly include low- and semi-skilled workers who may be unknowledgeable and uncomfortable with technology, along with knowledge workers providing professional services who are entirely reliant upon and comfortable with technology.

The changes brought about by demographics and technology will create a vastly more different and diverse workforce in the future. For HR, the key to creating and maintaining cohesive and productive workforces may require abandoning traditional human resource practices and allowing for extreme flexibility in all areas of workplace policies.

The role that technology can play in helping HR professionals capture and manage information—both the mundane and strategic—is staggering. Technology-driven innovation, combined with aggressive new entrants into the outsourcing market, will fundamentally change the way HR work is accomplished. There are at least three important catalysts for change operating in the market now:

- **Self-service.** Increasingly, employees will be able to conduct HR-related transactions through self-service. Managers will have desktop access to the kinds of information now provided by HR.

- **Call centers.** Services provided through call centers will become more sophisticated. Most generalist work will be handled through call centers.

- **Outsourcing.** There are outsourcing alternatives for every product and service now delivered by HR—including the option to outsource the entire function.

The Impact of Globalization

The complex interdependence of a global economy is evident in the movement of stock markets around the world. Changes in socioeconomic patterns, demographic changes or public policies in one part of the world can have a direct impact thousands of miles away. Globalization also presents a set of unique challenges and opportunities for employers. While the marketplace for goods, services and labor is now worldwide, competition for those same goods, services and labor is also worldwide, presenting employers with razor thin margins and little room for error.

Human resource professionals may operate under the same constraints and opportunities, as the pool of available talent grows but brings with it a new set of cultural expectations.

The New HR Professional

The primary responsibility for future HR professionals may become talent management. This area will involve traditional staffing concerns, but may also incorporate specific functions such as operating compensation, benefits and work/life programs, addressing poor performance and managing an overall organizational development program that provides continuous training. This holistic approach may in turn create a competitive advantage through the establishment of unique corporate cultures.

"In the new world of business we will find that competing for employees is often more difficult than competing for customers, building employee loyalty is as important as building customer loyalty, and treating employees right is the key to treating shareholders right." *Libby Sartain, SPHR, CCP, Senior Vice President and Chief People, Yahoo!*

All this won't happen through active involvement in the administration of workplace policies. Rather, much of the present HR function will be outsourced, made directly available to employees through the use of technology, or delegated to line managers. The focus for internal human resource practitioners will be on creating a work culture that nurtures talent by offering best-fit employment packages, rather than one-size-fits-all packages, by providing the freedom and responsibility needed by skilled workers and instilling a cohesive loyalty into diverse workforces.

The key for human resource professionals going forward may involve becoming true advocates of human capital. To do this, they will need to become adept at budgetary and financial goals and become knowledgeable about products, markets and strategies so that they are better able to coordinate with line managers to bring aboard and manage the talent needed to compete in global markets. By shedding much of the transactional work to vendors and to technology, they will be better positioned to manage talent and maximize performance.

The Bureau of Labor Statistics estimates that 19.1 million of the 19.5 million jobs created between 1998 and 2008 will be in the service sector. Though the service sector encompasses a huge array of industries and job functions, its focus on people binds it all together. From hospitality to high tech, the service industry depends on the knowledge and behavior of people, as opposed to the capabilities of machines. To ensure maximum productivity from all these knowledge workers, it may become imperative for human resource professionals to cast off much of their transactional duties so they can better focus on talent management and value creation.

Skills for Success

Sharafat Khan, partner and practice leader of strategy/organizational performance with Deloitte & Touche, suggests that to fulfill their new role, HR professionals will need the following skills:

- *Business/financial skills:* These include the ability to understand market/customer trends, develop financial forecasts, perform end-to-end financial transactions, analyze and solve complex financial/budget issues and assist line managers with budget preparation for HR services such as talent acquisition.

- *Professional/leadership skills:* These include the ability to respond with a high sense of urgency, understand and execute purchase orders, recognize and understand line manager drivers for success and leverage virtual technology to deliver solutions.

- *Functional skills:* These include the ability to execute projects on a real-time basis, translate people purchase orders to key HR actions, link people skills to work architecture to produce profits, provide credible advice and guidance to estimate scope of work, perform functional and business quality reviews, manage and integrate multiple projects and create options to pay for roles.

> *"The new goal for HR managers, indeed all managers, will be to manage markets. In the case of HR, the task is to anticipate what rapidly changing product markets and business strategies will require by way of human capabilities and find ways to deliver it."*
>
> *Peter Cappelli,*
> *George W. Taylor Professor of Management,*
> *The Wharton School, University of Pennsylvania*

HRCI Certification: Your Professional Edge

In addition to graduate studies, many HR professionals choose to broaden their human resource knowledge through professional certification. The Human Resource Certification Institute (HRCI), an affiliate of the Society for Human Resource Management (SHRM), certifies human resource professionals who have mastered the HR body of knowledge. HRCI offers two levels of professional certification: the PHR, "Professional in Human Resources," and the SPHR, "Senior Professional in Human Resources," designation. To earn your certification, you must have at least two years of exempt-level HR work experience and pass a 225-question multiple-choice exam. HRCI maintains the nationally recognized standards set by individuals working in the profession.

Though certification is not required to work in the HR field, professionals find that achieving certification benefits them in a number of ways. It provides an independent assessment of knowledge, similar to the CPA or bar exam for accountants and attorneys. As more HR practitioners become certified, the overall level of professionalism in the field increases, which in turn enhances the credibility and image of the profession. Human resource certification is a symbol of professional achievement. Beyond experience and education, the PHR or SPHR designation signifies that you have mastered the HR body of knowledge.

Since certification is voluntary, it demonstrates your motivation to employers and often provides an edge in the job market. As more employers turn to resume management systems and online recruitment, certification is increasingly used as a factor in narrowing the field of candidates for a position. Professional certification sends a clear message to your employer, your colleagues and the employees in your organization that you are challenging yourself to meet nationally recognized standards. Certification is not meant to replace or overshadow education or experience, but it does highlight your accomplishments and demonstrates that you have mastered the body of knowledge in all the core generalist areas of human resources.

Frequently Asked Questions
How do I decide whether I should take the PHR or SPHR exam?

Exams for both the PHR and SPHR require a minimum of two years of exempt-level HR experience. Although the eligibility requirement is the same, the focus of the certification levels is quite different. A candidate should choose the exam that most accurately reflects the type of experience he or she has. For example, the PHR exam focuses on the technical and operational aspects of HR, while the SPHR exam is more strategic and policy-oriented and requires more in-depth general management and applied HR knowledge.

HRCI strongly recommends that candidates attempting the PHR exam have two to four years of exempt-level HR experience, and that candidates attempting the SPHR exam have at least six years of exempt-level HR experience.

What if I don't have enough work experience to qualify for the PHR/SPHR exam?
You may be able to take the certification exam if you are an active student or recent graduate. Students and recent graduates are eligible to take the PHR exam no earlier than one year before their graduation date, and no later than one year after it. Upon passing the exam, the candidate is not considered a PHR until he or she gains two years of exempt-level work experience in the HR field. A current student or recent graduate who already has two years of exempt-level work experience may not take the exam under the student category.

Do I have to be a member of SHRM to become certified?
No. You do not have to be a member of SHRM in order to qualify for certification or to use the PHR or SPHR designations upon successful completion of the exam.

For more information on HRCI certification, visit **www.hrci.org**, *e-mail info@hrci.org or call (703) 548-3440.*

Which Degree Is Right for You?

As you look through this book, you will realize that there are a variety of degrees offered in the human resource field. Each degree program features its own combination of courses and overall emphasis, preparing students for slightly different career paths. To help you select the right degree program for your situation, we have categorized the degree programs into seven broad types.

No one program can be right for everyone. When selecting a program, consider your own background, your strengths and weaknesses, and your future career plans. For example, if you have an undergraduate degree in general business and you have selected human resources as your career, then a specialty degree such as an MS in HR would be a good choice to round out your education. However, if you majored in HR as an undergraduate and you would now like to learn more about general business, pursuing an MBA might open up new options for you.

The following is a general overview of each degree type. Keep in mind that there is considerable variation among the programs within each category, so an individual program may or may not fit this description. Use this information as a starting point to help you narrow your search. Next, consult the chart on "Programs by Degree Type" for a list of programs in each degree included in this book. For any program you are considering, review the required courses and most popular electives, as well as the points of excellence, to get a better sense of the degree's content and emphasis.

Business Administration (MBA, MBA/HRM, MBA/HR, MBA/HRIS). An MBA degree is highly respected in the business world. It demonstrates that graduates have a solid understanding of how a business operates and how HR fits into the big picture. An MBA program provides a broad overview of all business functions, including accounting, finance, marketing, strategy and human resources. This degree offers flexibility in future career options, as it will prepare you to move into other areas of business in addition to human resources. However, if you are seeking in-depth technical HR knowledge, then an MBA might not be the best choice for you. In most MBA programs, students take only a few HR courses. Obtaining professional HR certification in addition to an MBA is a good way to supplement a student's technical HR knowledge.

Human Resource Development (MSHRD, MAHRD). Traditionally, these programs place a strong emphasis on training and development and have a more narrow scope than a general business degree. Many HRD programs are very similar to the master's in human resources degree, as they provide in-depth technical knowledge of the HR function. Career paths include HR generalist, training specialist and consultant. These degree programs are often housed in the education or business school.

Human Resource Management (MSHRM, MSHR, MA/HRM, MHRM, MAHR, MAHRM, MHR). These programs provide a thorough base of knowledge in all aspects of human resource management and the employment relationship. Such a degree is a good choice for someone changing careers and entering human resources from another field or for someone interested in advancing within the HR profession. This program is also good preparation for achieving professional certification. Graduates may work as generalists or specialists in large organizations or as generalists in small to medium-size companies. Those who receive this degree are perceived as experts in human resources; however, they may or may not have acquired a broad understanding of general business concepts such as finance, marketing and accounting. To be credible in today's organizations, an individual must understand how the HR function fits into the overall mission of the organization and how HR adds value. If your HR master's program does not cover general business subjects, consider adding these as electives.

Industrial Relations/Labor Relations (MSILR, MILR, MAILR, MSIR, MIR, MALER; combined with HR: MHRIR, MA/HRIR, MLRHR, MLHR, MHRLR). Most industrial/labor relations programs were developed in the 1940s and 1950s in response to the growth of American labor unions. Though the names of these degrees have not changed, the curriculum has. In addition to the traditional focus on labor relations and collective bargaining, these programs now cover the full breadth of HR knowledge. For students interested in working in labor-management relations, this degree is the natural choice. It generally covers issues from both a management and an employee perspective giving graduates a thorough understanding of the employment relationship. Graduates work as HR generalists or as specialists in occupations such as labor relations, union representative or researcher, mediator or arbitrator. This can be a good complement to a law degree for people interested in working in labor and employment law.

Industrial/Organizational Psychology (MAP, MAOP, MA-I/O, MSIO, MAIOP, MSIOP, MAP-I/O, MSP-I/O). These programs focus on assessment, measurement and evaluation of human behavior in organizations. In "I/O psych" programs, courses like motivation, learning and cognition, and behavior modification help students to understand human behavior in the "real world." A "scientist/practitioner model" is developed, which helps the student understand the employee or person. Psychology students focus on data-based problem solving, and they rely on hard data to help avoid bias. Students develop strong data analysis skills in statistics and research and they learn to approach their work in a systematic and scientific way. The content area of I/O psychology covers a combination of HR, organizational behavior and some organizational theory, but I/O programs do not cover other areas of business such as accounting, marketing or economics. Education in HR topics is extensive, deep and technical. Career options include test validation, personnel assessment, selection, research and employment.

Management (MSM, MSOLE, MSM/HR/CM). These programs tend to focus on management and organizational behavior. They can be found in both business and arts schools. They are broader in scope than an HR master's degree; however, students will take fewer

HR courses. Career paths include management positions in public or private organizations.

Organizational Development/Organizational Behavior (MAOD, MOD, MSODA, MSHROD, MSOB). These degrees combine both organizational behavior and HR development, with an accent on organizational change. The programs are designed to provide theoretical, analytical, diagnostic and change agent skills. Courses focus on applied behavioral science areas such as leadership, motivation, planned change and research. This is a popular degree for those interested in consulting work.

Evaluating an Online Degree Program

By John Lavallee, former director, Champlain College Online

Today, many colleges and universities are adapting degree programs to meet the needs of adult students trying to fit ongoing education into already overcrowded schedules. For individuals who aren't able to travel to a regular college class across town, going to school online allows them to fit class time in during a weekend or after the kids have gone to bed.

"I really like taking classes online because I don't have to travel to class and I can arrange my schoolwork around my busy schedule," says Michael Pascal, an online student at Champlain College. "I look forward to completing my degree online." Champlain College, a four-year college located in Vermont, is a leader in distance learning and was one of the first to offer full degrees via the Internet.

Finding an online course can be a snap—there are many of them floating around in cyber-space and the number of choices is growing daily. But finding a quality online program where you can earn an entire degree is more of a challenge. When set up properly, with small classes and a high degree of student-instructor interaction, online degree programs are an excellent alternative to traditional classroom study.

To evaluate if online education is right for you, ask yourself the following questions:

Am I suited to online study?
Distance education is a terrific opportunity for disciplined and self-motivated students. Online students should be comfortable with computers and have good writing skills. Classwork can be completed at any time—day or night—so you choose when you're ready to "go to class." However, if you feel that you need more structure such as an assigned class time and place to keep you motivated, then online education might not be the best choice for you.

How will the program work?
Be sure to ask the college or university if you have the computer equipment needed to study online. When students connect to the Champlain College Online system via the World Wide Web, they find e-mail messages from their instructor and classmates in their mailbox or posted in the classroom forum. Lectures, exercises and assignments are presented via specially designed class web pages. Completed assignments are uploaded to the instructor electronically.

To determine the quality of an online degree program, consider the following questions before selecting a college or university:

Who is behind the program?

Today, online programs are offered by many sources, including for-profit learning centers and Internet start-up companies. Some may be new to the higher education market, so take time to find out whom you are dealing with. Online degree programs from established colleges are a good bet because online education is an extension of their educational mission.

Is the program self-paced or instructor-led?

Students in instructor-led programs tend to do better because they benefit from interacting with each other as new material is covered. Effective programs require the instructor to make a specified number of contacts with each student to ensure comprehension of the course material.

How big are the classes?

Class size is a key factor in effectiveness because it directly affects the level of interaction between students and instructors. Online classes can include up to several hundred students! However, the best programs limit class size to 15 to 20 students. As strange as it may seem, there is usually more interaction in a good online program than in many classroom settings because people are less intimidated about speaking up.

Is the program accredited?

Accreditation provides a stamp of approval for the education delivered. Make sure the degree is from a school that has been accredited by a regional accrediting organization. In New England, that can be the New England Association of Schools and Colleges, for example. To earn this accreditation, the online program must adhere to the same high standards as classroom programs.

Is the institution listed in college guidebooks?

Being included in standard college guidebooks like Peterson's or Barron's is another indicator of stability and accreditation. Also visit the college or university's web site, where you can get a sense of the overall institution. If the institution is an extension of a campus-based program, such as the Champlain College program, it is an indication of a solid track record in education.

Whom should I talk to?

Speak with the educators at the school you are considering. If you have any doubts about the quality of an online degree program, call and talk to the chairperson of the academic area you plan to study. Ask her to compare the institution's classroom program with its online degree program. If the content is the same and the online program culminates in the same degree as the traditional program, that is a good sign: The online program is probably an outgrowth of a campus-based program with a solid track record.

As with anything new, online education has its share of supporters and detractors, and both make some valid observations. But the undeniable fact is that online education is here to stay. Its convenience and accessibility are sure to make it an everyday part of the way many students learn in the near future. If you take the time to research various online programs and ask the right questions, you can feel confident that your degree program will offer you a quality learning experience.

Graduate School Application Timeline

Although some universities offer year-round "rolling" admissions, many programs still follow a traditional selection and admissions schedule. To allow yourself plenty of time to effectively research degree options, prepare for entrance exams, and apply to programs, follow this general timeline:

Summer:	Prepare for GRE or GMAT*
August:	Complete research on programs and select three programs to which you will apply
September:	Request letters of recommendation from professors or employers
October:	Complete GRE or GMAT exams
November:	Request personal interviews if appropriate
December:	Complete application packages
January:	Complete taxes so that financial aid forms can be completed. Mail application packages and follow up on receipt
March/April:	Admission decisions will be received
August/September:	Classes begin

Note: Taking prep courses greatly improves your score.

Degree Programs by State

State/University	Degree	Trad. Pgm	Enroll.	Even/ Wknd.	Avg. Age	Online	Tuition ($) In/Out State	Dist.	Starting Salary	Page #
ALABAMA										
Troy State University, Montgomery	MSHRM	N	75	Y	34	Y	2480/4960	Y	N/A	115
ARIZONA										
Troy State University, Western Region	MSHRM	N	30	Y	35	Y	6600	N	$30,000	116
CALIFORNIA										
Alliant International University	MAOP, MAOD	N	95	Y	33	N	500-650*	N	N/A	27
California State Polytechnic University, Pomona	MBA/HRM	N	600	Y	33	Y	1584/2568	Y in LA	$55,000	34
California State University, Fresno	MBA-HRM	N	134	Y	30	Y	1906/4428	Y	$52,000	35
California State University, Hayward	MBA-HRM	N	30	Y	32	N	2400/8000	N	N/A	36
California State University, Long Beach	MAIOP	Y	22	N	N/A	N	1822/3298	N	N/A	37
California State University, San Bernardino	MSIO	Y	12	N	28	N	292/502*	N	N/A	38
Chapman University, Bay Area	MSHR	N	N/A	Y	39	N	290*	N	N/A	42
Chapman University - Coachella Valley	MSHR	N	20	Y	35	N	265*	N	N/A	43
Chapman University	MSHR	N	301	Y	30	N	430*	Y	N/A	44
Chapman University, Sacramento	MSHR	N	9	Y	35	N	290*	N	N/A	45
Claremont Graduate University	MSHRD	N	36	N	30	N	1000*	N	$65,000	47
Monterey Institute of International Studies	MBA	Y	10	N	27	N	19988	N	N/A	81
San Francisco State University	MSP	N	38	Y	29	N	1904/3380	N	N/A	106
COLORADO										
Colorado State University – Denver Center	MSEHRS	N	60	Y	35	N	6500	N	N/A	49
University of Colorado at Denver	MSM	N	45	Y	30	Y	4428/15066	Y	N/A	122
CONNECTICUT										
University of New Haven	MA-I/O	N	80	Y	30	N	390*	N	$58,500	131
DIST. OF COLUMBIA										
American University	MSHRM	N	36	Y	37	N	18,160	N	N/A	28
National-Louis University	MS-HRM&D	N	22	Y	37	N	496*	N	N/A	83
FLORIDA										
Florida Institute of Technology	MSIOP	Y	25	Y	24	N	675*	N	N/A	55
National-Louis University	MS-HRM&D	N	22	Y	37	N	496*	N	N/A	83
Nova Southeastern University	MSHRM	N	108	Y	34	N	434*	Y	N/A	87
Rollins College	MHR	N	74	Y	36	Y	280*	N	N/A	97
University of Central Florida	MSM/HR/CM	N	40	Y	29	N	162/569*	N	N/A	120
University of North Florida	MHRM	N	30	Y	31	N	6000/18000	N	N/A	132
University of West Florida	MA-I/O	Y	29	N	N/A	N	156/535*	N	N/A	140
GEORGIA										
Georgia State University	MBA/HRM, MSHRM	N	66	Y	28	Y	130/518*	Y	$48,200	57
Kennesaw State University	MBA	Y	863	Y	32	Y	2648/9158	N	N/A	68
National-Louis University	MS-HRM&D	N	22	Y	37	N	496*	N	N/A	83
Troy State University, Ft. Benning	MSHRM	N	100	Y	N/A	Y	4350	Y	N/A	114

Degree Programs by State

DEGREE PROGRAMS BY STATE

State/University	Degree	Trad. Pgm	Enroll.	Even/ Wknd.	Avg. Age	Online	Tuition ($) In/Out State	Dist.	Starting Salary	Page #
HAWAII										
Hawaii Pacific University	MA/HRM	Y	1200	Y	30	N	410*	N	$54,600	58
University of Hawaii at Manoa	MHRM	N	N/A	Y	N/A	N	14000	N	N/A	124
ILLINOIS										
DePaul University	MBA, MSHR	N	4	Y	26	N	$362-$600*	N	N/A	52
Illinois Institute of Technology	MSPHRD	N	11	Y	N/A	N	590*	N	N/A	60
Keller Graduate School of Mgmt.	MHRM	N	6900	Y	34	Y	1420	Y	$63,000	66
Loyola University Chicago	MSHR, MSIR	N	200	Y	28	N	594*	Y	$65,000	71
National-Louis University	MS-HRM&D	N	22	Y	37	N	496*	N	N/A	83
Roosevelt University	MAP	N	70	Y	27	N	N/A	N	N/A	98
University of Illinois, Urbana-Champaign	MHRIR	Y	125	N	25	N	2121/5876	N	$58,000	127
INDIANA										
Indiana Institute of Technology	MBA/HRM	N	350	Y	40	N	250*	Y	N/A	62
Purdue University	MSHRM	Y	50	Y	26	N	4560/8996	Y	$60,000	92
IOWA										
Iowa State University	MSIR, MBA/HRM	Y	32	Y	25	N	3702/10898	Y	$45,000	64
KENTUCKY										
Western Kentucky University	MAP-I/O	Y	18	N	27	N	3044	N	$47,000	155
MARYLAND										
Towson University	MAHRD	Y	150	Y	N/A	Y	4336/9940	Y	$38,000	112
University of Baltimore	MS-I/O	Y	67	Y	33	N	7396/10708	N	N/A	119
University of Maryland	MBA-HC	Y	1100	Y	27	N	10798/15424	Y	$59,700	128
Western Maryland College	MSHRD	N	43	Y	31	N	240*	N	N/A	156
MICHIGAN										
Eastern Michigan University	MSHROD	N	50	Y	28	Y	215/440*	Y	$45,000	53
Marygrove College	MA-HRM	N	63	Y	32	N	360*	N	N/A	74
Michigan State University	MLRHR	Y	125	Y	27	N	244/494*	N	$65,500	78
MINNESOTA										
Capella University	MS O&M-HRM	N	125	Y	45	Y	325*	Y	N/A	39
Minnesota State University Mankato	MAIOP	Y	21	Y	24	N	3974/5980	N	$46,000	80
University of Minnesota	MA-HRIR	Y	240	Y	26	N	6785/12535	Y	$62,400	129
University of St. Thomas	MBA/HRM	Y	260	Y	33	Y	480*	Y	$54,000	134
MISSOURI										
National-Louis University	MS-HRM&D	N	22	Y	37	N	496*	N	N/A	83
Southwest Missouri State University	MSIOP	Y	20	N	N/A	N	2664/5328	N	$46,700	107
Washington University	MAHRM	N	50	Y	26	N	270*	N	N/A	151
Webster University-Ozarks Region	MAHR, MAHRD, MBAHRM, MBAHRD	N	132	Y	37	Y	345*	N	N/A	152

17

Degree Programs by State

State/University	Degree	Trad. Pgm	Enroll.	Even/ Wknd.	Avg. Age	Online	Tuition ($) In/Out State	Dist.	Starting Salary	Page #
MISSOURI continued										
Webster University - St. Louis	MAHRM	N	250	Y	27	Y	398*	N	N/A	153
MONTANA										
Troy State University, Western Region	MSHRM	N	30	Y	35	Y	6600	N	$30,000	116
NEBRASKA										
Nebraska Methodist College	MSHP	N	24	Y	33	Y	385*	Y	N/A	84
NEW JERSEY										
Fairleigh Dickinson University	MBA/HRM	Y	47	Y	30	N	550*	N	$50,000	54
Rutgers University	MHRM	Y	160	Y	30	N	7954/11704	Y	$59,900	99
NEW MEXICO										
Troy State University, Western Region	MSHRM	N	30	Y	35	Y	6600	N	$30,000	116
NEW YORK										
Baruch College, CUNY	MBA/HRM	Y	75	Y	N/A	N	6000/11,400	Y	$65,000	30
Baruch College, CUNY	MSILR	Y	75	Y	N/A	N	4200/5820	Y	$65,000	30
Cornell University	MILR	Y	140	N	28	N	13910	N	$69,400	50
Long Island University	MSHR	N	25	Y	27	N	505*	N	N/A	70
Manhattanville College	MSOMHR	N	180	Y	32	N	450*	Y	N/A	72
Mercy College	MSHRM	N	232	Y	35	N	435*	Y	N/A	77
New School University	MSHRM	N	215	Y	30	Y	690*	Y	$73,500	85
New York Institute of Technology	MSHRM/LR	N	140	Y	31	Y	545*	Y	32,000-40,000	86
Polytechnic University	MSHRM, MSOB	N	30	Y	30	N	695*	N	N/A	91
St. John Fisher College	MSHRD	N	42	Y	35	Y	465*/ N/A	Y	$40,000	102
St. Joseph's College	MSM	N	136	Y	N/A	N	399*	Y	N/A	103
University of Albany	MBA/HRIS	Y	20	N	26	N	4550/8230	N	$72,000	117
NORTH CAROLINA										
Appalachian State University	MA-I/O	Y	12	N	24	N	900/9000	N	$38,000	29
OHIO										
Bowling Green State University	MOD	Y	83	Y	26	N	7000/14,000	N	$55,000	31
Case Western Reserve University	MSODA	N	31	Y	35	N	834*	N	N/A	41
Cleveland State University	MAP	Y	26	Y	29	N	5964/11791	N	30,000-40,000	48
John Carroll University	MBA-HR	Y	266	Y	28	N	587*	N	N/A	65
Ohio State University	MLHR	Y	88	Y	28	N	7230/17301	N	$60,000	89
University of Cincinnati	MALER	N	76	Y	N/A	N	9096/16940	N	N/A	121
Xavier University	MAIOP	Y	20	Y	24	N	9353	N	$39,000	160
ONTARIO, CANADA										
Queen's University	MIR	Y	38	N	25	N	5500	N	$45,000	93

Degree Programs by State

State/University	Degree	Trad. Pgm	Enroll.	Even/ Wknd.	Avg. Age	Online	Tuition ($) In/Out State	Dist.	Starting Salary	Page #
PENNSYLVANIA										
Indiana University of Pennsylvania	MAILR	N	62	Y	26	N	1895/3305	N	$38,500	63
LaRoche College	MSHRM	Y	160	Y	32	Y	420*	Y	$38,000	69
Pennsylvania State University	MSIRHR	Y	11	N	28	N	7000/N/A	N	$55,000	90
Saint Francis University	MHRM	N	140	Y	35	Y	484*	Y	$52,000	101
University of Scranton	MSHR	N	70	Y	35	N	490*	N	N/A	136
Villanova University	MSHRM	N	80	Y	27	N	460*	Y	$51,000	148
West Chester University	MAIOP	N	30	Y	25	N	4140/7000	N	N/A	154
Widener University School of Business	MSHRM	N	49	Y	31	N	545*	N	N/A	159
RHODE ISLAND										
Salve Regina University	MAHR	N	79	Y	N/A	Y	300*	Y	N/A	105
University of Rhode Island	MSLRHR	N	24	Y	35	N	3540/5310	N	N/A	133
SOUTH CAROLINA										
University of South Carolina	MHR	Y	50	N	26	N	4014/8528	N	$62,500	137
TENNESSEE										
Middle Tennessee State University	MA-I/O	Y	23	N	N/A	N	3600/9400	N	$40,000	79
Trevecca Nazarene Univ.	MSM	N	100	Y	35	N	7000	N	N/A	113
University of Tennessee at Chattanooga	MSP-I/O	N	30	Y	25	N	175/275*	N	$35,000	138
Vanderbilt University	MBA-HR	Y	439	N	26	N	27560	N	$82,400	147
TEXAS										
Houston Baptist University	MS-HRM	N	16	Y	23	N	9600	N	N/A	59
St. Edward's University	MSOLE, MBA/HR	N	100	Y	32	Y	743*	N	N/A	100
Southwest Texas State University	MSHR	N	40	Y	32	Y	4584/13626	N	$42,000	108
Tarleton State University	MS-HRM	Y	55	Y	34	Y	1350/5000	Y	N/A	109
Texas A & M University	MSHRM	Y	40	N	25	Y	4000/7000	N	$62,000	110
University of Dallas	MBA	N	N/A	Y	33	Y	423*	Y	N/A	123
University of Houston, Clear Lake	MAHRM	N	52	Y	33	Y	217/352*	N	N/A	126
University of Texas at Arlington	MSHRM	N	20	Y	28	Y	4521/11331	N	$45,000	139
UTAH										
Brigham Young University	MBA	Y	58	N	29	N	342/512*	N	$60,000	32
Utah State University	MSSHRM	Y	60	Y	35	N	3711/11913	Y	N/A	146
VIRGINIA										
Marymount University	MA/HRM, MAHPS, MAOD	N	200	Y	32	N	480*	Y	$42,000	76
National-Louis University	MS-HRM&D	N	22	Y	37	N	496*	N	N/A	83
Radford University	MA-I/O	Y	27	N	23	N	3006/5814	N	$37,000	94
Regent University	MHRM,MORCD, MBA	Y	350	Y	34	Y	498*	Y	N/A	95
Virginia Commonwealth University	MSHRMIR	N	30	Y	28	N	2056/6013	N	N/A	150
WEST VIRGINIA										
West Virginia University	MSIR	Y	50	N	25	Y	1850/4300	Y	$55,000	157

Degree Programs by State

State/University	Degree	Trad. Pgm	Enroll.	Avg. Age	Even/ Wknd.	Online	Tuition ($) In/Out State	Dist.	Starting Salary	Page #
WISCONSIN										
Marquette University	MS-HR	Y	60	28	Y	N	500*	N	$40,000	73
University of Wisconsin - IR	MAIR	Y	27	30	N	N	5406/17110	N	$50,000	141
University of Wisconsin - MBA	MBA-HRM	Y	39	26	N	N	6524/18282	N	N/A	143
University of Wisconsin, Milwaukee	MHRLR	N	53	27	Y	N	1265/3759	N	N/A	144
University of Wisconsin, Whitewater	MBA-HR	N	20	30	Y	Y	4378/12750	Y	N/A	145

University — Name of college or university offering the degree program.

State — State where the college or university is located. Schools with locations in more than one state are noted as "mul."(multiple locations) on the "Programs by Degree Type" table. In the "Degree Programs by State" table, universities with locations in more than one state are listed under each of those states. Note: One Canadian university is included in the directory. 'ON' for 'Ontario' is listed in the state column.

Degree — The HR-related master's degree program offered. If a university offers multiple degrees, it is listed in multiple categories on the "Programs by Degree Type" table.

Tuition — Tuition figures are listed per year except where noted with an asterisk (*); these are per credit hour. The first figure lists tuition for in-state students; the second figure lists tuition for out-of-state students. If only one amount is listed, then the tuition is the same for both in-state and out-of-state students.

Trad. Program — Traditional program. Universities offering a traditional full-time day program have a 'Y' listed for yes.'

Even/Wknd. — Evening/Weekend program. 'Y' means the school offers at least some of its courses on a part-time evening or weekend basis.

Online — Online courses. 'Y' means the school offers at least some courses online, but may not offer an entire degree online.

Dist. — Distance learning. 'Y' means the university has some type of distance learning available.

Starting Salary — Average starting salary of program graduates. If the school did not provide this information, 'N/A' is listed. Note: Many non-traditional programs do not report starting salaries because the majority of these graduates are already employed.

Enrollment — Number of students enrolled in the program. (Note: Some universities may have supplied the total number of students in the school.)

Avg. Age — The average age of a student enrolled in the degree program.

SHRM Chptr — SHRM student chapter. 'Y' means the school has its own chapter of the Society for Human Resource Management.

Page # — Page number. Lists the page in the directory where the complete school profile can be found.

Y — Yes.

N — No.

N/A — Information not provided or not applicable.

Programs by Degree Type

University	State	Degree	Trad. Pgm	Enroll.	Even/ Wknd.	Avg. Age	Online	Tuition ($) In/Out State	Dist.	Starting Salary	Page #
BUSINESS ADMINISTRATION (MBA)											
Baruch College, CUNY	NY	MBA/HRM	Y	75	Y	N/A	N	6000/11,400	Y	$65,000	30
Brigham Young University	UT	MBA	Y	58	N	29	N	342/512*	N	$60,000	32
California State Polytechnic University, Pomona	CA	MBA/HRM	N	600	Y	33	Y	1584/2568	Y (LA)	$55,000	34
California State University, Fresno	CA	MBA-HRM	N	134	Y	30	Y	1906/4428	Y	$52,000	35
California State University, Hayward	CA	MBA-HRM	N	30	Y	32	N	2400/8000	N	N/A	36
DePaul University	IL	MBA	N	4	Y	26	N	$362-$600*	N	N/A	52
Fairleigh Dickinson University	NJ	MBA/HRM	Y	47	Y	30	N	550*	N	$50,000	54
Georgia State University	GA	MBA/HRM	N	66	Y	28	Y	130/518*	Y	$48,200	57
Indiana Institute of Technology	IN	MBA/HRM	N	350	Y	40	N	250*	Y	N/A	62
Iowa State University	IA	MBA/HRM	Y	32	Y	25	N	3702/10898	Y	$45,000	64
John Carroll University	OH	MBA-HR	Y	266	Y	28	N	587*	N	N/A	65
Kennesaw State University	GA	MBA	Y	863	Y	32	Y	2648/9158	N	N/A	68
Monterey Institute of International Studies	CA	MBA	Y	10	N	27	Y	19988	N	N/A	81
Regent University	VA	MBA	Y	350	Y	34	Y	498*	Y	N/A	95
St. Edward's University	TX	MBA/HR	N	100	Y	32	Y	743*	N	N/A	100
University of Albany	NY	MBA/HRIS	Y	20	N	26	N	4550/8230	N	$72,000	117
University of Dallas	TX	MBA	N	N/A	Y	33	Y	423*	Y	N/A	123
University of Maryland	MD	MBA-HC	Y	1100	Y	27	N	10798/15424	Y	$59,700	128
University of St. Thomas	MN	MBA/HRM	Y	260	Y	33	Y	480*	Y	$54,000	134
University of Wisconsin - MBA	WI	MBA-HRM	Y	39	N	26	N	6524/18282	N	N/A	143
University of Wisconsin, Whitewater	WI	MBA-HR	N	20	Y	30	Y	4378/12750	Y	N/A	145
Vanderbilt University	TN	MBA-HR	Y	439	N	26	N	27560	N	$82,400	147
Webster University-Ozarks Region	MO	MBAHRM, MBAHRD	N	132	Y	37	Y	345*	N	N/A	152
HUMAN RESOURCE DEVELOPMENT											
Colorado State University-Denver Center	CO	MSEHRS	N	60	Y	35	N	6500	N	N/A	49
Illinois Institute of Technology	IL	MSPHRD	N	11	Y	N/A	Y	590*	N	N/A	60
St. John Fisher College	NY	MSHRD	Y	42	Y	35	Y	465*/N/A	Y	$40,000	102
Towson University	MD	MAHRD	Y	150	Y	N/A	Y	4336/9940	Y	$38,000	112
Webster University-Ozarks Region	MO	MAHRD	N	132	Y	37	Y	345*	N	N/A	152
Western Maryland College	MD	MSHRD	N	43	Y	31	N	240*	N	N/A	156
HUMAN RESOURCES OR HUMAN RESOURCE MANAGEMENT											
American University	DC	MSHRM	N	36	Y	37	N	18,160	N	N/A	28
Chapman University	CA	MSHR	N	301	Y	30	N	430*	Y	N/A	44
Chapman University, Bay Area	CA	MSHR	Y	N/A	Y	39	N	290*	N	N/A	42
Chapman University - Coachella Valley	CA	MSHR	N	20	Y	35	N	265*	N	N/A	43
Chapman University, Sacramento	CA	MSHR	N	9	Y	35	N	290*	N	N/A	45
DePaul University	IL	MSHR	N	4	Y	26	N	$362-$600*	N	N/A	52
Georgia State University	GA	MSHRM	N	66	Y	28	Y	130/518*	Y	$48,200	57
Hawaii Pacific University	HI	MA/HRM	Y	1200	Y	30	N	410*	N	$54,600	58
Houston Baptist University	TX	MS-HRM	N	16	Y	23	N	9600	N	N/A	59

Programs by Degree Type

University	State	Degree	Trad. Pgm	Enroll.	Even/ Wknd.	Avg. Age	Online	Tuition ($) In/Out State	Dist.	Starting Salary	Page #
HUMAN RESOURCES OR HUMAN RESOURCE MANAGEMENT											
Keller Graduate School of Mgmt.	IL	MHRM	N	6900	Y	34	Y	1420	Y	$63,000	66
LaRoche College	PA	MSHRM	Y	160	Y	32	Y	420*	N	$38,000	69
Long Island University	NY	MSHR	N	25	Y	27	N	505*	Y	N/A	70
Loyola University Chicago	IL	MSHR	N	200	Y	28	N	594*	Y	$65,000	71
Marquette University	WI	MS-HR	Y	60	Y	28	N	500*	N	$40,000	73
Marygrove College	MI	MA-HRM	N	63	Y	32	N	360*	N	N/A	74
Marymount University	VA	MA/HRM	N	200	Y	32	N	480*	Y	$42,000	76
Mercy College	NY	MSHRM	N	232	Y	35	N	435*	Y	N/A	77
National-Louis University	Mul.	MS-HRM&D	N	22	Y	37	N	496*	N	N/A	83
New School University	NY	MSHRM	N	215	Y	30	Y	690*	Y	$73,500	85
Nova Southeastern University	FL	MSHRM	N	108	Y	34	Y	434*	Y	N/A	87
Polytechnic University	NY	MSHRM	N	30	Y	30	N	695*	Y	N/A	91
Purdue University	IN	MSHRM	Y	50	Y	26	N	4560/8996	Y	$60,000	92
Regent University	VA	MHRM	Y	350	Y	34	Y	498*	N	N/A	95
Rollins College	FL	MHR	N	74	Y	36	N	280*	Y	N/A	97
Rutgers University	NJ	MHRM	Y	160	Y	30	N	7954/11704	Y	$59,900	99
Saint Francis University	PA	MHRM	N	140	Y	35	Y	484*	Y	$52,000	101
Salve Regina University	RI	MAHR	N	79	Y	N/A	Y	300*	Y	N/A	105
Southwest Texas State University	TX	MSHR	Y	40	Y	32	N	4584/13626	N	$42,000	108
Tarleton State University	TX	MS-HRM	Y	55	Y	34	Y	1350/5000	Y	N/A	109
Texas A & M University	TX	MSHRM	Y	40	N	25	N	4000/7000	N	$62,000	110
Troy State University, Ft. Benning	GA	MSHRM	N	100	Y	N/A	Y	4350	Y	N/A	114
Troy State University, Montgomery	AL	MSHRM	N	75	Y	34	Y	2480/4960	Y	N/A	115
Troy State University, Western Region	Mul.	MSHRM	N	30	Y	35	Y	6600	N	$30,000	116
University of Hawaii at Manoa	HI	MHRM	N	N/A	Y	N/A	N	217/352*	N	N/A	124
University of Houston, Clear Lake	TX	MAHRM	N	52	Y	33	N	14000	N	N/A	126
University of North Florida	FL	MHRM	N	30	Y	31	Y	6000/18000	N	N/A	132
University of Scranton	PA	MSHR	N	70	Y	35	N	490*	N	N/A	136
University of South Carolina	SC	MHR	Y	50	N	26	N	4014/8528	N	$62,500	137
University of Texas at Arlington	TX	MSHRM	N	20	Y	28	Y	4521/11331	N	$45,000	139
Utah State University	UT	MSSHRM	Y	60	Y	35	N	3711/11913	Y	N/A	146
Villanova University	PA	MSHRM	N	80	Y	27	N	460*	N	$51,000	148
Washington University	MO	MAHRM	N	50	Y	26	Y	270*	Y	N/A	151
Webster University-Ozarks Region	MO	MAHR	N	132	Y	37	Y	345*	Y	N/A	152
Webster University-St. Louis	MO	MAHRM	N	250	Y	27	Y	398*	N	N/A	153
Widener University School of Business	PA	MSHRM	N	49	Y	31	N	545*	N	N/A	159
INDUSTRIAL RELATIONS/LABOR RELATIONS											
Baruch College, CUNY	NY	MSILR	Y	75	Y	N/A	N	4200/5820	Y	$65,000	30
Cornell University	NY	MILR	Y	140	N	28	N	13910	N	$69,400	50
Indiana University of Pennsylvania	PA	MAILR	N	62	Y	26	N	1895/3305	N	$38,500	63
Iowa State University	IA	MSIR	Y	32	Y	25	N	3702/10898	Y	$45,000	64
Loyola University Chicago	IL	MSIR	N	200	Y	28	N	594*	Y	$65,000	71

Programs by Degree Type

University	State	Degree	Trad. Pgm	Enroll.	Even/ Wknd.	Avg. Age	Online	Tuition ($) In/Out State	Dist.	Starting Salary	Page #
INDUSTRIAL RELATIONS/LABOR RELATIONS continued											
Michigan State University	MI	MLRHR	Y	125	Y	27	N	244/494*	N	$65,500	78
New York Institute of Technology	NY	MSHRM/LR	N	140	Y	31	Y	545*	Y	32,000-40,000	86
Ohio State University	OH	MLHR	Y	88	Y	28	N	7230/17301	N	$60,000	89
Pennsylvania State University	PA	MSIRHR	Y	11	N	28	N	7000/N/A	N	$55,000	90
Queen's University (Canada)	ON	MIR	Y	38	Y	25	N	5500	N	$45,000	93
University of Cincinnati	OH	MALER	N	76	Y	N/A	N	9096/16940	N	N/A	121
University of Illinois, Urbana-Champaign	IL	MHRIR	Y	125	N	25	N	2121/5876	N	$58,000	127
University of Minnesota	MN	MA-HRIR	Y	240	Y	26	N	6785/12535	N	$62,400	129
University of Rhode Island	RI	MSLRHR	N	24	Y	35	N	3540/5310	N	N/A	133
University of Wisconsin-IR	WI	MAIR	Y	27	N	30	N	5406/17110	N	$50,000	141
University of Wisc.-Milwaukee	WI	MHRLR	N	53	Y	27	N	1265/3759	N	N/A	144
Virginia Commonwealth University	VA	MSHRMIR	N	30	Y	28	N	2056/6013	N	N/A	150
West Virginia University	WV	MSIR	Y	50	N	25	Y	1850/4300	Y	$55,000	157
INDUSTRIAL/ORGANIZATIONAL PSYCHOLOGY; PSYCHOLOGY											
Alliant International University	CA	MAOP	N	95	Y	33	N	500-650*	N	N/A	27
Appalachian State University	NC	MA-I/O	Y	12	N	24	N	900/9000	N	$38,000	29
California State University, Long Beach	CA	MAIOP	Y	22	N	N/A	N	1822/3298	N	N/A	37
California State University, San Bernardino	CA	MSIO	Y	12	N	28	N	292/502*	N	N/A	38
Cleveland State University	OH	MAP	Y	26	Y	29	N	5964/11791	N	30,000-40,000	48
Florida Institute of Technology	FL	MSIOP	Y	25	Y	24	N	675*	N	N/A	55
Middle Tennessee State University	TN	MA-I/O	Y	23	Y	N/A	N	3600/9400	N	$40,000	79
Minnesota State University Mankato	MN	MAIOP	Y	21	Y	24	N	3974/5980	N	$46,000	80
Radford University	VA	MA-I/O	Y	27	N	23	N	3006/5814	N	$37,000	94
Roosevelt University	IL	MAP	N	70	Y	27	N	N/A	N	N/A	98
San Francisco State Univ.	CA	MSP	Y	38	N	29	N	1904/3380	N	N/A	106
Southwest Missouri State Univ.	MO	MSIOP	Y	20	N	N/A	N	2664/5328	N	$46,700	107
University of Baltimore	MD	MS-I/O	Y	67	Y	33	N	7396/10708	N	N/A	119
University of New Haven	CT	MA-I/O	N	80	Y	30	N	390*	N	$58,500	131
University of Tennessee-Chattanooga	TN	MSP-I/O	N	30	Y	25	N	175/275*	N	$35,000	138
University of West Florida	FL	MA-I/O	Y	29	N	N/A	N	156/535*	N	N/A	140
West Chester University	PA	MAIOP	N	30	Y	25	N	4140/7000	N	N/A	154
Western Kentucky University	KY	MAP-I/O	Y	18	N	27	N	3044	N	$47,000	155
Xavier University	OH	MAIOP	Y	20	Y	24	N	9353	N	$39,000	160
MANAGEMENT											
Capella University	MN	MS O&M-HRM	N	125	Y	45	Y	325*	Y	N/A	39
St. Edward's University	TX	MSOLE	N	100	Y	32	Y	743*	Y	N/A	100
St. Joseph's College	NY	MSM	N	136	Y	N/A	N	399*	N	N/A	103
Trevecca Nazarene Univ.	TN	MSM	N	100	Y	35	N	7000	N	N/A	113
University of Central Florida	FL	MSM/HR/CM	N	40	Y	29	N	162/569*	N	N/A	120

Programs by Degree Type

University	State	Degree	Trad. Pgm	Enroll.	Even/ Wknd.	Avg. Age	Online	Tuition ($) In/Out State	Dist.	Starting Salary	Page #
MANAGEMENT continued											
University of Colorado at Denver	CO	MSM	N	45	Y	30	Y	4428/15066	Y	N/A	122
ORGANIZATIONAL DEVELOPMENT/ ORGANIZATIONAL BEHAVIOR											
Alliant International University	CA	MAOD	N	95	Y	33	N	500-650*	N	N/A	27
Bowling Green State University	OH	MOD	Y	83	Y	26	N	7000/14,000	N	$55,000	31
Case Western Reserve University	OH	MSODA	N	31	Y	35	N	834*	N	N/A	41
Claremont Graduate University	CA	MSHRD	N	36	Y	30	Y	1000*	N	$65,000	47
Eastern Michigan University	MI	MSHROD	N	50	Y	28	Y	215/440*	Y	$45,000	53
Manhattanville College	NY	MSOMHR	N	180	Y	32	N	450*	N	N/A	72
Marymount University	VA	MAHPS, MAOD	N	200	Y	32	N	480*	Y	$42,000	76
Polytechnic University	NY	MSOB	N	30	Y	30	N	695*	Y	N/A	91
Regent University	VA	MORCD	Y	350	Y	34	Y	498*	Y	N/A	95
SPECIALTY: HEALTH PROMOTION											
Nebraska Methodist College	NE	MSHP	N	24	Y	33	Y	385*	Y	N/A	84

Note: Where classification of the program was not obvious, the list of required and elective courses was reviewed to determine the program's category.

University	Name of college or university offering the degree program.
State	State where the college or university is located. Schools with locations in more than one state are noted as "mul."(multiple locations) on the "Programs by Degree Type" table. In the "Degree Programs by State" table, universities with locations in more than one state are listed under each of those states. Note: One Canadian university is included in the directory. 'ON' for 'Ontario' is listed in the state column.
Degree	The HR-related master's degree program offered. If a university offers multiple degrees, it is listed in multiple categories on the "Programs by Degree Type" table.
Tuition	Tuition figures are listed per year except where noted with an asterisk (*); these are per credit hour. The first figure lists tuition for in-state students; the second figure lists tuition for out-of-state students. If only one amount is listed, then the tuition is the same for both in-state and out-of-state students.
Trad. Program	Traditional program. Universities offering a traditional full-time day program have a 'Y' listed for 'yes.'
Even/Wknd.	Evening/Weekend program. 'Y' means the school offers at least some of its courses on a part-time evening or weekend basis.
Online	Online courses. 'Y' means the school offers at least some courses online, but may not offer an entire degree online.
Dist.	Distance learning. 'Y' means the university has some type of distance learning available.
Starting Salary	Average starting salary of program graduates. If the school did not provide this information, 'N/A' is listed. Note: Many non-traditional programs do not report starting salaries because the majority of these graduates are already employed.
Enrollment	Number of students enrolled in the program. (Note: Some universities may have supplied the total number of students in the school.)
Avg. Age	The average age of a student enrolled in the degree program.
SHRM Chptr	SHRM student chapter. 'Y' means the school has its own chapter of the Society for Human Resource Management.
Page #	Page number. Lists the page in the directory where the complete school profile can be found.
Y	Yes.
N	No.
N/A	Information not provided or not applicable.

PROFILES OF

GRADUATE PROGRAMS IN

HUMAN RESOURCE MANAGEMENT

Alliant International University

San Francisco, California
College of Organizational Studies – SF Bay Campus

Degree
Masters in Organizational Psychology (MAOP)
Masters in Organizational Development (MAOD) (pending)

University Overview
Alliant International University (AIU) San Francisco Bay Campus is located in San Francisco, California.

Program Description
AIU is focused on the application of the behavioral sciences for understanding and resolving major social issues in a multi-cultural and global context.

Degree Requirements
Total Credits Required:	60 (MAOP), 43 (MAOD)
Average Credits per Course:	3
Course Schedule:	Semester
Total Courses Required:	Varies
HR/IR Courses Required:	Varies
Average Time for Completion:	Masters 2-3 years
Maximum Time Allowed for Completion:	7 years
Accepts Credits from Other Universities:	YES
Total:	Varies

Tuition
In-state	N/A	(per year)
	$500-$650	(per credit hour)
Out-of-state	N/A	(per year)
	$500-$650	(per credit hour)

Program Delivery
Traditional Day Program:	NO
Nontraditional Program:	YES
Evening Program:	YES
Weekend Program:	NO
Program Completed Evening/Weekend:	YES
Summer Courses:	YES
Some Courses Online:	NO
Full Program Online:	NO
Distance Learning/Offsite:	NO
Executive Education:	NO
Overseas Study Abroad:	YES

Faculty
Full-Time Faculty:	6
Part-Time Faculty:	6
Faculty to Student Ratio:	1:20

Primary Teaching Methods:
Experiential Learning Research
Field Projects Team Projects
Faculty Who Consult Outside: 50-74%
Faculty Involvement:
Newsletter Editor, Sociological Practice Section, American Sociological Association
Reviewer, Academy of Management, Research Methods Division
Reviewer, Academy of Management, Gender and Diversity in Organizations Division
Reviewer, *Journal of Management Education*
Top 5 Faculty Publications:
Qualitative Research Methods for Psychology: Instructive Empirical

Studies
What She Wants

Students
Total Enrollment:			95
Full-Time Enrollment:			
Men:	31%	Women:	69%
Hispanic:	3%	African-American:	17%
Other Minorities:	28%	International:	10%
Average Age:	33	Age Range:	20-54
Work Full Time:			25-49%
Have HR Experience:			25-49%
Speak 2nd Language:			25-49%

Minimum Admission Requirements:
UGPA:	3.0
GRE or GMAT Scores:	Not Required
Work Experience:	3 years recommended

Other Considerations:
Average Student Profile:
UGPA:	N/A
GMAT Score:	N/A
Work Experience:	N/A

Program Resources
Students Required to Have Computers:			YES
Video Teleconferencing:			YES
Physical Library Facilities:			YES
Online Library Facilities:			YES
HRCI Certification Preparation:			N/A
SHRM Student Chapter:			NO
URL:			
Fellowships:	NO	AMT:	
Scholarships:	NO	AMT:	
Assistantships:	YES	AMT:	$900/term
Eligibility:			N/A

Curriculum
Required Courses:
Organization Theory
Consulting Skills
Research Methods
Most Popular Elective Courses:
Communication and Integrity
The Enneagram
Knowledge in Organizations
Process Consulting
Strategic Management
Career Tracks/Concentrations:	N/A
Internship Required:	YES

Career Services
Career Services Offered:
Internships
Summer Internship Placement Rate:	N/A
Facilitate Placement:	N/A
Full-Time Placement Rate:	N/A
Internship Placement Rate:	N/A
Average Starting Salary (Full-Time Graduates):	N/A
Average Sign-on Bonus:	N/A
Companies Recruiting HR Master's Graduates:	N/A

Points of Excellence
Alliant International University (AIU) has a highly diverse student body, with roughly 49% coming from minority or international backgrounds. Classes have a high quality of student interaction and dialogue, due to the mix of doctoral and masters students. Most students are interested in the blend of research and practice. Individuals who succeed at AIU in Organizational Studies have excellent analytical, people and communication

skills, the ability to synthesize information, and a high degree of initiative and creativity, and are willing to work hard.

All organizational faculty are fully dedicated to graduate student training and education, as there are no undergraduate programs at the San Francisco Bay Campus.

Internships or practica assist students with later employment by allowing them opportunities to build skills and resumes. The instructional methods allow for considerable individualized attention. With the permission of the Program Director, students may take courses offered at one of the other AIU campuses, located in different parts of California.

Contact Information
Alliant International University, San Francisco Bay Campus
1005 Atlantic Avenue
Alameda, CA 94501
www.alliant.edu/cos/

Administrative Contact
Ned Doherty, Director of Admissions
Telephone: (510) 523-2300
ndoherty@alliant.edu

Faculty Contact
Kathryn Goldman Schuyler, Ph.D., Program Director
Telephone: (510) 814-8584
kgschuyler@alliant.edu

Admission Deadlines
February for Fall admissions
Online Application: YES

American University

Washington, DC
School of Public Affairs

Degree
Master of Science in Human Resource Management (MSHRM)

University Overview
American University (AU) was founded in 1893 by an act of Congress as a private, independent, coeducational institution, under the auspices of the United Methodist Church. Located in a very bucolic suburban area of the upper Northwest quadrant of Washington, DC, AU is literally 10 minutes by bus or subway from the centers of government and business.

Program Description
Our weekend program is designed for working HR professionals. It is noted for its development of HR professionals as strategic partners with management and for its faculty of leading scholar-practitioners from government, business, and other centers of power.

Degree Requirements
Total Credits Required:	39
Average Credits per Course:	3
Course Schedule:	Semester
Total Courses Required:	13
HR/IR Courses Required:	13
Average Time for Completion:	1¾ years
Maximum Time Allowed for Completion:	3 years
Accepts Credits from Other Universities:	NO
Total:	

Tuition
In-state	$18,160	(per year)
	$937	(per credit hour)
Out-of-state	$18,160	(per year)
	$937	(per credit hour)

Program Delivery
Traditional Day Program:	NO
Nontraditional Program:	YES
Evening Program:	NO
Weekend Program:	YES
Program Completed Evening/Weekend:	YES
Summer Courses:	YES
Some Courses Online:	NO
Full Program Online:	NO
Distance Learning/Offsite:	NO
Executive Education:	YES
Overseas Study Abroad:	NO

Faculty
Full-Time Faculty:	3
Part-Time Faculty:	13
Faculty to Student Ratio:	1:18

Primary Teaching Methods:

Case Study	Research
Student Presentation	Experiential Learning
Lecture	Group Discussion
Team Projects	

Faculty Who Consult Outside:	50-74%
Faculty Involvement:	N/A
Top 5 Faculty Publications:	N/A

Students
Total Enrollment:			36
Full-Time Enrollment:			0
Men:	6%	Women:	94%
Hispanic:	9.5%	African-American:	25%
Other Minorities:	5%	International:	16%
Average Age:	37	Age Range:	24-57
Work Full Time:			100%
Have HR Experience:			75-99%
Speak 2nd Language:			1-24%

Minimum Admission Requirements:
UGPA:	3.0
GRE or GMAT Scores	Not Required:
Work Experience:	3-5 years
Combined	N/A

Other Considerations:
After 6 years post graduation, less emphasis placed on undergrad GPA.

Average Student Profile:	N/A
UGPA:	3.3
GMAT Score:	N/A
Work Experience:	5-7 years

Program Resources
Students Required to Have Computers:			NO
Video Teleconferencing:			YES
Physical Library Facilities:			YES
Online Library Facilities:			YES
HRCI Certification Preparation:			NO
SHRM Student Chapter:			NO
URL:			
Fellowships:	NO	AMT:	
Scholarships:	NO	AMT:	
Assistantships:	NO	AMT:	
Eligibility:			N/A

Curriculum

Required Courses:
  HR Strategy
  International HR
  Compensation/Benefits
  Development/Training
  Recruitment/Retention
  Employment Law
  Management
  Employee Relations
  Labor Relations
  HR Measurement
  Managerial Economics
  Leadership
  Organizational Development
  Managing Diversity
  Performance Management

Most Popular Elective Courses:	N/A
Career Tracks/Concentrations:	N/A
Internship Required:	NO

Career Services

Career Services Offered:

Mentoring	Interview Training
Resume Services	Campus Interview

Summer Internship Placement Rate:	N/A
Facilitate Placement:	YES
Full-Time Placement Rate:	Students already employed. Most receive promotions or move to better jobs.
Internship Placement Rate:	N/A
Average Starting Salary (Full-Time Graduates):	N/A
Average Sign-on Bonus:	N/A
Companies Recruiting HR Master's Graduates:	N/A

Points of Excellence

Faculty consists of scholar-practitioners from the entire scope of government, business and organizations in the most powerful city in the world: an extraordinary resource.

Contact Information

American University
MS in Human Resources Program
School of Public Affairs
4200 Wisconsin Avenue NW, Suite 302
Washington, DC 20016

Administrative Contact
Elizabeth Lister, Associate Director
Telephone: (202) 885-2379
elister@american.edu

Faculty Contact
Dr. Arthur Freedman
Telephone: (202) 885-6207
afreed@american.edu

Admission Deadlines

April 1

Online Application:	YES

Appalachian State University

Boone, North Carolina
Department of Psychology

Degree

Master in Industrial/Organizational Psychology (MA-I/O)

University Overview

Appalachian State University, located in the Blue Ridge Mountains of North Carolina, is a state university with approximately 13,000 students.

Program Description

Traditional full-time day program. The I/O-HRM program offers an interdisciplinary approach with a core curriculum in Psychology and Business Management.

Degree Requirements

Total Credits Required:	42
Average Credits per Course:	3
Course Schedule:	Semester
Total Courses Required:	15
HR/IR Courses Required:	11
Average Time for Completion:	2 years
Maximum Time Allowed for Completion:	N/A
Accepts Credits from Other Universities:	YES
Total:	6 Hours

Tuition

In-state	$900	(per year)
	N/A	(per credit hour)
Out-of-state	$9,000	(per year)
	N/A	(per credit hour)

Program Delivery

Traditional Day Program:	YES
Nontraditional Program:	NO
Evening Program:	NO
Weekend Program:	NO
Summer Courses:	YES *
Some Courses Online:	NO
Full Program Online:	NO
Distance Learning/Offsite:	NO
Executive Education:	NO
Overseas Study Abroad:	NO

Internships and Independent Studies

Faculty

Full-Time Faculty:	5
Part-Time Faculty:	40
Faculty to Student Ratio:	1:3

Primary Teaching Methods:

Research	Team Projects
Student Presentation	Group Discussions

Faculty Who Consult Outside:	75-99%
Faculty Involvement:	See web site

Top 5 Faculty Publications:
  Journal of Applied Psychology (4 articles)
  Two books

Students

Total Enrollment:			12
Full-Time Enrollment:			100%
Men:	50%	Women:	50%
Hispanic:	0%	African-American:	8%
Other Minorities:	0%	International:	8%
Average Age:	24	Age Range:	23-35

Work Full Time:	1-24%
HR Experience:	1-24%
Speak 2nd Language:	1-24%
Minimum Admission Requirements:	
UGPA :	3.0
GRE Score:	1000 V&Q
Other Considerations:	

Research and/or Employment Experience

Average Student Profile:	
GRE Score:	1140 V&Q
Work experience:	1 year

Program Resources

Students Required to Have Computers:	YES
Video Teleconferencing:	NO
Physical Library Facilities:	YES
Online Library Facilities:	YES
HRCI Certification Preparation:	YES
Links students to local SHRM chapter study groups	
Offers SHRM Learning System as teaching tool	
Offers practice exams	
SHRM Student Chapter:	YES
Fellowships:	NO
In-state	$900 (per year)
Scholarships: 2 AMT:	Tuition
Assistantships: 12 AMT:	$6,250
Eligibility:	Full-Time Enrollment

Curriculum

Required Courses:
- HR Strategy
- Development/Training
- Employment Law
- Staffing
- HR Measurement
- Organizational Development
- Organizational Behavior
- Research Methodology
- Experimental Psychology
- Management

Most Popular Elective Courses:
- Labor Relations
- Compensation/Benefits

Career Tracks/Concentrations:	N/A
Internship Required:	NO

Career Services

Career Development Opportunities/Placement Service:

Mentoring	Field Trips
Resume Services	SHRM Student Chapter
Internships	

Summer Internship Placement Rate:	80%
Full-Time Placement Rate:	100%
Average Starting Salary (Full-Time Graduates):	$38,000
Average Sign-on Bonus:	N/A
Companies Recruiting HR Master's Graduates:	12

Points of Excellence

Faculty: Faculty and students within the program engage in productive scholarship activity in addition to an applied focus. Faculty and students have been successful in securing grants for research activities and have published in top journals of our field.

Contact Information

Department of Psychology
Appalachian State University
Boone, NC 28608
www.acs.appstate.edu/dept/psych/GradProg/io_info.htm

Dr. Timothy D. Ludwig, Director
Telephone: (828) 262-1280
ludwigtd@appstate.edu

Baruch College, CUNY

New York, New York

Degree
Master of Business Administration in Human Resource Management (MBA/HRM)
Master of Science in Industrial Labor Relations (MSILR)

University Overview
Baruch College is state funded with approximately 15,000 students. Located in New York City, it offers quality programs with low tuition rates.

Program Description
Offers both traditional and nontraditional programs. Courses, instructors, and internships provide practical, professional programs in Human Resource Management (MBAHRM) and Industrial Labor Relations (MSILR).

Degree Requirements

Total Credits Required:	54	MBA
	36	MSILR
Average Credits per Course:		3
Course Schedule:		Semester
Total Courses Required:	18	MBA
	12	MSILR
HR/IR Courses Required:	6	MBA
	11	MSILR
Average Time for Completion:	2 years	MBA
	3 years	MSILR
Maximum Time Allowed for Completion:		N/A
Accepts Credits from Other Universities:		NO
Total:		N/A

Tuition

In-state MBA	$6,000	(per year)
	$265	(per credit hour)
In-state MSILR	$4,200	(per year)
	$185	(per credit hour)
Out-of-state MBA	$11,400	(per year)
	$475	(per credit hour)
Out-of-state MSILR	$5,820	(per year)
	$320	(per credit hour)

Program Delivery

Traditional Day Program:	YES
Nontraditional Program:	YES
Evening Program:	YES
Weekend Program:	NO
Summer Courses:	N/A
Some Courses Online:	NO
Full Program Online:	NO
Distance Learning/Offsite:	YES
Executive Education:	N/A
Overseas Study Abroad:	NO

Faculty

Full-Time Faculty:	12
Part-Time Faculty:	6
Faculty to Student Ratio:	1:11

Primary Teaching Methods:

Case Study	Lecture
Team Projects	Field Projects
Simulations	Experiential Exercises

Faculty Who Consult Outside: 50%

Top 5 Faculty Publications:
Journal of Applied Psychology
Academy of Management Journal
Personnel Psychology
Journal of Vocational Behavior
Journal of Management

Students

Total Enrollment:			75
Full-Time Enrollment:			30%
Men:	N/A	Women:	N/A
Hispanic:	N/A	African-American:	N/A
Other Minorities:	N/A	International:	N/A
Average Age:	N/A	Age Range:	N/A
Work Full Time:			75-99%
HR Experience:		MBA/HRM	25-49%
		MSILR	75-99%
Speak 2nd Language:			25-49%

Minimum Admission Requirements:
GMAT Score: 550
Other Considerations:
GPA and work experience
Average Student Profile:
GMAT Score: 590

Program Resources

Students Required to Have Computers:		N/A
Video Teleconferencing:		NO
Physical Library Facilities:		N/A
Online Library Facilities:		N/A
HRCI Certification Preparation:		NO
SHRM Student Chapter:		NO
Fellowships:		NO
Scholarships:		NO
Assistantships:	5	AMT: $8,000
Eligibility:		Full-Time Enrollment

Curriculum

Required Courses (MBA):
Organizational Behavior
Managerial Skills
Business Functional Areas
Compensation/Benefits
Development/Training
Required Courses (MSILR):
Compensation/Benefits
Employment Law
Dispute Resolution
Development/Training
Labor Relations
Most Popular Elective Courses:
Organizational Development
Career Tracks/Concentrations: N/A
Internship Required: NO

Career Services

Career Development Opportunities/Placement Service:

Resume Services	Interview Training
Campus Interviews	Internships
Mentorship	Workshops

Summer Internship Placement Rate: N/A
Full-Time Placement Rate: N/A
Average Starting Salary (Full-Time Graduates): $65,000 (MBA)

Average Sign-on Bonus: N/A
Companies Recruiting HR Master's Graduates: N/A

Points of Excellence

Resources: Baruch's MSILR program utilizes its New York City location by developing internships, maintaining an active alumni organization, and incorporating practitioners as guest lecturers and adjuncts. The MSILR program has a cohort structure emphasizing a sequence of accumulated knowledge, commitment to consistent course scheduling, and educationally supportive peer relationships.

Placement: Most students are already working in HR, but graduate placement office places others. Graduate Student Advisor provides one-on-one mock interviews and feedback, and helps students prepare resumes. Access to New York City business community.

Contact Information

Baruch College, CUNY
1 Baruch Way
New York, NY 10010
www.Baruch.CUNY.edu

For MBA degree:
Dr. Donald Vredenburgh, Professor
Donald_Vredenburgh@Baruch.CUNY.edu

For MSILR degree:
Dr. Richard Kopelman, Professor
Telephone: (646) 312-3629   FAX: (646) 312-3621
Richard_Kopelman@Baruch.CUNY.edu

Admission Deadlines

February 28 (Full-Time MBA)
Online Application: YES
Telephone: (646) 312-3630   FAX: (646) 312-3621

Bowling Green State University

Bowling Green, Ohio
College of Business Administration

Degree

Master of Organizational Development (MOD)

University Overview

Bowling Green is a state-funded institution in Ohio.

Program Description

The degree is offered in both a traditional day program and an executive weekend program. MOD program uses the Action Research Model and focuses on empirically driven change strategies. The program has been in existence for more than 25 years.

Degree Requirements

Total Credits Required:	30-33
Average Credits per Course:	3
Course Schedule:	Semester
Total Courses Required:	10
HR/IR Courses Required:	1
Average Time for Completion:	1 ½ years
Maximum Time Allowed for Completion:	N/A
Accepts Credits from Other Universities:	NO
Total:	N/A

Tuition

In-state	$7,000	(per year)
	$250	(per credit hour)
Out-of-state	$14,000	(per year)
	$500	(per credit hour)

Program Delivery

Traditional Day Program:	YES
Nontraditional Program:	YES
Evening Program:	NO
Weekend Program:	YES (Executive)
Summer Courses:	N/A
Some Courses Online:	NO
Full Program Online:	NO
Distance Learning/Offsite:	NO
Executive Education:	N/A
Overseas Study Abroad:	NO

Faculty

Full-Time Faculty:	10
Part-Time Faculty:	Varies
Faculty to Student Ratio:	1:20

Primary Teaching Methods:

Case Study	Field Projects
Experiential Learning	Team Projects

Faculty Who Consult Outside:	50-74%

Faculty Involvement:
ODN Scholarship Committee; Editor, OD Journal

Top 5 Faculty Publications:
OD Journal
OD Practitioner
Academy of Management Review

Students

Total Enrollment:			83
Full-Time Enrollment:			22%
Men:	N/A	Women:	N/A
Hispanic:	N/A	African-American:	N/A
Other Minorities:	N/A	International:	N/A
Average Age:	26	Age Range:	N/A
Work Full Time:			50-74%
HR Experience:			25-49%
Speak 2nd Language:			1-24%

Minimum Admission Requirements:

GMAT Score:	500
Work experience:	3-5 years
UGPA:	2.7 +

Other Considerations:
Age and work experience

Average Student Profile:

GMAT Score:	580
Work experience:	3-5 years

Program Resources

Students Required to Have Computers:		N/A
Video Teleconferencing:		NO
Physical Library Facilities:		N/A
Online Library Facilities:		N/A
HRCI Certification Preparation:		NO
SHRM Student Chapter:		YES
Fellowships:		NO
Scholarships:		NO
Assistantships:	8	AMT: $3,550 + tuition
Eligibility:		Full-Time Enrollment

Curriculum

Required Courses:
HR Strategy
Management
HR Measurement
Statistics

Most Popular Elective Courses:
Internal OD
External OD
Business Process Analysis
Consulting

Career Tracks/Concentrations:	N/A
Internship Required:	YES

Career Services

Career Development Opportunities/Placement Service:

Mentoring	Field Trips
Resume Services	SHRM Student Chapter
Interview Training	Internships
Company Information Sessions	

Summer Internship Placement Rate:	N/A
Full-Time Placement Rate:	100%
Average Starting Salary (Full-Time Graduates):	$55,000
Average Sign-on Bonus:	N/A
Companies Recruiting HR Master's Graduates:	N/A

Points of Excellence

Placement: Strong alumni involvement built over 25 years and program reputation facilitates high-graduate placement rate.

Curriculum: Action research model orientation of curriculum, with a strong statistical component that blends theory and application. Typical internship program is 8-10 weeks (paid) with significant OD experiences. Outcome report is required for all internships.

Contact Information

Bowling Green State University
3009 College of Business Administration
Bowling Green, OH 43403
www.cba.bgsu.edu/html/mod.html

Joyce Steffan, Assistant Director
Telephone: (419) 372-8823   FAX: (419) 372-6057
jhyslop@cba.bgsu.edu

Brigham Young University

Provo, Utah
Marriott School of Management

Degree

Master of Business Administration (MBA)

University Overview

Brigham Young University (BYU) was founded in 1875 by Brigham Young, second president of the Latter Day Saints (LDS) Church. With more than 33,000 students, BYU is the largest privately owned church-sponsored institution in the United States.

Program Description

The MBA program, with an emphasis, or track, in Organizational Behavior/Human Resource Management, is a traditional professional degree program dedicated to creating compatibility between human values and organizational goals. Emphasizing the applied behavioral sciences, the two-year program prepares competent and ethical specialists who plan to take positions in the fields of organizational development, management training, and human resource management.

Degree Requirements

Total Credits Required:	64
Average Credits per Course:	3
Course Schedule:	Semester
Total Courses Required:	24
HR/IR Courses Required:	2
Average Time for Completion:	2 years
Maximum Time Allowed for Completion:	5 years
Accepts Credits from Other Universities:	YES
Total:	15 Hours

Tuition

LDS	N/A	(per year)
	$342	(per credit hour)
Non-LDS students	N/A	(per year)
	$512	(per credit hour)

Program Delivery

Traditional Day Program:	YES
Nontraditional Program:	NO
Evening Program:	NO
Weekend Program:	NO
Summer Courses:	NO
Some Courses Online:	NO
Full Program Online:	NO
Distance Learning/Offsite:	NO
Executive Education:	NO
Overseas Study Abroad:	NO

Faculty

Full-Time Faculty:	17
Part-Time Faculty:	2
Faculty to Student Ratio:	1:30

Primary Teaching Methods:

Case Study	Experiential Learning
Student Presentation	Team Projects
Faculty Who Consult Outside:	25-49%

Faculty Involvement:
Native-American tribal management consulting projects
President, Academy of Management

Top 5 Faculty Publications:
Harvard Business Review
Strategic Management Journal
Academy of Management Journal

Students

Total Enrollment:			58
Full-Time Enrollment:			100%
Men:	57%	Women:	43%
Hispanic:	13%	African-American:	1%
Other Minorities:	18%	International:	17%
Average Age:	29	Age Range:	22-49
Work Full Time:			1-24%
HR Experience:			1-24%
Speak 2nd Language:			50-74%

Minimum Admission Requirements:

GMAT Score:	500
UGPA:	3.6
Work experience:	2 years

Other Considerations:
Work experience helps offset lower test and GPA scores.

Average Student Profile:

GMAT Score:	617
Work experience:	2 years

Program Resources

Students Required to Have Computers:	YES
Video Teleconferencing:	NO
Physical Library Facilities:	YES
Online Library Facilities:	YES
HRCI Certification Preparation:	NO
SHRM Student Chapter:	YES

URL: marriottschool.byu.edu/clubs/shrm/

Fellowships:	N/A
Scholarships:	YES *
Assistantships:	YES *

*Most first-year students receive some scholarship assistance. Teaching and research assistantships are available to second-year students.

Eligibility:	Full-Time Enrollment

Curriculum

Required Courses:
Accounting
Finance
Marketing
HR Strategy
International HR
Employment Law
Development/Training

Most Popular Elective Courses:
Development/Training
Diversity
Labor Relations
Culture
Third World Development
Family-Owned Business

Career Tracks/Concentrations:
Organizational Development
Human Resource Management

Internship Required:	YES*

May substitute internship report in lieu of thesis

Career Services

Career Development Opportunities/Placement Service:

Online Job Search	SHRM Student Chapter
Resume Posting	Mentoring
Resume Services	Interview Training
Internships	Campus Interviews

Summer Internship Placement Rate:	N/A
Full-Time Placement Rate:	95%
Average Starting Salary (Full-Time Graduates):	$60,000
Average Sign-on Bonus:	$5,000
Companies Recruiting HR Master's Graduates:	30

Points of Excellence

Curriculum: The program is designed to equip individuals with theoretical, analytical, diagnostic, and "change-agent" skills. These skills help graduates gather appropriate organizational information and make appropriate interventions. Human resource management skills involving employee selection, training, compensation, and benefits and personnel law are also a central part of the curriculum.

A strong emphasis is given to applied behavioral science areas such as decision making, leadership, motivation, organization design, management of conflict, organization-environment interface, planned change, and research. Coursework is structured to give practical experience through special projects and research.

Placement: Internships are usually completed between first and second year. Longer internships for additional work experience are often suggested. Internship responsibilities can include consulting HRM, OD, training and development, and compensation analysis.

Contact Information

Master of Organizational Behavior Program
Marriott School of Management
Brigham Young University
790 TNRB
P.O. Box 23023
Provo, UT 84602
www.marriottschool.byu.edu/mob

Jean Hawkins, Graduate Program Advisor
Telephone: (801) 378-2665   FAX: (801) 378-8098
mob@byu.edu

Kate Kirkham, OB Program Director
Telephone: (801) 378-2664   FAX: (801) 378-8098
mob@byu.edu

Admission Deadlines

March 1 (Priority: January 15)
Online Application: YES

California State Polytechnic University

Pomona, California
School of Business

Degree

Master of Business Administration with an emphasis in Human Resource Management (MBA/HRM)

University Overview

Founded in 1966, Cal Poly Pomona is one of the 23 California state universities. It is located 30 miles east of Los Angeles and serves approximately 17,000 students. The College of Business emphasizes a practical, hands-on approach to learning.

Program Description

Evening program consisting of business core courses (accounting, finance, operations, marketing) with electives in Human Resources.

Degree Requirements

Total Credits Required:	48
Average Credits per Course:	4
Course Schedule:	Quarter
Total Courses Required:	12
HR/IR Courses Required:	5
Average Time for Completion:	2 ½ years
Maximum Time Allowed for Completion:	7 years
Accepts Credits from Other Universities:	YES
Total:	13 Hours (Quarter Units, 3 Classes)

Tuition

In-state	$1,584	(per year)
	N/A	(per credit hour)
Out-of-state	$1,584	(plus $164 per credit hour)
	N/A	

Program Delivery

Traditional Day Program:	NO
Nontraditional Program:	YES
Evening Program:	YES
Weekend Program:	NO
Summer Courses:	YES
Some Online Courses Offered:	YES
Full Program Online:	NO
Distance Learning/Offsite:	YES*
Executive Education:	NO
Overseas Study Abroad:	NO

Los Angeles County only

Faculty

Full-Time Faculty:	100
Part-Time Faculty:	25-30
Faculty to Student Ratio:	1:20
Primary Teaching Methods:	
Case Study	Lectures
Student Presentations	Research
Faculty Who Consult Outside:	50-74%
Faculty Involvement:	N/A
Top 5 Faculty Publications:	N/A

Students

Total Enrollment:			600
Full-Time Enrollment:			20%
Men:	59%	Women:	41%
Hispanic:	<10%	African-American:	<5%
Other Minorities:	N/A	International:	10%
Average Age:	33	Age Range:	22-58
Work Full Time:			75-99%
HR Experience:			1-24%
Speak 2nd Language:			1-24%
Minimum Admission Requirements:			
GMAT Score:			450
UGPA:			3.0
Supervisory/managerial work experience:			2 years
Other Considerations:			
Work experience and recommendation letters			
Average Student Profile:			
GMAT Score:			512
UGPA:			3.0
Work experience:			9 years

Program Resources

Students Required to Have Computers:	YES
Video Teleconferencing:	NO
Physical Library Facilities:	YES
Online Library Facilities:	YES
HRCI Certification Preparation:	NO
SHRM Student Chapter:	NO
Fellowships:	YES
Scholarships:	YES
Assistantships:	YES

Eligibility: Full-Time enrollment for fellowships and scholarships

Curriculum

Required Courses:
  Finance
  Accounting
  HR Strategy
  Marketing
  Development/Training
  Management
  Employee Relations
  Employment Law
Most Popular Elective Courses:
  Training & Development
  Compensation Plans
  Benefits & Services
  Leadership
  HR Information Management
  Staffing, Recruitment & Selection

Career Tracks/Concentrations:
Accounting
Entrepreneurship
Finance
Human Resources
Marketing
Internship Required: NO

Career Services
Career Development Opportunities/Placement Service:
Interview Training   Campus Interviews
Summer Internship Placement Rate: N/A
Full-Time Placement Rate: N/A
Average Starting Salary (Full-Time Graduates): $55,000
Average Sign-on Bonus: N/A
Companies Recruiting HR Master's Graduates: N/A

Points of Excellence
Curriculum: In addition to traditional testing methods, students are evaluated on the quality of their oral presentations, in-class experiential exercises, and team projects. Towards the end of the program, students have the option of a traditional thesis or a business project, which is frequently work-related. This gives students flexibility, but also provides the benefit of collaborating with professors with industry and/or consulting experience to help identify solutions to work-related challenges.

Contact Information
California State Polytechnic University College of Business
Graduate Programs
3801 W. Temple Ave.
Pomona, CA 91768
www.csupomona.edu

Dr. Cheryl Wyrick, SPHR
Professor of Management and Human Resources
Telephone: (909) 869-2431   FAX: (909) 869-4353
crwyrick@csupomona.edu

Admission Deadlines
June 1 for Fall admissions
Online Application: YES

California State University, Fresno

Fresno, California
Craig School of Business

Degree
Master of Business Administration with an emphasis in Human Resource Management (MBA-HRM)

University Overview
A public university, known for its commitment to excellence, ideally situated in central California with low cost of living, and close proximity to mountains (Yosemite).

Program Description
Our innovative program, taught by top faculty, is designed to address recent developments in HRM and provide the foundation for lifelong learning and performance.

Degree Requirements
Total Credits Required: 36
Average Credits per Course: 3
Course Schedule: Semester
Total Courses Required: 12

HR/IR Courses Required: 5 (9 units)
Average Time for Completion: 2
Maximum Time Allowed for Completion: 5
Accepts Credits from Other Universities: Yes
Total: 9 Credits

Tuition
In-state $1,906   (per year)
                              $103   (per credit hour)
Out-of-state $4,428   (per year)
                              $246   (per credit hour)

Program Delivery
Traditional Day Program: NO
Non-Traditional Programs: YES
    Evening Program: YES
    Weekend Program: YES
    Program Completed Evening/Weekend: YES
    Summer Courses: YES
    Some Courses Online: YES
    Full Program Online: NO
    Distance Learning/Offsite: YES
    Executive Education: YES
    Overseas Study Abroad: YES

Faculty
Full-Time Faculty: 4
Part-Time Faculty: 1
Faculty to Student Ratio: 1:20
Primary Teaching Methods:
    Case Study   Team Projects
    Experiential Learning   Group Discussion
Faculty Who Consult Outside: 25%-49%
Faculty Involvement:
    President, Academy of Legal Studies in Business
    Editor, Academy of Management, Conflict Resolution
    Division Newsletter
Top 5 Faculty Publications:
    Journal of Applied Psychology
    Innovations in Computerized Assessment
    Personnel Psychology

Students
Total Enrollment: 134
Full-Time Enrollment: 33%
    Men: 63%   Women: 37%
    Hispanic: 10%   African-American: 2%
    Other Minorities: 16%   International: 31%
    Average Age: 30   Age Range: 21-53
Work Full Time: 50%-74%
Have HR Experience: N/A
Speak 2nd Language: 50%-74%
Minimum Admission Requirements:
    UGPA: 2.5 (admission difficult below 3.0)
    GMAT Scores: GMAT   At least 25th percentile on all sections
Work Experience: 2 years
Other Considerations:
    GMAT weighed most heavily. A good GMAT score can out-
    weigh a lower GPA. The general formula is GMAT + (200 x
    GPA). Students offered admission generally score at least 1200
    points.
Average Student Profile:
    UGPA: 3.4
    GMAT score: 600
Work Experience: 7 years

Program Resources
Students Required to Have Computers: YES
Video Teleconferencing: YES

Physical Library Facilities: YES
Online Library Facilities: YES
HRCI Certification Preparation: YES
     Student study groups
     Local SHRM study groups
     Base curriculum on certification exam content
SHRM Student Chapter: YES
URL: www.csufresno.edu/StudentOrgs/SHRM/

Fellowships:	YES AMT:	$1,500
Scholarships:	YES AMT:	$1,500
Assistantships:	YES AMT:	$2,000

Eligibility: Full-time student for fellowships, part-time or full-time for scholarships and assistantships.

Curriculum

Required Courses:
     HR Strategy
     Leadership and Org. Behavior
     International HR
     Finance
     Compensation/Benefits
     Managerial Accounting
     Development/Training
     Marketing
     Recruitment/Retention
     HR Measurement
     Employment Law
     Strategic Management
     Management of Information Systems
     Government Regulation and Business Ethics
     Management Project
Most Popular Elective Courses:
     Negotiation
     Seminar in Workforce Issues
     Technology and HRM

Career Tracks/Concentrations:	N/A
Internship Required:	NO

Career Services

Career Development Opportunities/Placement Service:

Mentoring	Campus Interview
SHRM Student Chapter	Internships
Resume Services	Craig MBA web site/resume
Interview Training	posting & referral

Summer Internship Placement Rate:	N/A
Facilitate Placement:	YES
Full-Time Placement Rate:	N/A
Internship Placement Rate:	Some interns offered jobs
Average Starting Salary (Full-Time Graduates):	$52,000
Average Sign-on Bonus:	N/A
Companies Recruiting HR Master's Graduates:	N/A

Points of Excellence

We are committed to developing one of the top MBA-HRM programs in the nation. The internationally diverse faculty and students create a program that is truly global in perspective. Classes include discussions on proven theoretical concepts, as well as leading edge research testing innovative ideas. We stress the application of this knowledge in real-world situations by providing students with numerous opportunities to work closely with all types of organizations, from entrepreneurial start-ups to Fortune 500 companies. All HRM faculty are student-oriented and involve students in research ranging from alternative selection devices, test motivation, and workplace theft to training/managing virtual teams, employment law and alternative dispute resolution.

The HRM faculty have developed an innovative curriculum that allows the courses to be constantly updated according to recent changes or emphases in HRM, while still providing a very strong foundation in the core field of human resources. As a result, Craig MBA graduates are prepared to meet professional challenges and add value to their organizations.

Contact Information

The Craig MBA Program
California State University, Fresno
5245 N. Backer Ave.
M/S PB 7
Fresno, CA 93740
www.craig.csufresno.edu/mba/

Professor Mark Keppler
mkeppler@csufresno.edu
Telephone: (559) 278-2107

Professor Julie Olson-Buchanan
julieo@csufresno.edu
Telephone: (559) 278-4952

Admission Deadlines

April 1 (international applicants) and July 1 (U.S. applicants) for Fall admissions, November 1 (international applicants) and December 1 (U.S. applicants) for Spring admissions
Online Applications: YES

California State University, Hayward

Hayward, California
School of Business and Economics

Degree

Master of Business Administration with a concentration in Human Resource Management (MBA-HRM)

University Overview

Member of the California State University System, with more than 13,000 students located in the East Bay of the San Francisco Bay Area. CSUF Hayward is primarily a commuter campus.

Program Description

The HR option is an area of concentration within the MBA program. Courses are available in Strategic HRM and International HRM. Nine foundation courses are required as prerequisites.

Degree Requirements

Total Credits Required:	45
Average Credits per Course:	4
Course Schedule:	Quarter
Total Courses Required:	11
HR/IR Courses Required:	5
Average Time for Completion:	2-3 years
Maximum Time Allowed for Completion:	5 years
Accepts Credits from Other Universities:	YES
Total:	13 Graduate Hours

Tuition

In-state	$2,400	(per year)
	N/A	(per credit hour)
Out-of-state	$8,000	(per year)
	$164	(per credit hour)

Program Delivery

Traditional Day Program:	NO
Nontraditional Program:	YES
Evening Program:	YES
Weekend Program:	NO
Summer Courses:	N/A
Some Courses Online:	NO
Full Program Online:	NO
Distance Learning/Offsite:	NO
Executive Education:	NO
Overseas Study Abroad:	YES

Faculty

Full-Time Faculty:	6
Part-Time Faculty:	6
Faculty to Student Ratio:	1:20

Primary Teaching Methods:

Team Projects	Group Discussion
Student Presentations	Experiential Learning
Faculty Who Consult Outside:	50%

Faculty Involvement:
Advisor for SHRM Student Chapter

Top 5 Faculty Publications:	N/A

Students

Total Enrollment:			30
Full-Time Enrollment:			0
Men:	50%	Women	50%
Hispanic:	N/A	African-American:	N/A
Other Minorities:	N/A	International:	30%
Average Age:	32	Age Range:	N/A
Work Full Time:			75-99%
HR Experience:			N/A
Speak 2nd Language:			N/A

Minimum Admission Requirements:
GMAT score above 20% on verbal & quantitative

Other Considerations:
Upper-division GPA and GMAT score index
Work experience and recommendation letters

Average Student Profile:	N/A

Program Resources

Students Required to Have Computers:	N/A
Video Teleconferencing:	YES
Physical Library Facilities:	N/A
Online Library Facilities:	N/A
HRCI Certification Preparation:	YES

Encourages student study groups
Links students to local SHRM chapter study groups

SHRM Student Chapter:	YES
Fellowships:	N/A
Scholarships:	YES
Assistantships:	N/A
Eligibility:	N/A

Curriculum

Required Courses:
Accounting
Finance
Marketing
HR Strategy
Management
Labor Relations
Business Functional Areas

Most Popular Elective Courses:
International HRM
Compensation and Benefits
HR Training and Development

Career Tracks/Concentrations:	NO
Internship Required:	NO

Career Services

Career Development Opportunities/Placement Service:

SHRM Student Chapter	Interview Training
Campus Interviews	Internships
Summer Internship Placement Rate:	N/A
Full-Time Placement Rate:	N/A
Average Starting Salary (Full-Time Graduates):	N/A
Average Sign-on Bonus:	N/A
Companies Recruiting HR Master's Graduates:	5-10

Points of Excellence

Evening program for working professionals, small class sizes, location in San francisco Bay Area, Active Student Chapter of SHRM, access to Internships.

Contact Information

California State University, Hayward
School of Business and Economics
Graduate Programs
25800 Carlos Bee Blvd.
Hayward, CA 94542-3069
www.csuhayward.edu

Donna L. Wiley, Director of SBE Graduate Programs
Telephone: (510) 885-3964   FAX: (510) 885-2176
dwiley@csuhayward.edu

Candace M. King, Program Assistant
Telephone: (510) 885-2419   FAX: (510) 885-2176
clomg@csuhayward.edu

Admission Deadlines

June 14 for Fall admissions

Online Application:	YES

California State University, Long Beach

Long Beach, California
Department of Psychology

Degree

Master of Arts Industrial/Organizational Psychology (MAIOP)

University Overview

Public state university located in Long Beach, California, with access to the greater Los Angeles area.

Program Description

Designed for students who plan to use psychology in the solution of problems in business and industry, this program combines scientific discipline with professional practice.

Degree Requirements

Total Credits Required:	30
Average Credits per Course:	3
Course Schedule:	Semester
Total Courses Required:	9 + Thesis
HR/IR Courses Required:	9
Average Time for Completion:	2 years
Maximum Time Allowed for Completion:	7 years
Accepts Credits from Other Universities:	NO
Total:	

Tuition

In-state	$1,822	(per year)
	N/A	(per credit hour)
Out-of-state	$1,822	(per year)
	+$246	(per credit hour)

Program Delivery

Traditional Day Program:	YES
Nontraditional Program:	NO
Evening Program:	NO
Weekend Program:	NO
Program Completed Evening/Weekend:	NO
Summer Courses:	NO
Some Courses Online:	NO
Full Program Online:	NO
Distance Learning/Offsite:	NO
Executive Education:	NO
Overseas Study Abroad:	NO

Faculty

Full-Time Faculty:	3
Part-Time Faculty:	2
Faculty to Student Ratio:	1:10

Primary Teaching Methods:

Field Projects	Research
Lecture	Group Discussion

Faculty Who Consult Outside:	25-49%

Faculty Involvement:

Top 5 Faculty Publications:
Journal of Applied Psychology
Earthquake Spectra
Policy Studies Journal
Risk Analysis
Applied Psychological Measurement

Students

Total Enrollment:			22
Full-Time Enrollment:			14
Men:	23%	Women:	77%
Hispanic:	5%	African-American:	5%
Other Minorities:	27%	International:	9%
Average Age:	N/A	Age Range:	N/A
Work Full Time:			1-24%
Have HR Experience:			1-24%
Speak 2nd Language:			1-24%

Minimum Admission Requirements:

UGPA:	2.5
GRE or GMAT Scores:	NONE
Work Experience:	NONE

Other Considerations:

Average Student Profile:

UGPA:	3.6
GMAT Score:	1097 (V+Q)
Work Experience:	NONE

Program Resources

Students Required to Have Computers:			NO
Video Teleconferencing:			YES
Physical Library Facilities:			YES
Online Library Facilities:			YES
HRCI Certification Preparation:			NO
SHRM Student Chapter:			NO
URL:			
Fellowships:	YES	AMT:	$2,500/sem
Scholarships:	YES	AMT:	$1,250/sem
Assistantships:	YES	AMT:	$2,500/sem
Eligibility:	Full-Time Enrollment (Fellowships Only)		

Curriculum

Required Courses:
Development/Training
Advanced Statistics
Organizational Psychology
Personal Psychology
Test Construction
Practicum in I/O Psychology
Thesis Prep
Thesis

Most Popular Elective Courses:	N/A
Career Tracks/Concentrations:	N/A
Internship Required:	YES

Career Services

Career Services Offered:

Interview Training	Resume Services
Internships	

Summer Internship Placement Rate:	N/A
Facilitate Placement:	NO
Full-Time Placement Rate:	N/A
Internship Placement Rate:	N/A
Average Starting Salary (Full-Time Graduates):	N/A
Average Sign-on Bonus:	N/A
Companies Recruiting HR Master's Graduates:	N/A

Contact Information

Psychology Graduate Office, CSULB
1250 Bellflower Boulevard
Long Beach, CA 90840-0901
www.csulb.edu/~psych

Administrative Contact
Diane Roe
Telephone: (562) 985-5000
droe@csulb.edu

Faculty Contact
Dr. David Whitney
Telephone: (562) 985-5038
dwhitney@csulb.edu

Admission Deadlines

March 1 for Fall admissions

Online Application:	NO

California State University, San Bernardino

San Bernardino, California
MS Industrial/Organizational Psychology Program

Degree

MS Industrial/Organizational Psychology (MS IO)

University Overview

Public University at the foothills of the San Bernardino Mountains. One hour from Los Angeles.

Program Description

Master of Science degree covering all aspects of Industrial/Organizational Psychology, with an emphasis on applied knowledge and quantitative skills.

Degree Requirements

Total Credits Required:	78
Average Credits per Course:	4
Course Schedule:	Quarter

Total Courses Required:	18
HR/IR Courses Required:	12
Average Time for Completion:	2 years
Maximum Time Allowed for Completion:	5 years
Accepts Credits from Other Universities:	YES
Total:	12 Hours

Tuition

Part-Time		(per year)
	$292	(per credit hour)
Full-Time		(per year)
	$502	(per credit hour)

Program Delivery

Traditional Day Program:	YES
Nontraditional Program:	NO
Evening Program:	NO
Weekend Program:	NO
Program Completed Evening/Weekend:	NO
Summer Courses:	NO
Some Courses Online:	NO
Full Program Online:	NO
Distance Learning/Offsite:	NO
Executive Education:	NO
Overseas Study Abroad:	NO

Faculty

Full-Time Faculty:	4
Part-Time Faculty:	0
Faculty to Student Ratio:	1:20

Primary Teaching Methods:

Lecture	Research
Case Study	Student Presentation

Faculty Who Consult Outside:	50-74%
Faculty Involvement:	
Top 5 Faculty Publications:	

Students

Total Enrollment:			12
Full-Time Enrollment:			83%
Men:	40%	Women:	60%
Hispanic:	20%	African-American:	10%
Other Minorities:	N/A	International:	17%
Average Age:	28	Age Range:	25-50
Work Full Time:			1-24%
Have HR Experience:			1-24%
Speak 2nd Language:			1-24%

Minimum Admission Requirements:

UGPA:	3.4
GRE or GMAT Scores:	Not Required
Work Experience:	N/A

Other Considerations:

Average Student Profile:

UGPA:	3.5
GMAT Score:	N/A
Work Experience:	N/A

Program Resources

Students Required to Have Computers:	NO
Video Teleconferencing:	YES
Physical Library Facilities:	YES
Online Library Facilities:	YES
HRCI Certification Preparation:	NO
SHRM Student Chapter:	NO
URL:	

Fellowships:	NO	AMT:	
Scholarships:	YES	AMT:	Varies
Assistantships:	YES	AMT:	
Eligibility:			N/A

Curriculum

Required Courses:
Compensation/Benefits
Development/Training
Recruitment/Retention
Employment Law
Management
HR Measurement
Leadership
Motivation and Compensation
Group Dynamics
Professional Issues
Organizational Development
Personnel Selection
Research Methods advanced statistics
Law and Ethics

Most Popular Elective Courses:	All I/O Classes are required
Career Tracks/Concentrations:	None
Internship Required:	YES

Career Services

Career Services Offered:

Mentoring	Campus Interview

Summer Internship Placement Rate:	
Facilitate Placement:	YES
Full-Time Placement Rate:	N/A
Internship Placement Rate:	N/A
Average Starting Salary (Full-Time Graduates):	N/A
Average Sign-on Bonus:	N/A
Companies Recruiting HR Master's Graduates:	N/A

Points of Excellence

The balance of practice and research gives students many options for their future plans.

Contact Information

California State University, San Bernardino
Psychology Department
5500 University Parkway
San Bernardino, CA 92407-2397
www.csusb.edu or www.spiop.org

Administrative Contact:
Luci Van Loon
Telephone: (909) 880-5587
lvanloon@csusb.edu

Faculty Contact:
Janelle Gilbert
Telephone: (909) 880-5587
Janelle@csusb.edu

Admission Deadlines

March 1

Online Application:	YES

Capella University

Minneapolis, Minnesota
School of Business

Degree

Master of Science in Organization and Management with specialization in HR Management (MS O&M-HRM)

University Overview

Capella University is a private, online university offering MBA, Master's and PhD level degree programs in Business, Technology, Education, Psychology, and Human Services.

Program Description

HR managers and professionals gain the knowledge and strategic competencies needed to overcome the challenges of HR management while building strategic partnerships with other managers.

Degree Requirements

Total Credits Required:	48
Average Credits per Course:	4
Course Schedule:	Quarter
Total Courses Required:	12
HR/IR Courses Required:	4
Average Time for Completion:	2 ¼ years
Maximum Time Allowed for Completion:	4 years
Accepts Credits from Other Universities:	YES
Total:	12 Hours (Quarterly)

Tuition

In-state	$325	(per credit hour)
Out-of-state	$325	(per credit hour)

Program Delivery

Traditional Day Program:	NO
Nontraditional Program:	YES
Evening Program:	YES
Weekend Program:	YES
Program Completed Evening/Weekend:	YES
Summer Courses:	YES
Some Courses Online:	YES
Full Program Online:	YES
Distance Learning/Offsite:	YES
Executive Education:	YES
Overseas Study Abroad:	YES

Faculty

Full-Time Faculty:	5
Part-Time Faculty:	63
Faculty to Student Ratio:	1:20

Primary Teaching Methods:

Case Study	Team Projects
Field Projects	Group Discussion

Faculty Who Consult Outside:	100%
Faculty Involvement:	
Top 5 Faculty Publications:	

Students

Total Enrollment:			125
Full-Time Enrollment:			15%
Men:	33%	Women:	67%
Hispanic:	N/A	African-American:	N/A
Other Minorities:	N/A	International:	N/A
Average Age:	45	Age Range:	23-60
Work Full Time:			75-99%
Have HR Experience:			75-99%
Speak 2nd Language:			

Minimum Admission Requirements:

UGPA:	MS: 2.7
GRE or GMAT Scores:	N/A
Work Experience:	N/A
Combined:	N/A
Other Considerations:	N/A

Average Student Profile:

UGPA:	N/A
GMAT Score:	N/A
Work Experience:	N/A

Program Resources

Students Required to Have Computers:	YES
Video Teleconferencing:	NO
Physical Library Facilities:	NO
Online Library Facilities:	YES
HRCI Certification Preparation:	NO
SHRM Student Chapter:	NO
URL:	

Fellowships:	NO	AMT:	
Scholarships:	NO	AMT:	
Assistantships:	NO	AMT:	
Eligibility:			N/A

Curriculum

Required Courses:
- Accounting
- Finance
- Marketing
- Management
- Human Resource Management
- Information System Management
- Strategic Planning
- Management & Organizational Behavior

Most Popular Elective Courses:
- Gender and Diversity Issues
- Training and Development
- Conflict Management
- Performance Management
- Redefining the Workplace: The New Revolution

Career Tracks/Concentrations:	N/A
Internship Required:	NO

Career Services

Career Services Offered:
- Mentoring

Summer Internship Placement Rate:	N/A
Facilitate Placement:	NO
Full-Time Placement Rate:	N/A
Internship Placement Rate:	N/A
Average Starting Salary (Full-Time Graduates):	N/A
Average Sign-on Bonus:	N/A
Companies Recruiting HR Master's Graduates:	N/A

Points of Excellence

Capella University has a large online Organization and Management program, offering both a Master's and PhD with a specialization in Human Resource Management in the Capella University School of Business, adult learners can gain a graduate business education from an accredited institution through a flexible, online format that makes time for career, family and other commitments.

Courses in the Master's program are delivered in an instructor-led, asynchronous online format. Courses generally have 10-20 learners, have an established beginning and end date, and are 12 weeks in length. In addition to assigned course materials and case exercises, learners participate in weekly threaded discussions that cover key business topics. No set class meeting times exist; students typically invest 10 hours per week per course.

Capella faculty members are subject-matter experts of the highest caliber, each offering an ideal balance of in-depth theoretical knowledge and real-world practice to best prepare tomorrow's leaders. All of our faculty subscribe to a scholar-practitioner approach to advanced business education, encouraging learners to apply theoretical principles and research to their professional practice.

Capella was selected by the North Central Association of Colleges and Schools AQIP (Academic Quality Improvement Project) as its first online member, ensuring that Capella will stay on the leading edge of quality education.

Contact Information
Capella University
222 South 9th Street, 20th Floor
Minneapolis, MN 55402
www.capellauniversity.edu

Administrative Contact:
Wilson Garland
Telephone: (612) 252-4230
wgarland@capella.edu

Faculty Contact:
Nancy Johnson, Ph.D.
Telephone: (888) 227-3552
njohnson@capella.edu

Admission Deadlines
Students admitted monthly. Applications must be submitted during preceding month.

Online Application:	YES

Case Western Reserve University

Cleveland, Ohio
Weatherhead School of Management,
Department of Organizational Behavior

Degree
Master of Science in Organization Development and Analysis (MSODA)

University Overview
Case Western Reserve University is a private university created in 1967 through the federation of Western Reserve University (1826) and Case Institute of Technology (1880), with an enrollment of more than 9,500 students.

Program Description
Since 1975, the Department of Organization Behavior has offered a nontraditional master's degree program in organization development and analysis to meet the need for knowledgeable, action-oriented, and highly competent practitioners. Students meet in classes once a month for three days: Thursday, 9:00-9:00; Friday and Saturday, 9:00-5:00 plus two workshops per year of four to five days of intensive study.

Degree Requirements
Total Credits Required:	40
Average Credits per Course:	3-4
Course Schedule:	Semester
Total Courses Required:	12
HR/IR Courses Required:	11
Average Time for Completion:	2 years
Maximum Time Allowed for Completion:	N/A
Accepts Credits from Other Universities:	N/A
Total:	N/A

Tuition
In-state	N/A	(per year)
	$834	(per credit hour)
Out-of-state	N/A	(per year)
	$834	(per credit hour)

Program Delivery
Traditional Day Program:	NO
Nontraditional Program:	YES
Evening Program:	NO
Weekend Program:	YES
Summer Courses:	N/A
Some Courses Online:	NO
Full Program Online:	NO
Distance Learning/Offsite:	NO
Executive Education:	N/A
Overseas Study Abroad:	YES

Faculty
Full-Time Faculty:	14
Part-Time Faculty:	0
Faculty to Student Ratio:	1:10

Primary Teaching Methods:
Case Study	Lecture
Team Projects	Field Projects
Experiential Learning	Student Presentation
Group Discussion	

Faculty Who Consult Outside:	50-74%
Faculty Involvement:	See web site
Top 5 Faculty Publications:	See web site

Students
Total Enrollment:			31
Full-Time Enrollment:			100%
Men:	23%	Women:	77%
Hispanic:	3%	African-American:	23%
Other Minorities:	0%	International:	0%
Average Age:	35	Age Range:	25-55
Work Full Time:			100%
HR Experience:			100%
Speak 2nd Language:			N/A

Minimum Admission Requirements:
Full-Time employment
Work experience:	5 years
Other Considerations:	N/A

Average Student Profile:
Work experience:	5-25 years

Program Resources
Students Required to Have Computers:	N/A
Video Teleconferencing:	NO
Physical Library Facilities:	N/A
Online Library Facilities:	N/A
HRCI Certification Preparation:	NO
SHRM Student Chapter:	NO
Fellowships:	NO
Scholarships:	NO
Assistantships:	NO
Eligibility:	N/A

Curriculum
Required Courses:
Human Resource Systems
Team Building
Leadership Skills
Organizational Analysis
Human Systems
Group & Interpersonal Skills
Management of Change
Management of Work
Organization Development
Training Design
Career Planning
Professional Development
Organizations & the Environment

Most Popular Elective Courses:	N/A
Career Tracks/Concentrations:	N/A
Internship Required:	NO

41

Career Services

Career Development Opportunities/Placement Service:
    No placement activities

Summer Internship Placement Rate:	N/A
Full-Time Placement Rate:	N/A
Average Starting Salary (Full-Time Graduates):	N/A
Average Sign-on Bonus:	N/A
Companies Recruiting HR Master's Graduates:	N/A

Points of Excellence

Curriculum: This Organization Development program embodies an action-based approach to learning. Program goals were conceived in terms of what practitioners in the field must be able to do, and learning activities are geared to the achievement of these goals. Students are evaluated in terms of their action skills and their theoretical knowledge. The method of program delivery enables the full-time working professional to obtain a master's degree within the same amount of time as the traditional student.

Contact Information

Case Western Reserve University
Weatherhead School of Management
Cleveland, OH 44106-7235
www.weather.cwru.edu/orbh

Eric H. Neilsen, Professor & Program Director
Telephone: (216) 368-2055   FAX: (216) 368-4785
ehn@po.cwru.edu

Retta Holdorf, Department Administrator
Telephone: (216) 368-2055   FAX: (216) 368-4785
rmh2@po.cwru.edu

Admission Deadlines

Online Application:	NO

Chapman University, Bay Area

Fairfield, California

Degree

Master of Science in Human Resources (MSHR)

University Overview

Chapman University is an independent non-profit institution. The main campus is in Orange, California. We have approximately 26 regional campuses from Phoenix, Arizona, to Seattle, Washington.

Program Description

While the Orange campus targets anyone desiring a quality education, the regional campuses are set up to enable busy, working adults to receive quality education at their own pace.

Degree Requirements

Total Credits Required:	36
Average Credits per Course:	3
Course Schedule:	Semester
Total Courses Required:	12
HR/IR Courses Required:	8
Average Time for Completion:	2 years
Maximum Time Allowed for Completion:	7 years
Accepts Credits from Other Universities:	YES
Total:	9 Hours

Tuition

In-state		(per year)
	$290	(per credit hour)
Out-of-state		(per year)
	$290	(per credit hour)

Program Delivery

Traditional Day Program:	YES
Nontraditional Program:	YES
Evening Program:	YES
Weekend Program:	NO
Program Completed Evening/Weekend:	YES
Summer Courses:	YES
Some Courses Online:	NO
Full Program Online:	NO
Distance Learning/Offsite:	NO
Executive Education:	NO
Overseas Study Abroad:	NO

Faculty

Full-Time Faculty:	N/A
Part-Time Faculty:	125
Faculty to Student Ratio:	1:10

Primary Teaching Methods:
Case Study	Research
Student Presentation	Lecture

Faculty Who Consult Outside:
Faculty Involvement:
Top 5 Faculty Publications:

Students

Total Enrollment:
Full-Time Enrollment:

Men:	30%	Women:	70%
Hispanic:	5%	African-American:	7%
Other Minorities:	33%	International:	
Average Age:	39	Age Range:	18-56+

Work Full Time:	75-99%
Have HR Experience:	25-49%
Speak 2nd Language:	1-24%

Minimum Admission Requirements:
    UGPA: 2.5-2.99 with appropriate entrance exam. 3.0 without
    GRE or GMAT Scores:

Work Experience:	NO

Other Considerations:
Average Student Profile:

UGPA:	3.2
GMAT Score:	1100
Work Experience:	N/A

Program Resources

Students Required to Have Computers:	NO
Video Teleconferencing:	NO
Physical Library Facilities:	NO
Online Library Facilities:	YES
HRCI Certification Preparation:	YES
SHRM Student Chapter:	NO

URL:
Fellowships:	NO	AMT:
Scholarships:	NO	AMT:
Assistantships:	NO	AMT:
Eligibility:		N/A

Curriculum

Required Courses:
    HR Strategy
    Recruitment/Retention
    Compensation/Benefits
    Employment Law

HR Systems
Organizational Dynamics
Organizational Change
Organizational Research Methods
Most Popular Elective Courses:
    Conflict and Negotiation
    Training and Development
    Career Management
    Leadership and Team Development
Career Tracks/Concentrations:
    Human Resource   Organizational Leadership
Internship Required: NO

Career Services

Career Services Offered:	NO
Summer Internship Placement Rate:	N/A
Facilitate Placement:	N/A
Full-Time Placement Rate:	N/A
Internship Placement Rate:	N/A
Average Starting Salary (Full-Time Graduates):	N/A
Average Sign-on Bonus:	N/A
Companies Recruiting HR Master's Graduates:	N/A

Points of Excellence

The goal of the Human Resources program at Chapman University, University College, is to provide students with specialized knowledge of the systems of human resources in organizations. The program focuses on theories and practical applications of human resources, as well as the role of the human resource practitioner as a change agent and strategic partner.

The degree program is a unique interdisciplinary course of study, specifically designed to provide the working professional with the specialized skills and knowledge to address cultural, regulatory, behavioral and social changes in today's diverse society, and to deal with them effectively, efficiently, and with sensitivity and compassion.

Through the use of case studies, group discussion, and research, students learn current issues in the Human Resource field that organizations face today. The Human Resources program prepares its graduates to attract, retain, and develop needed talent in organizations (public, private, military, or non-profit), and to become partners with top management in policy making and strategic decision making.

Contact Information

Chapman University Bay Area
450 Chadbourne Road
Fairfield, CA 94585
www.chapman.edu

Administrative and Faculty Contact
Jerrold Strong, M.A., Program Manager
Telephone: (707) 438-2125
strong@chapman.edu

Admission Deadlines

May 5 for Fall admissions
Online Application: NO

Chapman University

Palm Desert, California
Betty Hutton Williams-Coachella Valley Campus

Degree
Master of Science in Human Resources (MSHR)

University Overview
Chapman University is a private liberal arts university. The main campus is in Orange, California. The Betty Hutton Williams-Coachella Valley Campus is a branch of the university and is located in Palm Desert, California.

Program Description
The Master of Science in Human Resources is a non-traditional generalist HR degree program aimed at mid-level managers and designed for working professionals.

Degree Requirements

Total Credits Required:	36
Average Credits per Course:	3
Course Schedule:	Semester
Total Courses Required:	12
HR/IR Courses Required:	12
Average Time for Completion:	1 ¼ years
Maximum Time Allowed for Completion:	7 years
Accepts Credits from Other Universities:	YES
Total:	9 Hours

Tuition

In-state	N/A	(per year)
	$265	(per credit hour)
Out-of-state	N/A	(per year)
	$265	(per credit hour)

Program Delivery

Traditional Day Program:	NO
Nontraditional Program:	YES
Evening Program:	YES
Weekend Program:	NO
Program Completed Evening/Weekend:	YES
Summer Courses:	YES
Some Courses Online:	NO
Full Program Online:	NO
Distance Learning/Offsite:	NO
Executive Education:	NO
Overseas Study Abroad:	NO

Faculty

Full-Time Faculty:	1
Part-Time Faculty:	6
Faculty to Student Ratio:	1:10

Primary Teaching Methods:

Case Study	Team Projects
Student Presentation	Experiential learning
Computer-aided Instruction	

Faculty Who Consult Outside:	1-24%
Faculty Involvement:	
Top 5 Faculty Publications:	

Students

Total Enrollment:			20
Full-Time Enrollment:			0
Men:	60%	Women:	40%
Hispanic:	15%	African-American:	0%
Other Minorities:	5%	International:	0%
Average Age:	35	Age Range:	25-55

Work Full Time:	75-99%
Have HR Experience:	50-74%
Speak 2nd Language:	25-49%

Minimum Admission Requirements:
UGPA: 2.5-2.99 with appropriate entrance exam. 3.0 without

GRE or GMAT Scores:	GRE 900 on 2 of 3 tests
Work Experience:	NO

Other Considerations:
Average Student Profile:

UGPA:	3.2
GMAT Score:	N/A
Work Experience:	N/A

Program Resources

Students Required to Have Computers:	NO
Video Teleconferencing:	NO
Physical Library Facilities:	YES
Online Library Facilities:	YES
HRCI Certification Preparation:	YES
SHRM Student Chapter:	NO
URL:	
Fellowships:	NO AMT:
Scholarships:	NO AMT:
Assistantships:	NO AMT:
Eligibility:	N/A

Curriculum

Required Courses:
HR Strategy
Compensation/Benefits
Development/Training
Recruitment/Retention
Employment Law
Strategic Management
Employee Relations
HR Measurement
Organizational Dynamics
Organizational Research

Most Popular Elective Courses:
Conflict Resolution
Consulting
Training and Development
HR Information Systems
Internship

Career Tracks/Concentrations:
Human Resources Manager   HR Specialist positions
Career Counselor   Consultant
Trainer or Facilitator

Internship Required: NO

Career Services

Career Services Offered:
Mentoring   Interview Training
Internships

Summer Internship Placement Rate:	N/A
Facilitate Placement:	YES – limited on-site career center
Full-Time Placement Rate:	N/A
Internship Placement Rate:	N/A
Average Starting Salary (Full-Time Graduates):	N/A
Average Sign-on Bonus:	N/A
Companies Recruiting HR Master's Graduates:	N/A

Contact Information

Chapman University Betty Hutton Williams-Coachella Valley
42-600 Cook Street, Suite 134
Palm Desert, CA 92211

Administrative Contact
Ron Stephens
Telephone: (760) 341-8051
Stephens@chapman.edu

Faculty Contact
Johann Von Flue, Ph.D.
Telephone: (760) 341-8051
jvonflue@chapman.edu

Chapman University

Orange, California
Department of Human Resources

Degree
Master of Science in Human Resources (MSHR)

University Overview
Chapman University is a private liberal arts university in Orange, California, with an enrollment of approximately 3,700 students. Additionally, branch campuses throughout California and Washington offer the MSHR program.

Program Description
The Master of Science in Human Resources (MSHR) program is a nontraditional, generalist HR degree program aimed at mid-level managers. This highly experimental program emphasizes student-centered learning.

Degree Requirements

Total Credits Required:	36
Average Credits per Course:	3
Course Schedule:	Semester
Total Courses Required:	12
HR/IR Courses Required:	12
Average Time for Completion:	2-3 years
Maximum Time Allowed for Completion:	7 years
Accepts Credits from Other Universities:	YES
Total:	9 Hours

Tuition

In-state	N/A	(per year)
	$430	(per credit hour)
Out-of-state	N/A	(per year)
	$430	(per credit hour)

Program Delivery

Traditional Day Program:	NO
Nontraditional Program:	YES
Evening Program:	YES
Weekend Program:	NO
Summer Courses:	YES
Some Courses Online:	NO
Full Program Online:	NO
Distance Learning/Offsite:	YES
Executive Education:	NO
Overseas Study Abroad:	NO

Faculty

Full-Time Faculty:	5
Part-Time Faculty:	3
Faculty to Student Ratio:	1:18

Primary Teaching Methods:
Case Study   Student Presentation
Team Projects   Experiential Learning
Computer-Aided Instruction

Faculty Who Consult Outside:		1-24%

Faculty Involvement:
  2002 Chair, SHRM Foundation Board
  National Executive Board of Academy of Management for
  Careers Division
Top 5 Faculty Publications:
  Journal of Vocational Behavior
  Group and Organization Management
  Women in Management Review
  Corporate Reputation Review
  Human Resource Management Review

Students

Total Enrollment:		301
Full-Time Enrollment:		17%
Men:	32%	Women: 68%
Hispanic:	9%	African-American: 3%
Other Minorities:	11%	International: 3%
Average Age:	30	Age Range: 25-55
Work Full Time:		75-99%
HR Experience:		75-99%
Speak 2nd Language:		1-24%

Minimum Admission Requirements:
  GRE Score: 900 on 2 of 3 or
  (UGPA X 200) + GMAT: 1000
Other Considerations:
  If UGPA above 3.0, no entrance exam required.
Average Student Profile:
  Work experience: 3-15 years

Program Resources

Students Required to Have Computers:		NO
Video Teleconferencing:		NO
Physical Library Facilities:		YES
Online Library Facilities:		YES
HRCI Certification Preparation:		YES

  Student study groups
  Offers SHRM Learning System as a teaching tool

SHRM Student Chapter:		YES
Fellowships:		NO
Scholarships:	3	AMT: $1,800
Assistantships:		NO
Eligibility:		All Students

Curriculum

Required Courses:
  HR Systems
  Organizational Change
  Organizational Dynamics
  Recruitment/Retention
  Compensation/Benefits
  Employment Law
  HR Measurement
  Strategic HR
  Accounting
Most Popular Elective Courses:
  Training/Development
  Team Building
  Consulting
  HRIS
  Career Management
  Conflict/Negotiation

Career Tracks/Concentrations:	N/A
Internship Required:	NO

Career Services

Career Development Opportunities/Placement Service:
  Mentoring   Resume Services
  SHRM Student Chapter   Interview Training
  Campus Interviews   Internships

Summer Internship Placement Rate:	N/A
Full-Time Placement Rate:	N/A
Average Starting Salary (Full-Time Graduates):	N/A
Average Sign-on Bonus:	N/A
Companies Recruiting HR Master's Graduates:	N/A

Points of Excellence

Faculty: The use of practitioners to support the program is a point of excellence. The Advisory Board composed of HR executives from Orange County is very involved. These executives work closely with students. In addition, the Executive Human Resource Forum of Orange County sponsors an Executive Lecture Series.

Curriculum: Another point of excellence is the method for continuously evaluating and updating the curriculum. The faculty reviews all syllabi, textbooks, and resources yearly. The Human Resource Advisory Board reviews all changes.

Contact Information

Chapman University
Master of Science in Human Resources
One University Drive
Orange, CA 92866
www.chapman.edu

Becky Ballestero, Program Coordinator
Telephone: (714) 628-7319   FAX: (714) 997-6641
balleste@chapman.edu

Dr. Amy E. Hurley, Associate Professor, Program Chair
SHRM Student Chapter Advisor
Telephone: (714) 628-7312   FAX: (714) 997-6641
ahurley@chapman.edu

Chapman University, Sacramento

Sacramento, California

Degree

Master of Science Human Resources (MSHR)

University Overview

Chapman University is a 140 year-old independent institution of liberal arts and professional training dedicated to providing students with a solid foundation of knowledge. Chapman's mission is to provide personalized education of distinction that leads to inquiring, ethical, and productive lives as global citizens.

Degree Requirements

Total Credits Required:	36
Average Credits per Course:	3
Course Schedule:	10-week terms
Total Courses Required:	12
HR/IR Courses Required:	12
Average Time for Completion:	2 years
Maximum Time Allowed for Completion:	7 years
Accepts Credits from Other Universities:	YES
Total:	9 Hours

Tuition

In-state	N/A	(per year)
	$290	(per credit hour)
Out-of-state	N/A	(per year)
	$290	(per credit hour)

Program Delivery

Traditional Day Program:	NO
Nontraditional Program:	YES
Evening Program:	YES
Weekend Program:	NO
Program Completed Evening/Weekend:	YES
Summer Courses:	YES
Some Courses Online:	NO
Full Program Online:	NO
Distance Learning/Offsite:	NO
Executive Education:	NO
Overseas Study Abroad:	NO

Faculty

Full-Time Faculty:	0
Part-Time Faculty:	11
Faculty to Student Ratio:	1:10

Primary Teaching Methods:

Case Study	Team Projects
Group Discussion	Lecture

Faculty Who Consult Outside:	N/A
Faculty Involvement:	
Top 5 Faculty Publications:	

Students

Total Enrollment:			9
Full-Time Enrollment:			0
Men:	0%	Women:	100%
Hispanic:	0%	African-American:	0%
Other Minorities:	11%	International:	0%
Average Age:	35	Age Range:	29-44
Work Full Time:			75-99%
Have HR Experience:			50-74%
Speak 2nd Language:			1-24%

Minimum Admission Requirements:

UGPA:	3.0
GRE or GMAT Scores:	900 on two sections of GRE
Work Experience:	0 years
Other Considerations:	

Average Student Profile:

UGPA:	
GMAT Score:	
Work Experience:	0 years

Program Resources

Students Required to Have Computers:			NO
Video Teleconferencing:			NO
Physical Library Facilities:			NO
Online Library Facilities:			YES
HRCI Certification Preparation:			YES
SHRM Student Chapter:			NO
URL:			
Fellowships:	NO	AMT:	
Scholarships:	NO	AMT:	
Assistantships:	NO	AMT:	
Eligibility:			N/A

Curriculum

Required Courses:
 Accounting
 HR Strategy
 Compensation/Benefits
 Recruitment/Retention
 Employment Law
 Management
 HR Measurement
 Organizational Leadership
 Organizational Research Methods
 Leading Organizational Change
 Organizational Dynamics

Most Popular Elective Courses:
 Leadership & Team Development
 Self, Systems & Leadership
 Foundations of Organizational Leadership
 Democracy, Ethics & Leadership
 Training & Development
 Consulting

Career Tracks/Concentrations:	NONE
Internship Required:	NO

Career Services

Career Services Offered:	NO
Summer Internship Placement Rate:	N/A
Facilitate Placement:	NO
Full-Time Placement Rate:	N/A
Internship Placement Rate:	N/A
Average Starting Salary (Full-Time Graduates):	N/A
Average Sign-on Bonus:	N/A
Companies Recruiting HR Master's Graduates:	N/A

Points of Excellence

At Chapman, Human Resources students are exposed to faculty and students from other disciplines such as organizational leadership, health administration, or criminal justice. Human resources colleagues in the classroom are working in human resources and offer both a professional and personal source of networking and support. Class schedules are designed for working professionals with all classes held in the evenings.

Chapman's program provides through, broad coverage of all the human resources "subsystems" such as recruitment, selection, training, and compensation. Chapman also offers a diverse selection of electives that focus on contemporary issues facing both organizations and human resources practitioners working within those organizations.

Contact Information

Chapman University Sacramento
855 Howe Avenue
Sacramento, CA 95825
www.chapman.edu

Administrative and Faculty Contact
Susan Osborn, Ph.D.
Telephone: (916) 561-1961
sosborn@chapman.edu

Admission Deadlines

None. Students accepted start at the beginning of next term.

Claremont Graduate University

Claremont, California
School of Behavioral and Organizational Sciences

Degree
Master of Science in Human Resources Design

University Overview
Founded in 1925, Claremont Graduate University (CGU) is a private university located in Southern California, approximately 35 miles east of Los Angeles. CGU has 2,000 students in 22 fields of study.

Program Description
The Human Resources Design (HRD) program is designed to enable students to become organizational strategic partners in their companies. Target student is a full-time working professional.

Degree Requirements
Total Credits Required:	36
Average Credits per Course:	2
Course Schedule:	Semester
Total Courses Required:	12
HR/IR Courses Required:	5
Average Time for Completion:	1 ½ years
Maximum Time Allowed for Completion:	5 years
Accepts Credits from Other Universities:	YES
Total:	6 Hours

Tuition
In-state	N/A	(per year)
	$1,000	(per credit hour)
Out-of-state	N/A	(per year)
	$1,000	(per credit hour)

Program Delivery
Traditional Day Program:	NO
Nontraditional Program:	YES
Evening Program:	YES
Weekend Program:	YES
Program Completed Evening/Weekend:	YES
Summer Courses:	YES
Some Courses Online:	NO
Full Program Online:	NO
Distance Learning/Offsite:	NO
Executive Education:	YES
Overseas Study Abroad:	YES

Certain classes have a travel component to them. These are optional classes.

Faculty
Full-Time Faculty:	2
Part-Time Faculty:	19
Faculty to Student Ratio:	1:10

Primary Teaching Methods:
Case Study	Team Projects
Student Presentation	Group Discussion

Faculty Who Consult Outside:	75-99%
Faculty Involvement:	
Top 5 Faculty Publications:	

Students
Total Enrollment:			36
Full-Time Enrollment:			7
Men:	25%	Women:	75%

Hispanic:	17%	African-American:	3%
Other Minorities:	19%	International:	0%
Average Age:	30	Age Range:	22-45
Work Full Time:			50-74%
Have HR Experience:			50-74%
Speak 2nd Language:			50-74%

Minimum Admission Requirements:
UGPA:	N/A
GRE or GMAT Scores:	N/A
Work Experience:	Not required, but prefer 5+ years
Other Considerations:	

Average Student Profile:
UGPA:	3.5
GMAT Score:	550-600
Work Experience:	7 years

Program Resources
Students Required to Have Computers:	NO
Video Teleconferencing:	YES
Physical Library Facilities:	YES
Online Library Facilities:	YES
HRCI Certification Preparation:	YES
SHRM Student Chapter:	NO
URL:	

Fellowships:	YES	AMT:	Varies
Scholarships:	NO	AMT:	
Assistantships:	YES	AMT:	Varies
Eligibility:			

Curriculum
Required Courses:
- Accounting
- Finance
- HR Strategy
- Employment Law
- HR Measurement
- Organizational Behavior and Change Management
- Strategic Management
- Organization Behavior Theory
- Inquiry Skills

Most Popular Elective Courses:
- Consulting
- Arbitration & Dispute Resolution
- Labor Relations
- International HR
- Compensation & Benefits

Career Tracks/Concentrations:
Human Resources	Organizational Behavior/
Evaluation	Psychology
Management	

Internship Required:	NO

Career Services
Career Services Offered:
Field Trips	Interview Training
Resume Services	Campus Interview
Internships	

Summer Internship Placement Rate:	N/A
Facilitate Placement:	YES
Full-Time Placement Rate:	10%
Internship Placement Rate:	N/A
Average Starting Salary (Full-Time Graduates):	$65,000
Average Sign-on Bonus:	N/A
Companies Recruiting HR Master's Graduates:	N/A

Points of Excellence
Education at Claremont Graduate University (CGU) is student centered, characterized by personal attention and flexibility. Working closely with a responsive staff and engaged faculty, stu-

dents have the opportunity to create, within the limits of degree requirements, a course of study and research that is best suited for their needs and interests. In addition, CGU's limited enrollment lends itself to small classes, close faculty-student relationships, and individual attention. CGU's unique status as the only comprehensive independent graduate institution in the country enables it to provide students with an incomparable environment in which to excel.

As a member of the prestigious Claremont Colleges Consortium, CGU provides its students with the best of two worlds often considered mutually exclusive: intimate education and the facilities and academic breadth of a much larger institution. In addition, many of the 550 faculty members from the undergraduate Claremont colleges – Pomona, Scripps, Claremont McKenna, Harvey Mudd, and Pitzer colleges and affiliated institutions participate actively in the graduate University's academic programs.

Specifically designed for the working adult, all Master of Science Human Resources Design (MSHRD) courses are offered in the evening or on Saturdays. Students may choose to take elective courses in the MSHRD program, or with approval, at another CGU academic unit, including the Peter F. Drucker Graduate School of Management and the Information Science Department.

Finally, the curriculum is reviewed annually by the faculty and an advisory committee.

Contact Information
Claremont Graduate University, SBOS/HRD
123 E. 8th Street
Claremont, CA 91711
www.cgu.edu/sbos/hrd

Administrative Contact
Donna Monika
Telephone: (909) 607-3286
hrd@cgu.edu

Faculty Contact
Dale Berger
Dale.berger@cgu.edu

Admission Deadlines
Rolling admissions, February 15 for institutional aid
Online Application: YES

Cleveland State University

Cleveland, Ohio
Department of Psychology

Degree
Master of Arts in Psychology (MAP)

University Overview
Cleveland State University (CSU) is located in downtown Cleveland, Ohio.

Program Description
The Consumer and Industrial Research Program (CIRP) is a unique mix between consumer behavior and Industrial/Organizational psychology. CIRP prepares students to apply psychological concepts and research techniques in business and organizational settings. It combines advanced quantitative research with hands-on experience involving problems and issues encountered in the workplace.

Degree Requirements
Total Credits Required:	43
Average Credits per Course:	4
Course Schedule:	Semester
Total Courses Required:	11
HR/IR Courses Required:	4
Average Time for Completion:	2 years
Maximum Time Allowed for Completion:	5 years
Accepts Credits from Other Universities:	YES
Total:	Varies

Tuition
In-state	$5,964	(per year)
	$249	(per credit hour)
Out-of-state	$11,791	(per year)
	$491	(per credit hour)

Program Delivery
Traditional Day Program:	YES
Nontraditional Program:	YES
Evening Program:	YES
Weekend Program:	NO
Program Completed Evening/Weekend:	NO
Summer Courses:	YES
Some Courses Online:	NO
Full Program Online:	NO
Distance Learning/Offsite:	NO
Executive Education:	NO
Overseas Study Abroad:	NO

Faculty
Full-Time Faculty:	3
Part-Time Faculty:	Varies
Faculty to Student Ratio:	1:10
Primary Teaching Methods:	
Lecture	Research
Team Projects	Group Discussion
Faculty Who Consult Outside:	25-49%
Faculty Involvement:	
SIOP Program Review Committee	

Top 5 Faculty Publications:
Personality and Individual Differences
Journal of Applied Social Psychology
Handbook of Quantitative Methods in Public Administration
Evaluation in Practice: A Methodological Approach

Students
Total Enrollment:			26
Full-Time Enrollment:			26
Men:	31%	Women:	69%
Hispanic:	4%	African-American:	4%
Other Minorities:	4%	International:	12%
Average Age:	29	Age Range:	23-66
Work Full Time:			1-24%
Have HR Experience:			1-24%
Speak 2nd Language:			1-24%
Minimum Admission Requirements:			
UGPA:			3.0
GRE or GMAT Scores:		500 Verbal, 500 Quantitative on GRE	
Work Experience:			NO
Other Considerations:			
Average Student Profile:			
UGPA:			3.5
GMAT Score:		550V, 550Q on GRE	
Work Experience:			0

Program Resources

Students Required to Have Computers:		NO
Video Teleconferencing:		YES
Physical Library Facilities:		YES
Online Library Facilities:		YES
HRCI Certification Preparation:		NO
SHRM Student Chapter:		YES
URL:		
Fellowships:	NO	AMT:
Scholarships:	NO	AMT:
Assistantships:	YES	AMT: $5,964
Eligibility:		Full-Time Enrollment

Curriculum

Required Courses:
Marketing
Recruiting/Retention
International HR
HR Measurement
Development/Training
Personnel Psychology
Organization Psychology
Marketing Research
Most Popular Elective Courses:
Job Analysis and Performance Appraisal
Consumer Psychology
Career Tracks/Concentrations:

Marketing Researchers	HR Managers
HR Consultants	

Internship Required: NO

Career Services

Career Services Offered:

Resume Services	Interview Training
Campus Interview	Internships

Summer Internship Placement Rate:	N/A
Facilitate Placement:	YES
Full-Time Placement Rate:	50%
Internship Placement Rate:	N/A
Average Starting Salary (Full-Time Graduates):	$30-40,000
Average Sign-on Bonus:	N/A
Companies Recruiting HR Master's Graduates:	N/A

Points of Excellence

The graduate specialization in Consumer Industrial Research (CIRP), which leads to the degree of Master of Arts in Psychology, prepares students to apply psychological concepts and research techniques in business and institutional settings. The program is designed to be completed in two years, culminating with a Master's thesis or an applied research project. To ensure that the program is geared to one's strengths and interests, a close working relationship is encouraged between each student and a specific faculty member. Additionally, it is expected that all students will have the opportunity to participate in actual research projects, often in conjunction with members of the faculty. This practical experience, whatever the form, occurs primarily after completion of the first year of study.

Contact Information

Cleveland State University
Department of Psychology
2300 Chester Avenue
Cleveland, OH 44114
www.csuohio.edu/psy

Administrative Contact
Barb Durfey
Telephone: (216) 687-2544
b.durfey@csuohio.edu

Faculty Contact
Dr. Chieh-Chen Bowen
Telephone: (216) 687-2582
c.c.bowen@csuohio.edu

Admission Deadlines

February 15, April 15
Online Application: NO

Colorado State University – Denver Center

Denver, Colorado
School of Education

Degree

Master of Education in Education and Human Resource Studies (MSEHRS)

University Overview

Colorado State University – Denver Center is located in downtown Denver, Colorado. The university is designated as the land grant university for Colorado, focusing on teaching, research, extension, and public service.

Program Description

The Denver-based Human Resource Development Master's degree is geared toward working professionals in the fields of training, management, and human resources.

Degree Requirements

Total Credits Required:	36
Average Credits per Course:	3
Course Schedule:	Semester
Total Courses Required:	11
HR/IR Courses Required:	11
Average Time for Completion:	1¾ years
Maximum Time Allowed for Completion:	10 years
Accepts Credits from Other Universities:	NO
Total:	

Tuition

In-state	$6,500	(per year)
	N/A	(per credit hour)
Out-of-state	$6,500	(per year)
	N/A	(per credit hour)

Program Delivery

Traditional Day Program:	NO
Nontraditional Program:	YES
Evening Program:	YES
Weekend Program:	NO
Program Completed Evening/Weekend:	YES
Summer Courses:	YES
Some Courses Online:	NO
Full Program Online:	NO
Distance Learning/Offsite:	NO
Executive Education:	NO
Overseas Study Abroad:	YES

Faculty

Full-Time Faculty:	7
Part-Time Faculty:	4
Faculty to Student Ratio:	1:20

Primary Teaching Methods:

Case Study	Research
Team Projects	Group Discussion

Faculty Who Consult Outside:	25-49%

Faculty Involvement:
Board of Directors, Academy of Human Resource Development
Series Editor, New Perspectives of Organizational Learning, Performance, and Change

Top 5 Faculty Publications:
Performance Improvement Quarterly
Performance Improvement Journal
HRD Quarterly
HRD International
Journal of Education Reform

Students

Total Enrollment:			60
Full-Time Enrollment:			
Men:	N/A	Women:	N/A
Hispanic:		African-American:	
Other Minorities:		International:	5%
Average Age:	35	Age Range:	25-60
Work Full Time:			75-99%
Have HR Experience:			50-74%
Speak 2nd Language:			1-24%

Minimum Admission Requirements:

UGPA:	N/A
GRE or GMAT Scores:	1350 GRE
Work Experience:	2 years

Other Considerations:
Average Student Profile:

UGPA:	3.0
GMAT Score:	1350 GRE
Work Experience:	5 years

Program Resources

Students Required to Have Computers:		NO
Video Teleconferencing:		YES
Physical Library Facilities:		NO
Online Library Facilities:		YES
HRCI Certification Preparation:		NO
SHRM Student Chapter:		YES
URL: www.colostate.edu/Depts/HRD/DenverCenter/SHRM		
Fellowships:	NO	AMT:
Scholarships:	NO	AMT:
Assistantships:	NO	AMT:
Eligibility:		N/A

Curriculum

Required Courses:
HR Strategy
International HR
Development/Training
Management
Career Development
Organization Development

Most Popular Elective Courses:	N/A
Career Tracks/Concentrations:	N/A
Internship Required:	NO

Career Services

Career Services Offered:

SHRM Student Chapter	Resume Services
Career support services	Networking

Summer Internship Placement Rate:	N/A
Facilitate Placement:	YES
Full-Time Placement Rate:	10-20%
Internship Placement Rate:	N/A
Average Starting Salary (Full-Time Graduates):	N/A
Average Sign-on Bonus:	N/A
Companies Recruiting HR Master's Graduates:	N/A

Points of Excellence

US News and World Report ranked Colorado State University's Human Resource Development (HRD) program in the top 10 career and technical graduate programs in the country. The program is cohort based and includes a variety of team and group activities. The graduation rate from the program is extremely high – over 90% of the individuals who start the program graduate. There is a strong alumni base of HRD graduates who meet regularly. The majority of students who attend the 22-month program are working professionals. The program was formatted to allow professionals to continue working while completing their master's degree. The program is taught by tenure track faculty who are experts in the field.

Contact Information

Colorado State University – Denver Center
110 16th Street, Suite 110
Denver, CO 80202

Administrative Contact
Kate Pennella
Telephone: (303) 573-6318
kpennella@learn.colostate.edu

Faculty Contact
Jerry W. Gilley
Telephone: (970) 491-2918
Jerry.Gilley@CAHS.colostate.edu

Admission Deadlines

July 31

Online Application:	NO

Cornell University

Ithaca, New York
School of Industrial and Labor Relations

Degree
Master in Industrial and Labor Relations (MILR)

University Overview
Cornell is both a private Ivy League university and a land-grant institution of New York State with about 18,000 students. It is located on a hill overlooking Cayuga Lake in the New York Finger Lakes region.

Program Description
The MILR program is a traditional day program designed to increase students' knowledge in all aspects of the field as well as specific functional areas, which include human resources, organizational behavior, international comparative labor, social statistics, labor economics, international comparative labor, and collective bargaining, labor law, and labor history. Most MILR students complete a well-paid internship between their first and second years.

Degree Requirements

Total Credits Required:	30-48
Average Credits per Course:	3-4
Course Schedule:	Semester

Total Courses Required:	16
HR/IR Courses Required:	6
Average Time for Completion:	2 years
Maximum Time Allowed for Completion:	4 years
Accepts Credits from Other Universities:	NO
Total:	N/A

Tuition

In-state	$13,910	(per year)
	N/A	(per credit hour)
Out-of-state	$13,910	(per year)
	N/A	(per credit hour)

Program Delivery

Traditional Day Program:	YES
Nontraditional Program:	NO
Evening Program:	NO
Weekend Program:	NO
Summer Courses:	YES
Some Courses Online:	NO
Full Program Online:	NO
Distance Learning/Offsite:	NO
Executive Education:	YES*
Overseas Study Abroad:	YES

Certificate Programs
(www.ILR.cornell.edu/extension/home/mgmt.html)

Faculty

Full-Time Faculty:	50
Part-Time Faculty:	0
Faculty to Student Ratio:	1:3
Primary Teaching Methods:	
Case Study	Team Projects
Student Presentation	Lecture
Faculty Who Consult Outside:	N/A
Faculty Involvement:	See web site
Top 5 Faculty Publications:	See web site

Students

Total Enrollment:			140
Full-Time Enrollment:			100%
Men:	40%	Women:	60%
Hispanic:	2%	African-American:	4%
Other Minorities:	4%	International:	37%
Average Age:	28	Age Range:	21-55
Work Full Time:			0%
HR Experience:			25-49%
Speak 2nd Language:			25-49%
Minimum Admission Requirements:			
GRE Score:		1500 (V&Q&A Combined)	
Other Considerations:			
Research Experience			
Average Student Profile:			
GRE Scores:			726 Quantitative
			537 Verbal
			602 Analytical

Program Resources

Students Required to Have Computers:			NO
Video Teleconferencing:			YES
Physical Library Facilities:			YES
Online Library Facilities:			YES
HRCI Certification Preparation:			NO
SHRM Student Chapter:			YES
Fellowships:	16	AMT:	$6,000
Scholarships:			YES
Assistantships:	60	AMT:	$13,200 +tuition
Eligibility:			Full-Time Enrollment

Curriculum

Required Courses:
  Employment Law
  Management
  HR Measurement
  Employee Relations
  Labor Relations
Most Popular Elective Courses:
  Organizational Behavior
  Collective Bargaining
  Labor Market Policies
Career Tracks/Concentrations:

Human Resources and	Labor Market Policies
Organizations	Collective Representation
Dispute Resolution	

Internship Required:	NO

Career Services

Career Development Opportunities/Placement Service:

Mentoring	Interview Training
Resume Services	SHRM Student Chapter
Internships	Campus Interviews

Summer Internship Placement Rate:	N/A
Full-Time Placement Rate:	100%
Average Starting Salary (Full-Time Graduates):	$69,400
Average Sign-on Bonus:	$9,500
Companies Recruiting HR Master's Graduates:	100 +

Points of Excellence

Faculty: The faculty consists of the most recognized names in the academic community and best-known practitioners in the field. They specialize in many areas including absenteeism, Labor Market Trends and Analysis, Compensation and Employee Benefits, Conflict Prevention and Resolution, Occupational Safety and Health, Organizational Theory and Behavior, Staffing and Personnel Selection.

Placement: Most students complete a well-paid internship during the summer between their first and second years. Most are offered full-time jobs with the companies with which they intern upon graduation.

Resources: ILIR's Catherwood Library is the third largest library of its kind in the country, after the Library of Congress and the Department of Labor.

Contact Information

ILR Graduate Office
216 Ives Hall
Cornell University
Ithaca, NY 14853-3901
www.ilr.cornell.edu/gradprograms/index2.html

Dr. Robert Stern, Director of Graduate Studies
RNS1@Cornell.edu

Ms. Janet Frand, Administrative Director
Telephone: (607) 255-2227   FAX: (607) 254-1251
JAF4@cornell.edu

Admission Deadlines

February 15 (for academic aid), April 1 for Fall admissions

Online Application:	YES

DePaul University

Chicago, Illinois
Kellstadt Graduate School of Business

Degree
Master of Science in Human Resources (MSHR)
M.B.A. with a concentration in Human Resources (MBA)

University Overview
DePaul is a private university located in downtown Chicago. The business school is ranked #4 in the U.S. for its part-time business program.

Program Description
The focus is on those who wish to (1) enter or advance in HR; (2) prepare for the SHRM certification exam; and/or (3) develop knowledge in core HR functions, people management areas, and business/public administration areas. Business classes are offered at the main downtown campus and at three suburban locations.

Degree Requirements
Total Credits Required: 48 quarter hours (equivalent to 32 semester hours)

Average Credits per Course:	4
Course Schedule:	Quarter
Total Courses Required:	12
HR/IR Courses Required:	9
Average Time for Completion:	2 years
Maximum Time Allowed for Completion:	6 years
Accepts Credits from Other Universities:	YES
Total:	12 quarter hours

Tuition
In-state	N/A	(per year)
	$362-$600	(per credit hour)
Out-of-state	N/A	(per year)
	$362-$600	(per credit hour)

Program Delivery
Traditional Day Program:	NO
Non-Traditional Programs:	YES
Evening Program:	YES
Weekend Program:	NO
Program Completed Evening/Weekend:	YES
Summer Courses:	YES
Some Courses Online:	NO
Full Program Online:	NO
Distance Learning/Offsite:	NO
Executive Education:	NO
Overseas Study Abroad:	YES

Faculty
Full-Time Faculty:	16
Part-Time Faculty:	10
Faculty to Student Ratio:	1:30

Primary Teaching Methods:

Case Study	Lecture
Student Presentation	Team Projects
Group Discussion	

Faculty Who Consult Outside: N/A
Faculty Involvement:
Proceedings Editor, National Association of Arbitrators
Planning Committee for AACSB International's Graduate Program Conference
Top 5 Faculty Publications:
Academy of Management Executive
Human Relations
Labor Law Journal
Organizational Behavior and Human Decision Processes
Personnel Psychology

Students
Total Enrollment:			4
Full-Time Enrollment:			0
Men:	25%	Women:	75%
Hispanic:	0	African-American:	0
Other Minorities:	0	International:	0
Average Age:	26	Age Range:	24-28
Work Full Time:			100%
Have HR Experience:			50-74%
Speak 2nd Language:			None

Minimum Admission Requirements:
UGPA:	no minimum
GRE or GMAT Scores:	no minimum
Work Experience:	no minimum

Other Considerations:
compensatory model used; trade off test scores, undergrad GPA and work experience

Average Student Profile:
UGPA:	3.15

GMAT score: 660; 585 average on the three sub-scores of GRE
Work Experience: 3 ½ years

Program Resources
Students Required to Have Computers:	NO
Video Teleconferencing:	NO
Physical Library Facilities:	YES
Online Library Facilities:	YES
HRCI Certification Preparation:	YES

Base the curriculum on the certification exam content

SHRM Student Chapter:			NO
URL:			N/A
Fellowships:	NO	AMT:	N/A
Scholarships:	NO	AMT:	N/A
Assistantships:	NO	AMT:	N/A
Eligibility:			N/A

Curriculum
Required Courses:
HR Strategy
Compensation/Benefits
Development/Training
Recruitment/Retention
Management

Most Popular Elective Courses:
Negotiation Skills
Change Management
Resolving Conflict
Motivation
Leadership

Career Tracks/Concentrations:
Professional in Human Resources	Industrial/Organizational Psychology
Employee Counseling	Labor Policy
Public Services	

Internship Required: NO

Career Services
Career Services Offered:
Resume Services	Interview Training
Campus Interview	Internships

Summer Internship Placement Rate:	N/A
Facilitate Placement:	YES
Full-Time Placement Rate:	N/A (new program)
Internship Placement Rate:	N/A

Average Starting Salary (Full-Time Graduates):   N/A
(new program)
Average Sign-on Bonus: N/A
Companies Recruiting HR Master's Graduates: N/A

Points of Excellence

The MSHR program is housed in the Kellstadt Graduate School of Business at DePaul University. Our part-time graduate business program has been rated #4 in the U.S. by U.S. News and World Report. Students in the MSHR program take many classes in this highly ranked business school.

The MSHR program is a joint effort by the business school, the college of liberal arts, and the law school. Students must take at least six courses in the business school. Students can take up to six courses in the college of liberal arts and/or the law school. However, if they wish, they can take all 12 courses in the business school.

The curriculum is built around three areas:

(1) Core HR courses (5 required): Organizational Behavior, Strategic Human Resource Management, Staffing, Compensation, and Employee Development.

(2) HR electives (4 required): 23 choices from the following areas: Management, Psychology, Public Services, Law, Economics, Internship

(3) Business electives (3 required): 13 choices from the following areas: Management, Public Services, Marketing, Accounting/MIS, Economics, and Finance

We have an advisory board made up of 19 HR professionals from companies and unions in the Chicago area.

Contact Information

Kellstadt Graduate School of Business
1 E. Jackson Blvd.
Chicago, IL 60604
www.depaul.edu/~mshr

Christine Munoz
Director of Student Services
Kellstadt Graduate School of Business
(312) 362-8810
cmunoz@depaul.edu

Dr. Daniel Koys
Associate Dean of the College of Commerce and Director of the MSHR
(312) 362-6782
dkoys@depaul.edu

Admission Deadlines

July 1 for Autumn quarter
October 1 for Winter quarter
February 1 for Spring quarter
April 1 for Summer quarter
Online Application: YES

Eastern Michigan University

Ypsilanti, Michigan
College of Business

Degree

Master of Science in Human Resources and Organizational Development (MSHROD)

University Overview

Eastern Michigan is a state-funded university with small-town charm and state-of-the-art facilities. With more than 23,000 students it has nearly 200 academic programs. EMU is one of the nation's 50 largest universities. *U.S. News and World Report* has recognized its commitment to diversity. The College of Business has partnerships with organizations in the Greater Detroit and Ann Arbor area.

Program Description

Courses, instructors, and internships provide practical, professional programs in Human Resource Management and Organizational Development in a nontraditional format.

Degree Requirements

Total Credits Required:	30
Average Credits per Course:	3
Course Schedule:	Semester
Total Courses Required:	10
HR/IR Courses Required:	10
Average Time for Completion:	2 years
Maximum Time Allowed for Completion:	6 years
Accepts Credits from Other Universities:	YES
Total:	6 Hours

Tuition

In-state	N/A	(per year)
	$215	(per credit hour)
Out-of-state	N/A	(per year)
	$440	(per credit hour)

Program Delivery

Traditional Day Program:	NO
Nontraditional Program:	YES
Evening Program:	YES
Weekend Program:	YES
Summer Courses:	YES
Some Courses Online:	YES
Full Program Online:	NO
Distance Learning/Offsite:	YES
Executive Education:	NO
Overseas Study Abroad:	YES

Faculty

Full-Time Faculty:	12
Part-Time Faculty:	2
Faculty to Student Ratio:	1:20

Primary Teaching Methods:

Case Study	Team Projects
Student Presentation	Group Discussion

Faculty Who Consult Outside: 50-74%
Faculty Involvement:
Organizational assessments and HRD projects in both profit and not-for-profit organizations
Top 5 Faculty Publications:
Journal of Business Research
Leadership in OD Journal
HRD Quarterly

Students

Total Enrollment:			50
Full-Time Enrollment:			100%
Men:	25%	Women:	75%
Hispanic:	2%	African-American:	5%
Other Minorities:	5%	International:	5%
Average Age:	28	Age Range:	22-45
Work Full Time:			75-99%
HR Experience:			50-74%
Speak 2nd Language:			1-24%

Minimum Admission Requirements:
  GPA of 2.75 or 3.0 on last 60 units (3.5 for master's work)
Other Considerations:
  Formula to index GPA & GMAT
Average Student Profile:
  GMAT Score: 500
  Work experience: 5 years

Program Resources
Students Required to Have computers:		NO
Video Teleconferencing:		NO
Physical Library Facilities:		YES
Online Library Facilities:		YES
HRCI Certification Preparation:		YES

  Encourages student study groups
  Offers SHRM Learning System as a teaching tool
  Offers practical exams

SHRM Student Chapter:			YES
Fellowships:	6	AMT:	N/A
Scholarships:	3	AMT:	N/A
Assistantships:	10	AMT:	N/A
Eligibility:			Full-Time Enrollment

Curriculum
Required Courses:
  HR Development
  Practicum or Thesis
  Basic HR
  Basic OD
  HR Measurement
  Accounting
  Finance
  Marketing
Most Popular Elective Courses:
  Compensation
  Special Topics in HR
  Communications & OD
  Staffing
  Mediation
  Employment Law
  Mgmt. in Unionized Settings Org.
  Design & Strategy
Career tracks/Concentrations:
  Human Resource Management
  Organizational Development
Internship Required: NO

Career Services
Career Development Opportunities/Placement Service:
  Resume Services   Field Trips
  Campus Interviews   Internships
  SHRM Student Chapter

Summer Internship Placement Rate:	N/A
Full-Time Placement Rate:	100%
Average Starting Salary (Full-Time Graduates):	$45,000
Average Sign-on Bonus:	N/A
Companies Recruiting HR Master's Graduates:	10-15

Points of Excellence
Curriculum: Each student completes a portfolio with projects and a reflective essay to demonstrate how he or she has met program goals. Faculty meet with the students to assess HR and OD competencies as well as to evaluate their program portfolio. Class team projects and field projects provide an application-orientation approach to HR & OD. Practitioners and alumni support the program by serving as part-time lecturers and guest speakers. They also provide networking opportunities for students.

Placement: Most interns are offered full-time jobs with companies they interned with. Students have interned with Ford, Chrysler, and Ingersoll-Rand.

Contact Information
Eastern Michigan University
College of Business
300 W. Michigan Ave., Room 466
Ypsilanti, MI 48197
www.emich.edu

Fraya Wagner-Marsh
Professor/Dept. Head of Management Dept.
Co-Director of MSHROD
Telephone: (734) 487-3240   FAX: (734) 487-4100
fraya.wagner@emich.edu

Admission Deadlines
May 16 for Fall admissions
Online Application: NO

Fairleigh Dickinson University

Madison, New Jersey
Center for Human Resource Management Studies,
Samuel J. Silberman College of Business
Administration

Degree
Master of Business Administration with a concentration on Human Resource Management (MBA/HRM)

University Overview
Private university with approximately 9,500 students. Campuses are located in Madison, NJ; Teaneck, NJ; Wroxton, England; and Tel Aviv, Israel.

Program Description
FDU offers one of the largest MBA programs in HRM in the United States. It offers both traditional day and nontraditional programs, and is known for its competency-based learning and for providing opportunities for students to work with businesses and dialogue with top executives. The curriculum, which was developed in conjunction with top HR executives, emphasizes the strategic orientation and transformational aspects of HR. The program is managed through the Center for Human Resource Management Studies (www.CHRMS.org).

Degree Requirements
Total Credits Required:	60
Average Credits per Course:	3
Course Schedule:	Semester
Total Courses Required:	21
HR/IR Courses Required:	5
Average Time for Completion:	2-3 years
Maximum Time Allowed for Completion:	5 years
Accepts Credits from Other Universities:	YES
Total:	N/A

Tuition
In-state	N/A	(per year)
	$550	(per credit hour)
Out-of-state	N/A	(per year)
	$550	(per credit hour)

Program Delivery

Traditional Day Program:	YES
Nontraditional Program:	YES
Evening Program:	YES
Weekend Program:	YES
Summer Courses:	YES
Some Courses Online:	NO
Full Program Online:	NO
Distance Learning/Offsite:	NO
Executive Education:	YES*
Overseas Study Abroad:	NO

*Executive MBA/HRM program is a cohort
program that meets evenings and weekends*

Faculty

Full-Time Faculty:	7
Part-Time Faculty:	7
Faculty to Student Ratio:	1:10

Primary Teaching Methods:

Case Study	Research
Student Presentation	Team Projects
Computer Simulations	

Faculty Who Consult Outside:	25-49%

Faculty Involvement:
Board of Governors, American Society for Competitiveness
Board Member & University Partner, LearnShare
Member, Academy of Management
Organizer, Practitioner Series, Academy of Management
President, Eastern Academy of Management

Top 5 Faculty Publications:
Journal of Organizational Behavior
Employee Rights and Policy Journal
Journal of Global Competitiveness

Students

Total Enrollment:			47
Full-Time Enrollment:			40%
Men:	30%	Women:	70%
Hispanic:	0%	African-American:	9%
Other Minorities:	1%	International:	6%
Average Age:	30	Age Range:	22-49
Work Full Time:			50-74%
HR Experience:			50-74%
Speak 2nd Language:			1-24%

Minimum Admission Requirements:
Uses an index score computed from GPA & GMAT

Other Considerations:	None
Average Student Profile:	N/A

Program Resources

Students Required to Have Computers:		NO
Video Teleconferencing:		NO
Physical Library Facilities:		YES
Online Library Facilities:		YES
HRCI Certification Preparation:		NO
SHRM Student Chapter:		YES
Fellowships:		NO
Scholarships:		NO
Assistantships:	5	AMT:	$13,900
Eligibility:		Full-Time Enrollment

Curriculum

Required Courses:
Accounting
Finance
Marketing
HR Strategy
Development/Training

Employment Law
Management
HR Measurement
Employment Relations
Business Functional Areas

Most Popular Elective Courses:
Consulting Skills
Corporate Communications
HR Information Systems
International Business
Personnel Psychology
HR Development

Career Tracks/Concentrations:

Any HR career track	Any OD career track
A combination business/HR career track	

Internship Required:	NO

Career Services

Career Development Opportunities/Placement Service:

Mentoring	Field Trips
Resume Services	SHRM Student Chapter
Interview Training	Campus Interviews
Internships	Company Information Sessions

Summer Internship Placement Rate:	N/A
Full-Time Placement Rate:	100%
Average Starting Salary (Full-Time Graduates):	$50,000
Average Sign-on Bonus:	N/A
Companies Recruiting HR Master Graduates:	20

Points of Excellence

Curriculum: The capstone course for the HRM/MBA requires teams of four or five students to analyze real business problems (through CHRMS). They use benchmarking, surveys, and research to analyze the problem and present solution recommendations to the company that they are working with. Full-time HRM/MBA students are mentored by executives from Fortune 500 programs that are involved with CHRMS.

Contact Information

Fairleigh Dickinson University
285 Madison Ave.
Mailcode M-MS1-05
Madison, NJ 07940
www.FDU.edu or www.CHRMS.org
information@chrms.org

Greg Hammill, Executive Director, CHRMS
Telephone: (973) 443-8977   FAX: (973) 443-8506
hammill@fdu.edu

Dr. Daniel F. Twomey
CHRMS Director & Professor of Management
Telephone: (973) 443-8802   FAX: (973) 443-8506
dtwomey@fdu.edu

Admission Deadlines

Online Application:	NO

Florida Institute of Technology

Melbourne, Florida
School of Psychology

Degree

Industrial Organizational Psychology (I/O Psychology)

University Overview

Florida Institute of Technology (Florida Tech) is an accredited, coeducational, independently controlled, and supported university. Florida Tech was originally founded, in 1958, to offer continuing education opportunities to scientists, engineers, and technicians at what is now NASA's Kennedy Space Center. Florida Tech is rich in history with many fascinating links to the development of Brevard County and our nation's space program.

Program Description

Florida Tech's doctoral degree in Industrial Organizational Psychology provides training and research opportunities in the complex issues associated with the management of human resources in the international business community. It is designed to provide a more advanced level of education as well as the opportunity to continue independent research.

Degree Requirements

Total Credits Required:	45
Average Credits per Course:	3
Course Schedule:	Semester
Total Courses Required:	15
HR/IR Courses Required:	N/A
Average Time for Completion:	2 years
Maximum Time Allowed for Completion:	NONE
Accepts Credits from Other Universities:	YES
Total:	19 Hours

Tuition

In-state	N/A	(per year)
	$675	(per credit hour)
Out-of-state	N/A	(per year)
	$675	(per credit hour)

Program Delivery

Traditional Day Program:	YES
Nontradtional Day Program:	YES
Evening Program:	YES
Weekend Program:	NO
Program Completed Evening/Weekend:	NO
Summer Courses:	YES
Some Courses Online:	NO
Full Program Online:	NO
Distance Learning/Offsite:	NO
Executive Education:	NO
Overseas Study Abroad:	NO

Faculty

Full-Time Faculty:	3
Part-Time Faculty:	5
Faculty to Student Ratio:	1:10
Primary Teaching Methods:	N/A
Faculty Who Consult Outside:	N/A
Faculty Involvement:	
Associate Editor, TIP	
Top 5 Faculty Publications:	

Students

Total Enrollment:			25
Full-Time Enrollment:			88%
Men:	25%	Women:	75%
Hispanic:	4%	African-American:	8%
Other Minorities:	24%	International:	24%
Average Age:	24	Age Range:	22-46
Work Full Time:			1-24%
Have HR Experience:			1-24%
Speak 2nd Language:			1-24%
Minimum Admission Requirements:			

UGPA:	3.3
GRE or GMAT Scores:	Combined 1000
Work Experience:	NONE
Other Considerations:	
Average Student Profile:	
UGPA:	3.6
GMAT Score:	1100
Work Experience:	NONE

Program Resources

Students Required to Have Computers:	NO
Video Teleconferencing:	YES
Physical Library Facilities:	YES
Online Library Facilities:	YES
HRCI Certification Preparation:	NO
SHRM Student Chapter:	NO
URL:	

Fellowships:	NO	AMT:	
Scholarships:	NO	AMT:	
Assistantships:	YES	AMT:	
Eligibility:		Full-Time enrollment	

Curriculum

Required Courses:
- International HR
- Recruitment/Retention
- Development/Training
- Employment Law
- HR Measurement
- Tests and Measures
- Group and Team Development
- Organization Psychology
- Organization Change
- Applied Research Methods

Most Popular Elective Courses:
- Chaos Theory
- Leadership
- Organization Survey Methods

Career Tracks/Concentrations:	NONE
Internship Required:	NO

Career Services

Career Services Offered:

Mentoring	Interview Training
Internships	

Summer Internship Placement Rate:	N/A
Facilitate Placement:	NO
Full-Time Placement Rate:	N/A
Internship Placement Rate:	N/A
Average Starting Salary (Full-Time Graduates):	N/A
Average Sign-on Bonus:	N/A
Companies Recruiting HR Master's Graduates:	N/A

Points of Excellence

Contact Information

Florida Institute of Technology
School of Psychology
150 W. University Avenue
Melbourne, FL 32901
www.fit.edu/AcadRes/psych/io/index.htm

Administrative Contact
Lori Sorum
Telephone: (321) 674-8104
lsorum@fit.edu

Faculty Contact
Dr. Richard Griffith
Telephone: (321) 674-8104
Griffith@fit.edu

Admission Deadlines
February 1
Online Application: YES

Georgia State University

Atlanta, Georgia
W.T. Beebe Institute of Personnel and Employment Relations

Degree
Master of Business Administration/Human Resource Management (MBA/HRM)
Master of Science in Human Resource Management (MSHRM)

University Overview
State university located in urban Atlanta, Georgia. Offers undergraduate, master's, and doctoral-level studies.

Program Description
Traditional day and nontraditional programs designed to prepare students for practice in HRM and Change Management. Business-based curriculum combines academics with practical world.

Degree Requirements
Total Credits Required:	30+
Average Credits per Course:	3
Course Schedule:	Semester
Total Courses Required:	15-18 (MBA/HRM)
	10-14 (MS/HRM
HR/IR Courses Required:	6 (MBA/HRM)
	10 (MS/HRM)
Average Time for Completion:	2-3 years (MBA/HRM)
	1-2 years (MS/HRM)
Maximum Time Allowed for Completion:	5 years
Accepts Credits from Other Universities:	YES
Total:	N/A

Tuition
In-state	N/A	(per year)
	$130	(per credit hour)
Out-of-state	N/A	(per year)
	$518	(per credit hour)

Program Delivery
Traditional Day Program:	YES
Nontraditional Program:	YES
Evening Program:	YES
Weekend Program:	YES
Summer Courses:	N/A
Some Courses Online:	YES (MBA classes)
Full Program Online:	NO
Distance Learning/Offsite:	YES
Executive Education:	N/A
Overseas Study Abroad:	YES

Faculty
Full-Time Faculty:	8
Part-Time Faculty:	1
Faculty to Student Ratio:	1:10

Primary Teaching Methods:
Case Study	Team Projects
Student Presentation	Experiential Learning

Faculty Who Consult Outside: 25-49%
Faculty Involvement:
President, Southern Management Association
GOALS Board of Directors
President, University Consortium of IR and HR Programs
Program Chair and President of HRM Division, Academy of Management
Chair, Teaching Committee on HR, Academy of Management
Top 5 Faculty Publications:
Academy of Management Journal
Personnel Psychology
Journal of Vocational Behavior
Books

Students
Total Enrollment:			66
Full-Time Enrollment:			42%
Men:	15%	Women:	85%
Hispanic:	4%	African-American:	19%
Other Minorities:	2%	International:	0%
Average Age:	28	Age Range:	23-37
Work Full Time:			75-99%
HR Experience:			50-74%
Speak 2nd Language:			25-49%

Minimum Admission Requirements:
GMAT Score:	550
UGPA:	3.0

Other Considerations:
Uses composite UGPA and GMAT. Also, significant work experience and evidence of leadership potential.
Average Student Profile:
GMAT Score:	580
Work experience:	5 years

Program Resources
Students Required to Have Computers:	N/A
Video Teleconferencing:	YES
Physical Library Facilities:	N/A
Online Library Facilities:	N/A
HRCI Certification Preparation:	YES

Encourages student study groups
Links students to local SHRM chapter study groups
Bases curriculum on certification exam

SHRM Student Chapter:			YES
Fellowships:	2	AMT:	$9,000
Scholarships:	4	AMT:	$1,000
Assistantships:	20	AMT:	$900 + tuition
Eligibility:			All Students

Curriculum
Required Courses:
Accounting
Finance
HR Strategy
Compensation/Benefits
Recruitment/Retention
Employment Law
Management
Labor Relations
Negotiations
Business Functional Areas
Most Popular Elective Courses:
Project Management
HR Information Systems
Performance Management

Industrial Psychology
Managerial Economics
Benefits and Pension Systems
Legal & Ethical Environment in HRM

Career Tracks/Concentrations:	N/A
Internship Required:	NO

Career Services

Career Development Opportunities/Placement Service:

Interview Training	Field Trips
Resume Services	SHRM Student Chapter
Internships	Campus Interviews
Job Posting	Internship Services

Summer Internship Placement Rate:	N/A
Full-Time Placement Rate:	100%
Average Starting Salary (Full-Time Graduates):	$48,200
Average Sign-on Bonus:	N/A
Companies Recruiting HR Master's Graduates:	10

Points of Excellence

Curriculum: The Beebe Institute structure brings together business leaders, students, faculty, administrators, alumni, and professional associations (SHRM, ACA, etc.) and allows extensive and significant interaction. Workshops, seminars, and a newsletter (HR Atlanta) involve students in Institute activities. The HR Roundtable of executives encourages constructive curriculum adjustments. A field research class (co-sponsored with local SHRM chapter) is a student consulting course. In addition to coursework, students take two free training modules (day-long seminars) on HR topics (e.g., Decision Making, Team Building) taught by top-flight consultants or faculty members.

Contact Information

W.T. Beebe Institute
University Plaza
Atlanta, GA 30303
www.gsu.edu

Dr. Richard H. Deane
Interior Director
Telephone: (404) 651-3118   FAX: (404) 651-1700
Rdeane@qsu.edu

Dr. Lucy McClurg
Advisor
Telephone: (404) 651-2863   FAX: (404) 651-1700
mgtlnm@langate.gsu.edu

Admission Deadlines

May 1 for Fall admissions
Online Application: YES

Hawaii Pacific University

Honolulu, Hawaii

Degree

Master of Arts in Human Resource Management (MA/HRM)

University Overview

Hawaii Pacific University is the largest private college or university in Hawaii, with more than 1,200 graduate students.

Program Description

The program emphasizes the study and practice of human relations and managing personnel. As a foundation for the program, students must have successfully completed undergraduate courses in statistics, microcomputer applications to management, and research methods and writing.

Degree Requirements

Total Credits Required:	42
Average Credits per Course:	3
Course Schedule:	Semester
Total Courses Required:	14
HR/IR Courses Required:	14
Average Time for Completion:	2-3 years
Maximum Time Allowed for Completion:	7 years
Accepts Credits from Other Universities:	YES
Total:	12 Hours

Tuition

In-state	N/A	(per year)
	$410	(per credit hour)
Out-of-state	N/A	(per year)
	$410	(per credit hour)

Program Delivery

Traditional Day Program:	YES
Nontraditional Program:	YES
Evening Program:	YES
Weekend Program:	YES
Summer Courses:	YES
Some Courses Online:	NO
Full Program Online:	NO
Distance Learning/Offsite:	NO
Executive Education:	NO
Overseas Study Abroad:	NO

Faculty

Full-Time Faculty:	40
Part-Time Faculty:	21
Faculty to Student Ratio:	1:20

Primary Teaching Methods:

Experiential Learning	Team Projects
Student Presentation	Lecture

Faculty Who Consult Outside:	N/A
Faculty Involvement:	N/A
Top 5 Faculty Publications:	N/A

Students

Total Enrollment:			1,200
Full-Time Enrollment:			840
Men:	56%	Women:	44%
Hispanic:	N/A	African-American:	N/A
Other Minorities:	N/A	International:	N/A
Average Age:	30	Age Range:	21-64
Work Full Time:			25-49%
HR Experience:			N/A
Speak 2nd Language:			N/A
Minimum Admission Requirements:			N/A

Other Considerations:
Ability and motivation to do graduate-level work.

Average Student Profile:	N/A

Program Resources

Students Required to Have Computers:	NO
Video Teleconferencing:	NO
Physical Library Facilities:	YES
Online Library Facilities:	YES
HRCI Certification Preparation:	YES

Encourages student study groups
Bases the curriculum on the certification exam content

SHRM Student Chapter:			YES
Fellowships:			NO
Scholarships:	20	AMT:	N/A
Assistantships:	10	AMT:	N/A
Eligibility:			Full-Time Enrollment

Curriculum

Required Courses:
    Compensation/Benefits
    Development/Training
    Recruitment/Retention
    Employment Law
    Management
    Employee Relations
    Labor Relations
    HR Measurement

Most Popular Elective Courses:	N/A
Career Tracks/Concentrations:	N/A
Internship Required:	NO

Career Services

Career Development Opportunities/Placement Service:
    SHRM Student Chapter   Resume Services
    Interview Training   Internships

Summer Internship Placement Rate:	YES
Full-Time Placement Rate:	N/A
Average Starting Salary (Full-Time Graduates):	$54,600
Average Sign-on Bonus:	N/A
Companies Recruiting HR Master's Graduates:	60

Points of Excellence

Faculty: A major strength is the highly respected and accomplished faculty. Known for their research and teaching skills, the faculty of Hawaii Pacific University (HPU) have extensive experience working in business, consulting for corporations, serving on advisory councils, and leading not-for-profit organizations. This experience enables them to bring a balance of theory and practice into every class they teach. The faculty's international character complements a curriculum that embraces global philosophies and ideas. Their expertise extends to all areas of business, education, nursing, management, information systems, human resources, history, and communication.

Resources: HPU has assistantship and scholarship opportunities. Students have the opportunity to utilize a Career Services Center, Computer Center, Learning Assistance Lab, and two libraries with over 150,000 volumes. HPU also has a Media Technology Center equipped with state-of-the-art technology for class work and projects.

Contact Information

Hawaii Pacific University
1164 Bishop St.
Suite 911
Honolulu, HI 96813
www.hpu.edu

Harry Byerly, Assistant Dean
Director of Graduate Admissions and Marketing
Telephone: (808) 544-1120   FAX: (808) 544-0280
hbyerly@hpu.edu

Larry Zimmerman
Dean of Professional Studies
Telephone: (808) 544-0236   FAX: (808) 544-0247
lzimmerm@hpu.edu

Admission Deadlines

Rolling admissions

Online Application:	YES

Houston Baptist University

Houston, Texas
College of Business and Economics

Degree
Master of Science in Human Resource Management (MS-HRM)

University Overview
The campus of Houston Baptist University (HBU) consists of 158 acres in southwest Houston. HBU is accredited by the Southern Association of Colleges and Schools.

Program Description
The MSHRM program is designed for the working professional. Students will gain a deep understanding of the elements that are critical to building high performing organizations. Courses incorporate an integrating thread to ensure appreciation and understanding of the importance to align human resources with business strategy, culture, and leadership.

Degree Requirements

Total Credits Required:	36
Average Credits per Course:	3
Course Schedule:	Quarter
Total Courses Required:	12
HR/IR Courses Required:	12
Average Time for Completion:	1 ½ years
Maximum Time Allowed for Completion:	5 years
Accepts Credits from Other Universities:	YES
Total:	6 Hours

Tuition

In-state	$9,600	(per year)
	$400	(per credit hour)
Out-of-state	$9,600	(per year)
	$400	(per credit hour)

Program Delivery

Traditional Day Program:	NO
Nontraditional Program:	YES
Evening Program:	YES
Weekend Program:	YES
Program Completed Evening/Weekend:	YES
Summer Courses:	YES
Some Courses Online:	NO
Full Program Online:	NO
Distance Learning/Offsite:	NO
Executive Education:	NO
Overseas Study Abroad:	NO

Faculty

Full-Time Faculty:	16
Part-Time Faculty:	5
Faculty to Student Ratio:	1:10

Primary Teaching Methods:
    Case Study   Experiential Learning
    Lecture   Team Projects

Faculty Who Consult Outside:	1-24%

Faculty Involvement:
Top 5 Faculty Publications:

Students

Total Enrollment:			16
Full-Time Enrollment:			0
Men:	13%	Women:	87%
Hispanic:	13%	African-American:	25%
Other Minorities:	0%	International:	0%
Average Age:	23	Age Range:	23-57

Work Full Time:	75-99%
Have HR Experience:	75-99%
Speak 2nd Language:	1-24%

Minimum Admission Requirements:

UGPA:	2.5
GRE or GMAT Scores:	GMAT 450 total w/3.0 analyt. writing
Work Experience:	N/A

Other Considerations:

Average Student Profile:

UGPA:	2.97
GMAT Score:	510
Work Experience:	N/A

Program Resources

Students Required to Have Computers:	YES
Video Teleconferencing:	YES
Physical Library Facilities:	YES
Online Library Facilities:	YES
HRCI Certification Preparation:	NO
SHRM Student Chapter:	YES
URL:	
Fellowships:	NO	AMT:
Scholarships:	NO	AMT:
Assistantships:	NO	AMT:
Eligibility:	N/A

Curriculum

Required Courses:
HR Strategy
Recruitment/Retention
International HR
Employment Law
Compensation/Benefits
Management
Development/Training
Labor Relations
Strategic HRM Change Interventions
Organizational Diagnosis & Transformation
HR Technology

Most Popular Elective Courses:	N/A
Career Tracks/Concentrations:	N/A
Internship Required:	NO

Career Services

Career Services Offered:
SHRM Student Chapter   Campus Interview
Internships

Summer Internship Placement Rate:	N/A
Facilitate Placement:	NO
Full-Time Placement Rate:	N/A
Internship Placement Rate:	N/A
Average Starting Salary (Full-Time Graduates):	N/A
Average Sign-on Bonus:	N/A
Companies Recruiting HR Master's Graduates:	N/A

Points of Excellence

Students enrolled in the MS-HRM program at HBU come from a variety of backgrounds and industries. They reflect various perspectives and experiences, which contribute to a rich learning environment. Class sizes are small, allowing for extensive interaction with the faculty. In addition, you will have opportunities to interact with executive decision makers in the Houston community. Your learning experience at HBU will be eclectic, thought provoking and relevant to the human resources and business issues facing organizations today.

The MS-HRM program at HBU has an excellent reputation with the Houston business community and is given high praise by former graduates of the program. As one graduate said,

"My MS in Human Resources Management, even while I was still working on the degree, made a huge difference in my career." We promise a supportive, stimulating, active, and fun experience that will further your career and professional insights in many positive ways.

Contact Information

MS-HRM Program
Houston Baptist University
7502 Fondren Road
Houston, TX 77074-3298
www.hbu.edu/Pages/acad/H3MNhrm.html
or
www2.hbu.edu/bus&econ/

Administrative Contact:
Susan Bubeck
Telephone: (281) 649-3265
Sbubeck@hbu.edu

Faculty Contact:
Douglas Gehrman
Telephone: (281) 649-3396
Dgehrman@hbu.edu

Admission Deadlines

60 days prior to registration
Online Application: NO

Illinois Institute of Technology

Chicago, Illinois
Institute of Psychology

Degree

Master of Science in Personnel and Human Resource Development (MSPHRD)

University Overview

Illinois Institute of Technology (IIT), located in Chicago, is a private PhD-granting University, established in 1890, with programs in Engineering, Sciences, Psychology, Architecture, Business, Design, and Law.

Program Description

The Personnel and Human Resource Development (PHRD) degree has balanced coverage of personnel, organizational behavior, and statistical topics. It is designed for individuals who work, or plan to work, in human resources areas.

Degree Requirements

Total Credits Required:	43
Average Credits per Course:	3
Course Schedule:	Semester
Total Courses Required:	15
HR/IR Courses Required:	N/A
Average Time for Completion:	2 years
Maximum Time Allowed for Completion:	6 years
Accepts Credits from Other Universities:	NO
Total:	

Tuition

In-state	N/A	(per year)
	$590	(per credit hour)
Out-of-state	N/A	(per year)
	$590	(per credit hour)

Program Delivery

Traditional Day Program:	NO
Nontraditional Program:	YES
Evening Program:	YES
Weekend Program:	NO
Program Completed Evening/Weekend:	NO
Summer Courses:	NO
Some Courses Online:	NO
Full Program Online:	NO
Distance Learning/Offsite:	NO
Executive Education:	NO
Overseas Study Abroad:	NO

Faculty

Full-Time Faculty:	5
Part-Time Faculty:	2
Faculty to Student Ratio:	1:10

Primary Teaching Methods:

Case Study	Field Projects
Student Presentation	Team Projects
Lecture	Group Discussion

Faculty Who Consult Outside: 25-49%

Faculty Involvement:
Member of Executive Board, Organizational Psychology
Division, International Association of Applied Psychology
Member of Council of Representatives, American
Psychological Association

Top 5 Faculty Publications:
Group & Organizational Management: An International Journal
International Journal of Selection and Assessment
Personnel Psychology
Journal of Applied Psychology

Students

Total Enrollment:			11
Full-Time Enrollment:			11
Men:	36%	Women:	64%
Hispanic:	9%	African-American:	0%
Other Minorities:	55%	International:	45%
Average Age:	N/A	Age Range:	N/A
Work Full Time:			NONE
Have HR Experience:			1-24%
Speak 2nd Language:			50-74%

Minimum Admission Requirements:

UGPA:	3.1
GRE or GMAT Scores:	1000 cumulative Verbal & Quantitative GRE score
Work Experience:	NONE

Other Considerations:
Average Student Profile:

UGPA:	3.36
GMAT Score:	1051 cumulative Verbal & Quantitative GRE score
Work Experience:	N/A

Program Resources

Students Required to Have Computers:			NO
Video Teleconferencing:			YES
Physical Library Facilities:			YES
Online Library Facilities:			YES
HRCI Certification Preparation:			NO
SHRM Student Chapter:			NO
URL:			
Fellowships:	NO	AMT:	
Scholarships:	YES	AMT:	$2,655/semester
Assistantships:	YES	AMT:	$6,475/semester
Eligibility:			Full-Time enrollment

Curriculum

Required Courses:
Marketing
Recruitment/Retention
Compensation/Benefits
Employment Law
Development/Training
HR Measurement
Organizational Behavior
Statistics and Psychometric Theory
Personnel Psychology

Most Popular Elective Courses:
Selection
Performance Appraisal
Leadership and Group Dynamics
Organizational Attitudes and Behavior
Job Analysis and Utility Analysis

Career Tracks/Concentrations:

Management Consulting	HR Specialist
Compensation Analysis	Training Evaluator/ Performance Management

Project Manager

Internship Required: YES

Career Services

Career Services Offered:

Mentoring	Interview Training
Field Trips	Resume Services
Internships	

Summer Internship Placement Rate:	N/A
Facilitate Placement:	YES
Full-Time Placement Rate:	N/A
Internship Placement Rate:	N/A
Average Starting Salary (Full-Time Graduates):	N/A
Average Sign-on Bonus:	N/A
Companies Recruiting HR Master's Graduates:	N/A

Points of Excellence

The MS in PHRD degree is housed within the Industrial and Organizational Psychology PhD program. It is designed to provide a balanced exposure to personnel issues and organizational behavior issues. Students are expected to develop competencies in areas such as statistical models and SPSS, presentation skills, report writing, proposal writing, interviewing, team facilitation, developing and conducting organizational surveys. Our students and our program are not only assessed by our traditional grading system, they are also assessed by the experts and employers outside of the Illinois Institute of Technology. Our program has modified its offerings through the years based on expansion of the field and the needs of the job market.

Students are selected based on their academic competencies by a committee of faculty with consulting experience. The teaching philosophy of our faculty is guided by the scientist/practitioner model. Students are exposed to both practical issues and research design in our classes. They are provided a strong theoretical foundation in various fields.

The design of our program emphasizes both traditional class sessions and practical experience gained through internships. Students are evaluated by both faculty and supervisors of their projects. They also receive individual feedback on the skills they are developing. The program has hands-on training sessions, workshops and short courses to give students more focused time to develop these various skills. Students are individually coached and empowered to improve on their skills and knowledge.

Contact Information
Institute of Psychology
Illinois Institute of Technology
3101 South Dearborn
Chicago, IL 60637
www.iit.edu/colleges/psych/

Administrative Contact
Angeles Anaya
Telephone: (312) 567-3500
anaya@iit.edu

Faculty Contact
Dr. Roya Ayman
Telephone: (312) 567-3516
ayman@iit.edu

Admission Deadlines
February 15 for Fall admission
Online Application: YES

Indiana Institute of Technology

Fort Wayne, Indiana
College of Business and Arts

Degree
Master of Business Administration with a concentration in Human Resource Management (MBA-HRM)

University Overview
Indiana Institute of Technology is a small private college founded in 1930.

Program Description
The Indiana Institute of Technology's MBA in HRM is a new nontraditional program. The first class graduated in May 2001. The program has a special focus of preparing graduate students for the SHRM certification exam. All students have the opportunity to attend the SHRM National Conference and receive graduate credit for taking the Senior Professional Human Resources (SPHR) certification exam.

Degree Requirements

Total Credits Required:	39
Average Credits per Course:	3
Course Schedule:	Quarter
Total Courses Required:	13
HR/IR Courses Required:	4
Average Time for Completion:	1-2 years
Maximum Time Allowed for Completion:	7 years
Accepts Credits from Other Universities:	YES
Total:	9 Hours

Tuition

In-state	N/A	(per year)
	$250	(per credit hour)
Out-of-state	N/A	(per year)
	$250	(per credit hour)

Program Delivery

Traditional Day Program:	NO
Nontraditional Program:	YES
Evening Program:	YES
Weekend Program:	NO
Summer Courses:	YES

Some Courses Online:	NO
Full Program Online:	NO
Distance Learning/Offsite:	YES
Executive Education:	YES*
Overseas Study Abroad:	NO

Indiana Tech offers an accelerated program with courses offered one night per week, for six weeks. Classes are held Monday through Thursday evenings and Saturday mornings within eight, six-week sessions throughout a calendar year

Faculty

Full-Time Faculty:		15
Part-Time Faculty:		45
Faculty to Student Ratio:		1:10
Primary Teaching Methods:		
Case Study	Lecture	
Team Projects	Student Presentation	
Computer Simulations		
Faculty Who Consult Outside:		75-99%
Faculty Involvement:		
SHRM National College Relations Committee		
Top 5 Faculty Publications:		N/A

Students

Total Enrollment:			350
Full-Time Enrollment:			100%
Men:	64%	Women:	36%
Hispanic:	1%	African-American:	15%
Other Minorities:	5%	International:	4%
Average Age:	40	Age Range:	21-64
Work Full Time:			75-99%
HR Experience:			25-49%
Speak 2nd Language:			1-24%
Minimum Admission Requirements:			
UGPA:			2.5
Work experience:			2 years
Other Considerations:			
A score of 200 X UGPA + GMAT > 1000 points			
Average Student Profile:			
Work experience:			14 years

Program Resources

Students Required to Have Computers:	YES
Video Teleconferencing:	NO
Physical Library Facilities:	YES
Online Library Facilities:	YES
HRCI Certification Preparation:	YES
Encourages student study groups	
Links students with local SHRM chapter study groups	
Offers SHRM Learning System as a teaching tool	
Offers practice exams	
Bases curriculum on the certification exam content	
SHRM Student Chapter:	YES
Fellowships:	NO
Scholarships:	YES
Assistantships:	NO
Eligibility:	N/A

Curriculum
Required Courses:
Finance
Accounting
Marketing
HR Strategy
Employment Law
Management

Most Popular Elective Courses:
  Health & Safety
  Training & Development
  Compensation
  HR Planning
  Labor Relations
Career Tracks/Concentrations:
  Entrepreneurship   Human Resources
  Marketing   Management
Internship Required: NO

Career Services
Career Development Opportunities/Placement Service:
  Mentoring   Field Trips
  Internships   SHRM Student Chapter
  Resume Services   Interview Training
  Campus Interviews
Summer Internship Placement Rate: N/A
Full-Time Placement Rate: N/A
Average Starting Salary (Full-Time Graduates):   N/A
Average Sign-on Bonus: N/A
Companies Recruiting HR Master's Graduates: N/A

Points of Excellence
Curriculum: The Indiana Institute of Technology MBA program is designed for graduate students who are employed in full-time positions. All graduate students of the program have the opportunity to attend the SHRM National Conference, take the SPHR certification exam, and receive graduate credit for this learning experience.

Contact Information
Indiana Institute of Technology
College of Business and Arts
1600 E. Washington Blvd.
Fort Wayne, IN 46803
www.indtech.edu

Dr. Jeffrey L. Walls, EdD, SPHR, Professor of Business
Telephone: (219) 422-5561, ext. 2267   FAX: (219) 422-1518
walls@indtech.edu

Jim Bishop, VP of Extended Studies
Telephone: (219) 422-5561, ext. 2209   FAX: (219) 422-1518
bishop@indtech.edu

Admission Deadlines
Online Application: NO

Indiana University of Pennsylvania

Indiana, Pennsylvania
Graduate Program in Industrial and Labor Relations

Degree
Master of Arts in Industrial and Labor Relations (MAILR)

University Overview
Indiana University of Pennsylvania is recognized as a "Public Ivy" because of cost and quality of educational programs. IUP is the only state-owned university to grant doctoral degrees in the state system of higher education.

Program Description
The Master of Arts in Industrial and Labor Relations is a multi-disciplinary graduate degree program designed to prepare professional practitioners in the field of Industrial and Labor Relations in public and private management, unions, government agencies, and service organizations.

Degree Requirements
Total Credits Required: 42
Average Credits per Course: 3
Course Schedule: Semester
Total Courses Required: 14
HR/IR Courses Required: 14
Average Time for Completion: 1-3 years
Maximum Time Allowed for Completion: 5 years
Accepts Credits from Other Universities: YES
Total: 6 Hours

Tuition
In-state $1,895   (per semester)
                          $210   (per credit hour)
Out-of-state $3,305   (per semester)
                          $367   (per credit hour)

Program Delivery
Traditional Day Program: NO
Nontraditional Program: YES
  Evening Program: YES
  Weekend Program: NO
  Summer Courses: YES
  Some Courses Online: NO
  Full Program Online: NO
  Distance Learning/Offsite: NO
  Executive Education: YES*
  Overseas Study Abroad: NO
*Two-year cohort program at the Monroeville Campus in the greater Pittsburgh area. Students take two courses each term for two years and receive the degree. The program assumes experience in Human Resources or Labor Relations.

Faculty
Full-Time Faculty: 6
Part-Time Faculty: 0
Faculty to Student Ratio: 1:10
Primary Teaching Methods:
  Case Study   Lecture
  Student Presentation   Experiential Learning
Faculty Who Consult Outside: 50-74%
Faculty Involvement:
  Chapter Executive Director, Western PA IRRA
  President, Western PA IRRA
  President, PA Labor History Society
  Editorial Board, NAA Chronicle
Top 5 Faculty Publications:
  Prezeglad Political Science Review

Students
Total Enrollment: 62
Full-Time Enrollment: 52%
  Men: 45%   Women: 55%
  Hispanic   0%   African-American: 8%
  Other Minorities: 0%   International: 3%
  Average Age: 26   Age Range: 22-58
Work Full Time: 25-49%
Have HR Experience: 1-24%
Speak 2nd Language: N/A
Minimum Admission Requirements:
  UGPA: 3.0
Other Considerations:
  Practitioners may enroll with a GPA below 3.0.
Average Student Profile:
  Work Experience: 1.5 years

Program Resources

Students Required to Have Computers:		NO
Video Teleconferencing:		NO
Physical Library Facilities:		YES
Online Library Facilities:		YES
HRCI Certification Preparation:		NO
SHRM Student Chapter:		YES
URL:		www.iup.edu/ilr/shrm
Fellowships:		N/A
Scholarships:		N/A
Assistantships:	11	AMT: $5,660 + tuition
Eligibility:		Full-Time enrollment

Curriculum

Required Courses:
  Employment Law
  Employee Relations
  Labor Relations
  HR Measurement
  Human Resources
  Labor Law
  Dispute Resolution, Theory & Development
Most Popular Elective Courses:
  Compensations & Benefits
  Conflict Resolution
  Training
  Negotiations
  International HR
  Labor History
  Current Topics
Career Tracks/Concentrations:
  Employee Relations   Human Resource Management
  Labor Relations

Internship Required:	YES

Career Services

Career Development Opportunities/Placement Service:
  Internships   SHRM Student Chapter
  Interview Training   Campus Interviews
  Annual Regional HR/LR Conference

Summer Internship Placement Rate:	N/A
Full-Time Placement Rate:	90%
Average Starting Salary (Full-Time Graduates):	$38,500
Average Sign-on Bonus:	$3,000
Companies Recruiting HR Master's Graduates:	25

Points of Excellence

Students: Students are a mix of traditional and nontraditional from an experience level. About half come straight from undergraduate programs. About one-third come from HR or Labor Relations majors with the rest from psychology, political science, safety science, history, sociology, and education undergraduate work. Students with substantial coursework or professional experience may be permitted to waive required courses. Required courses are a balance of HR and LR subjects. Students are permitted to attend arbitration hearings conducted by faculty. Students may be hired to assist consultants in project work.

Faculty: Faculty are practitioners who are professionally active in specialty areas as arbitrators or consultants.

Contact Information

Indiana University of Pennsylvania
Graduate Program in Industrial and Labor Relations
3E Keith Hall
Indiana, PA 15705
www.iup.edu/Ilr

Admission Deadlines

Rolling admissions

Online Application:	NO

Iowa State University

Ames, Iowa
Industrial Relations Center

Degree

Master of Science in Industrial Relations (MSIR)
Master of Business Administration with a concentration in Human Resource Management (MBA/HRM)

University Overview

Iowa State University is a state-funded institution with approximately 24,000 students. It is located 30 miles north of Des Moines, Iowa.

Program Description

For over a quarter of a century, this multidisciplinary program has offered students a choice of either Human Resource Management or Labor/Management Relations concentrations through the full-time, traditional day or international program. Students typically come from a number of backgrounds such as business, economics, political science, psychology, and sociology. Students may complete either a thesis or combination of practical internship and creative component.

Degree Requirements

Total Credits Required:		36
Average Credits per Course:		2-4
Course Schedule:		Semester
Total Courses Required:	12	MSIR
	16	MBA/HRM
HR/IR Courses Required:	5	MSIR
	4	MBA/HRM
Average Time for Completion:	1 ½-2 years	(MSIR)
	2 years	(MBA/HRM)
Maximum Time Allowed for Completion:		5 years
Accepts Credits from Other Universities:		YES
Total:		9 Hours

Tuition

In-state	$3,702	(per year)
	$206	(per credit hour)
Out-of-state	$10,898	(per year)
	$206	(per credit hour)

Program Delivery

Traditional Day Program:	YES
Nontraditional Program:	YES
Evening Program:	YES
Weekend Program:	YES
Summer Courses:	YES
Some Courses Online:	NO
Full Program Online:	NO
Distance Learning/Offsite:	YES
Executive Education:	NO
Overseas Study Abroad:	NO

Faculty

Full-Time Faculty:	18
Part-Time Faculty:	0
Faculty to Student Ratio:	1:2

Primary Teaching Methods:
  Lecture   Team Projects
  Student Presentation Group Discussion

Faculty Who Consult Outside:		1-24%
Faculty Involvement:		See web site

Top 5 Faculty Publications:
Journal of Human Resources
Human Resource Management Review
Journal of Vocational Behavior
Journal of Organizational Behavior

Students

Total Enrollment:			32
Full-Time Enrollment:			50%
Men:	25%	Women:	75%
Hispanic	4%	African-American:	4%
Other Minorities:	10%	International:	18%
Average Age:	25	Age Range:	22-45
Work Full Time:			50-74%
HR Experience:			50-74%
Speak 2nd Language:			1-24%

Minimum Admission Requirements:
GMAT Score:	540
GPA Score:	letters of reference

Other Considerations:
GPA and research experience
Average Student Profile:
Standardized test scores in the 50th percentile
UGPA:	3.2
Work experience:	4 years

Program Resources

Students Required to Have Computers:		NO
Video Teleconferencing:		YES
Physical Library Facilities:		YES
Online Library Facilities:		YES
HRCI Certification Preparation:		YES

Encourages student study groups
Links students to local SHRM chapter study groups

SHRM Student Chapter:		YES
Fellowships:		NO
Scholarships:		NO
Assistantships:	6	AMT: $5,200 + tuition
Eligibility:		Full-Time Enrollment

Curriculum

Required Courses:
Employee Relations
Labor Relations
Statistics
Management
Most Popular Elective Courses:
Finance
Compensation/Benefits
Training & Development
Recruitment/Retention
Career Tracks/Concentrations:	N/A
Internship Required:	NO

Career Services

Career Development Opportunities/Placement Service:
Interview Training	Field Trips
Resume Services	SHRM Student hapter
Internships	Campus Interviews

Summer Internship Placement Rate:	N/A
Full-Time Placement Rate:	100%
Average Starting Salary (Full-Time Graduates):	$45,000
Average Sign-on Bonus:	N/A
Companies Recruiting HR Master's Graduates:	10

Points of Excellence

Curriculum: Faculty and students within the program engage in productive scholarship activity in addition to an applied focus. Faculty and students have been successful in securing grants for research activities and have published in top journals of field. Program is very strong in technological applications and computer areas. Statistics are genuinely world class.

Faculty: Many are internationally acclaimed in their subject areas. Students choose three faculty members to work with them individually, thereby creating a program driven by student interest in HRM or IR.

Contact Information

Industrial Relations Center, Department of Economics
280 Heady Hall
Iowa State University
Ames, IA 50011-1070
www.econ.iastate.edu/industrialrelations/ircenter.htm

Dr. Peter Orazem, Professor
Telephone: (515) 294-8656   FAX: (515) 294-0221
pfo@iastate.edu

Deanna Ward, Program Assistant
Telephone: (515) 294-2701   FAX: (515) 294-0221
pfo@iastate.edu

Admission Deadlines

March 12 for Fall admissions, November 1 for Spring admissions
Online Application: YES

John Carroll University

University Heights, Ohio

Degree

Master of Business Administration with concentration in Human Resources (MBA-HR)

University Overview

A private, coeducational, Catholic and Jesuit University established in 1886 with enrollment of approximately 4,500 students located in a suburb of Cleveland, Ohio. The university's mission is to prepare students for intellectual and professional leadership.

Program Description

HR is one of several career tracks available in the MBA program. Emphasis on negotiations and strategic HR are typical HR electives. Full-time program was instituted in 2000.

Degree Requirements

Total Credits Required:	36
Average Credits per Course:	3
Course Schedule:	Semester
Total Courses Required:	12
HR/IR Courses Required:	3
Average Time for Completion:	1 ½-2 ½ years
Maximum Time Allowed for Completion:	5 years
Accepts Credits from Other Universities:	YES
Total:	N/A

Tuition

In-state	N/A	(per year)
	$587	(per credit hour)
Out-of-state	N/A	(per year)
	$587	(per credit hour)

Program Delivery

Traditional Day Program:	YES
Nontraditional Program:	YES
Evening Program:	YES
Weekend Program:	YES
Summer Courses:	N/A
Some Courses Online:	NO
Full Program Online:	NO
Distance Learning/Offsite:	NO
Executive Education:	N/A
Overseas Study Abroad:	YES

Faculty

Full-Time Faculty:	3
Part-Time Faculty:	3
Faculty to Student Ratio:	1:20

Primary Teaching Methods:

Case Study	Research
Student Presentation	Experiential Learning
Field Projects	Lecture
Team Projects	Group Discussion
Computer Simulations	

Faculty Who Consult Outside:	25-49%
Faculty Involvement:	N/A
Top 5 Faculty Publications:	None

Students

Total Enrollment:			266
Full-Time Enrollment:			8%
Men:	56%	Women:	44%
Hispanic	N/A	African-American:	N/A
Other Minorities:	N/A	International:	N/A
Average Age:	28	Age Range:	N/A
Work Full Time:			75-99%
HR Experience:			75-99%
Speak 2nd Language:			25-49%

Minimum Admission Requirements:

GMAT Score:	400
Other Considerations:	NO
Average Student Profile:	N/A

Program Resources

Students Required to Have Computers:		N/A
Video Teleconferencing:		YES
Physical Library Facilities:		N/A
Online Library Facilities:		N/A
HRCI Certification Preparation:		YES
Links students to local SHRM chapter study groups		
Offers the SHRM Learning System as a teaching tool		
SHRM Student Chapter:		YES
Fellowships:		NO
Scholarships:		NO
Assistantships:	6	AMT: $8,000
Eligibility:		Full-Time Enrollment

Curriculum

Required Courses:
  Accounting
  Finance
  Marketing
  HR Strategy
  International HR
  Management
  Business Functional Areas

Most Popular Elective Courses:	N/A
Career Tracks/Concentrations:	N/A
Internship Required:	NO

Career Services

Career Development Opportunities/Placement Service:

Field Trips	Resume Services
Interview Training	Campus Interview
Internships	Diversity
Organizational Change	Negotiations
Staffing	

Summer Internship Placement Rate:	N/A
Full-Time Placement Rate:	N/A
Average Starting Salary (Full-Time Graduates):	N/A
Average Sign-on Bonus:	N/A
Companies Recruiting HR Master's Graduates:	N/A

Points of Excellence

Curriculum: Students receive an extensive evaluation of their leadership and managerial skills. Using an assessment center process as well as personality measures, self-report measures, and experiential learning, students have the opportunity to discover their strengths and weaknesses. In a structured classroom setting, students create a career development plan. In addition to placement and counseling services, students have available a career coach who meets with each student to assist with date/information analysis and with the creation of the comprehensive career plan.

Faculty: Faculty expertise is in labor relations, negotiations, staffing, and organizational change. Faculty are highly collaborative and seek to provide an integrated learning experience.

Contact Information

John Carroll University
Graduate School/MBA Program
20700 N. Park Blvd.
University Heights, OH 44118
www.jcu.edu/graduate

Dr. James M. Daley
Associate Dean and Director MBA Program
Telephone: (216) 397-4391   FAX: (216) 397-1728
mmauk@jcu.edu

Dr. Sandra Washington
Assistant Professor
Telephone: (216) 397-1605   FAX: (216) 397-1728
swashington@jcu.edu

Admission Deadlines

Online Application:	NO

Keller Graduate School of Management

Oakbrook Terrace, Illinois

Degree

Master of Human Resource Management (MHRM)

University Overview

Keller is accredited by NCA and has 47 centers (including online) serving approximately 7,000 students nationwide. Keller's reputation is based on providing a high-quality management education, a practitioner orientation, and exceptional service to working adults through a nontraditional program.

Program Description

The MHRM program prepares students to be more productive in their organizations by teaching concepts and skills needed to plan, control, and direct organizational requirements for effective and efficient use of human resources. Coursework is taught from the practitioner's perspective.

Degree Requirements

Total Credits Required:	60
Average Credits per Course:	3
Course Schedule:	Quarter
Total Courses Required:	15
HR/IR Courses Required:	7
Average Time for Completion:	2 ⅓ years
Maximum Time Allowed for Completion:	5 years
Accepts Credits from Other Universities:	YES
Total:	12 Hours (Quarterly, 3 Courses)*

Students in California may receive transfer credit for up to two courses.

Tuition

In-state	$1,420	(per year)
	N/A	(per credit hour)
Out-of-state	$1,420	(per year)
	N/A	(per credit hour)

Program Delivery

Traditional Day Program:	NO
Nontraditional Program:	YES
Evening Program:	YES
Weekend Program:	YES
Summer Courses:	YES
Some Courses Online:	YES
Full Program Online:	YES
Distance Learning/Offsite:	YES
Executive Education:	NO
Overseas Study Abroad:	YES

Faculty

Full-Time Faculty:	20
Part-Time Faculty:	860
Faculty to Student Ratio:	1:10
Primary Teaching Methods:	
Case Study	Group Discussion
Experiential Learning	Lecture
Faculty Who Consult Outside:	1-24%
Faculty Involvement:	See web site
Top 5 Faculty Publications:	N/A

Students

Total Enrollment:			6,900
Full-Time Enrollment:			26%
Men:	54%	Women:	46%
Hispanic	4%	African-American:	24%
Other Minorities:	17%	International:	2%
Average Age:	34	Age Range:	22-64
Work Full Time:			50-74%
HR Experience:			N/A
Speak 2nd Language:			N/A
Minimum Admission Requirements:			
GRE Score:			500 Math, 430 Verbal
GMAT Score:			27 Math, 25 Verbal
Other Considerations:			N/A
Average Student Profile:			N/A

Program Resources

Students Required to Have Computers:	YES
Video Teleconferencing:	NO
Physical Library Facilities:	NO
Online Library Facilities:	YES
HRCI Certification Preparation:	YES
Curriculum based on exam content	

SHRM Student Chapter:	NO
Fellowships:	NO
Scholarships:	NO
Assistantships:	NO
Eligibility:	N/A

Curriculum

Required Courses:
- Accounting
- Finance
- Management
- Marketing
- HR Strategy
- Business Functional Areas
- Employment Law
- Recruitment/Retention
- Compensation/Benefits
- Development/Training

Most Popular Elective Courses:
- Negotiation Skills
- Labor Relations
- Managing Global Diversity
- International HR Management

Career Tracks/Concentrations:	N/A
Internship Required:	NO

Career Services

Career Development Opportunities/Placement Service:
- Online job leads
- Workshops
- Career Counseling

Summer Internship Placement Rate:	N/A
Full-Time Placement Rate:	N/A
Average Starting Salary (Full-Time Graduates):	$63,000
Average Sign-on Bonus:	N/A
Companies Recruiting HR Master's Graduates:	11%

Points of Excellence

Curriculum: Keller recognizes the challenges facing managers today. To this end, we work diligently to bridge the gap between the typical academic classroom experience and the day-to-day demands of business. Our faculty of practicing business professionals are successful managers who have a strong desire to teach and approach management theories from a practical point of view. They provide a unique education that's immediately useful on the job. At Keller, management theories and concepts focus directly on the realities of current business. Keller offers six master's degree programs relevant to today's business world, with coursework in each offered both onsite and online.

Contact Information

Keller Graduate School of Management
1751 Pinnacle Drive
McLean, VA 22102
www.keller.edu

Ron Stone, MHRM Program Manager
Telephone: (703) 556-9669
rstone@keller.edu

Admission Deadlines

Online Application:	YES

Kennesaw State University

Kennesaw, Georgia

Degree
Master of Business Administration (MBA)

University Overview
A regional state university with 14,000 students located near Atlanta.

Program Description
General Human Resources Program is available in both traditional and nontraditional formats. The program accents career goals.

Degree Requirements
Total Credits Required:	36
Average Credits per Course:	3
Course Schedule:	Semester
Total Courses Required:	12
HR/IR Courses Required:	4
Average Time for Completion:	2-3 years
Maximum Time Allowed for Completion:	6 years
Accepts Credits from Other Universities:	YES
Total:	N/A

Tuition
In-state	$2,648	(per year)
	$94	(per credit hour)
Out-of-state	$9,158	(per year)
	$376	(per credit hour)

Program Delivery
Traditional Day Program:	YES
Nontraditional Program:	YES
Evening Program:	YES
Weekend Program:	YES
Summer Courses:	N/A
Some Courses Online:	YES
Full Program Online:	NO
Distance Learning/Offsite:	NO
Executive Education:	N/A
Overseas Study Abroad:	NO

Faculty
Full-Time Faculty:	50
Part-Time Faculty:	0
Faculty to Student Ratio:	1:17

Primary Teaching Methods:
Experiential Learning   Field Projects
Student Presentation   Team Projects
Lecture

Faculty Who Consult Outside:	25-49%
Faculty Involvement:	N/A

Top 5 Faculty Publications:
Journal of Vocational Behavior
Journal of Business and Psychology

Students
Total Enrollment:			863
Full-Time Enrollment:			
Men:	59%	Women:	41%
Hispanic	3%	African-American:	13%
Other Minorities:	47%	International:	N/A
Average Age:	32	Age Range:	25-63%
Work Full Time:			75-99%
HR Experience:			N/A
Speak 2nd Language:			N/A

Minimum Admission Requirements:
Combined GPA-2.8/GMAT 475

Other Considerations:	Personal Goals/Resume
Average Student Profile:	GPA 3.6, GMAT 478

Program Resources
Students Required to Have Computers:	N/A
Video Teleconferencing:	YES
Physical Library Facilities:	N/A
Online Library Facilities:	N/A
HRCI Certification Preparation:	NO
SHRM Student Chapter:	YES
Fellowships:	None
Scholarships:	None
Assistantships:	None
Eligibility:	N/A

Curriculum
Required Courses:
Human Resource Management and Development
Employment Law
Advanced Topics in Human Resource Management
Most Popular Elective Courses:
Consulting Services
Cyber Law
Entrepreneurship for e-Business
International Management Practices
Organizational Effectiveness

Career Tracks/Concentrations:	N/A
Internship Required:	NO

Career Services
Career Development Opportunities/Placement Service:
Field Trips   Campus Interview
Internships

Summer Internship Placement Rate:	N/A
Full-Time Placement Rate:	N/A
Average Starting Salary (Full-Time Graduates):	N/A
Average Sign-on Bonus:	N/A
Companies Recruiting HR Master's Graduates:	N/A

Points of Excellence
Placement: Our "Career Services Center" has a full schedule of visiting companies seeking high quality individuals for employment from the metro-Atlanta area as well as firms outside Atlanta. However, most part-time Career Growth MBA students are employed full-time and remain with their organizations upon graduation. In addition students are continually visiting web sites during their MBA programs of study to seek employment alternatives.

Contact Information
Michael J. Coles
College of Business
Kennesaw State University
1000 Chastain Rd.
Kennesaw, GA 30149
www.kennesaw.edu

Dr. Harry J. Lasher, Director
Career Growth MBA, MAcc and WebMBA Programs
Telephone: (770) 423-6041   FAX: (770) 423-6141
harry_lesher@coles2.kennesaw.edu

Admission Deadlines
Online Application:	YES

LaRoche College

Pittsburgh, Pennsylvania

Degree
Master of Science in Human Resource Management (MSHRM)

University Overview
A private Catholic college with an enrollment of 1,900 students.

Program Description
Available in both full-time traditional day and nontraditional programs, this comprehensive Human Resource program offers concentrations in HR Administration, HR Development, and HR Strategy. It also encourages special talents in HR Information Systems (HRIS), Organizational Development, and HR Strategy.

Degree Requirements
Total Credits Required:	42
Average Credits per Course:	3
Course Schedule:	Semester
Total Courses Required:	14
HR/IR Courses Required:	14
Average Time for Completion:	2-3 years
Maximum Time Allowed for Completion:	5 years
Accepts Credits from Other Universities:	YES
Total:	N/A

Tuition
In-state	N/A	(per year)
	$420	(per credit hour)
Out-of-state	N/A	(per year)
	$420	(per credit hour)

Program Delivery
Traditional Day Program:	YES
Nontraditional Program:	YES
Evening Program:	YES
Weekend Program:	YES
Summer Courses:	N/A
Some Courses Online:	YES
Full Program Online:	NO
Distance Learning/Offsite:	YES
Executive Education:	N/A
Overseas Study Abroad:	NO

Faculty
Full-Time Faculty:	6
Part-Time Faculty:	10
Faculty to Student Ratio:	1:10

Primary Teaching Methods:
Research	Group Discussion
Lecture	Experiential Learning

Faculty Who Consult Outside: 1-24%

Faculty Involvement:
Member, Editorial Board for Human Communication Research
Editor, Organization Communication Subseries Hampton, Press Editor
Member, International Communication Assoc.

Top 5 Faculty Publications:
Journal of Organizational Change

Students
Total Enrollment:			160
Full-Time Enrollment:			10%
Men:	35%	Women:	65%
Hispanic	0%	African-American:	2%
Other Minorities:	1%	International:	6%
Average Age:	32	Age Range:	N/A

Work Full Time:	75-99%
HR Experience:	50-74%
Speak 2nd Language:	1-24%
Minimum Admission Requirements:	N/A

Other Considerations:
Demonstration of significant professional accomplishment
And/or very good GRE/GMAT scores

Average Student Profile:
GRE Score:	1050
UGPA:	3.5
Work experience:	9 years

Program Resources
Students Required to Have Computer:	N/A
Video Teleconferencing:	NO
Physical Library Facilities:	N/A
Online Library Facilities:	N/A
HRCI Certification Preparation:	YES

Encourages student study groups
Bases curriculum on certification content

SHRM Student Chapter:	YES
Fellowships:	0

Scholarships:	varies	AMT:	full ride
Assistantships:	1	AMT:	$1,000/mo
Eligibility:			All Students

Curriculum
Required Courses:
Finance
Accounting
HR Strategy
Employment Law
Development/Training
Management
HR Measurement
HRIS

Most Popular Elective Courses:
Leadership
Recruitment
Advanced Legal
Advanced HRIS
Web-based Training
International HR
Safety & Wellness
Compensation
Benefits
Organizational Analysis

Career Tracks/Concentrations:	N/A
Internship Required:	NO

Career Services
Career Development Opportunities/Placement Service:
Mentoring	Resume Services
Interview Training	SHRM Student Chapter
Internships	

Summer Internship Placement Rate:	N/A
Full-Time Placement Rate:	100%
Average Starting Salary (Full-Time Graduates):	$38,000
Average Sign-on Bonus:	N/A
Companies Recruiting HR Master's Graduates:	N/A

Points of Excellence
Program Resources: Only program in the region that offers a Certificate Program in HRIS. This four-course program teaches students the various ways technology interfaces with HRM. The certificate program can be earned as part of the student's master curriculum or separately for alumni and others who are interested in specialized HR skills. Other certificate programs are offered

in Legal Aspects of HRM, Financial Aspects of HRM, Training and Development, and HR Generalist.

Students: LaRoche College offers HRM scholarships to international students coming from war-torn countries, including Bosnia, Rwanda, and Uganda. Students are handpicked by their respective governments. The program is called "Pacem in Terris" and is supported by grants from the U.S. government and the World Bank.

Curriculum: Student and alumni involvement in the governance of program is very innovative. Students and alumni provide annual feedback on everything from program content and course requirements to teaching evaluation format and content. For example, students and alumni championed a new concentration in Strategic HR and Leadership. They also asked for and received a reduction in core program requirements and an increase in electives. They do this through the HRM Graduate Student Advisory Council, which meets with faculty monthly.

Contact Information
LaRoche College
9000 Babcock Blvd.
Pittsburgh, PA 15237
www.laroche.edu

Dr. Howard Ishiyama, Chair, Graduate Program in HRM
Telephone: (412) 536-1193   FAX: (412) 536-1179
ishiyah1@laroche.edu

Admission Deadlines
Rolling admissions
Online Application: YES

Long Island University

Brooklyn, New York

Degree
Master of Science in Human Resources (MSHR)

University Overview
Long Island University is the eighth largest private university in enrollment in the United States. The MSHR program, serving the New York Metropolitan area, is located in the downtown Brooklyn Campus, which serves more than 11,000 students.

Program Description
The MSHR program is designed to prepare students to enter the profession at the generalist level by providing a broad overview of the functional areas of HRM. Most students work full-time. The program stresses the integration of HRM within the context of managerial planning, organizing, and leading as a strategic partner who contributes to organizational success.

Degree Requirements
Total Credits Required:	36
Average Credits per Course:	3
Course Schedule:	Semester
Total Courses Required:	12
HR/IR Courses Required:	6
Average Time for Completion:	2 years
Maximum Time Allowed for Completion:	5 years
Accepts Credits from Other Universities:	YES
Total:	6 Approved Transfer Credits

Tuition
In-state	N/A	(per year)
	$505	(per credit hour)
Out-of-state	N/A	(per year)
	$505	(per credit hour)

Program Delivery
Traditional Day Program:	NO
Nontraditional Program:	YES
Evening Program:	YES
Weekend Program:	YES
Summer Courses:	YES
Some Courses Online:	NO
Full Program Online:	NO
Distance Learning/Offsite:	Under Development
Executive Education:	NO
Overseas Study Abroad:	NO

Faculty
Full-Time Faculty:	4
Part-Time Faculty:	4
Faculty to Student Ratio:	1:20

Primary Teaching Methods:
Case Study	Lecture
Student Presentation	Group Discussion

Faculty Who Consult Outside:	50-74%
Faculty Involvement:	See web site
Top 5 Faculty Publications:	N/A

Students
Total Enrollment:			25
Full-Time Enrollment:			25%
Men:	32%	Women:	68%
Hispanic:	15%	African-American:	45%
Other Minorities:	8%	International:	28%
Average Age:	27	Age Range:	23-40
Work Full Time:			75-99%
HR Experience:			1-24%
Speak 2nd Language:			25-49%

Minimum Admission Requirements:
  Not publicized
Other Considerations:
  Limited matriculation to 12 credits until GPA of 3.25 achieved
Average Student Profile:
Work experience:	5 years

Program Resources
Students Required to Have Computers:	NO
Video Teleconferencing:	YES
Physical Library Facilities:	YES
Online Library Facilities:	YES
HRCI Certification Preparation:	YES

  Encourages student study groups
  Will offer SHRM Learning System in spring 2001
SHRM Student Chapter:			YES
Fellowships:			NO
Scholarships:			NO
Assistantships:	3	AMT:	N/A
Eligibility:			Full-Time Enrollment

Curriculum
Required Courses:
  International HR
  Compensation
  Development/Training
  Recruitment/Retention
  Employment Law
  Management
  Employee Relations
  Labor Relations
  Business Functional Areas

Most Popular Elective Courses:
   Employee Benefits

Career Tracks/Concentrations: N/A

Internship Required: NO

Career Services
Career Development Opportunities/Placement Service:

Mentoring	Internships
Resume Services	SHRM Student Chapter
Interview Training	Campus Interviews

Summer Internship Placement Rate: N/A

Full-Time Placement Rate: 90-100%

Average Starting Salary (Full-Time Graduates): N/A

Average Sign-on Bonus: N/A

Companies Recruiting HR Master's Graduates: 15

Points of Excellence
Faculty: The MSHR faculty are truly practitioner/educators and bring many years of experience in areas of corporate training and development, gender bias, ADA, international studies, recruiting, and employee development. The program encourages students to use the program as a laboratory to address relevant workplace issues. Under the supervision of a senior faculty member, students prepared a business plan for a start-up, not-for-profit organization that was to offer disability training to firms interested in employing individuals with disabilities. Another project involved the development of a proposal to obtain a $1.2 million grant from the New York State Department of Health for the hiring of culturally sensitive and linguistically appropriate staff to work in the emergency department of a major New York City hospital.

Contact Information
Long Island University, H-700
1 University Plaza
Brooklyn, NY 11201-5372
www.liu.edu

Linette Williams, Academic Advisor
Telephone: (718) 488-1072   FAX: (718) 488-1125
Linette.williams@liu.edu

Dr. Jordan Kaplan
Director, HR Management Program
Telephone: (718) 488-1148   FAX: (718) 488-1125
Jordan.kaplan@liu.edu

Admission Deadlines
One month prior to the semester for which applying

Online Application: N/A

Loyola University

Chicago, Illinois
Institute of Human Resources and Industrial Relations

Degree
Master of Science in Human Resources (MSHR)
Master of Science in Industrial Relations (MSIR)

University Overview
Loyola, a private Jesuit College, is located along the magnificent mile in Chicago's Gold Coast. Established in 1870, Loyola Chicago has an enrollment of more than 13,000 students.

Program Description
Loyola's HR/IR program is one of the oldest programs, established in 1941. Most students work full-time and attend the program on a part-time basis. The HR/IR program has several areas of concentration including HR, IR, Organization Development, and Global Human Resources & Training. Member of GOALS Consortium.

Degree Requirements
Total Credits Required: 42

Average Credits per Course: 3

Course Schedule: Quarter

Total Courses Required: 14

HR/IR Courses Required: 8

Average Time for Completion: 2 ½ years

Maximum Time Allowed for Completion: 5 years

Accepts Credits from Other Universities: YES

Total: 6 Hours (2 Classes)

Tuition

In-state	N/A	(per year)
	$594	(per credit hour)
Out-of-state	N/A	(per year)
	$594	(per credit hour)

Program Delivery
Traditional Day Program: NO

Nontraditional Program: YES

   Evening Program: YES

   Weekend Program: YES

   Summer Courses: YES

   Some Courses Online: NO

   Full Program Online: NO

   Distance Learning/Offsite: YES

   Executive Education: NO

   Overseas Study Abroad: YES

Faculty
Full-Time Faculty: 9

Part-Time Faculty: 15

Faculty to Student Ratio: 1:30

Primary Teaching Methods:

Case Study	Experiential Learning
Team Projects	Group Discussion
Computer Simulations	

Faculty Who Consult Outside: 50-74%

Faculty Involvement:
   Board member, Personnel Management Association
   Editorial Board, leading academic journals
   GOALS

Top 5 Faculty Publications: N/A

Students

Total Enrollment:			200
Full-Time Enrollment:			80%
Men:	25%	Women:	75%
Hispanic	5%	African-American:	10%
Other Minorities:	5%	International:	1%
Average Age:	28	Age Range:	22-55
Work Full Time:			75-99%
HR Experience:			50-74%
Speak 2nd Language:			1-24%

Minimum Admission Requirements:

   GRE Score: 1550

   GMAT Score: 500

   Work experience: NONE*

Other Considerations:

   Work experience: 10 years as experienced professional

Students with less than three years of work experience must take additional coursework.

Average Student Profile:
GRE Score:	1560
GMAT Score:	510
Work experience:	8 years

Program Resources
Students Required to Have Computers:	NO
Video Teleconferencing:	YES
Physical Library Facilities:	YES
Online Library Facilities:	YES
HRCI Certification Preparation:	NO
SHRM Student Chapter:	YES
Fellowships:	NO
Scholarships:	NO
Assistantships: 4	AMT: $25,000
Eligibility:	Full-Time Enrollment

Curriculum
Required Courses:
  Analytical Problem Solving
  Employment Law
Most Popular Elective Courses:
  Labor Relations
  Compensation/Benefits
  Performance Management
  Global HR
  Strategic HR Planning
  Development/Training
  Organization Development
  Staffing
Career Tracks/Concentrations:
  Compensation and Benefits   Generalist
  Global   Organization Development
  Training
Internship Required: NO

Career Services
Career Development Opportunities/Placement Service:
  Mentoring   Campus Interviews
  Resume Services   SHRM Student Chapter
  Internships   Interview Training
Summer Internship Placement Rate:	N/A
Full-Time Placement Rate:	90-100%
Average Starting Salary (Full-Time Graduates):	$65,000
Average Sign-on Bonus:	N/A
Companies Recruiting HR Master's Graduates:	15

Points of Excellence
Curriculum: Loyola has had a Global HR concentration for 10 years. There are established courses in global expatriate compensation, expatriate management, global training, and global HR. An option is available for students to do research in other countries. Each year, there is an overseas seminar. Locations have included Cuba, Hong Kong, England, Germany, and France.

Placements: Loyola has strong relationships with the many global corporations located in the Chicago area that facilitate career placement for students. There are a full-time manager of career services and an online job listing updated weekly. A resume book is sent electronically to 75 companies twice a year. Most students have jobs but many make career moves as a result of the program.

Students: Loyola is proud to have such a diverse student population and attribute this success to our involvement with programs like GOALS and endowed scholarship programs from GM and EEOC.

Contact Information
Institute of Human Resources and Industrial Relations
820 N. Michigan Ave.
Chicago, IL 60611
www.luc.edu/depts/hrir

Dr. Fran Daly, Associate Director
Telephone: (312) 915-6598   FAX: (312) 915-6231
fdaly@luc.edu

Nicole DeLuca, Program Coordinator
Telephone: (312) 915-6595   FAX: (312) 915-6231
ndeluca@luc.edu

Dr. Arup Varma, Associate Professor
SHRM Student Chapter Advisor
Telephone: (312) 915-6664   FAX: (312) 915-6231
avarma@luc.edu

Admission Deadlines
August 3 for Fall admissions
Online Application: YES

Manhattanville College

Purchase, New York
School of Graduate and Professional Studies

Degree
Master of Science in Organizational Management and Human Resource Development (MSOMHR)

University Overview
Manhattanville College is an independent, coeducational, liberal arts institution founded in 1841. The campus is located in Purchase, New York, approximately 30 miles north of New York City.

Program Description
The MSOMHR program is ideal for current human resource professionals as well as for those seeking to enter the HR field. It emphasizes a strong theoretical background plus the development of practical management and leadership skills.

Degree Requirements
Total Credits Required:	36
Average Credits per Course:	3
Course Schedule:	Semester
Total Courses Required:	12
HR/IR Courses Required:	9
Average Time for Completion:	3 years
Maximum Time Allowed for Completion:	5 years
Accepts Credits from Other Universities:	YES
Total:	6 Hours

Tuition
In-state	N/A	(per year)
	$450	(per credit hour)
Out-of-state	N/A	(per year)
	$450	(per credit hour)

Program Delivery
Traditional Day Program:	NO
Nontraditional Program:	YES
Evening Program:	NO
Weekend Program:	YES
Program Completed Evening/Weekend:	YES
Summer Courses:	YES
Some Courses Online:	NO

Full Program Online:	NO
Distance Learning/Offsite:	NO
Executive Education:	NO
Overseas Study Abroad:	NO

Faculty

Full-Time Faculty:	3
Part-Time Faculty:	15
Faculty to Student Ratio:	1:15

Primary Teaching Methods:
Case Study	Team Projects
Student Presentation	Lecture
Group Discussion	

Faculty Who Consult Outside:	NONE
Faculty Involvement:	
Top 5 Faculty Publications:	

Students

Total Enrollment:	180
Full-Time Enrollment:	0

Men:	11%	Women:	89%
Hispanic:	9%	African-American:	20%
Other Minorities:	2%	International:	1%
Average Age:	32	Age Range:	22-62

Work Full Time:	75-99%
Have HR Experience:	75-99%
Speak 2nd Language:	1-24%

Minimum Admission Requirements:
UGPA:	2.75
GRE or GMAT Score:	N/A
Work Experience:	2 years

Other Considerations:
Breadth of experience after 5+ years from undergraduate studies.

Average Student Profile:
UGPA:	3.4
GRE/GMAT Score:	N/A
Work Experience:	8 years

Program Resources

Students Required to Have Computers:	NO
Video Teleconferencing:	NO
Physical Library Facilities:	YES
Online Library Facilities:	YES
HRCI Certification Preparation:	YES
Offer SHRM Learning System	
SHRM Student Chapter:	NO
URL:	

Fellowships:	NO	AMT:
Scholarships:	NO	AMT:
Assistantships:	NO	AMT:
Eligibility:		

Curriculum

Required Courses:
Finance
Employment Law
HR Strategy
Development/Training
Research Techniques
Overview of the HR Field

Most Popular Elective Courses:
Leading Change
Diverse Workforce
Staffing & Recruitment
Total Rewards: Trends, Strategies and Practices

Career Tracks/Concentrations:
Generalist

Internship Required:	NO

Career Services

Career Services Offered:
Mentoring	Interview Training
Resume Services	Campus Interview
Internships	

Summer Internship Placement Rate:	N/A
Facilitate Placement:	YES
Full-Time Placement Rate:	N/A
Internship Placement Rate:	N/A
Average Starting Salary (Full-Time Graduates):	N/A
Average Sign-on Bonus:	N/A
Companies Recruiting HR Master's Graduates:	N/A

Points of Excellence

Manhattanville College offers the student an experienced faculty along with easy access to counseling by both faculty and deans. The college's Corporate Educational Advisory Board allows for adjustment to the curriculum to maintain relevance and value to the student. Students' thesis projects are generally related to areas of interest in their workplace.

Contact Information

School of Graduate & Professional Studies
Manhattanville College
2900 Purchase Street
Purchase, NY 10577
www.mville.edu/graduate

Administrative Contact
Donald J. Richards, Ph.D., Associate Dean
Telephone: (914) 694-3425
gps@mville.edu

Faculty Contact
William G. Stopper
Telephone: (203) 431-1333
wgstopper@msn.com

Admission Deadlines

Rolling admissions
Online Application:	NO

Marquette University

Milwaukee, Wisconsin
College of Business

Degree

Master of Science in Human Resources (MS-HR)

University Overview

Marquette University is a private, Jesuit Catholic university with more than 11,000 students, located in downtown Milwaukee.

Program Description

Courses are offered in all traditional areas of human resources strategy, HRIS, and organization change. Study abroad courses with an HR emphasis are available.

Degree Requirements

Total Credits Required:	36
Average Credits per Course:	3
Course Schedule:	Semester
Total Courses Required:	13
HR/IR Courses Required:	7
Average Time for Completion:	2-4 years
Maximum Time Allowed for Completion:	6 years
Accepts Credits from Other Universities:	YES
Total:	N/A

Tuition

In-state	N/A	(per year)
	$500	(per credit hour)
Out-of-state	N/A	(per year)
	$500	(per credit hour)

Program Delivery

Traditional Day Program:	YES
Nontraditional Program:	YES
Evening Program:	YES
Weekend Program:	YES
Summer Courses:	N/A
Some Courses Online:	NO
Full Program Online:	NO
Distance Learning/Offsite:	NO
Executive Education:	N/A
Overseas Study Abroad:	NO

Faculty

Full-Time Faculty:	7
Part-Time Faculty:	4
Faculty to Student Ratio:	1:20

Primary Teaching Methods:

Case Study	Team Projects
Student Presentation	Group Discussion
Computer Simulations	

Faculty Who Consult Outside: N/A

Faculty Involvement:
Executive Board, National Industrial Relations Research Association

Top 5 Faculty Publications:
Academy of Management Journal
Journal of Applied Psychology
Journal of Vocational Behavior

Students

Total Enrollment:			60
Full-Time Enrollment:			10
Men:	30%	Women:	70%
Hispanic	5%	African-American:	5%
Other Minorities:	7%	International:	7%
Average Age:	28	Age Range:	21-50
Work Full Time:			75-99%
HR Experience:			50-74%
Speak 2nd Language:			1-24%

Minimum Admission Requirements:
GMAT or GRE, UGPA, and diligent study habits

Other Considerations:
Case by case; high probability of success

Average Student Profile:
4 years of work experience

GMAT/GRE Score:	60th percentile

Program Resources

Students Required to Have Computers:			N/A
Video Teleconferencing:			NO
Physical Library Facilities:			N/A
Online Library Facilities:			N/A
HRCI Certification Preparation:			NO
SHRM Student Chapter:			YES
Fellowships:			NO
Scholarships:	6	AMT:	$4,500
Assistantships:	1	AMT:	$20,000
Eligibility:		Full-Time Enrollment	

Curriculum

Required Courses:
HR Strategy
Compensation/Benefits
Development/Training
Recruitment/Retention
Labor Relations
HR Measurement
Social Responsibility of Business

Most Popular Elective Courses:
Employment Law
Diversity
Employee Benefit Systems
Negotiations
Dispute Resolution
HR Information Systems
Organization Change
Organization Development
Using Technology for Instruction

Career Track/Concentrations:	N/A
Internship Required:	NO

Career Services

Career Development Opportunities/Placement Service:

Mentoring	Interview Training
Campus Interview	Internships
Resume Services	

Summer Internship Placement Rate:	N/A
Full-Time Placement Rate:	75-80%
Average Starting Salary (Full-Time Graduates):	$40,000
Average Sign-on Bonus:	N/A
Companies Recruiting HR Master's Graduates:	49

Points of Excellence

Faculty: Tenure-track faculty have active high-quality research programs that lead to publications in major academic journals. Adjunct faculty bring specialization.

Students: Typical student works in HR and has a wealth of experience. Consequently, the course content is focused on relevant issues facing HR professionals.

Contact Information

Marquette University
Human Resources Program
College of Business
P.O. Box 1881
Milwaukee, WI 53201-1881
www.grad.mu.edu

Timothy Keaveny
Director, MS. In Human Resources Program
Telephone: (414) 288-3643   FAX: (414) 288-5754
tim.keaveny@marquette.edu

Admission Deadlines

One month prior to the semester for which applying

Online Application:	YES

Marygrove College

Detroit, Michigan

Degree

Master of Arts in Human Resource Management (MA-HRM)

University Overview

An urban private college located in Detroit with a total enrollment of more than 5,000 students. A large number are enrolled in a distance-learning program in teacher education.

Program Description
Nontraditional program offers two concentrations: Management and HRM sequences.

Degree Requirements
Total Credits Required:	36
Average Credits per Course:	2-3
Course Schedule:	Semester
Total Courses Required:	16
HR/IR Courses Required:	12
Average Time for Completion:	2-3 years
Maximum Time Allowed for Completion:	6 years
Accepts Credits from Other Universities:	YES
Total:	N/A

Tuition
In-state	N/A	(per year)
	$360	(per credit hour)
Out-of-state	N/A	(per year)
	$360	(per credit hour)

Program Delivery
Traditional Day Program:	NO
Nontraditional Program:	YES
Evening Program:	YES
Weekend Program:	YES
Summer Courses:	N/A
Some Courses Online:	NO
Full Program Online:	NO
Distance Learning/Offsite:	NO
Executive Education:	N/A
Overseas Study Abroad:	NO

Faculty
Full-Time Faculty:	1
Part-Time Faculty:	4
Faculty to Student Ratio:	1:10

Primary Teaching Methods:

Case Study	Lecture
Research	Student Presentations
Team Projects	Field Projects
Group Discussion	

Faculty Who Consult Outside:	50-74%
Faculty Involvement:	See web site
Top 5 Faculty Publications:	N/A

Students
Total Enrollment:			63
Full-Time Enrollment:			0%
Men:	35%	Women:	65%
Hispanic:	3%	African-American:	85%
Other Minorities:	0%	International:	N/A
Average Age:	32	Age Range:	22-49
Work Full Time:			75-99%
HR Experience:			1-24%
Speak 2nd Language:			1-24%

Minimum Admission Requirements:
Other admissions based on academic record, work experience, and other factors.

Other Considerations:	NO
Average Student Profile:	N/A

Program Resources
Students Required to Have Computers:	N/A
Video Teleconferencing:	NO
Physical Library Facilities:	N/A
Online Library Facilities:	N/A
HRCI Certification Preparation:	NO
SHRM Student Chapter:	YES

Fellowships:	NO
Scholarships:	NO
Assistantships:	NO
Eligibility:	N/A

Curriculum
Required Courses:
- Finance
- HR Strategy
- Development/Training
- Recruitment/Retention
- Employment Law
- Management
- Employee Relations
- Labor Relations
- Business Functional Areas

Most Popular Elective Courses:
- Collective Bargaining
- Labor Economics
- Diversity
- Ethics & Human Behavior

Career Tracks/Concentrations:	N/A
Internship Required:	NO

Career Services
Career Development Opportunities/Placement Service:

Field Trips	SHRM Student Chapter

Summer Internship Placement Rate:	N/A
Full-Time Placement Rate:	N/A
Average Starting Salary (Full-Time Graduates):	N/A
Average Sign-on Bonus:	N/A
Companies Recruiting HR Master's Graduates:	10

Points of Excellence
Students: Staff and adjuncts are available to working adult students for encouragement and support. Students are admitted on a basis of undergraduate success, work experience, and a personal interview. Students assess faculty performance each semester. Program content is reviewed every two years. Financial assistance is available by virtue of state of Michigan grants and personal loans. The Marygrove Financial Aid staff is ready and able to assist students with these opportunities. Faculty and staff provide informal mentoring and career coaching.

Contact Information
Marygrove College
8425 W. McNichols Rd.
Detroit, MI 48221-2599
www.marygrove.edu

Richard Laurent-Barnett, Ph.D., Graduate Dean
Telephone: (313) 927-1496   FAX: (313) 927-1490
rlbarnett@marygrove.edu

John A. Candela, Ed.D., Assistant Professor
Telephone: (313) 927-1466   FAX: (313) 927-1444
jcandela@marygrove.edu

Admission Deadlines
Online Application:	N/A

Marymount University

Arlington, Virginia
School of Business Administration,
Human Resources Department

Degree
Master in Human Resource Management (MA/HRM)
Master in Human Performance System (MAHPS)
Master in Organization Development (MAOD)

University Overview
Private Catholic university with approximately 3,600 students located near Washington, DC.

Program Description
Focus of nontraditional program is on performance-based systems approach. Emphasis is on learning practical skills and transfer to workplace performance. Offers three concentrations: MA in Human Resource Management; MA in Human Performance Systems; and MA in Organization Development.

Degree Requirements
Total Credits Required:	36
Average Credits per Course:	6
Course Schedule:	Semester
Total Courses Required:	12
HR/IR Courses Required:	9
Average Time for Completion:	1-4 years
Maximum Time Allowed for Completion:	5 years
Accepts Credits from Other Universities:	YES
Total:	12 Hours

Tuition
In-state	N/A	(per year)
	$480	(per credit hour)
Out-of-state	N/A	(per year)
	$480	(per credit hour)

Program Delivery
Traditional Day Program:	NO
Nontraditional Program:	YES
Evening Program:	YES
Weekend Program:	YES
Summer Courses:	N/A
Some Courses Online:	NO
Full Program Online:	NO
Distance Learning/Offsite:	YES (corporate delivery)
Executive Education:	N/A
Overseas Study Abroad:	YES

Faculty
Full-Time Faculty:	5
Part-Time Faculty:	12
Faculty to Student Ratio:	1:20

Primary Teaching Methods:
Case Study	Experiential Learning
Team Projects	Group Discussion

Faculty Who Consult Outside:	100%

Faculty Involvement:
ASTD, Research Committee
ASTD, Publications Committee
OD Consulting
Top 5 Faculty Publications:	N/A

Students
Total Enrollment:	200
Full-Time Enrollment:	5%

Men:	15%	Women:	85%
Hispanic	3%	African-American:	20%
Other Minorities:	3%	International:	8%
Average Age:	32	Age Range:	23-65
Work Full Time:			75-99%
HR Experience:			50-74%
Speak 2nd Language:			1-24%

Minimum Admission Requirements:
Work experience: 2 years where ability is in question
Other Considerations:
Satisfactory master's level work
Significant work experience
Average Student Profile:
GRE Score:	1650
GMAT Score:	550
Work experience:	8 years

Program Resources
Students Required to Have Computers:	N/A
Video Teleconferencing:	NO
Physical Library Facilities:	N/A
Online Library Facilities:	N/A
HRCI Certification Preparation:	YES

Refers students to local preparation courses
SHRM Student Chapter:	YES
Fellowships:	NO
Scholarships:	NO
Assistantships:	5 AMT: $300/month + tuition
Eligibility:	Full-Time Enrollment

Curriculum
Required Courses:
HR Strategy
Development/Training
Recruitment/Retention
Compensation/Benefits
Employment Law
HR Measurement
Research Design/Evaluation
HR Planning
Most Popular Elective Courses:
Business Statistics
Group Decision Making
Project Management
HRIS
International HR
Labor Relations
Career Tracks/Concentrations:	N/A
Internship Required:	YES

Career Services
Career Development Opportunities/Placement Service:
Field Trips	SHRM Student Chapter
Mentoring	Resume Services
Campus Interviews	Internships
Networking with Alumni	

Summer Internship Placement Rate:	N/A
Full-Time Placement Rate:	75-100%
Average Starting Salary (Full-Time Graduates):	$42,000
Average Sign-on Bonus:	N/A
Companies Recruiting HR Master's Graduates:	20

Points of Excellence
Placement: Strong alumni network provides tremendous support to students. This network facilitates idea sharing, partnering for research and consulting, practicum, and job placement opportunities. Most courses include hands-on projects that students complete within local organizations or one of the many nonprofit organizations within the DC area.

Curriculum: The Human Performance Systems Program is one of the few of its kind in the United States, focusing on performance consulting, improvement, and technology. Each student must complete a three-credit practicum at either his or her current workplace or at another organization.

Contact Information
Marymount University
School of Business Administration, HR Dept.
2807 N. Glebe Rd.
Arlington, VA 22207
www.marymount.edu

Dr. Karen Medsker, Chair, Human Resources Department
Telephone: (703) 284-5959   FAX: (703) 527-3830
kmedsker@marymount.edu

Dr. Virginia Bianco-Mathis, Professor
Telephone: (703) 698-8418   FAX: (703) 527-3830
vmathis@aol.com

Admission Deadlines
Online Application: YES

Mercy College

Dobbs Ferry, New York

Degree
Master of Science in Human Resource Management (MSHRM)

University Overview
Mercy College is a comprehensive, private college with a total enrollment of more than 8,000 students at its main and three branch campuses. The college's main campus is located in Dobbs Ferry, NY.

Program Description
The program is designed to prepare students for careers as professionals in the field and to enhance the skills of those already in the field. The program presents an application-oriented, real-world focus for those wishing to build highly developed management skills and is offered in a nontraditional format.

Degree Requirements
Total Credits Required:	36
Average Credits per Course:	3
Course Schedule:	Quarter
Total Courses Required:	12
HR/IR Courses Required:	12
Average Time for Completion:	1 ½ years
Maximum Time Allowed for Completion:	5 years
Accepts Credits from Other Universities:	YES
Total:	N/A

Tuition
In-state	N/A	(per year)
	$435	(per credit hour)
Out-of-state	N/A	(per year)
	$435	(per credit hour)

Program Delivery
Traditional Day Program:	NO
Nontraditional Program:	YES
Evening Program:	YES
Weekend Program:	YES
Summer Courses:	N/A
Some Courses Online:	NO
Full Program Online:	NO

Distance Learning/Offsite:	YES
Executive Education:	N/A
Overseas Study Abroad:	NO

Faculty
Full-Time Faculty:	5
Part-Time Faculty:	12
Faculty to Student Ratio:	1:20

Primary Teaching Methods:

Research	Student Presentations
Lecture	Group Discussion
Computer Simulation	

Faculty Who Consult Outside:	50-74%
Faculty Involvement:	See web site
Top 5 Faculty Publications:	N/A

Students
Total Enrollment:			232
Full-Time Enrollment:			10%
Men:	45%	Women:	55%
Hispanic	N/A	African-American:	N/A
Other Minorities:	N/A	International:	N/A
Average Age:	35	Age Range:	23-65
Work Full Time:			75-99%
HR Experience:			50-74%
Speak 2nd Language:			25-49%

Minimum Admission Requirements:
UGPA:	3.5

Other Considerations:
   Work experience

Average Student Profile:
Work experience:	5 years

Program Resources
Students Required to Have Computers:			N/A
Video Teleconferencing:			NO
Physical Library Facilities:			N/A
Online Library Facilities:			N/A
HRCI Certification Preparation:			YES

   Encourages student study groups
   Links students to local SHRM chapter study groups

SHRM Student Chapter:			YES
Fellowships:			NO
Scholarships:	5	AMT:	$500
Assistantships:	12	AMT:	$15,000
Eligibility:			All Students

Curriculum
Required Courses:
   Accounting
   HR Strategy
   Employment Law
   Management
   HR Measurement
   Business Functional Areas
   Business Research
   Business Communication
Most Popular Elective Courses:
   Recruitment/Selection
   Training/Development
   Organizational Behavior
   Labor Relations
   International HR
   Compensation
   Benefits
   Health, Safety & EAPs

Career Tracks/Concentrations:	N/A
Internship Required:	NO

Career Services

Career Services Offered:

Mentoring	SHRM Student Chapter
Resume Services	Interview Training
Internships	

Summer Internship Placement Rate:	N/A
Full-Time Placement Rate:	N/A
Average Starting Salary (Full-Time Graduates):	N/A
Average Sign-on Bonus:	N/A
Companies Recruiting HR Master's Graduates:	N/A

Points of Excellence

Students: HRM internships and Capstone Thesis are supervised by faculty mentors and evaluated by a second member. Students are encouraged to designate a mentor based on their potential for an effective working relationship rather than on the mentor's area of expertise. Alumni participate in information sessions for prospective students by making presentations to groups and individuals about their experiences as students in the program and after graduation. Alumni are also invited to the annual program convocation that honors new and former graduates.

Curriculum: All faculty submit syllabi copies to the program office for review (objectives, outcomes, measures, etc.). Students are evaluated against expected outcomes. In addition to traditional testing methods, students are evaluated on the quality of their oral presentations, in-class experiential exercises, and out-of-class group projects. Students are required to perform original research in HRM by completing a thesis.

Contact Information

Mercy College
555 Broadway
Dobbs Ferry, NY 10522
www.mercynet.edu
grad.mercynet.edu/humanresource

Linda A. Jerris, Director, Graduate Program in HR Management
Telephone: (914) 674-7632   FAX: (914) 674-7479
ljerris@mercynet.edu

Admission Deadlines

Online Application:

Michigan State University

East Lansing, Michigan
School of Labor & Industrial Relations

Degree

Master of Labor Relations and Human Resources (MLRHR)

University Overview

Founded in 1855, Michigan State University (MSU) was one of the first publicly funded land grant institutions of higher learning. MSU, located in East Lansing, near the state capital, has a total enrollment of more than 43,000 with more than 7,700 graduate students. As a leader in scientific and technological advancement, MSU has more Rhodes Scholars than any other Big Ten University in this generation.

Program Description

Master of Labor Relations and Human Resources (MLRHR) is available in full-time traditional day and nontraditional program and is structured to give well-rounded competencies in human resources, labor relations, and quantitative methods.

Degree Requirements

Total Credits Required:	36
Average Credits per Course:	3
Course Schedule:	Semester
Total Courses Required:	12
HR/IR Courses Required:	7
Average Time for Completion:	1 ½-2 years
Maximum Time Allowed for Completion:	6 years
Accepts Credits from Other Universities:	YES
Total:	6 Hours

Tuition

In-state	N/A	(per year)
	$244	(per credit hour)
Out-of-state	N/A	(per year)
	$494	(per credit hour)

Program Delivery

Traditional Day Program:	YES
Nontraditional Program:	YES
Evening Program:	YES
Weekend Program:	NO
Summer Courses:	YES
Some Courses Online:	NO
Full Program Online:	NO
Distance Learning/Offsite:	Under Development
Executive Education:	NO
Overseas Study Abroad:	YES

Faculty

Full-Time Faculty:	19
Part-Time Faculty:	0
Faculty to Student Ratio:	1:20

Primary Teaching Methods:

Case Study	Lecture
Student Presentation	Group Discussion

Faculty Who Consult Outside:	75-99%

Faculty Involvement:
United Association for Labor Education
Workers' Compensation Research
National Gender & Diversity in Organizations
National Academy of Management
Wharton Business School Work/Life Roundtable
Board of Directors, GOALS

Top 5 Faculty Publications:	See web site

Students

Total Enrollment:			125
Full-Time Enrollment:			75%
Men:	42%	Women:	58%
Hispanic	4%	African-American:	18%
Other Minorities:	3%	International:	19%
Average Age:	27	Age Range:	22-51
Work Full Time:			1-24%
HR Experience:			25-49%
Speak 2nd Language:			1-24%

Minimum Admission Requirements:

GRE Score:	1000 (V&Q Combined)

Other Considerations:
UGPA

Average Student Profile:

GMAT Score:	540
GRE Score:	1043 (V & Q)

Program Resources

Students Required to Have Computers:	NO
Video Teleconferencing:	NO
Physical Library Facilities:	YES
Online Library Facilities:	YES

HRCI Certification Preparation:			NO
SHRM Student Chapter:			YES
Fellowships:	2	AMT:	$6,000
Scholarships:	15	AMT:	$800
Assistantships:	19	AMT:	$5,479 + tuition
Eligibility:			Full-Time Enrollment

Curriculum

Required Courses:
- HR Strategy
- Compensation/Benefits
- Employment Law
- Recruitment/Retention
- Labor Relations
- Employment Relations
- Research Methods
- Organizational Behavior
- Statistics

Most Popular Elective Courses:
- HRIS
- Conflict Resolution
- Grievance & Arbitration
- EEO & OSHA
- Finance
- Group Dynamics & Leadership
- High-Performance Work Systems

Career Tracks/Concentrations:
- HR Management
- Labor Relations & Collective Bargaining

Internship Required: NO

Career Services

Career Services Offered:

Mentoring	Field Trips
Resume Services	SHRM Student Chapter
Internships	Interview Training
Camput Interviews	Company Information Sessions

Summer Internship Placement Rate:	90%
Full-Time Placement Rate:	95%
Average Starting Salary (Full-Time Graduates):	$65,500
Average Sign-on Bonus:	$7,300
Companies Recruiting HR Master's Graduates:	65

Points of Excellence

Program Highlights: The program is taught by full-time faculty. The core requires students to obtain substantive knowledge in three basic knowledge areas of labor relations, human resource management, and behavioral sciences. Embedded in the courses is the provision of multiple skills and competencies. These include business and institutional knowledge and awareness, international awareness, appreciation of diversity and multi-cultural issues, change management skills, process skills, oral and written presentations skills, group process skills, and technological expertise.

Contact Information

Graduate Program, School of Labor & Industrial Relations
401 S. Kedzie Hall
Michigan State University
East Lansing, MI 48824-1032
www.lir.msu.edu

Connie Nichols, Graduate Student Advisor
Telephone: (517) 432-2800   FAX: (517) 355-7656
nicho138@msu.edu

Dr. Richard Block, Associate Director
Telephone: (517) 353-3896   FAX: (517) 355-7656
block@msu.edu

Admission Deadlines

July for Fall admissions

Online Application:	YES

Middle Tennessee State University

Murfreesboro, Tennessee
Psychology Department

Degree

Master of Arts in Industrial/Organizational Psychology (MA-I/O)

University Overview

State university with approximately 18,000 students centrally located in the Middle Tennessee area, a major economic growth area.

Program Description

Full-time traditional day program follows the Society for Industrial and Organizational Psychology (SIOP) guidelines for master-level education, providing broad coverage of the I/O Psychology area. The curriculum provides a strong theoretical and research foundation that also provides numerous applied experiences.

Degree Requirements

Total Credits Required:	45
Average Credits per Course:	3
Course Schedule:	Semester
Total Courses Required:	17
HR/IR Courses Required:	11
Average Time for Completion:	2- 2 ½ years
Maximum Time Allowed for Completion:	6 years
Accepts Credits from Other Universities:	NO
Total:	N/A

Tuition

In-state	$3,600	(per year)
	$137	(per credit hour)
Out-of-state	$9,400	(per year)
	$361	(per credit hour)

Program Delivery

Traditional Day Program:	YES
Nontraditional Program:	NO
Evening Program:	NO
Weekend Program:	NO
Summer Courses:	N/A
Some Courses Online:	NO
Full Program Online:	NO
Distance Learning/Offsite:	NO
Executive Education:	N/A
Overseas Study Abroad:	NO

Faculty

Full-Time Faculty:	8
Part-Time Faculty:	0
Faculty to Student Ratio:	1:4

Primary Teaching Methods:

Research	Team Projects
Student Presentation	Field Projects

Faculty Who Consult Outside:	25-49%
Faculty Involvement:	See web site

Top 5 Faculty Publications:
Journal of Applied Psychology
Journal of Quality Management
Psychological Reports
Quality Progress

Students

Total Enrollment:			23
Full-Time Enrollment:			100%
Men:	44%	Women:	56%
Hispanic	4%	African-American:	0%
Other Minorities:	0%	International:	8%
Average Age:	N/A	Age Range:	N/A
Work Full Time:			1-24%
HR Experience:			0%
Speak 2nd Language:			1-24%

Minimum Admission Requirements:
GRE Score:	900 (A&Q)
UGPA:	3.0

Other Considerations:
NONE

Average Student Profile:
GRE Score:	1180 (A&Q)
UGPA:	3.5

Program Resources

Students Required to Have Computers:			N/A
Video Teleconferencing:			NO
Physical Library Facilities:			N/A
Online Library Facilities:			N/A
HRCI Certification Preparation:			YES

Encourage student study groups
Links students to local SHRM chapter study groups

SHRM Student Chapter:			YES
Fellowships:			NO
Scholarships:			NO
Assistantships:	12	AMT:	N/A
Eligibility:			Full-Time Enrollment

Curriculum

Required Courses:
Statistics
Research Methods in HRM
Organizational Psychology
Training & Development
Selection & Placement
Perf. Appraisal/Job Analysis
Professional Issues
Practicum (Internship)
Wage & Salary Admin.
Moral, Attitudes & Motivation
Org. Change & Dev.
Work Group Effectiveness

Most Popular Elective Courses:
Organizational Skills
Organizational Effectiveness
Collective Bargaining
TQM
Psychological Testing
Employee Benefits
Group Dynamics
Health & Safety

Career Tracks/Concentrations:	N/A
Internship Required:	YES

Career Services

Career Services Offered:
Mentoring	Field Trips
Resume Services	SHRM Student Chapter
Internships	Interview Training

Summer Internship Placement Rate:	N/A
Full-Time Placement Rate:	100%
Average Starting Salary (Full-Time Graduates):	$40,000
Average Sign-on Bonus:	N/A
Companies Recruiting HR Master's Graduates:	N/A

Points of Excellence

Faculty: At least one internship is required, but most students do more. Students work in an organization or with faculty on consulting projects. Most are paid and focus in areas such as training, selection, job analysis, performance appraisal, and survey design and evaluation. Two examples of organizational project work by students (under the direction of faculty) are:

1. Development of an employee selection system to support an organizational culture change by hiring/promoting individuals who fit the new culture; and

2. Administration of periodic team process and team leadership surveys to assess and feed back data regarding the organization's change to team functioning.

Contact Information

Department of Psychology
MTSU Box 87
Murfreesboro, TN 37132
www.mtsu.edu/-iopsych

Dr. Richard G. (Rick) Moffett III, Assistant Professor
Telephone: (615) 898-5943   FAX: (615) 898-5027
rmoffett@mtsu.edu

Admission Deadlines

Online Application:	YES

Minnesota State University, Mankato

Mankato, Minnesota
Department of Psychology

Degree

Master of Arts in Industrial/Organizational Psychology (MAIOP)

University Overview

Minnesota State University, Mankato, is a state supported school with an enrollment of 13,000 students. MSU is located about 60 miles south of Minneapolis.

Program Description

The goal of the program is to provide broad theoretical and technical training for individuals who will function as consultants, HR researchers, and HR generalists.

Degree Requirements

Total Credits Required:	44
Average Credits per Course:	3
Course Schedule:	Semester
Total Courses Required:	14
HR/IR Courses Required:	14
Average Time for Completion:	2 years
Maximum Time Allowed for Completion:	6 years

Accepts Credits from Other Universities:		YES
Total:		8 Hours (Semester)

Tuition

In-state	$3,974	(per year)
	$180	(per credit hour)
Out-of-state	$5,980	(per year)
	$271	(per credit hour)

Program Delivery

Traditional Day Program:	YES
Nontraditional Program:	YES
Evening Program:	YES
Weekend Program:	NO
Program Completed Evening/Weekend:	NO
Summer Courses:	NO
Some Courses Online:	NO
Full Program Online:	NO
Distance Learning/Offsite:	NO
Executive Education:	NO
Overseas Study Abroad:	NO

Faculty

Full-Time Faculty:		3
Part-Time Faculty:		2
Faculty to Student Ratio:		1:5

Primary Teaching Methods:

Research	Team Projects
Group Discussion	Lecture

Faculty Who Consult Outside:	1-24%

Faculty Involvement:

Top 5 Faculty Publications:
Personality and Social Psychology Bulletin
Journal of Social Psychology
Personality & Individual Differences
Educational and Psychological Measurement

Students

Total Enrollment:			21
Full-Time Enrollment:			16
Men:	24%	Women:	76%
Hispanic:	5%	African-American:	0%
Other Minorities:	14%	International:	14%
Average Age:	24	Age Range:	22-30
Work Full Time:			1-24%
Have HR Experience:			1-24%
Speak 2nd Language:			1-24%

Minimum Admission Requirements:

UGPA:	3.0
GRE or GMAT Scores:	950
Work Experience:	NONE

Other Considerations:

Average Student Profile:

UGPA:	3.6
GMAT Score:	1150 GRE
Work Experience:	NONE

Program Resources

Students Required to Have Computers:	NO
Video Teleconferencing:	NO
Physical Library Facilities:	YES
Online Library Facilities:	YES
HRCI Certification Preparation:	NO
SHRM Student Chapter:	NO

URL:

Fellowships:	NO	AMT:	
Scholarships:	NO	AMT:	
Assistantships:	YES	AMT:	$7,000
Eligibility:			Full-Time Enrollment

Curriculum

Required Courses:
Development/Training
HR Measurement
Selection, Statistics
Performance Evaluation
Motivation, Ethics, Human Factors

Most Popular Elective Courses:
Compensation

Career Tracks/Concentrations:

Management Consulting	Market Research
HR Generalist	HR Researcher

Internship Required:	YES

Career Services

Career Services Offered:

Field Trips	Campus Interview
Internships	

Summer Internship Placement Rate:	N/A
Facilitate Placement:	YES
Full-Time Placement Rate:	N/A
Internship Placement Rate:	N/A
Average Starting Salary (Full-Time Graduates):	$46,000
Average Sign-on Bonus:	N/A
Companies Recruiting HR Master's Graduates:	N/A

Points of Excellence

The Minnesota State University I/O program is a student-centered program that primarily prepares students to work in industry and consulting. Consequently, we emphasize strong teaching, skill building assignments, opportunities for students to work with businesses, and a high degree of student/faculty contact. All students participate on a research team with a faculty member. Most students work on some form of consulting project. All students complete internships. Students complete the program as a cohort group.

Contact Information

MSU I/O Psychology Program
Minnesota State University
23 Armstrong Hall
Mankato, MN 56001
www.mnsu.edu/iopsych

Administrative & Faculty Contact
Daniel Sachau, Ph.D.
Telephone: (507) 389-2724 or (507) 389-5829
Sachau@mnsu.edu

Admission Deadlines

March 1 for Fall Admission

Online Application:	NO

Monterey Institute of International Studies

Monterey, California
Fisher Graduate School of International Business

Degree

Master of Business Administration with International HR and Cross-Cultural Focus (MBA)

University Overview

Monterey Institute of International Studies is a private institute with four graduate schools, all having an international focus.

Program Description

This MBA program is a full-time traditional day program providing a specialized course track in International HR and cross-cultural management. Program provides 14 paid fieldwork internships and 100% placement rate.

Degree Requirements

Total Credits Required:	64
Average Credits per Course:	3
Course Schedule:	Semester
Total Courses Required:	20
HR/IR Courses Required:	6
Average Time for Completion:	1-2 years
Maximum Time Allowed for Completion:	6 years
Accepts Credits from Other Universities:	YES
Total:	12 Hours

Tuition

In-state	$19,988	(per year)
	$840	(per credit hour)
Out-of-state	$19,988	(per year)
	$840	(per credit hour)

Program Delivery

Traditional Day Program:	YES
Nontraditional Program:	NO
Evening Program:	NO
Weekend Program:	NO
Summer Courses:	YES
Some Courses Online:	NO
Full Program Online:	NO
Distance Learning/Offsite:	NO
Executive Education:	NO
Overseas Study Abroad:	NO

Faculty

Full-Time Faculty:	1
Part-Time Faculty:	4
Faculty to Student Ratio:	1:10

Primary Teaching Methods:

Lecture	Field Projects
Team Projects	Group Discussion

Faculty Who Consult Outside:	1-24%

Faculty Involvement:
SHRM Chapter Board Member
Board Member, Education Alliance
Board Member & VP, SHRM Global Forum
Track Chair, International Management Development Association

Top 5 Faculty Publications:
International HR Development
HR World

Students

Total Enrollment:			10
Full-Time Enrollment:			100%
Men:	40%	Women:	60%
Hispanic	0%	African-American:	0%
Other Minorities:	0%	International:	50%
Average Age:	27	Age Range:	22-50
Work Full Time:			0%
HR Experience:			1-24%
Speak 2nd Language:			100%

Minimum Admission Requirements:

GMAT Score:	530, Bilingual
Work experience:	4 years (preferably international)

Other Considerations:
International work and living experience; languages

Average Student Profile:

GMAT Score:	531 (U.S.); 501 (International)
Work experience:	4.5 years

Program Resources

Students Required to Have Computers:			NO
Video Teleconferencing:			YES
Physical Library Facilities:			YES
Online Library Facilities:			YES
HRCI Certification Preparation:			YES

Encourages student study groups
Links students to local SHRM chapter study groups
Offers SHRM Learning System as a teaching tool
Offers practice exams
Bases curriculum on certification exam content
Mentoring by successful alumni in the field

SHRM Student Chapter:			YES
Fellowships:			NO
Scholarships:	2	AMT:	N/A
Assistantships:	2	AMT:	N/A
Eligibility:			Full-Time Enrollment

Curriculum

Required Courses: (with an international emphasis)
Accounting
Finance
Marketing
HR Strategy
International HR
Compensation/Benefits
Development/Training
Recruitment/Retention
Employment Law
Management
Employee Relations
Labor Relations
HR Measurement
Business Functional Areas

Most Popular Elective Courses:
All electives are in the international HR/cross-cultural track
Languages

Career Tracks/Concentrations:	N/A
Internship Required:	YES

Career Services

Career Services Offered:

Mentoring	SHRM Student Chapter
Resume Services	Interview Training
Campus Interviews	Internships

Summer Internship Placement Rate:	100%
Full-Time Placement Rate:	100%
Average Starting Salary (Full-Time Graduates):	N/A
Average Sign-on Bonus:	N/A
Companies Recruiting HR Master's Graduates:	5-10

Points of Excellence

Curriculum: Monterey has the largest concentration of International HR courses in any MBA program. The faculty are multilingual and multicultural and have done HR field research in many countries. Students with international experience and language skills are selected. Students can participate in International HR summer field research/internships abroad to acquire multilingual and HR proficiency.

Contact Information

Fisher Graduate School of International Business
425 Van Buren St.
Monterey, CA 93940
www.fgsib.miis.edu

Christy Gibson Herlick, Academic Programs Associate
Telephone: (831) 647-6586   FAX: (831) 647-6504
christy.gibson@miis.edu

Lisbeth Claus, Professor
Telephone: (831) 647-6501   FAX: (831) 647-6506
lclaus@miis.edu

Admission Deadlines
One month prior to semester for which applying
Online Application: YES

National-Louis University

**Washington, DC; Tampa, Florida;
Atlanta, Georgia; Chicago, Illinois;
St. Louis, Missouri; McLean, Virginia
College of Management and Business**

Degree
Master of Science in Human Resource Management &
Development (MS-HRM&D)

University Overview
National-Louis University is a private, independent,
not-for-profit, comprehensive university located in Chicago. This
nontraditional program is also offered in Tampa; Atlanta; St.
Louis; McLean, VA; and Washington, DC.

Program Description
The program emphasizes HR Strategy & Planning,
Organizational Behavior, Training & Development, and the HR
functional areas.

Degree Requirements
Total Credits Required:	36
Average Credits per Course:	3-4
Course Schedule:	Semester
Total Courses Required:	9
HR/IR Courses Required:	9
Average Time for Completion:	1-2 years
Maximum Time Allowed for Completion:	10 years
Accepts Credits from Other Universities:	YES
Total:	N/A

Tuition
In-state	N/A	(per year)
	$496	(per credit hour)
Out-of-state	N/A	(per year)
	$496	(per credit hour)

Program Delivery
Traditional Day Program:	NO
Nontraditional Program:	YES
Evening Program:	YES
Weekend Program:	NO
Summer Courses:	N/A
Some Courses Online:	NO
Full Program Online:	NO
Distance Learning/Offsite:	NO
Executive Education:	N/A
Overseas Study Abroad:	NO

Faculty
Full-Time Faculty:	26
Part-Time Faculty:	175
Faculty to Student Ratio:	1:20

Primary Teaching Methods:
Case Study	Research
Computer-Aided Instruction	Experiential Learning
Field Projects	Lecture
Team Projects	Student Presentations
Group Discussion	

Faculty Who Consult Outside:	25-49%

Faculty Involvement:
American College Personnel Association
Chair, Florida Employment Council
Enrollment Management Center, Inc.
Top 5 Faculty Publications:
HR Magazine
HR Development Quarterly
Management OB Classics

Students (Tampa only)
Total Enrollment:			22
Full-Time Enrollment:			100%
Men:	36%	Women:	64%
Hispanic:	9%	African-American:	36%
Other Minorities:	0%	International:	0%
Average Age:	37	Age Range:	24-50
Work Full Time:			75-99%
HR Experience:			75-99%
Speak 2nd Language:			1-24%

Minimum Admission Requirements: (for 6 locations)
Use own writing and critical thinking skill assessment
instrument
Other Considerations:
Experience, Academic/Professional References
Average Student Profile:	N/A

Program Resources
Students Required to Have Computers:			N/A
Video Teleconferencing:			NO
Physical Library Facilities:			N/A
Online Library Facilities:			N/A
HRCI Certification Preparation:			YES (Tampa only)

Links students to local SHRM chapter study groups
Offers practice exams
Bases the curriculum on certification exam content
SHRM Student Chapter:			YES
Fellowships:			NO
Scholarships:	8	AMT:	$1,000
Assistantships:			NO
Eligibility:			Full-Time Enrollment

Curriculum
Required Courses:
HR Strategy
Compensation/Benefits
Development/Training
Recruitment/Retention
Employment Law
Management
Employee Relations
Labor Relations
HR Measurement
Most Popular Elective Courses:
No electives
Career Tracks/Concentrations:	N/A
Internship Required:	NO

Career Services
Career Services Offered:
Mentoring	Field Trips
SHRM Student Chapter	SHRM Chapter Affiliation

Summer Internship Placement Rate:	N/A
Full-Time Placement Rate:	N/A
Average Starting Salary (Full-Time Graduates):	N/A
Average Sign-on Bonus:	N/A
Companies Recruiting HR Master's Graduates:	N/A

Points of Excellence

Curriculum: All courses are reviewed annually. Major revisions to instructor guides are made on a three-year cycle. A full-time faculty member assigned by the Dean ensures that the program is current (texts, guides, deliverables, etc.).

Students: This program is for working adults; most already work in HR. A cohort group begins the program together and progresses through the sequence of coursework until program completion. Each cohort has the opportunity to build strong relationships with their peers and a lifelong network of professionals.

Contact Information

National-Louis University (Main Campus)
College of Management and Business
122 S. Michigan Ave.
Chicago, IL 60603
www.nl.edu

Dr. Howard Zacks, Dean
College of Management & Business
Telephone: (800) 443-5522, ext. 4378   FAX: (630) 668-5883
hzac@whe2.nl.edu

Admission Deadlines

Online Application:	NO

Nebraska Methodist College

Omaha, Nebraska

Degree

Master of Science in Health Promotion (MSHP)

University Overview

Nebraska Methodist College is a private institution that focuses on whole-person education and development.

Program Description

The MS in Health Promotions (corporate focus) with emphasis in Human Resource Management is an accelerated nontraditional program. Most students are employed in companies and wish to enhance their positions and contributions.

Degree Requirements

Total Credits Required:	37
Average Credits per Course:	2-3
Course Schedule:	Trimester
Total Courses Required:	13
HR/IR Courses Required:	3
Average Time for Completion:	2 years
Maximum Time Allowed for Completion:	6 years
Accepts Credits from Other Universities:	YES
Total:	9 Hours

Tuition

In-state	N/A	(per year)
	$385	(per credit hour)
Out-of-state	N/A	(per year)
	$385	(per credit hour)

Program Delivery

Traditional Day Program:	NO
Nontraditional Program:	YES
Evening Program:	YES
Weekend Program:	NO
Summer Courses:	YES
Some Courses Online:	YES
Full Program Online:	NO
Distance Learning/Offsite:	YES
Executive Education:	YES*
Overseas Study Abroad:	NO

Evenings and an occasional weekend

Faculty

Full-Time Faculty:			4
Part-Time Faculty:			12
Faculty to Student Ratio:			1:10
Primary Teaching Methods:			
Case Study		Lecture	
Experiential Learning		Research	
Faculty Who Consult Outside:			75-99%
Faculty Involvement:			
President, Wellness Council of America			
President, Silverstone Consulting (HR Consulting Firm)			
President, Human Resources Institute			
Top 5 Faculty Publications:			N/A

Students

Total Enrollment:			24
Full-Time Enrollment:			100%
Men:	13%	Women:	87%
Hispanic	0%	African-American:	0%
Other Minorities:	0%	International:	5%
Average Age:	33	Age Range:	24-55
Work Full Time:			75-99%
HR Experience:			25-49%
Speak 2nd Language:			1-24%
Minimum Admission Requirements:			
UGPA :			3.0
Other Considerations:			
Work experience, essay, and interview results			
Average Student Profile:			
Work experience:			10 years

Program Resources

Students Required to Have Computers:			YES
Video Teleconferencing:			YES
Physical Library Facilities:			YES
Online Library Facilities:			YES
HRCI Certification Preparation:			YES
SHRM Student Chapter:			YES
Fellowships:			NO
Scholarships:			NO
Assistantships:	7	AMT:	$6,500
Eligibility:			Full-Time Enrollment

Curriculum

Required Courses:
Cultural Anthropology and Organizational Behavior
Human Resources and Labor Relations
Health Promotion Research and Statistics
Community Diagnosis and Needs Assessment
Advanced Fitness Physiology
Health Care Utilization Management
Management Communications, Leadership & Marketing
Program Design and Evaluation
Employee Benefits Management
Psychological Aspects of Behavior/Adult Education

Holistic Interventions and Diverse Populations
Research Proposal and Thesis Writing
Thesis

Most Popular Elective Courses:	No electives
Career Tracks/Concentrations:	

Health Promotion	Human Resources
Management Positions	

Internship Required:	NO

Career Services

Career Services Offered:

Mentoring	Interview Training
Resume Services	SHRM Student Chapter

Summer Internship Placement Rate:	N/A
Full-Time Placement Rate:	N/A
Average Starting Salary (Full-Time Graduates):	N/A
Average Sign-on Bonus:	N/A
Companies Recruiting HR Master's Graduates:	N/A

Points of Excellence

Curriculum: Program utilizes the most renowned expert practitioners in the field who teach on campus or through distance delivery technology. A systematic outcome assessment plan is modeled after a performance review in the corporate sector that provides students with feedback on all dimensions of their academic performance. Course content combines the highest level of competencies of Health Promotion with Human Resource Management to create a professional who can influence an organizational culture.

Contact Information

Nebraska Methodist College
8501 W. Dodge Rd.
Omaha, NE 68114
www.methodistcollege.edu

Jeannie Hannan, Coordinator of Health Promotions
Telephone: (402) 354-4933   FAX: (402) 354-8875
jhannan@nmhs.org

Admission Deadlines

Online Application:	YES

New School University

New York, New York
Milano Graduate School of Management and Urban Policy

Degree

Master of Science in Human Resources Management (MSHRM)

University Overview

New School is a private university with seven academic divisions. The Milano Graduate School has a mission that is consistent with New School's tradition as an innovative urban university.

Program Description

The program in Human Resources Management is designed to equip students with the skills and knowledge needed to meet the challenges of the HR profession. The nontraditional program is geared to the adult learner in terms of both content and course design.

Degree Requirements

Total Credits Required:	42
Average Credits per Course:	3

Course Schedule:	Semester
Total Courses Required:	14
HR/IR Courses Required:	11
Average Time for Completion:	2-3 years
Maximum Time Allowed for Completion:	10 years
Accepts Credits from Other Universities:	YES
Total:	N/A

Tuition

In-state	N/A	(per year)
	$690	(per credit hour)
Out-of-state	N/A	(per year)
	$690	(per credit hour)

Program Delivery

Traditional Day Program:	NO
Nontraditional Program:	YES
Evening Program:	YES
Weekend Program:	YES
Summer Courses:	N/A
Some Courses Online:	YES
Full Program Online:	NO
Distance Learning/Offsite:	YES
Executive Education:	N/A
Overseas Study Abroad:	NO

Faculty

Full-Time Faculty:	3
Part-Time Faculty:	27
Faculty to Student Ratio:	1:10

Primary Teaching Methods:

Lecture	Experiential Learning
Field Projects	Group Discussion

Faculty Who Consult Outside:	75-99%

Faculty Involvement:
Students may be involved in faculty consulting projects.

Top 5 Faculty Publications:	N/A

Students

Total Enrollment:			215
Full-Time Enrollment:			7%
Men:	40%	Women:	60%
Hispanic:	5%	African-American:	30%
Other Minorities:	5%	International:	5%
Average Age:	30	Age Range:	24-65%
Work Full Time:			75-99%
HR Experience:			75-99%
Speak 2nd Language:			1-24%

Minimum Admission Requirements:
UGPA, essay, letters of recommendation, interview
Other Considerations:
Work experience
Average Student Profile:

Work experience:	7 years

Program Resources

Students Required to Have Computers:			N/A
Video Teleconferencing:			YES
Physical Library Facilities:			N/A
Online Library Facilities:			N/A
HRCI Certification Preparation:			NO
SHRM Student Chapter:			YES
Fellowships:			NO
Scholarships:	56	AMT:	$3,200
Assistantships:	2	AMT:	$10,000
Eligibility:			Full-Time Enrollment

Curriculum

Required Courses:
  HR Strategy
  Management
  HR Measurement
  Economics
  Statistics
  Policy Analysis
Most Popular Elective Courses:
  Recruitment
  Organizational Development
  Interviewing/Assessment
  Development/Training
  Compensation Management
  Employment Legislation
  Group Processes
  Facilitation & Intervention

Career Tracks/Concentrations:	N/A
Internship Required:	YES

Career Services

Career Services Offered:
  SHRM Student Chapter   Resume Services
  Interview Training   Internships

Summer Internship Placement Rate:	N/A
Full-Time Placement Rate:	N/A
Average Starting Salary (Full-Time Graduates):	$73,500
Average Sign-on Bonus:	N/A
Companies Recruiting HR Master's Graduates:	10

Points of Excellence

Curriculum: Curriculum is reviewed annually and changes are made to both required courses and electives to ensure that students graduate with the core competencies required of HRM professionals. For example, the course Financial Impact of HRM Strategies was added as a course two years ago when it became clear that HR was increasingly being held accountable for its contribution to the organization's bottom line.

Faculty: New York City is the home of some of the world's most progressive organizations and most respected HRM consulting firms and practitioners. The HRM program taps these assets in a number of ways. Prominent professionals serve as adjunct faculty and guest lecturers as well as advisors on curriculum development. Strong links are maintained with the professional community, and students are challenged to address the real issues they will face in their careers.

Students: The program's major strength is the diversity of the student body. Students come from across United States and a number of foreign countries and reflect New York City's multifaceted population.

Contact Information

Milano Graduate School of Management and Urban Policy
72 5th Ave.
New York, NY 10011
www.newschool.edu

Mark Lipton, Ph.D., Chair
Telephone: (212) 229-5311, ext. 1611   FAX: (212) 807-1913
lipton@newschool.edu

Admission Deadlines

Online Application:	N/A

New York Institute of Technology

**New York, New York; Old Westbury, New York
School of Management, Center for Labor and
Industrial Relations**

Degree

Master of Science in Human Resources Management and Labor Relations (MSHRM/LR)

University Overview

New York Institute of Technology (NYIT) is a fully accredited, nonsectarian and nonprofit institution of higher learning that provides career-oriented education, both graduate and undergraduate. Nearly 10,000 students are enrolled at campuses in Manhattan, Long Island, New York, and in programs in Fort Lauderdale, Florida, as well as overseas.

Program Description

A professionally oriented program for qualified human resource and employee/labor relations practitioners and aspirants. Four program locations and Evening/Saturday classes meet the needs of students who are employed full-time. The program has a strong core curriculum with a variety of electives to select from.

Degree Requirements

Total Credits Required:	42
Average Credits per Course:	3
Course Schedule:	Semester
Total Courses Required:	14
HR/IR Courses Required:	14
Average Time for Completion:	2 ½ years
Maximum Time Allowed for Completion:	5 years
Accepts Credits from Other Universities:	YES
Total:	9 Hours

Tuition

In-state	N/A	(per year)
	$545	(per credit hour)
Out-of-state	N/A	(per year)
	$545	(per credit hour)

Program Delivery

Traditional Day Program:	NO
Nontraditional Program:	YES
Evening Program:	YES
Weekend Program:	YES
Program Completed Evening/Weekend:	YES
Summer Courses:	YES
Some Courses Online:	YES
Full Program Online:	NO
Distance Learning/Offsite:	YES
Executive Education:	NO
Overseas Study Abroad:	NO

Faculty

Full-Time Faculty:	3
Part-Time Faculty:	8
Faculty to Student Ratio:	1:20

Primary Teaching Methods:
  Case Study   Experiential Learning
  Lecture   Group Discussion

Faculty Who Consult Outside:	75-99%

Faculty Involvement:
  Industrial Relations Research Association
  Society for Human Resource Management

WorldatWork

Society for Professionals in Dispute Resolution

Top 5 Faculty Publications:

Journal of Collective Negotiations

Journal of Employee Ownership Law

Students

Total Enrollment:			140
Full-Time Enrollment:			30
Men:	35%	Women:	65%
Hispanic:	N/A	African-American:	N/A
Other Minorities:	N/A	International:	15%
Average Age:	31	Age Range:	23-58
Work Full Time:			75-99%
Have HR Experience:			50-74%
Speak 2nd Language:			1-24%
Minimum Admission Requirements:			
UGPA:			2.85
GRE or GMAT Scores:			N/A
Work Experience:			N/A
Other Considerations:			
Average Student Profile:			
UGPA:			3.15
GMAT Score:			N/A
Work Experience:			N/A

Program Resources

Students Required to Have Computers:			NO
Video Teleconferencing:			YES
Physical Library Facilities:			YES
Online Library Facilities:			YES
HRCI Certification Preparation:			YES
Encourage study groups			
Offer SHRM Learning System			
SHRM Student Chapter:			YES
URL:			
Fellowships:	NO	AMT:	
Scholarships:	YES	AMT:	⅓ of Tuition
Assistantships:	YES	AMT:	Varies
Eligibility:			

Curriculum

Required Courses:

Accounting

Employment Law

HR Strategy

Labor Relations

Organizational Behavior

Research Methods

HRIS

Labor Economics

Human Resource Management

Collective Bargaining

Industrial Relations

Most Popular Elective Courses:

Training

Staffing

Compensation

Alternative Dispute Resolution

Benefits

Career Tracks/Concentrations:

Human Resources Management	Labor Relations
Internship Required:	NO

Career Services

Career Services Offered:

Mentoring	Interview Training
SHRM Student Chapter	Internships
Resume Services	Campus Interview

Summer Internship Placement Rate:	N/A
Facilitate Placement:	YES
Full-Time Placement Rate:	N/A
Internship Placement Rate:	N/A
Average Starting Salary (Full-Time Graduates):	$32-$40,000
Average Sign-on Bonus:	N/A
Companies Recruiting HR Master's Graduates:	N/A

Points of Excellence

This program is oriented towards the needs of practitioners in the fields of HRM and employee/labor relations. There is a strong core curriculum, which emphasizes the fundamentals, in addition to a wide selection of advanced elective courses. Role of HR policies and employment law, role of HRM in strategic management, and HR metrics are integrated throughout the curriculum. A full curriculum in labor relations is also offered. Three campuses in the New York metropolitan region provides students with considerable flexibility in scheduling classes.

The student body is ethnically diverse, with most employed full time, or participating in internships or assistantships, while pursuing their degree. There is an active alumni chapter, comprised of graduates who have achieved managerial and leadership positions in the field, who provide mentoring, career-oriented programs, and networking opportunities to students. In addition, students are actively involved in the activities of professional societies such as SHRM, IRRA, and ASTD. These organizations also sponsor scholarships and award competitions annually. There is an on-campus student SHRM chapter.

Contact Information

New York Institute of Technology

Room 517, Center for Labor and Industrial Relations

Old Westbury, NY 11568-8000

www.nyit.edu

Administrative & Faculty Contact

Dr. Richard Dibble

Telephone: (516) 686-7722

rdibble@nyit.edu

Admission Deadlines

90 days prior to beginning of semester of planned enrollment

Online Application:	YES

Nova Southeastern University

Ft. Lauderdale, Florida
Huizenga School of Business

Degree

Master of Science in Human Resource Management (MSHRM)

University Overview

Nova Southeastern University (NSU) is Florida's largest private university, with an enrollment of more than 16,000. NSU is located in Ft. Lauderdale and offers both traditional and distance programs.

Program Description

The NSU HR program emphasizes managerial and development aspects of the HR function within an organization. Students are working adults with five or more years of experience in HR or other areas of business. This program is also offered in Aiken, South Carolina; Nassau, Bahamas; Kingston, Jamaica; and Jacksonville, Florida.

Degree Requirements

Total Credits Required:	43
Average Credits per Course:	3-4
Course Schedule:	Quarter
Total Courses Required:	14
HR/IR Courses Required:	11
Average Time for Completion:	1-2 years
Maximum Time Allowed for Completion:	5 years
Accepts Credits from Other Universities:	YES
Total:	N/A

Tuition

In-state	N/A	(per year)
	$434	(per credit hour)
Out-of-state	N/A	(per year)
	$434	(per credit hour)

Program Delivery

Traditional Day Program:	NO
Nontraditional Program:	YES
Evening Program:	YES
Weekend Program:	YES
Summer Courses:	N/A
Some Courses Online:	NO
Full Program Online:	NO
Distance Learning/Offsite:	YES
Executive Education:	N/A
Overseas Study Abroad:	YES

Faculty

Full-Time Faculty:	4
Part-Time Faculty:	17
Faculty to Student Ratio:	1:20

Primary Teaching Methods:

Case Study	Lecture
Student Presentation	Research
Field Projects	Group Discussions

Faculty Who Consult Outside:	1-24%

Faculty Involvement:
Co-Chair, Management History Division, American Management Association
Leadership positions within community organizations
Editorial boards for national journals

Top 5 Faculty Publications:
AMACOM books
Leadership and Organization Development Journal
Productivity and Quality Management

Students

Total Enrollment:			108
Full-Time Enrollment:			0%
Men:	42%	Women:	58%
Hispanic	6%	African-American:	8%
Other Minorities:	3%	International:	39%
Average Age:	34	Age Range:	24-42
Work Full Time:			75-99%
HR Experience:			50-74%
Speak 2nd Language:			1-24%

Minimum Admission Requirements:

GMAT Score:	450
GRE Score:	1000
UGPA:	3.0

Other Considerations:
Corporate sponsorship

Average Student Profile:

GMAT Score:	465
GRE Score:	1040
Work experience:	7 years

Program Resources

Students Required to Have Computers:			N/A
Video Teleconferencing:			NO
Physical Library Facilities:			N/A
Online Library Facilities:			N/A
HRCI Certification Preparation:			NO
SHRM Student Chapter:			NO
Fellowships:			NO
Scholarships:	1	AMT:	$10,000
Assistantships:			NO
Eligibility:			Full-Time Enrollment

Curriculum

Required Courses:
HR Strategy
Compensation/Benefits
Development/Training
Recruitment/Retention
Employment Law
Management
Employee Relations
Labor Relations
Business Functional Areas

Most Popular Elective Courses:	N/A
Career Tracks/Concentrations:	N/A
Internship Required:	NO

Career Services

Career Services Offered:

Resume Services	Interview Training

Summer Internship Placement Rate:	N/A
Full-Time Placement Rate:	N/A
Average Starting Salary (Full-Time Graduates):	N/A
Average Sign-on Bonus:	N/A
Companies Recruiting HR Master's Graduates:	N/A

Points of Excellence

Placement: The Huizenga School provides biannual three-day workshops on job searching, resume writing, and job interviewing. They are led by outplacement professionals from the community in conjunction with full-time faculty who consult in the HR field. Workshops include group lectures, one-on-one resume reviews, and videotaping of role-played job interviews with one-on-one critiques by the experts.

Curriculum: The Huizenga School, in keeping with the Nova Southeastern University mission, brings education to the students. As a result, the MS HRM program has been or is being delivered in three foreign countries. This requires having work culture, processes, and laws governing the human resource function in each country. Professionals from the country who have terminal degrees are recruited to customize the coursework content according to the needs of the country when possible.

Contact Information

Nova Southeastern University
3100 SW 9th Ave.
Ft. Lauderdale, FL 33315-3025
www.huizenga.nova.edu

Kelly Ferguson, Associate Director of MS/HRM
Telephone: (954) 262-5021   FAX: (954) 262-3829
kellyg@huizenga.nova.edu

Admission Deadlines

Online Application:	NO

Ohio State University

Columbus, Ohio
Fisher College of Business

Degree
Master in Labor and Human Resources (MLHR)

University Overview
The Ohio State University is one of the largest universities in America. The Columbus campus, located in the 18th largest metropolitan area in the United States, enrolls nearly 55,000 students.

Program Description
The MLHR is the foremost program in educating and developing individuals to be effective internal and external HR consultants and policy makers. The program focuses on analytical and leadership process skills, and functional content knowledge needed to increase effectiveness within organizations. An alumni network is available.

Degree Requirements
Total Credits Required:	76
Average Credits per Course:	4
Course Schedule:	Quarter
Total Courses Required:	18
HR/IR Courses Required:	17
Average Time for Completion:	2-3 years
Maximum Time Allowed for Completion:	6 years
Accepts Credits from Other Universities:	YES
Total:	16 Hours (Quarterly)

Tuition
In-state	$7,230	(per year)
	$300	(per credit hour)
Out-of-state	$17,301	(per year)
	$636	(per credit hour)

Program Delivery
Traditional Day Program:	NO
Nontraditional Program:	YES
Evening Program:	YES
Weekend Program:	NO
Program Completed Evening/Weekend:	YES
Summer Courses:	NO
Some Courses Online:	NO
Full Program Online:	NO
Distance Learning/Offsite:	NO
Executive Education:	NO
Overseas Study Abroad:	YES (Peace Corps program)

Faculty
Full-Time Faculty:	4
Part-Time Faculty:	16
Faculty to Student Ratio:	1:15

Primary Teaching Methods:

Case Study	Lecture
Computer-Aided Instruction	Experiential Learning
Field Projects	Research
Team Projects	Student Presentations
Group Discussion	

Faculty Who Consult Outside: 1-24%

Faculty Involvement:
Past Chairs, Business Policy & Strategy Division (1999), Organizational Behavior Division (1999), Human Resources Division (1998), Conflict Management Division (1998), Academy of Management Chair, GOALS Board of Directors

Top 5 Faculty Publications:
Academy of Management
Journal of Applied Psychology

Students
Total Enrollment:			88
Full-Time Enrollment:			60%
Men:	25%	Women:	75%
Hispanic:	2%	African-American:	16%
Other Minorities:	1%	International:	16%
Average Age:	28	Age Range:	21-43
Work Full Time:			25-49%
HR Experience:			50-74%
Speak 2nd Language:			25-49%

Minimum Admission Requirements:
GMAT Score:	450
UGPA:	3.0

20 hours of social sciences in UGP

Other Considerations:
Composite, GPA, GRE, work experience, and letters of recommendation

Average Student Profiles:
GRE Score:	V:474 Q:553 A:578
UGPA:	3.4
Work experience:	5 years

Program Resources
Students Required to Have Computers:		NO
Video Teleconferencing:		YES
Physical Library Facilities:		YES
Online Library Facilities:		YES
HRCI Certification Preparation:		YES
Encourages student study groups		
SHRM Student Chapter:		YES
Fellowships:	3	AMT: $1,200/mo + tuition
Scholarships:	NO	
Assistantships:	15	AMT: $1,000/mo + tuition
Eligibility:		Full-Time Enrollment

Curriculum
Required Courses:
HR Strategy
Compensation/Benefits
Development/Training
Recruitment/Retention
Employment Law
Management
Employee Relations
Labor Relations
Business Functional Areas
HR Measurement
HRIS
Research Methods
Economic Policy
Labor Law & Diversity
Organizational Behavior

Most Popular Elective Courses:
Managerial Negotiations
Reengineering the Corporation

Career Tracks/Concentrations:	N/A
Internship Required:	YES

Career Services
Career Services Offered:

Mentoring	Interview Training
Field Trips	Campus Interviews
SHRM Student Chapter	Internships
Resume Services	Executive Lunches

Summer Internship Placement Rate:		95-100%
Full-Time Placement Rate:		95-100%
Average Starting Salary (Full-Time Graduates):		$60,000
Average Sign-on Bonus:		N/A
Companies Recruiting HR Master's Graduates:		N/A

Points of Excellence

Resources: Program is located in a large metropolitan area where MLHR students interact frequently with HR professionals. This interaction occurs with class projects, guest speakers, internships, independent studies, and part/full-time employment.

Curriculum: Program offers MLHR students the opportunity to apply the analytical skills learned in the curriculum by working on research projects in areas such as reward systems, new forms of the employment relationship, and international HR practices. Companies involved in this research include Monsanto, Motorola, The Travelers, Federal Express, AT&T, IBM, Swiss firms, General Motors, and the U.S. Department of Labor.

Contact Information

Fisher College of Business, OSU
2100 Neil Ave.
Columbus, OH 43210-1144
www.osu.edu

Dr. Robert L. Heneman
Associate Professor & Program Director
Telephone: (614) 292-4587   FAX: (614) 292-7062
heneman.1@osu.edu

Admission Deadlines

July 1 for Fall admissions, October 1 for Winter admissions, February 1 for Spring admissions
Online Application: YES

Pennsylvania State University

University Park, Pennsylvania
Department of Labor Studies
and Industrial Relations

Degree

Master of Science in Industrial Relations and Human Resources (MSIRHR)

University Overview

Penn State, part of the state university system, is located in central Pennsylvania, with 40,000 students.

Program Description

Full-time traditional day program emphasizes work/life integration, industrial relations, dispute management, and diversity management. Half of all students have international backgrounds. Most have prior work experience.

Degree Requirements

Total Credits Required:	36
Average Credits per Course:	3
Course Schedule:	Semester
Total Courses Required:	12
HR/IR Courses Required:	7
Average Time for Completion:	2 years
Maximum Time Allowed for Completion:	8 years
Accepts Credits from Other Universities:	YES
Total:	N/A

Tuition

In-state	$7,000	(per year)
	$400	(per credit hour)
Out-of-state	N/A	(per year)
	N/A	(per credit hour)

Program Delivery

Traditional Day Program:	YES
Nontraditional Program:	NO
Evening Program:	NO
Weekend Program:	NO
Summer Courses:	N/A
Some Courses Online:	NO
Full Program Online:	NO
Distance Learning/Offsite:	NO
Executive Education:	N/A
Overseas Study Abroad:	YES

Faculty

Full-Time Faculty:	11
Part-Time Faculty:	0
Faculty to Student Ratio:	1:5

Primary Teaching Methods:

Case Study	Research
Student Presentation	Group Discussion

Faculty Who Consult Outside:	1-24%

Faculty Involvement:
President, National Association for Black Studies

Top 5 Faculty Publications:
Industrial and Labor Relations Review
Monthly Labor Review
Work and Occupations

Students

Total Enrollment:			11
Full-Time Enrollment:			90%
Men:	50%	Women:	50%
Hispanic	0%	African-American:	0%
Other Minorities:	0%	International:	50%
Average Age:	28	Age Range:	22-35
Work Full Time:			1-24%
HR Experience:			25-49%
Speak 2nd Language:			25-49%

Minimum Admission Requirements:

GMAT Score:	550
GRE Score:	1500
Other Considerations:	NONE

Average Student Profile:

GMAT Score:	600
GRE Score:	1650
Work experience:	2 years

Program Resources

Students Required to Have Computers:		N/A
Video Teleconferencing:		YES
Physical Library Facilities:		N/A
Online Library Facilities:		N/A
HRCI Certification Preparation:		NO
SHRM Student Chapter:		YES
Fellowships:		NO
Scholarships:		NO
Assistantships:	9	AMT:	$11,500
Eligibility:		Full-Time Enrollment

Curriculum

Required Courses:
    HR Strategy
    Employment Law
    Employee Relations

Labor Relations
Diversity

Most Popular Elective Courses:
HR Measurement
Development/Training
Recruitment/Retention
Grievance & Arbitration
Contract Administration
Work/Life Integration

Career Tracks/Concentrations:	N/A
Internship Required:	NO

Career Services

Career Services Offered:

Mentoring	Field Trips
SHRM Student Chapter	Resume Services
Interview Training	Campus Interviews
Internships	

Summer Internship Placement Rate:	N/A
Full-Time Placement Rate:	75%
Average Starting Salary (Full-Time Graduates):	$55,000
Average Sign-on Bonus:	N/A
Companies Recruiting HR Master's Graduates:	5

Points of Excellence

Faculty: Most students participate in faculty research projects, which include studying work/life integration processes, aspects of part-time and temporary employment, recruitment and retention of women and minorities, contract administration, and dispute/grievance handling.

Placement: Alumni group comes to campus twice a year to offer mentoring, placement, and career development sessions. Alumni provide numerous internship and job opportunities.

Contact Information

Department of Labor Studies and Industrial Relations
133 Willard Building
University Park, PA 16802
www.la.psu.edu

Amy Dietz, Administrative Assistant
Telephone: (814) 865-5425
ard5@psu.edu

Mark Wardell, Head of Department
Telephone: (814) 865-5425
mlw9@psu.edu

Admission Deadlines

Online Application:	YES

Polytechnic University

Brooklyn, New York
Department of Management

Degree

Master of Science in Organizational Behavior (MSOB)
Master of Science in Management with an HRM concentration (MSHRM)

University Overview

Polytechnic University is the oldest private technology university in the nation (established in 1854).

Program Description

This nontraditional program places emphasis on integrating and utilizing people and technology to achieve organizational effectiveness.

Degree Requirements

Total Credits Required:	36
Average Credits per Course:	3
Course Schedule:	Semester
Total Courses Required:	12
HR/IR Courses Required:	10
Average Time for Completion:	1-2 years
Maximum Time Allowed for Completion:	5 years
Accepts Credits from Other Universities:	YES
Total:	9 Hours

Tuition

In-state	N/A	(per year)
	$695	(per credit hour)
Out-of-state	N/A	(per year)
	$695	(per credit hour)

Program Delivery

Traditional Day Program:	NO
Nontraditional Program:	YES
Evening Program:	YES
Weekend Program:	NO
Summer Courses:	YES
Some Courses Online:	NO
Full Program Online:	NO
Distance Learning/Offsite:	YES
Executive Education:	NO
Overseas Study Abroad:	YES

Faculty

Full-Time Faculty:	2
Part-Time Faculty:	8
Faculty to Student Ratio:	1:10

Primary Teaching Methods:

Research	Team Projects
Field Projects	Student Presentations
Lectures	

Faculty Who Consult Outside:	1-24%
Faculty Involvement:	N/A
Top 5 Faculty Publications:	N/A

Students

Total Enrollment:			30
Full-Time Enrollment:			30%
Men:	50%	Women:	50%
Hispanic:	10%	African-American:	30%
Other Minorities:	10%	International:	20%
Average Age:	30	Age Range:	20-50
Work Full Time:			75-99%
HR Experience:			1-24%
Speak 2nd Language:			1-24%
Minimum Admission Requirements:			N/A

Other Considerations:
Work experience and letters of recommendation

Average Student Profile:	N/A

Program Resources

Students Required to Have Computers:	NO
Video Teleconferencing:	NO
Physical Library Facilities:	YES
Online Library Facilities:	YES
HRCI Certification Preparation:	YES

Links students with alumni who have taken the exam

SHRM Student Chapter:	YES

Fellowships:			NO
Scholarships:	Several	AMT:	$6,000
Assistantships:			NO
Eligibility:			All Students

Curriculum

Required Courses:
- HR Strategy
- International HR
- Compensation/Benefits
- Development/Training
- Recruitment/Retention
- Employment Law
- Employee Relations
- Labor Relations
- HR Measurement
- Career Management
- Organizational Design
- Technological Design

Most Popular Elective Courses: N/A

Career Tracks/Concentrations:
- Human Resource Management
- Human Resource Information Systems
- Management of Change
- Training & Development

Internship Required: NO

Career Services

Career Services Offered:
- Mentoring
- Field Trips
- SHRM Student Chapter
- Resume Services
- Interview Training
- Campus Interviews
- Internships

Summer Internship Placement Rate:	N/A
Full-Time Placement Rate:	N/A
Average Starting Salary (Full-Time Graduates):	N/A
Average Sign-on Bonus:	N/A
Companies Recruiting HR Master's Graduates:	5

Points of Excellence

Faculty: HR practitioners are utilized in teaching most courses. Most are PhDs in I/O Psychology. Practitioners also participate in program's SHRM Forums scheduled at the end of each semester to address important issues in HR and to provide networking opportunities.

Placement: Alumni are utilized as mentors and help students network for jobs. They serve as guest speakers at seminars and at an annual forum, and help in career development and placement by providing coaching and internship opportunities.

Contact Information

Polytechnic University
6 Metrotech Center
Brooklyn, NY 11201
www.poly.edu

Harold G. Kaufman, Professor & Director
Organizational Behavior Program
Telephone: (718) 260-3485   FAX: (718) 260-3874
hkaufman@poly.edu

Admission Deadlines

Online Application: YES

Purdue University

West Lafayette, Indiana
Krannert Graduate School of Management

Degree
Master of Science in Human Resource Management (MSHRM)

University Overview
Founded in 1869, Purdue is a public university located 125 miles from Chicago and 65 miles from Indianapolis. The West Lafayette campus enrolls almost 38,000 students.

Program Description
The MSHRM program trains individuals to play an essential role in upper management and adapt to the needs of contemporary organizations. The plan of study integrates three components: human resources, a strong emphasis on business functions, and a distinctive analytical orientation.

Degree Requirements

Total Credits Required:	61
Average Credits per Course:	2
Course Schedule:	Semester
Total Courses Required:	30
HR/IR Courses Required:	12
Average Time for Completion:	2 years
Maximum Time Allowed for Completion:	6 years
Accepts Credits from Other Universities:	N/A
Total:	N/A

Tuition

In-state	$4,560	(per semester)
	N/A	(per credit hour)
Out-of-state	$8,996	(per semester)
	N/A	(per credit hour)

Program Delivery

Traditional Day Program:	YES
Nontraditional Program:	YES
Evening Program:	YES
Weekend Program:	NO
Summer Courses:	N/A
Some Courses Online:	NO
Full Program Online:	NO
Distance Learning/Offsite:	YES
Executive Education:	N/A
Overseas Study Abroad:	N/A

Faculty

Full-Time Faculty:	N/A
Part-Time Faculty:	N/A
Faculty to Student Ratio:	1:20

Primary Teaching Methods:
- Case Study
- Research
- Group Discussion
- Lecture
- Team Projects
- Group Presentations

Faculty Who Consult Outside:	N/A
Faculty Involvement:	N/A

Top 5 Faculty Publications:

Students

Total Enrollment:			50
Full-Time Enrollment:			100%
Men:	68%	Women:	32%
Hispanic:	N/A	African-American:	N/A
Other Minorities:	N/A	International:	N/A
Average Age:	26	Age Range:	22-42
Work Full Time:			1-24%

HR Experience:	1-24%
Speak 2nd Language:	1-24%
Minimum Admission Requirements:	
GMAT	
UGPA	
Other Considerations:	
Work experience, leadership experience, recommendations	
Average Student Profile:	N/A

Program Resources

Students Required to Have Computers:	N/A
Video Teleconferencing:	N/A
Physical Library Facilities:	N/A
Online Library Facilities:	N/A
HRCI Certification Preparation:	YES
SHRM Student Chapter:	YES
Fellowships:	NO
Scholarships:	NO
Assistantships:	NO
Eligibility:	N/A

Curriculum

Required Courses:
  Accounting
  Marketing
  Quantitative Methods
  Organizational Behavior
  Financial Management
  HR Systems
  Mgmt. Communications
  Staffing
  Labor Economics
  HRIS
  Compensation
  Research Methods
  Functional Management
  Industrial Relations

Most Popular Elective Courses:
  Advanced Benefits
  Advanced Reward Sys.
  HRIS II
  Negotiations
  Staffing Tools
  Team Work

Career Tracks/Concentrations:	N/A
Internship Required:	NO

Career Services

Career Services Offered:

Mentoring	Campus Interviews
Interview Training	Resume Services
SHRM Student Chapter	Internships

Summer Internship Placement Rate:	N/A
Full-Time Placement Rate:	90-100%
Average Starting Salary (Full-Time Graduates):	$60,000
Average Sign-on Bonus:	$7,000
Companies Recruiting HR Master's Graduates:	50

Points of Excellence

Curriculum: In response to the demand for leaders with team skills, Krannert assigns entering students to a cohort team during their first module of classes. Team members are cross-functional (from management industrial administration and HRM programs) and are required to complete assignments together. Krannert students also practice leadership skills by leading consulting projects, volunteer groups, and professional organizations. Students are responsible for all aspects of these activities, from budgets to program planning and implementation.

Contact Information

Krannert Graduate School of Management
1310 Krannert Building
West Lafayette, IN 47907-1310
www.mgmt.purdue.edu/masters/shrm

Cyntha G. Emrich, Ph.D., Assistant Professor of Management
Telephone: (765) 494-4511   FAX: (765) 494-9658
cindy@mgmt.purdue.edu

Chuck Johnson, Director of Professional MS Programs
Telephone: (765) 496-3668   FAX: (765) 494-4360
cjohnson@mgmt.purdue.edu

Admission Deadlines

July 15 for Fall admissions

Online Application:	YES

Queen's University

Kingston, Ontario, Canada
School of Industrial Relations

Degree
Master of Industrial Relations (MIR)

University Overview
One of the oldest universities in Canada, Queen's University was founded in 1841 in Kingston, Ontario, Canada. Today more than 16,000 students are enrolled.

Program Description
The Master of Industrial Relations Program is multidisciplinary, allowing students to concentrate on labor relations, human resource management, or labor law.

Degree Requirements

Total Credits Required:	5.5
Average Credits per Course:	.5
Course Schedule:	Semester
Total Courses Required:	11
HR/IR Courses Required:	8
Average Time for Completion:	1-3 years
Maximum Time Allowed for Completion:	5 years
Accepts Credits from Other Universities:	NO
Total:	N/A

Tuition

In-state	$5,500	(per year)
	N/A	(per credit hour)
Out-of-state	$5,500	(per year)
	N/A	(per credit hour)

Program Delivery

Traditional Day Program:	YES
Nontraditional Program:	NO
Evening Program:	NO
Weekend Program:	NO
Summer Courses:	N/A
Some Courses Online:	NO
Full Program Online:	NO
Distance Learning/Offsite:	NO
Executive Education:	N/A
Overseas Study Abroad:	NO

Faculty

Full-Time Faculty:	3
Part-Time Faculty:	2
Faculty to Student Ratio:	N/A

Primary Teaching Methods:
Case Study   Experiential Learning
Team Projects   Group Discussion
Computer Simulation

Faculty Who Consult Outside: 25-49%

Faculty Involvement:
Research Committee, Canadian Industrial Relations Association
Member, Federal Government Taskforce on Working Time and the Distribution of Work
Organizer, Human Resources Division of the Administrative Science Association of Canada
Vice Chair, Public Service Grievance Board
Adjudicator, Board of Inquiry of the Human Rights Commission

Top 5 Faculty Publications: N/A

Students

Total Enrollment:			38
Full-Time Enrollment:			92%
Men:	47%	Women:	53%
Hispanic:	N/A	African-American:	N/A
Other Minorities:	N/A	International:	N/A
Average Age:	25	Age Range:	22-64
Work Full Time:			1-24%
HR Experience:			1-24%
Speak 2nd Language:			75-99%

Minimum Admission Requirements:
UGPA & TOEFL Score: 600
Other Considerations: N/A
Average Student Profile: N/A

Program Resources

Students Required to Have Computers:			N/A
Video Teleconferencing:			YES
Physical Library Facilities:			N/A
Online Library Facilities:			N/A
HRCI Certification Preparation:			NO
SHRM Student Chapter:			NO
Fellowships:	6	AMT:	$8,000
Scholarships:	10	AMT:	$2,000
Assistantships:			NO
Eligibility:			Full-Time Enrollment

Curriculum

Required Courses:
HR Strategy
Compensation/Benefits
Development/Training
Employment Law
HR Measurement
Labor Relations

Most Popular Elective Courses:
Quantitative Methods
Economics of the Labor Market
Management of Change
Organizational Leadership
Conflict Management
Industrial Dispute Law

Career Tracks/Concentrations: N/A
Internship Required: N/A

Career Services

Career Services Offered:
Resume Services   Interview Training
Internships

Summer Internship Placement Rate: N/A
Full-Time Placement Rate: 90-100%

Average Starting Salary (Full-Time Graduates):	$45,000
Average Sign-on Bonus:	N/A
Companies Recruiting HR Master's Graduates:	20

Points of Excellence

Curriculum: The MIR curriculum is focused to provide a challenging standard of excellence in the field. Core courses in HR, IR, and Canadian Labor Law are supplemented with Analytical & Research Skills Seminars covering the latest innovations in the field.

Contact Information

School of Industrial Relations
Queen's University
Kingston, Ontario
Canada K7L 3N6
qsilver.queensu.ca/irl/

Grier Owen, MIR Program Administrator
Telephone: (613) 533-6000 ext. 7732   FAX: (613) 533-2560
go4@post.queensu.ca

Admission Deadlines

Online Application: YES

Radford University

Radford, Virginia
Department of Psychology

Degree

Master of Industrial/Organizational Psychology (MA-I/O)

University Overview

Radford University is a public university with an enrollment approaching 9,000. It is located close to the beautiful Blue Ridge Mountains, 35 miles from Roanoke, Virginia.

Program Description

The two-year, full-time traditional day program has an applied orientation designed to prepare students for jobs in a variety of HR careers. Though the faculty is involved in consulting and is well published, the program's primary focus is on the students.

Degree Requirements

Total Credits Required:	36
Average Credits per Course:	3
Course Schedule:	Semester
Total Courses Required:	12
HR/IR Courses Required:	11
Average Time for Completion:	2 years
Maximum Time Allowed for Completion:	10 years
Accepts Credits from Other Universities:	YES
Total:	6 Hours

Tuition

In-state	$3,006	(per year)
	$167	(per credit hour)
Out-of-state	$5,814	(per year)
	$323	(per credit hour)

Program Delivery

Traditional Day Program:	YES
Nontraditional Program:	NO
Evening Program:	NO
Weekend Program:	NO
Summer Courses:	NO
Some Courses Online:	NO
Full Program Online:	NO

Distance Learning/Offsite:		NO
Executive Education:		NO
Overseas Study Abroad:		NO

Faculty
Full-Time Faculty:		3
Part-Time Faculty:		0
Faculty to Student Ratio:		1:10
Primary Teaching Methods:		
Team Projects	Lecture	
Experiential Learning	Student Presentations	
Faculty Who Consult Outside:		25-49%

Faculty Involvement:
Board of Directors for IPMAAC

Top 5 Faculty Publications:
Human Relations In Business
Applied Industrial/Organizational Psychology

Students
Total Enrollment:			27
Full-Time Enrollment:			100%
Men:	30%	Women:	70%
Hispanic:	0%	African-American:	3%
Other Minorities:	3%	International:	3%
Average Age:	23	Age Range:	22-30
Work Full Time:			1-24%
HR Experience:			1-24%
Speak 2nd Language:			1-24%

Minimum Admission Requirements:
Enters GRE, GPA (last 60 units), and recommendations into regression equation

Other Considerations:	NONE
Average Student Profile:	
Work experience:	1 year
GRE Score:	1080

Program Resources
Students Required to Have Computers:		NO
Video Teleconferencing:		NO
Physical Library Facilities:		YES
Online Library Facilities:		YES
HRCI Certification Preparation:		NO
SHRM Student Chapter:		YES
Fellowships:	7	AMT:	$8,680
Scholarships:			NO
Assistantships:	23	AMT:	$3,720
Eligibility:		Full-Time Enrollment

Curriculum
Required Courses:
HR Strategy
Compensation/Benefits
Development/Training
Recruitment/Retention
Employment Law
Management
Labor Relations
HR Measurement

Most Popular Elective Courses:	N/A
Career Tracks/Concentrations:	N/A
Internship Required:	YES

Career Services
Career Services Offered:
Mentoring	Interview Training
Field Trips	Campus Interviews
SHRM Student Chapter	Internships
Resume Services	

Summer Internship Placement Rate: N/A

Full-Time Placement Rate:	N/A
Average Starting Salary (Full-Time Graduates):	$37,000
Average Sign-on Bonus:	N/A
Companies Recruiting HR Master's Graduates:	N/A

Points of Excellence
Curriculum: Perhaps the most unusual aspect of the program at Radford is the Community Human Resource Center (CHRC). The CHRC is a not-for-profit human resource consulting group that provides free consulting to public and nonprofit agencies, while at the same time providing graduate students with applied experience. Recent projects include Conducting Job Analyses and Writing Job Descriptions; Analyzing Salary Survey Data; Presenting Training Programs to Organizations; and Creating Performance Appraisal Systems.

Students: Radford I/O graduate students have presented more papers at the national graduate conference in industrial-organizational psychology and organizational behavior (IOOB) than any other master's degree program in the country. The I/O Program represents a diverse group of students.

Contact Information
Department of Psychology
Radford University
Radford, VA 24142-6946
www.radford.edu/~psych-web/Io-psych/

Mike Aamodt, Professor
Telephone: (540) 831-5913　　　　FAX: (540) 831-6113
maamodt@runet.edu

Admission Deadlines
March 1 for Fall admissions
Online Application: NO

Regent University

Virginia Beach, Virginia
School of Business

Degree
Master of Human Resources Management (MHRM)
Master of Organizational Change and Development (MORCD)
Master of Business Administration with concentration in Human Resources Management (MBAHRM)

University Overview
Founded in the late 1960s, Regent University is a Christian graduate school. It is one of the fastest growing graduate schools, serving over 2,500 students worldwide through both on-campus and distance programs. Degree programs are taught from a Judeo-Christian worldview emphasizing leadership and best business practices.

Program Description
Professors within the Graduate School of Business are generally full-time faculty as well as PhD-level trained and/or senior experienced practitioners within their disciplines. Students are given the opportunity to develop a plan that best suits their career needs and goals at the MBA, MA, or Graduate Certificate level.

Degree Requirements
Total Credits Required:	33-48
Average Credits per Course:	3
Course Schedule:	Semester

95

Total Courses Required:		14	(MBAHRM)
		9	(MHRM and MORCD)
HR/IR Courses Required:			4
Average Time for Completion:			1 ½-2 years
Maximum Time Allowed for Completion:			5 years
Accepts Credits from Other Universities:			YES
Total:			N/A

Tuition

In-state	N/A	(per year)
	$498	(per credit hour)
Out-of-state	N/A	(per year)
	$498	(per credit hour)

Program Delivery

Traditional Day Program:	YES
Nontraditional Program:	YES
Evening Program:	YES
Weekend Program:	YES
Summer Courses:	N/A
Some Courses Online:	YES
Full Program Online:	NO
Distance Learning/Offsite:	YES
Executive Education:	N/A
Overseas Study Abroad:	YES

Faculty

Full-Time Faculty:	8
Part-Time Faculty:	4
Faculty to Student Ratio:	1:20

Primary Teaching Methods:

Case Study	Field Projects
Lecture	Research
Group Discussion	Computer Simulations

Faculty Who Consult Outside:	1-24%
Faculty Involvement:	N/A

Top 5 Faculty Publications:
Journal for Leadership Studies
Drug Information Journal
Books

Students

Total Enrollment:			350
Full-Time Enrollment:			57%
Men:	N/A	Women:	N/A
Hispanic:	N/A	African-American:	N/A
Other Minorities:	N/A	International:	N/A
Average Age:	34	Age Range:	23-55
Work Full Time:			25-49%
HR Experience:			50-74%
Speak 2nd Language:			25-49%

Minimum Admission Requirements:

GPA:	2.75
Work experience:	5 years

Other Considerations:
Work experience and achievements
Average Student Profile:

Work experience:	9 years

Program Resources

Students Required to Have Computers:			N/A
Video Teleconferencing:			YES
Physical Library Facilities:			N/A
Online Library Facilities:			N/A
HRCI Certification Preparation:			YES
Encourage student study groups			
SHRM Student Chapter:			NO
Fellowships:	2	AMT:	$10,000 + tuition

Scholarships:	Varies	AMT:	$5,000
Assistantships:	10	AMT:	$7,500
Eligibility:			Full-Time Enrollment

Curriculum

Required Courses:
Accounting
Finance
Marketing
HR Strategy
Employment Law
Management
Business Functional Areas

Most Popular Elective Courses:	N/A
Career Tracks/Concentrations:	N/A
Internship Required:	NO

Career Services

Career Development Opportunities/Placement Service:

Mentoring	Interview Training
Resume Services	Campus Interview
Internships	

Summer Internship Placement Rate:	NO
Full-Time Placement Rate:	N/A
Average Starting Salary (Full-Time Graduates):	N/A
Average Sign-on Bonus:	N/A
Companies Recruiting HR Master's Graduates:	N/A

Points of Excellence

Curriculum: Students enjoy significant access to their professors and use of one of the most extensive electronic databases in the nation, whether as a distance or on-campus student. Emphasis is placed on real-world application and leadership within the discipline rather than flavor-of-the-month theory. Projects and evidence of the ability to apply theory in workplace rather than examinations are the norm. Heavy use of technology both in training and coursework is expected.

Placement: The graduate School of Business includes Career Services, an active alumni network, and Executive Recruiter and Corporate Relations, all of which assist students in placement in all sectors. On-campus career fairs are also held on an ongoing basis, with nationally known firms recruiting at Regent.

Contact Information

Regent University
Graduate School of Business
1000 Regent University Dr.
Virginia Beach, VA 23456
www.regent.edu/acad/schbus

Paul E. Rondeau
Manager, Executive Recruitment & Education
Telephone: (757) 226-4386   FAX: (757) 226-4823
paulron@regent.edu

Dail L. Fields, Ph.D.
Associate Professor of Management
Telephone: (800) 477-3642   FAX: (757) 226-4369
dailfie@regent.edu

Michael A. Zigarelli, Ph.D.
Associate Professor of Management
Telephone: (800) 477-3642   FAX: (757) 226-4369
michig@regent.edu

Admission Deadlines

Online Application:	NO

Rollins College

Winter Park, Florida
Interdisciplinary Program

Degree
Master of Human Resources (MHR)

University Overview
Rollins College, established in 1885, is a private university located near Orlando, Florida.

Program Description
This nontraditional program is an interdisciplinary, stand-alone program that draws its faculty primarily from the colleges of business and psychology. It is designed to prepare talented working people for positions of organizational leadership and professional responsibility in the field of Human Resource Management.

Degree Requirements
Total Credits Required:	40
Average Credits per Course:	4
Course Schedule:	Semester
Total Courses Required:	12
HR/IR Courses Required:	6
Average Time for Completion:	1 ½-2 years
Maximum Time Allowed for Completion:	7 years
Accepts Credits from Other Universities:	YES
Total:	6 Hours (Semester, 2 Courses)

Tuition
In-state	N/A	(per year)
	$280	(per credit hour)
Out-of-state	N/A	(per year)
	$280	(per credit hour)

Program Delivery
Traditional Day Program:	NO
Nontraditional Program:	YES
Evening Program:	YES
Weekend Program:	YES
Summer Courses:	YES
Some Courses Online:	YES
Full Program Online:	NO
Distance Learning/Offsite:	NO
Executive Education:	NO
Overseas Study Abroad:	YES

Faculty
Full-Time Faculty:	10
Part-Time Faculty:	6
Faculty to Student Ratio:	1:11

Primary Teaching Methods:

Experiential Learning	Team Projects
Field Projects	Student Presentations
Computer Simulation	

Faculty Involvement:
Faculty Who Consult Outside:	50-74%

Faculty Involvement:
Member, SHRM College Relations Committee

Top 5 Faculty Publications:
Five HR books In the last three years
22 academic or professional articles

Students
Total Enrollment:			74
Full-Time Enrollment:			100%
Men:	35%	Women:	65%
Hispanic:	30%	African-American:	8%
Other Minorities:	4%	International:	0%
Average Age:	36	Age Range:	25-70
Work Full Time:			75-99%
HR Experience:			75-99%
Speak 2nd Language:			25-49%

Minimum Admission Requirements:
GRE and GMAT Scores:	Above the 50th percentile
Work experience:	2 years

Other Considerations:
Considers "whole person" (experience, test scores, GPA, references, and personal statement)

Average Student Profile:
GRE Score:	75th percentile
Work experience:	8.5 years

Program Resources
Students Required to Have Computers:	YES
Video Teleconferencing:	NO
Physical Library Facilities:	YES
Online Library Facilities:	YES
HRCI Certification Preparation:	YES
Encourages student study groups	
Links students to local SHRM chapter study groups	
SHRM Student Chapter:	YES
Fellowships:	NO
Scholarships:	NO
Assistantships:	NO
Eligibility:	N/A

Curriculum
Required Courses:
HR Strategy
Organization Development
Employment & Labor Law
Recruitment/Retention
Training & Development
Future of HR Management

Popular Elective Courses:
Employee Relations
Dispute Resolution
Compensation
Organizational Psychology
Management Consulting
Performance Consulting
HR Measurement
International HR
Finance for HR Managers
Leading the HR Department
Career & Succession Planning
Human Performance Improvement

Career Tracks/Concentrations:

Human Resource Management (HRM)	Human Resource Development (HRD)
Organizational Development (OD)	Management Consulting (MC)
Employee Relations (ER)	

Internship Required:	NO

Career Services
Career Services Offered:

Field Trips	Interview Training
SHRM Student Chapter	Internships
Resume Services	Networking

Summer Internship Placement Rate:	10%*
Full-Time Placement Rate:	100%*
Average Starting Salary (Full-Time Graduates):	N/A
Average Sign-on Bonus:	N/A

Companies Recruiting HR Master's Graduates:	40

Most students already have HR jobs

Points of Excellence

Curriculum: The MHR Program is designed for working HR professionals. Courses are taught in executive-style classrooms with individual Internet links. Some course syllabi with chat rooms are on the campus web. The program gives HR people the competencies necessary to function as leaders and managers of HR departments; as members of top management teams; and as senior level consultants. Since Rollins is an elite Liberal Arts college, personal effectiveness, leadership skills, communication skills, managerial decision-making, project management, and strategic thinking skills are emphasized more than mere knowledge

Contact Information

Rollins College
Masters in Human Resources
1000 Holt Ave.
Winter Park, FL 32789-4499
www.rollins.edu

Donald P. Rogers, Director, MHR Program
Telephone: (407) 646-2348   FAX: (407) 646-1566
drogers@rollins.edu

Admission Deadlines

Rolling admissions

Online Application:	YES

Roosevelt University

Chicago, Illinois
School of Psychology

Degree

Master of Arts Psychology (Industrial/Organizational Psychology)

University Overview

Roosevelt University is an independent, nonsectarian, coeducational institution with two campuses in Chicago, Illinois and a third in Schaumburg, Illinois.

Program Description

Action-oriented, applied program with strong statistical approach; thesis or practicum alternative; practicum is 1,000 hours of experience, typically paid.

Degree Requirements

Total Credits Required:	30
Average Credits per Course:	3
Course Schedule:	Semester
Total Courses Required:	10
HR/IR Courses Required:	0
Average Time for Completion:	3 years
Maximum Time Allowed for Completion:	6 years
Accepts Credits from Other Universities:	YES
Total:	9 Hours

Tuition

In-state	N/A	(per year)
	N/A	(per credit hour)
Out-of-state	N/A	(per year)
	N/A	(per credit hour)

Program Delivery

Traditional Day Program:	NO
Nontraditional Program:	YES
Evening Program:	YES
Weekend Program:	YES
Program Completed Evening/Weekend:	YES
Summer Courses:	YES
Some Courses Online:	NO
Full Program Online:	NO
Distance Learning/Offsite:	NO
Executive Education:	NO
Overseas Study Abroad:	NO

Faculty

Full-Time Faculty:	15
Part-Time Faculty:	3
Faculty to Student Ratio:	1:20

Primary Teaching Methods:

Research	Lecture
Student Presentation	Group Discussion

Faculty Who Consult Outside:	100%
Faculty Involvement:	
Top 5 Faculty Publications:	

Students

Total Enrollment:			70
Full-Time Enrollment:			25
Men:	35%	Women:	65%
Hispanic:	15%	African-American:	35%
Other Minorities:	4%	International:	2%
Average Age:	27	Age Range:	22-50
Work Full Time:			75-99%
Have HR Experience:			1-24%
Speak 2nd Language:			1-24%

Minimum Admission Requirements:

UGPA:	3.0
GRE or GMAT Scores:	N/A
Work Experience:	N/A
Other Considerations:	
Average Student Profile:	
UGPA:	N/A
GMAT Score:	N/A
Work Experience:	N/A

Program Resources

Students Required to Have Computers:	NO
Video Teleconferencing:	YES
Physical Library Facilities:	YES
Online Library Facilities:	YES
HRCI Certification Preparation:	NO
SHRM Student Chapter:	YES
URL:	

Fellowships:	YES	AMT:	$5,000 plus tuition
Scholarships:	YES	AMT:	Varies
Assistantships:	N/A	AMT:	
Eligibility:		Full-Time Enrollment (for Fellowships)	

Curriculum

Required Courses:
   Management
   Compensation/Benefits
   Development/Training

Most Popular Elective Courses:	N/A
Career Tracks/Concentrations:	N/A
Internship Required:	NO

Career Services

Career Services Offered:	N/A
Summer Internship Placement Rate:	N/A
Facilitate Placement:	NO
Full-Time Placement Rate:	20-30%
Internship Placement Rate:	98%
Average Starting Salary (Full-Time Graduates):	N/A
Average Sign-on Bonus:	N/A
Companies Recruiting HR Master's Graduates:	N/A

Points of Excellence

Contact Information
Roosevelt University
430 South Michigan Avenue
Chicago, Illinois 60605

Edward J. Wygonik, Ph.D.
ewygonik@roosevelt.edu   (312) 341-3760

Admission Deadlines
Rolling admissions; students accepted each semester.

Online Application:	YES

Rutgers University

New Brunswick, New Jersey
School of Management & Labor Relations

Degree
Master of Human Resource Management (MHRM)

University Overview
Rutgers University, the eighth oldest college in the nation, was chartered in 1766 as Queen's College and designated the State University of New Jersey in 1956. It is made up of 29 degree-granting schools and colleges with an enrollment of more than 48,000 students.

Program Description
The MHRM curriculum prepares students to assume leadership positions in the management of firms as well as to have more traditional careers in HRM. The new curriculum also emphasizes comparative and international HRM and strategies for enhancing firm competitiveness through the use of human capital.

Degree Requirements

Total Credits Required:	48
Average Credits per Course:	3
Course Schedule:	Semester
Total Courses Required:	16
HR/IR Courses Required:	14
Average Time for Completion:	2-4 Years
Maximum Time Allowed for Completion:	10 Years
Accepts Credits from Other Universities:	YES
Total:	12 Hours

Tuition

In-state	$7,954	(per year)
	$328	(per credit hour)
Out-of-state	$11,704	(per year)
	N/A	(per credit hour)

Program Delivery

Traditional Day Program:	YES
Nontraditional Program:	YES
Evening Program:	YES
Weekend Program:	YES

Summer Courses:	YES
Some Courses Online:	NO
Full Program Online:	NO
Distance Learning/Offsite:	YES
Executive Education:	NO
Overseas Study Abroad:	YES

Faculty

Full-Time Faculty:	16
Part-Time Faculty:	4
Faculty to Student Ratio:	1:25

Primary Teaching Methods:

Case Study	Team Projects
Lecture	Group Discussion
Computer Simulations	

Faculty Who Consult Outside:	25-49%

Faculty Involvement:
Editor, *Human Resource Management Journal*, Industrial Relations Research Association, Human Resource Planning, Academy of Management Review
Recipient of SHRM's Yoder-Heneman Scholarly Achievement Award
President, Academy of Management's Division of Organizational Behavior
Board of Directors, GOALS

Top 5 Faculty Publications:	See web site

Students

Total Enrollment:			160
Full-Time Enrollment:			100%
Men:	21%	Women:	79%
Hispanic:	1.5%	African-American:	4.6%
Other Minorities:	3.8%	International:	25%
Average Age:	30	Age Range:	22-60+
Work Full Time:			50-74%
HR Experience:			50-74%
Speak 2nd Language:			1-24%

Minimum Requirements:

GMAT Score:	500
GRE Score:	500
TOEFL Score:	575 for foreign Students
UGPA:	3.0

Other Considerations:
Applicants with 5+ years of HR management-level experience are exempt from GRE/GMAT.

Average Student Profile:

Work experience:	6 years
GMAT Score:	556
GRE Score:	486V, 598Q, 609A
UGPA:	3.19

Program Resources

Students Required to Have Computers:		NO
Video Teleconferencing:		YES
Physical Library Facilities:		YES
Online Library Facilities:		YES
HRCI Certification Preparation:		NO
SHRM Student Chapter:		YES
Fellowships:	2 AMT:	$10,000
Scholarships:		NO
Assistantships:		NO
Eligibility:		Full-Time Enrollment

Curriculum
Required Courses:
HR Strategy
HR Decision Making
HR Measurement

Developing Human Capital
Managing Workforce Flow
Managing Rewards Systems
Governance Systems Design
Labor Economics
Managing Global Workforce
Employment Law
Business and Functional Areas, Finance
Change Management
Most Popular Elective Courses:
    Designing & Management Organizational Change
    Managing Teams
    Internal Consulting Skills
    Managing Workforce Diversity

Career Tracks/Concentrations:	N/A
Internship Required:	NO

Career Services

Career Services Offered:

Mentoring	Interview Training
SHRM Student Chapter	Campus Interview
Resume Services	Internships
Career Fairs	

Summer Internship Placement Rate:	N/A
Full-Time Placement Rate:	N/A
Average Starting Salary (Full-Time Graduates):	$59,889
Average Sign-on Bonus:	N/A
Companies Recruiting HR Master's Graduates:	20-25

Points of Excellence

Resources: The Center for Global Strategic Human Resource Management (CGSHRM) has established partnerships with corporations, other universities and centers, government agencies, and professional organizations for the advancement of research and the development of effective practice in global strategic HRM. The Department provides limited support to enable students to attend a class in our Singapore MHRM program. Students can take additional classes in the affiliated Master's in Labor and Employment Relations program. The Center for Women and Work supports research and programs on the role of women in the modern workplace.

Faculty: The faculty and staff of the Human Resource Management (HRM) Department focus on the strategic deployment of human resources; the role of human resource policies and practices in firm performance; improving the practice of human resource management at the firm, corporate, and global level; and public policy related to employment. The faculty conduct research, provide graduate and professional education, and engage in a variety of service activities related to the profession, their disciplines, and the academic community.

Contact Information

School of Management and Labor Relations
216 B Janice Levin Building
New Brunswick, NJ 08854-8054
www.rci.rutgers.edu/~smlr

Judy Von Loewe, administrative assistant, HRM
Telephone: (732) 445-5917   FAX: (732) 445-2830
jvloewe@rci.rutgers.edu

Prof. Charles H. Fay, Director, Graduate Programs in HRM
Telephone: (732) 445-5831   FAX: (732) 445-2830
cfay@rci.rutgers.edu

Admission Deadlines

May 1 for Fall admissions, November 1 for Spring admissions

Online Application:	YES

St. Edward's University

Austin, Texas
School of Adult and Professional Education

Degree

Master of Science in Organizational Leadership and Ethics (MSOLE)
Master of Business Administration with HR concentration (MBA/HR)

University Overview

Private Catholic university with 600 graduate students. Most students are adults who work part time.

Program Description

The program emphasizes the development of abilities associated with superior managerial effectiveness as well as the importance of relating theoretical knowledge to issues or problems found in the students' workplaces.

Degree Requirements

Total Credits Required:	36
Average Credits per Course:	3
Course Schedule:	Trimester (MSOLE-7 week schedule)
Total Courses Required:	12
HR/IR Courses Required:	5
Average Time for Completion:	2-3 years
Maximum Time Allowed for Completion:	6 years
Accepts Credits from Other Universities:	YES
Total:	12 Hours

Tuition

In-state	N/A	(per year)
	$743	(per course)
Out-of-state	N/A	(per year)
	$743	(per course)

Program Delivery

Traditional Day Program:	NO
Nontraditional Program:	YES
Evening Program:	YES
Weekend Program:	YES
Summer Courses:	YES
Some Courses Online:	YES
Full Program Online:	YES
Distance Learning/Offsite:	NO
Executive Education:	Under Development
Overseas Study Abroad:	NO

Faculty

Full-Time Faculty:	9
Part-Time Faculty:	20
Faculty to Student Ratio:	1:20

Primary Teaching Methods:

Case Study	Group Discussion
Experiential Learning	Team Projects
Computer-Aided Instruction	

Faculty Who Consult Outside:	75-99%

Faculty Involvement:
  HR Advisor, Human Resources Management

Top 5 Faculty Publications:	N/A

Students

Total Enrollment:			100
Full-Time Enrollment:			15%
Men:	48%	Women:	52%
Hispanic:	12%	African-American:	10%

Other Minorities:	10%	International:	15%
Average Age:	32	Age Range:	23-65
Work Full Time:			75-99%
HR Experience:			25-49%
Speak 2nd Language:			1-24%

Minimum Admission Requirements:

Work experience:	3 years
GMAT:	500
GRE:	1000
UGPA:	3.0
Other Considerations:	None

Average Student Profile:

Work experience:	8 years

Program Resources

Students Required to Have Computers:		NO
Video Teleconferencing:		YES
Physical Library Facilities:		YES
Online Library Facilities:		YES
HRCI Certification Preparation:		YES
SHRM Student Chapter:		YES
Fellowships:		NO
Scholarships:	2	AMT: $1,000
Assistantships:		NO
Eligibility:		All Students

Curriculum

Required Courses:
Managing the Organization
HR Development
Financial Statement Analysis
Compensation Management
Business Law & Ethics
Financial Management
Marketing Management
HR Management
Personnel Law
Global HRM and Labor Relations or Org Behavior

Most Popular Elective Courses:	N/A
Career Tracks/Concentrations:	
Internship Required:	NO

Career Services

Career Development Opportunities/Placement Service:

SHRM Student Chapter	Interview Training
Resume Services	Resume Writing

Summer Internship Placement Rate:	N/A
Full-Time Placement Rate:	N/A
Average Starting Salary (Full-Time Graduates):	N/A
Average Sign-on Bonus:	N/A
Companies Recruiting HR Master's Graduates:	N/A

Contact Information

St. Edward's University
3001 S. Congress, CM 961
Austin, TX 78704
www.stedwards.edu

Allan E. Pevoto, Ph.D.
Associate Professor
Telephone: (512) 448-8678   FAX: (512) 416-5819
allanp@admin.stedwards.edu

Admission Deadlines

July 1 (priority), August 1 for Fall admissions

Online Application:	YES

Saint Francis University

Loretto, Pennsylvania
**Graduate School of Human Resource Management
and Industrial Relations**

Degree
Master of Human Resource Management (MHRM)

University Overview
A private college with nearly 2,000 students.

Program Description
Nontraditional evening program serves both the HR professional established in a career and those aspiring to enter the field. Ninety percent of the students are employed full-time. The Master of Arts program is career focused, comprehensive in scope, and structured to meet the needs of working professionals as well as persons studying full-time to earn the degree. This program is also offered at Dixon University Center in Harrisburg and in downtown Pittsburgh.

Degree Requirements

Total Credits Required:	33
Average Credits per Course:	3
Course Schedule:	Semester
Total Courses Required:	11
HR/IR Courses Required:	9
Average Time for Completion:	2 ½ - 3 years
Maximum Time Allowed for Completion:	5 years
Accepts Credits from Other Universities:	YES
Total:	N/A

Tuition

In-state	N/A	(per year)
	$484	(per credit hour)
Out-of-state	N/A	(per year)
	$484	(per credit hour)

Program Delivery

Traditional Day Program:	NO
Nontraditional Program:	YES
Evening Program:	YES
Weekend Program:	NO
Summer Courses:	N/A
Some Courses Online:	YES
Full Program Online:	NO
Distance Learning/Offsite:	YES
Executive Education:	N/A
Overseas Study Abroad:	NO

Faculty

Full-Time Faculty:	1
Part-Time Faculty:	28
Faculty to Student Ratio:	1:15

Primary Teaching Methods:

Case Study	Experiential Learning
Lecture	Student Presentations

Faculty Who Consult Outside:	1-24%

Faculty Involvement:
Co-editor, *Journal of Individual Employment Rights*
Member, writing panel for HRCI-SHRM
Top 5 Faculty Publications:
Books
Chapters

Students

Total Enrollment:			140
Full-Time Enrollment:			3%
Men:	31%	Women:	69%
Hispanic:	0%	African-American:	7%
Other Minorities:	1%	International:	0%
Average Age:	35	Age Range:	23-56
Work Full Time:			75-99%
HR Experience:			50-74%
Speak 2nd Language:			1-24%

Minimum Admission Requirements:
Two letters of recommendation
Other Considerations:
Work experience and letters of recommendation
Average Student Profile:

Work experience:	14 years

Program Resources

Students Required to Have Computers:			N/A
Video Teleconferencing:			YES
Physical Library Facilities:			N/A
Online Library Facilities:			N/A
HRCI Certification Preparation:			YES

Encourages student study groups
Links students to local SHRM chapter study groups
Bases the curriculum on the certification exam

SHRM Student Chapter:			YES
Fellowships:			NO
Scholarships:	9	AMT:	$1,000
Assistantships:	3-6	AMT:	$12,000
Eligibility:			All Students

Curriculum

Required Courses:
Performance Management
Compensation/Benefits
Development/Training
Recruitment/Retention
Employment Law
Employee Relations
Labor Relations
HR Measurement

Most Popular Elective Courses:	N/A
Career Tracks/Concentrations:	N/A
Internship Required:	NO

Career Services

Career Services Offered:

SHRM Student Chapter	Resume Services
Interview Training	Internships

Summer Internship Placement Rate:	N/A
Full-Time Placement Rate:	N/A
Average Starting Salary (Full-Time Graduates):	$52,000
Average Sign-on Bonus:	N/A
Companies Recruiting HR Master's Graduates:	N/A

Points of Excellence

Curriculum: Content derived from HRCI Body of Knowledge to link validated concerns of practitioners with academic program content. Students then take either the PHR or SPHR exam at the end of their program in lieu of a traditional comprehensive exam. This instructional approach reinforces the link between theory and practice and the value of critical thinking in addressing the practical concerns of people employed in the HR field.

Contact Information

Graduate School of HRMIR
Scotus Hall
Loretto, PA 15940-0600
www.francis.edu

Phillip Benham, Ph.D., SPHR, Director
Telephone: (814) 472-3026   FAX: (814) 472-3369
pbenham@francis.edu

Admission Deadlines:
Rolling admissions

Online Application:	NO

St. John Fisher College

Pittsford, New York

Degree
Master of Science in Human Resource Development (MSHRD)

University Overview
St. John Fisher College is a private, coeducational liberal arts college located in Pittsford, New York. The 125-acre campus has 1,500 full-time and 500 part-time students. The college offers 26 academic majors in the humanities, social sciences, sciences, business, and nursing. It also offers 12 graduate programs through the School of Graduate Education.

Program Description
The MS in Human Resource Development is for anyone interested in learning about organizational systems that focus on learning and training development, organization development, and career development. The program meets strictly in a weekend format, every other weekend, and can be completed in 20 months.

Degree Requirements

Total Credits Required:	33
Average Credits per Course:	3
Course Schedule:	Semester
Total Courses Required:	11
HR/IR Courses Required:	10
Average Time for Completion:	1¾ years
Maximum Time Allowed for Completion:	N/A
Accepts Credits from Other Universities:	YES
Total:	6 Hours

Tuition

In-state	N/A	(per year)
	$465	(per credit hour)
Out-of-state	N/A	(per year)
	N/A	(per credit hour)

Program Delivery

Traditional Day Program:	YES
Nontraditional Program:	YES
Evening Program:	NO
Weekend Program:	YES
Program Completed Evening/Weekend:	YES
Summer Courses:	N/A
Some Courses Online:	YES
Full Program Online:	NO
Distance Learning/Offsite:	YES
Executive Education:	YES
Overseas Study Abroad:	NO

Faculty

Full-Time Faculty:	1
Part-Time Faculty:	6
Faculty to Student Ratio:	1:10

Primary Teaching Methods:

Case Study	Research
Field Projects	Experiential Learning

Faculty Who Consult Outside:	100%

Faculty Involvement:
Top 5 Faculty Publications:

Students

Total Enrollment:			42
Full-Time Enrollment:			0%
Men:	33%	Women:	67%
Hispanic:	5%	African-American:	7%
Other Minorities:	0%	International:	0%
Average Age:	35	Age Range:	22-55
Work Full Time:			100%
Have HR Experience:			50-74%
Speak 2nd Language:			1-24%

Minimum Admission Requirements:

UGPA:	3.0
GRE or GMAT Scores:	N/A
Work Experience:	2 years

Other Considerations:

Extensive Work Experience	GRE
Conditional Matriculation for 12 credits to prove ability	

Average Student Profile:

UGPA:	3.3
GMAT Score:	N/A
Work Experience:	N/A

Program Resources

Students Required to Have Computers:		YES
Video Teleconferencing:		NO
Physical Library Facilities:		YES
Online Library Facilities:		YES
HRCI Certification Preparation:		YES
Offered as 3-credit course		
SHRM Student Chapter:		NO
URL:		
Fellowships:	NO	AMT:
Scholarships:	NO	AMT:
Assistantships:	NO	AMT:
Eligibility:		N/A

Curriculum

Required Courses:
- HR Strategy
- Management
- Development/Training
- HR Measurement
- Research Methods
- Organizational Development and Career
- Applied Research
- Interpersonal Communication and Group Dynamics
- Self Exploration
- Role of HRD in Organizations

Most Popular Elective Courses:
- HRCI Certification Prep
- Self Management Teams
- HR Management
- Leadership
- Grantwriting

Career Tracks/Concentrations:
- Human Resource Development

Internship Required:	NO

Career Services

Career Services Offered:

Mentoring	Interview Training
Field Trips	Campus Interview
Resume Services	Internships

Summer Internship Placement Rate:	N/A
Facilitate Placement:	YES
Full-Time Placement Rate:	60%
Internship Placement Rate:	N/A
Average Starting Salary (Full-Time Graduates):	$40,000
Average Sign-on Bonus:	N/A
Companies Recruiting HR Master's Graduates:	N/A

Points of Excellence

The mission of the Master of Science in Human Resource Development Program is to prepare graduates who can anticipate and recognize rapid changes in jobs, careers, work groups and organizations, contribute to workplace learning, and take a leadership role in providing strategies and practical solutions to the global business challenge affecting the workplace.

The M.S. in Human Resource Development at St. John Fisher College produces exemplary professionals in the field who have mastered a scholarly program of theory, research, and best practices and are recognized as leaders in the field.

Contact Information

St. John Fisher College
3690 East Avenue
Rochester, NY 14618
www.sjfc.edu

Administrative Contact
Holly Smith
Telephone: (716) 385-8045
hsmith@sjfc.edu

Faculty Contact
Dr. Marilynn Butler
Telephone: (716) 385-8157
mbutler@sjfc.edu

Admission Deadlines

August 1

Online Application:	YES

St. Joseph's College

Brooklyn, New York; Patchogue, New York
School of Adult and Professional Education

Degree

Master of Science in Management (MSM)

University Overview

St. Joseph's College is a private, coeducational institution with more than 4,000 students. It serves a diverse population of students who live within commuting distance of either the Brooklyn campus or the Suffolk County branch campus located in Patchogue, Long Island.

Program Description

The MS in Management began in 1999. It is designed for working adults holding leadership positions in the public service, private, and nonprofit sectors. Students may elect concentrations in Human Resources Management, Organizational Management, or Healthcare Management. The program emphasizes the development of abilities associated with superior managerial effectiveness as well as the importance of relating theoretical knowledge to issues or problems found in the students' workplaces.

Degree Requirements

Total Credits Required:	36
Average Credits per Course:	3
Course Schedule:	Semester
Total Courses Required:	12
HR/IR Courses Required:	3
Average Time for Completion:	2 years
Maximum Time Allowed for Completion:	N/A
Accepts Credits from Other Universities:	YES
Total:	6 Hours

Tuition

In-state	N/A	(per year)
	$399	(per credit hour)
Out-of-state	N/A	(per year)
	$399	(per credit hour)

Program Delivery

Traditional Day Program:	NO
Nontraditional Program:	YES
Evening Program:	YES
Weekend Program:	YES
Summer Courses:	YES
Some Courses Online:	NO
Full Program Online:	NO
Distance Learning/Offsite:	NO
Executive Education:	YES*
Overseas Study Abroad:	NO

Classes are scheduled one weekday evening and Saturdays, eight meetings per course, every other week, over 16 weeks.

Faculty

Full-Time Faculty:	7
Part-Time Faculty:	5
Faculty to Student Ratio:	1:8

Primary Teaching Methods:

Case Study	Research
Lecture	Group Discussion

Faculty Who Consult Outside:	25-49%
Faculty Involvement:	N/A

HR Advisor
Human Resources Management

Top 5 Faculty Publications:
Guide to Employee Handbook
Essential Facts of Employment
Guide to Corporate HR Policies & Procedures Manuals
HR Advisor

Students

Total Enrollment:			136
Full-Time Enrollment:			54%
Men:	28%	Women:	72%
Hispanic:	4%	African-American:	28%
Other Minorities:	2%	International:	2%
Average Age:	N/A	Age Range:	25-62
Work Full Time:			75-99%
HR Experience:			1-24%
Speak 2nd Language:			25-49%

Minimum Requirements:

Work experience:	2 years
UGPA:	3.0

Other Considerations:
Essay, strong work experience, and letters of reference

Average Student Profile:

UGPA:	3.32

Program Resources

Students Required to Have Computers:	NO
Video Teleconferencing:	YES
Physical Library Facilities:	YES
Online Library Facilities:	YES
HRCI Certification Preparation:	NO
SHRM Student Chapter:	YES
Fellowships:	NO
Scholarships:	NO
Assistantships:	NO
Eligibility:	N/A

Curriculum

Required Courses:
Accounting
Finance
HR Strategy
Development/Training
Employment Law
Management
Business Functional Areas
Statistics
Research Methods
Economics
Recruitment/Retention
Compensation/Benefits

Most Popular Elective Courses:
Strategic HR Management
Operations Management
Strategic Planning

Career Tracks/Concentrations:

Health Care Management	Human Resource Management
Organizational Management	

Internship Required:	NO

Career Services

Career Services Offered:

SHRM Student Chapter	Interview Training
Resume Services	

Summer Internship Placement Rate:	N/A
Full-Time Placement Rate: (all students employed)	N/A
Average Starting Salary:	N/A
Average Sign-on Bonus:	N/A
Companies Recruiting HR Master's Graduates:	N/A

Points of Excellence

Curriculum Effectiveness: The program identifies and promotes 20 specific abilities associated with superior managerial performance. These abilities are divided into three broad categories as follows:

- Goal and Action Management Abilities;
- People Management Abilities; and
- Analytic Reasoning Abilities.

Students assess data from self-assessment and diagnostic instruments and create an individualized plan to target those abilities they wish to develop over the course of the degree. Each course requires a Self-Directed Managerial Applications Component, which addresses an appropriate issue/problem/task within an actual organization. Integrative in purpose, the project will apply the knowledge from the course and will provide for the development of one or more of the managerial-effectiveness abilities discussed above.

Contact Information
School of Adult and Professional Education
MS in Management
155 W. Roe Blvd.
Patchogue, NY 11772
www.sjcny.edu

Mary A. Chance, MS, CPA, Director, MS in Management
Telephone: (631) 447-3390   FAX: (631) 654-1782
mchance@sjcny.edu

Admission Deadlines
Online Application: N/A

Salve Regina University

Newport, Rhode Island

Degree
Master of Arts in Human Resources (MAHR)

University Overview
Private institution based on the Catholic tradition, located next to the ocean in lovely Newport, Rhode Island.

Program Description
This nontraditional program is designed to provide a new approach to leadership and managerial education. The curriculum provides students with insight and education in human development, social values, ethics, and behavioral dynamics and their relationship to the management process. This program is recommended particularly for those students interested in human resource management or those working in not-for-profit organizations.

Degree Requirements
Total Credits Required:	36
Average Credits per Course:	3
Course Schedule:	Semester
Total Courses Required:	12
HR/IR Courses Required:	8
Average Time for Completion:	2-3 years
Maximum Time Allowed for Completion:	5 years
Accepts Credits from Other Universities:	YES
Total:	N/A

Tuition
In-state	N/A	(per year)
	$300	(per credit hour)
Out-of-state	N/A	(per year)
	$300	(per credit hour)

Program Delivery
Traditional Day Program:	NO
Nontraditional Program:	YES
Evening Program:	YES
Weekend Program:	NO
Summer Courses:	N/A
Some Courses Online:	YES
Full Program Online:	NO
Distance Learning/Offsite:	YES
Executive Education:	N/A
Overseas Study Abroad:	NO

Faculty
Full-Time Faculty:	4
Part-Time Faculty:	10
Faculty to Student Ratio:	1:10

Primary Teaching Methods:
Case Study	Team Projects
Lecture	Group Discussion

Faculty Who Consult Outside:	25-49%
Faculty Involvement:	N/A
Top 5 Faculty Publications:	N/A

Students
Total Enrollment:			79
Full-Time Enrollment:			12%
Men:	N/A	Women:	N/A
Hispanic:	N/A	African-American:	N/A
Other Minorities:	N/A	International:	N/A
Average Age:	N/A	Age Range:	25-45
Work Full Time:			75-99%
HR Experience:			75-99%
Speak 2nd Language:			N/A
Minimum Requirements:			N/A

Other Considerations:
Workplace achievement
Average Student Profile:
Work experience:	5 years

Program Resources
Students Required to Have Computers:		N/A
Video Teleconferencing:		NO
Physical Library Facilities:		N/A
Online Library Facilities:		N/A
HRCI Certification Preparation:		NO
SHRM Student Chapter:		NO
Fellowships:		NO
Scholarships:	8	AMT: N/A
Assistantships:		NO
Eligibility:		All Students

Curriculum
Required Courses:
Finance
Marketing
HR Strategy
International HR
Employment Law
Management
Employee Relations
Labor Relations
HR Measurement
Most Popular Elective Courses:
HR for Nonprofits
Career Tracks/Concentrations:	N/A
Internship Required:	NO

Career Services
Career Services Offered:
Resume Services	Interview Training
Campus Interviews	Internships

Summer Internship Placement Rate:	N/A
Full-Time Placement Rate:	N/A
Average Starting Salary (Full-Time Graduates):	N/A
Average Sign-on Bonus:	N/A
Companies Recruiting HR Master's Graduates:	N/A
Most students employed full-time

Points of Excellence
Faculty: The faculty is the program's most valuable resource. Faculty are chosen for the quality of their academic training and research, for their knowledge of managerial practice, and for their superior teaching skills. As graduates of leading doctoral, MBA, and law programs, they bring a wide variety of backgrounds and perspectives to the classroom.

Contact Information
Salve Regina University
100 Ochre Point Ave.
Newport, RI 02840
www.salve.edu

Linda Perry, Director of Post Baccalaureate Marketing &
Recruitment
Telephone: (401) 341-3241   FAX: (401) 341-2973
perryl@salve.edu

Admission Deadlines
Online Application: NO

San Francisco State University

San Francisco, California
Psychology Department

Degree
Master of Science in Psychology (Concentration in
Industrial/Organizational Psychology) (MSP)

University Overview
San Francisco State is a public institution, part of the California
State University System. The campus is located in the southwest-
ern part of the city, a short distance from the Pacific Ocean.

Program Description
The program takes a science/practitioner approach and provides
a strong theoretical and methodological education. It is a terminal degree program with the aims of preparing students for professional level work in organizational behavior, organizational
research and human resources functions, as well as continued
higher education in the field of Industrial/Organizational
Pyschology.

Degree Requirements
Total Credits Required:	36
Average Credits per Course:	3
Course Schedule:	Semester
Total Courses Required:	12
HR/IR Courses Required:	N/A
Average Time for Completion:	2 ½ years
Maximum Time Allowed for Completion:	7 years
Accepts Credits from Other Universities:	YES
Total:	6 Hours

Tuition
In-state	$1,904	(per year)
	N/A	(per credit hour)
Out-of-state	$1,904	(per year)
	+$246	(per credit hour)

Program Delivery
Traditional Day Program:	NO
Nontraditional Program:	YES
Evening Program:	YES
Weekend Program:	NO
Program Completed Evening/Weekend:	YES
Summer Courses:	NO
Some Courses Online:	NO
Full Program Online:	NO
Distance Learning/Offsite:	NO
Executive Education:	NO
Overseas Study Abroad:	NO

Faculty
Full-Time Faculty:		3
Part-Time Faculty:		2
Faculty to Student Ratio:		1:15
Primary Teaching Methods:		
Field Projects	Research	
Student Presentation	Group Discussion	
Faculty Who Consult Outside:		1-24%
Faculty Involvement:		
Top 5 Faculty Publications:		
Employee Selection		

Students
Total Enrollment:			38
Full-Time Enrollment:			63%
Men:	18%	Women:	82%
Hispanic:	5%	African-American:	3%
Other Minorities:	11%	International:	8%
Average Age:	29	Age Range:	23-43
Work Full Time:			1-24%
Have HR Experience:			25-49%
Speak 2nd Language:			25-49%
Minimum Admission Requirements:			
UGPA:			3.0
GRE or GMAT Scores:			1550
Work Experience:			NONE
Other Considerations:			
Average Student Profile:			
UGPA:			3.5
GMAT Score:			1600
Work Experience:			1 year

Program Resources
Students Required to Have Computers:		NO
Video Teleconferencing:		NO
Physical Library Facilities:		YES
Online Library Facilities:		YES
HRCI Certification Preparation:		NO
SHRM Student Chapter:		NO
URL:		
Fellowships:	NO	AMT:
Scholarships:	YES	AMT:	Varies
Assistantships:	YES	AMT:	$10-12/Hr
Eligibility:	Full-Time Enrollment (for Scholarship)

Curriculum
Required Courses:
Overview of Industrial/Organizational Psychology
Seminar in Industrial Psychology
Seminar in Organizational Psychology
Research Methods
Data Analysis – Multiple Regression
Most Popular Elective Courses:
Human Resources
International Business Courses
Compensation
Instructional Technology Courses
Career Tracks/Concentrations:
Human Resources   Organizational Development
Internship Required: YES

Career Services
Career Services Offered:
Internships
Summer Internship Placement Rate:	N/A
Facilitate Placement:	NO
Full-Time Placement Rate:	N/A
Internship Placement Rate:	N/A

Average Starting Salary (Full-Time Graduates):	N/A
Average Sign-on Bonus:	N/A
Companies Recruiting HR Master's Graduates:	N/A

Contact Information
San Francisco State University
1600 Holloway Avenue
San Francisco, CA 94132
www.sfsu.edu

Faculty Contact
Dr. Kathleen Mosier
Telephone: (415) 338-1059
kmosier@sfsu.edu

Admission Deadlines
March 1 for Fall admission
Online Application: YES

Southwest Missouri State University

Springfield, Missouri
Department of Psychology

Degree
Master of Science in Industrial and Organizational Psychology
(MSIOP)

University Overview
State university with approximately 17,000 students, is located in Springfield, Missouri.

Program Description
Following a scientist-practitioner model, the program reflects standards promulgated by the Counsel for Applied Master's Programs and curricular guidelines developed by the Society for Industrial and Organizational Psychology. Designed to develop research skills and general knowledge of Industrial/Organizational content areas, the program's focus is on application of psychological principles and research methods in business, industry, government and nonprofit organizations.

Degree Requirements

Total Credits Required:	47
Average Credits per Course:	3
Course Schedule:	Semester
Total Courses Required:	16
HR/IR Courses Required:	10
Average Time for Completion:	2 ¼ years
Maximum Time Allowed for Completion:	8 years
Accepts Credits from Other Universities:	YES
Total:	14 Hours

Tuition

In-state	$2,664	(per year)
	$111	(per credit hour)
Out-of-state	$5,328	(per year)
	$222	(per credit hour)

Program Delivery

Traditional Day Program:	YES
Nontraditional Program:	NO
Evening Program:	NO
Weekend Program:	NO
Program Completed Evening/Weekend:	NO
Summer Courses:	YES

Some Courses Online:	NO
Full Program Online:	NO
Distance Learning/Offsite:	NO
Executive Education:	NO
Overseas Study Abroad:	NO

Faculty

Full-Time Faculty:	5
Part-Time Faculty:	1
Faculty to Student Ratio:	1:4

Primary Teaching Methods:

Field Projects	Lecture
Student Presentation	Group Discussion

Faculty Who Consult Outside:
Faculty Involvement:
Membership Committee, Society for Industrial and Organizational Psychology
Program Committee, Society for Industrial and Organizational Psychology
Program Committee, Academy of Management
Presenter, 2001 Professional Development Workshop, Academy of Management
Top 5 Faculty Publications:
Small Group Research
Military Psychology
Journal of Business Psychology
International Journal of Conflict Management

Students

Total Enrollment:			20
Full-Time Enrollment:			20
Men:	35%	Women:	65%
Hispanic:	10%	African-American:	10%
Other Minorities:	N/A	International:	10%
Average Age:	N/A	Age Range:	N/A
Work Full Time:			N/A
Have HR Experience:			N/A
Speak 2nd Language:			N/A

Minimum Admission Requirements:

UGPA:	3.0
GRE Scores: 1000 V&Q (no less than 470 on either); 550 Psych	
Work Experience:	NONE

Other Considerations:
Average Student Profile:

UGPA:	3.5
GMAT Score:	GRE (V&Q) 1024; GRE Psych 529
Work Experience:	NONE

Program Resources

Students Required to Have Computers:			NO
Video Teleconferencing:			YES
Physical Library Facilities:			YES
Online Library Facilities:			YES
HRCI Certification Preparation:			NO
SHRM Student Chapter:			YES
URL:			
Fellowships:	NO	AMT:	
Scholarships:	NO	AMT:	
Assistantships:	YES	AMT:	$6,150/yr
Eligibility:		Full-Time Enrollment	

Curriculum
Required Courses:
Development/Training
Multivariate Statistics
Research Methods
Social Psychology
Professional and Ethical Issues

Personnel Psychology
Organizational Psychology
Selection and Placement
Personnel Practicum
Organizational Practicum
Most Popular Elective Courses:
Group Processes
Performance Appraisal
Occupational Health
Compensation Management
Labor Law and Employment Discrimination
Career Tracks/Concentrations:
HR practitioner   Applied Researcher
Consulting
Internship Required: NO

Career Services
Career Services Offered:	N/A
Summer Internship Placement Rate:	N/A
Facilitate Placement:	YES
Full-Time Placement Rate:	N/A
Internship Placement Rate:	N/A
Average Starting Salary (Full-Time Graduates):	$46,728
Average Sign-on Bonus:	N/A
Companies Recruiting HR Master's Graduates:	N/A

Points of Excellence
This program offers many advantages to qualified students, including small class size (average 10 students) and a low faculty-student ratio (1:4). All of students seeking graduate funding have received funding through departmental or university assistantships that pay tuition for Fall, Spring and Summer semesters and provide a yearly stipend. Students receive organizational experience through practicum and applied class projects. Most students seeking internships receive paid internships. Students have an opportunity to be involved in faculty research projects. Many develop their own projects and gain supervisory experience of research assistants. Many have their work accepted for panel or poster presentations at various national conferences. An active graduate network offering current students internship opportunities, mentoring, and job placement information.

Contact Information
Department of Psychology
Southwest Missouri State University
901 South National Avenue
Springfield, MO 65804
psychology.smsu.edu/io

Administrative Contact
Carol F. Shoptaugh, Associate Professor/Program Coordinator
Telephone: (417) 836-5788 or (417) 836-4790
FAX: (417) 836-8330
cfs280f@smsu.edu

Admission Deadlines
March 1 for early admission, mid-August for late applications (if vacancies available)
Online Application: N/A

Southwest Texas State University

San Marcos, Texas
Department of Health Services Research

Degree
Master of Human Resources (MSHR)

University Overview
Comprehensive public university offering undergraduate and graduate programs to more than 23,000 students. San Marcos is approximately 35 miles from San Antonio and Austin, in one of the fastest growing high-tech areas in the country.

Program Description
The program is designed for the working adult and offers Internet-based courses. The program emphasis is on basic content for Human Resource Development (Training) and Human Resource Management (Personnel). All students are encouraged to take the SHRM exam. Technology content is emphasized in courses on HR Information Systems, Internet-based training, and HR metrics and decision support systems. Courses help to prepare HR professionals as equal partners in strategic planning and the company bottom line.

Degree Requirements
Total Credits Required:	38-40
Average Credits per Course:	3
Course Schedule:	Semester
Total Courses Required:	13
HR/IR Courses Required:	10
Average Time for Completion:	2 Years
Maximum Time Allowed for Completion:	6 Years
Accepts Credits from Other Universities:	YES
Total:	6 Hours

Tuition
In-state	$4,584	(per year)
	$150	(per credit hour)
Out-of-state	$13,626	(per year)
	$350	(per credit hour)

Program Delivery
Traditional Day Program:	NO
Nontraditional Program:	YES
Evening Program:	YES
Weekend Program:	YES
Summer Courses:	YES
Some Courses Online:	YES
Full Program Online:	NO
Distance Learning/Offsite:	Under Development
Executive Education:	NO
Overseas Study Abroad:	YES

Faculty
Full-Time Faculty:	3
Part-Time Faculty:	5
Faculty to Student Ratio:	1:10

Primary Teaching Methods:
Team Projects   Student Presentations
Lecture   Web-based Instruction
Computer Simulations
Faculty Who Consult Outside:	25-49%

Faculty Involvement:
Board member, Accessible Web Authoring Resources and Education Center (AWARE)
Program Chair, Universal Web Accessibility Symposium 2000

Top 5 Faculty Publications: N/A

Students

Total Enrollment:			40
Full-Time Enrollment:			20%
Men:	30%	Women:	70%
Hispanic:	15%	African-American:	32%
Other Minorities:	4%	International:	0%
Average Age:	32	Age Range:	24-50
Work Full Time:			75-99%
HR Experience:			25-49%
Speak 2nd Language:			1-24%

Minimum Admission Requirements:
UGPA:	2.75 (for last 60 units)
GRE:	800

Other Considerations:
Conditional admission, work experience

Average Student Profile:
GRE Score:	920

Program Resources

Students Required to Have Computers:			NO
Video Teleconferencing:			YES
Physical Library Facilities:			YES
Online Library Facilities:			YES
HRCI Certification Preparation:			YES

Encourages student study groups
Links students to local SHRM chapter study groups
Offers the SHRM Learning System as a teaching tool
Bases the curriculum on the certification exam content

SHRM Student Chapter:			YES
Fellowships:	0	AMT:	N/A
Scholarships:	0	AMT:	N/A
Assistantships:	2	AMT:	$12,000
Eligibility:			All Students

Curriculum

Required Courses:
HR Management
Innovations in Multimedia for Health Care
Research Methods
Human Resource Development
Program Design
Interpersonal Relations
Training Needs Analysis

Most Popular Elective Courses:
Public Relations
Compensation & Benefits
HR System Metrics
Management of Occupational Health & Safety
Healthcare Labor Relations
Trends
Employment Law
Grant Writing

Career Tracks/Concentrations:	N/A
Internship Required:	YES

Career Services

Career Services Offered:
Mentoring	Field Trips
SHRM Student Chapter	Resume Services
Internships	

Summer Internship Placement Rate:	N/A
Full-Time Placement Rate:	75-80%

Average Starting Salary (Full-Time Graduates):	$42,000
Average Sign-on Bonus:	N/A
Companies Recruiting HR Master's Graduates:	N/A

Points of Excellence

The program is individualized to meet the needs of full-time or part-time students and experienced and non-experienced students. There is a high level of interaction among students and the faculty. The student body is highly diversified. Students report high satisfaction with program.

Contact Information

Healthcare Human Resources
Southwest Texas State University
601 University Dr.
San Marcos, TX 78666-4616
www.swt.edu

Dr. Charles Johnson, Chair, Health Services & Research
Telephone: (512) 245-3492   FAX: (512) 245-8712
Charles.Johnson@swt.edu

Dr. Deanie French, HHR Program Director
Telephone: (512) 245-3497   FAX: (512) 245-8712
elearn@Deanie.org

Admission Deadlines

June 15 for Fall admissions
Online Application:	NO

Tarleton State University

Killeen, Texas
College of Business Administration

Degree

Master of Science in Human Resource Management (MS-HRM)

University Overview

Tarleton State University is a member of the Texas A&M public coeducational institution. The student population is as diverse as the city of Killeen, which has been named one of the most diverse cities in the United States.

Program Description

The MS-HRM is designed to improve the strategic, technical, and interpersonal skills of professionals engaged in the management and development of human resources. Students develop critical skills in research and job analysis, recruitment and selection, training and development, compensation and benefits, labor relations, and organizational effectiveness.

Degree Requirements

Total Credits Required:	36
Average Credits per Course:	3
Course Schedule:	Semester
Total Courses Required:	12
HR/IR Courses Required:	7
Average Time for Completion:	2-3 years
Maximum Time Allowed for Completion:	6 years
Accepts Credits from Other Universities:	YES
Total:	N/A

Tuition

In-state	$1,350	(per year)
	$74	(per credit hour)
Out-of-state	$5,000	(per year)
	$278	(per credit hour)

Program Delivery

Traditional Day Program:	YES
Nontraditional Program:	YES
Evening Program:	YES
Weekend Program:	NO
Summer Courses:	N/A
Some Courses Online:	YES
Full Program Online:	NO
Distance Learning/Offsite:	YES
Executive Education:	N/A
Overseas Study Abroad:	YES

Faculty

Full-Time Faculty:	6
Part-Time Faculty:	0
Faculty to Student Ratio:	1:20

Primary Teaching Methods:

Experiential Learning	Team Projects
Lecture	Student Presentations
Seminars	Guest Speakers
Computer Simulations	

Faculty Who Consult Outside:	1-24%

Faculty Involvement:
Local SHRM chapter
Chair, Southwest Academy of Management, HR track program
Rotary international business exchange liaison

Top 5 Faculty Publications:	N/A

Students

Total Enrollment:			55
Full-Time Enrollment:			100%
Men:	46%	Women:	54%
Hispanic:	27%	African-American:	24%
Other Minorities:	3%	International:	1%
Average Age:	34	Age Range:	26-58
Work Full Time:			75-99%
HR Experience:			1-24%
Speak 2nd Language:			1-24%

Minimum Admission Requirements:

UGPA:	3.0
GMAT:	550

Other Considerations:
GRE or GMAT scores compensate for lower UGPA
Average Student Profile:

Work experience:	7 years; approx. 50% military

Program Resources

Students Required to Have Computers:			N/A
Video Teleconferencing:			YES
Physical Library Facilities:			N/A
Online Library Facilities:			N/A
HRCI Certification Preparation:			YES

Encourages student study groups
Links students to local SHRM chapter study groups
Bases the curriculum on certification course content

SHRM Student Chapter:			YES
Fellowships:			N/A
Scholarships:	10	AMT:	N/A
Assistantships:			N/A
Eligibility:			All Students

Curriculum

Required Courses:
HR Strategy
Compensation/Benefits
Development/Training
Recruitment/Retention
Employment Law
Management
Labor Relations
Job Design/Analysis
Organization Theory
Research Methods
Most Popular Elective Courses:
I/O Psychology

Career Tracks/Concentrations:	N/A
Internship Required:	NO

Career Services

Career Services Offered:

SHRM Student Chapter	Resume Services
Internships	

Summer Internship Placement Rate:	N/A
Full-Time Placement Rate:	N/A
Average Starting Salary (Full-Time Graduates):	N/A
Average Sign-on Bonus:	N/A
Companies Recruiting HR Master's Graduates:	N/A

Points of Excellence

Curriculum: Content is developed through a competency-based instructional system design process model and is centered on the HRCI "HR Body of Knowledge." It is focused on developing HR professionals who are technically competent and confident in all functional areas, and many of the courses focus on experiential outcomes, combining theory-based pedagogy with applied processes.

All students are required to pass a program-comprehensive examination during their final semester. Further, regular review of course evaluations and statistical assessment of outcomes are performed to evaluate the extent to which courses provide academically challenging experiences to students. Professional advisory council suggestions are integrated to improve the program's overall effectiveness.

Students: HRM students are rich in diversity. Many students have traveled the world and bring uncommon insights to class discussions and presentations.

Contact Information

MS Human Resource Management Program
1901 S. Clear Creek Rd.
Killeen, TX 76549
www.tarleton.edu/~blyon

Dr. Barbara Lyon, SPHR, Associate Professor
Telephone: (254) 519-5444   FAX: (254) 526-8403
lyon@tarleton.edu

Admission Deadlines

Online Application:	YES

Texas A&M University

College Station, Texas
Management, Lowry Mays College of Business

Degree
Master of Science in Human Resource Management (MSHRM)

University Overview
State university in small college town with 43,000 uniquely loyal and devoted students.

Program Description

This full-time traditional day program offers a strong business/management-based generalist program. Through a combination of core courses, electives, and leadership development opportunities, the MS program develops and deepens the competencies needed for entry-level and long-term career effectiveness. All students can be made eligible for in-state tuition.

Degree Requirements

Total Credits Required:	51
Average Credits per Course:	3
Course Schedule:	Semester
Total Courses Required:	17
HR/IR Courses Required:	13
Average Time for Completion:	1 ½-2 years
Maximum Time Allowed for Completion:	5 years
Accepts Credits from Other Universities:	YES
Total:	12 Hours

Tuition

In-state	$4,000	(per year)
	$114	(per credit hour)
Out-of-state	$7,000	(per year)
	N/A	(per credit hour)

Program Delivery

Traditional Day Program:	YES
Nontraditional Program:	NO
Evening Program:	NO
Weekend Program:	NO
Summer Courses:	YES*
Some Courses Online:	Under Development
Full Program Online:	NO
Distance Learning/Offsite:	NO
Executive Education:	NO
Overseas Study Abroad:	YES

Only core and internship

Faculty

Full-Time Faculty:	23
Part-Time Faculty:	12
Faculty to Student Ratio:	1:10

Primary Teaching Methods:

Field Projects	Experiential Learning
Student Presentation	Lecture

Faculty Who Consult Outside:	1-24%

Faculty Involvement:
Chair, BPS Division, Academy of Management
Program Chair, Society Industrial/Organizational Psychology
Chair-elect, OB Division, Academy of Management
Executive Committee, HR Division of Academy of Management
Program Chair, AIB

Top 5 Faculty Publications:	See web site

Students

Total Enrollment:			40
Full-Time Enrollment:			92%
Men:	35%	Women:	65%
Hispanic:	10%	African-American:	0%
Other Minorities:	13%	International:	20%
Average Age:	25	Age Range:	23-34
Work Full Time:			1-24%
HR Experience:			1-24%
Speak 2nd Language:			1-24%

Minimum Admission Requirements:

GMAT Score:	525
GRE Score:	1050
UGPA:	3.0
Work experience:	0

Other Considerations:
HR-related work experience compensates for low scores

Average Student Profile:

Work experience:	1.5 years
GMAT Score:	570
GRE Score:	1100
UGPA:	3.6

Program Resources

Students Required to Have Computers:			NO
Video Teleconferencing:			YES
Physical Library Facilities:			YES
Online Library Facilities:			YES
HRCI Certification Preparation:			NO
SHRM Student Chapter:			YES
Fellowships:			NO
Scholarships:	20	AMT:	$1,000
Assistantships:	10	AMT:	$4,600 + summer
Eligibility:			Full-Time Enrollment

Curriculum

Required Courses:
HR Strategy
International HR
Development & Training
Compensation/Benefits
Recruitment/Retention
Employment Law
Employee Relations
Business Functional Areas
Research Methods
Business Statistics
Org. Development & Practicum Change Internship

Most Popular Elective Courses:
Negotiations
Managing Creativity

Career Services Offered:

SHRM Student Chapter	Interview Training
Resume Services	Campus Interviews
Internships	

Career Tracks/Concentrations:	N/A
Internship Required:	YES

Career Services

Career Services Offered:

SHRM Student Chapter	Interview Training
Resume Services	Campus Interviews
Internships	

Summer Internship Placement Rate:	100%
Full-Time Placement Rate:	100%
Average Starting Salary (Full-Time Graduates):	$62,000
Average Sign-on Bonus:	$3,000
Companies Recruiting HR Master's Graduates:	70

Points of Excellence

Placement: Working with employers that have operations in Texas ensures that internship assignments are meaningful, well paid, and likely to lead to permanent employment. These internships, along with the smaller size of our program, are major factors in ensuring that all of our graduates find full-time employment in HR by the time they graduate.

Network of former students provides access to HR managers throughout the United States and the world. These managers return to campus to conduct workshops for students on how to interview, how to prepare resumes, and career counseling in general. They actively help graduates obtain jobs.

Contact Information
Department of Management
Texas A & M University
TAMU 4221
College Station, TX 77843-4221
www.tamu.edu

Dr. Ramona Paetzold
Telephone: (979) 845-5429   FAX: (979) 845-3420
Rpaetzold@tamu.edu

Admission Deadlines
Online Application: YES

Towson University

Towson, Maryland
Department of Psychology

Degree
Master of Human Resource Development (MSHRD)

University Overview
Member of the University of Maryland System with approximately 12,000 students.

Program Description
This interdisciplinary program is designed to provide students with specific knowledge and practical skills within a variety of human resource fields. Focusing on disciplines of psychology, management, instructional technology, education, and communications, the curriculum is designed to meet the needs of individuals with varied academic backgrounds and professional experience. Most students work full time.

The Educational Leadership Track is designed for certified teachers and other licensed professionals working in schools who aspire to become educational leaders and administrators at local and state levels. This interdisciplinary program is approved by the Maryland State Department of Education for those seeking certification as Administrator I.

Degree Requirements
Total Credits Required:	36
Average Credits per Course:	3
Course Schedule:	Semester
Total Courses Required:	12
HR/IR Courses Required:	7
Average Time for Completion:	2 years
Maximum Time Allowed for Completion:	7 years
Accepts Credits from Other Universities:	YES
Total:	18 Hours

Tuition
In-state	$4,336	(per year)
	$211	(per credit hour)
Out-of-state	$9,940	(per year)
	$425	(per credit hour)

Program Delivery
Traditional Day Program:	YES
Nontraditional Program:	YES
Evening Program:	YES
Weekend Program:	NO
Summer Courses:	YES
Some Courses Online:	YES
Full Program Online:	NO
Distance Learning/Offsite:	YES

Executive Education:	NO
Overseas Study Abroad:	YES

Faculty
Full-Time Faculty:	3
Part-Time Faculty:	6
Faculty to Student Ratio:	1:20

Primary Teaching Methods:

Case Study	Team Projects
Computer-Aided Instruction	Experiential Learning
Field Projects	Student Presentations
Lecture	Group Discussion

Faculty Who Consult Outside:	25-49%
Faculty Involvement:	
Maryland Chapter, ASTD	
Top 5 Faculty Publications:	N/A

Students
Total Enrollment:			150
Full-Time Enrollment:			25%
Men:	22%	Women:	78%
Hispanic:	2%	African-American:	23%
Other Minorities:	1%	International:	7%
Average Age:	N/A	Age Range:	N/A
Work Full Time:			75-99%
HR Experience:			50-74%
Speak 2nd Language:			1-24%
Minimum Admission Requirements:			
Work Experience and UGPA			
Other Considerations:			N/A
Average Student Profile:			
Work experience:			10 years

Program Resources
Students Required to Have Computers:	NO
Video Teleconferencing:	NO
Physical Library Facilities:	YES
Online Library Facilities:	YES
HRCI Certification Preparation:	NO
SHRM Student Chapter:	YES
Fellowships:	NO
Scholarships:	YES
Assistantships:	1 AMT: $4,000
Eligibility:	Full-Time Enrollment (Part-Time for Scholarship)

Curriculum
Required Courses:
- Introduction to HR
- HRD
- Training & Development
- Change in the Workplace
- Organizational Behavior

Most Popular Elective Courses:
- Conflict Management
- Labor Economics & Relations
- Personnel Selection
- Business Writing
- Employee Relations
- Team Building

Career Tracks/Concentrations:

General Track	Educational Leadership Track

Internship Required:	NO

Career Services
Career Services Offered:

SHRM Student Chapter	Resume Services
Interview Training	Internships

Summer Internship Placement Rate:	N/A

Full-Time Placement Rate:	N/A
Average Starting Salary (Full-Time Graduates):	$38,000
Average Sign-on Bonus:	N/A
Companies Recruiting HR Master's Graduates:	N/A

Points of Excellence

Students: The HRD program is designed for individuals seeking to enter the human resource field, mid-career professionals seeking opportunities for professional development and career advancement, working adults seeking a career change, and recent undergraduates who wish to pursue graduate study. Applicants do not need prior work experience in human resources to be eligible for admission.

Contact Information

Department of Psychology
Towson University
8000 York Rd.
Towson, MD 21252-0001
www.towson.edu

Dr. Larry Froman, Program Director, HRD
Telephone: (410) 704-2678   FAX: (410) 704-3800
lfroman@towson.edu

Admission Deadlines

Rolling admissions
Online Application: YES

Trevecca Nazarene University

Nashville, Tennessee
School of Business and Management

Degree

Master of Science in Management (MSM)

University Overview

Trevecca Nazarene University is a private liberal arts university in the heart of downtown Nashville, Tennessee. Trevecca Nazarene University is part of the Church of the Nazarene Denomination.

Program Description

This program focuses on training entry-level and upper-level management students for success in the changing business market. The program has the traditional business core classes, as well as a focus on Quality Management and Human Resources.

Degree Requirements

Total Credits Required:	36
Average Credits per Course:	3
Course Schedule:	Semester
Total Courses Required:	10
HR/IR Courses Required:	1
Average Time for Completion:	1 ¾ years
Maximum Time Allowed for Completion:	6 years
Accepts Credits from Other Universities:	YES
Total:	6 Hours

Tuition

In-state	$7,000	(per year)
	N/A	(per credit hour)
Out-of-state	$7,000	(per year)
	N/A	(per credit hour)

Program Delivery

Traditional Day Program:	NO
Nontraditional Program:	YES
Evening Program:	YES
Weekend Program:	NO
Program Completed Evening/Weekend:	YES
Summer Courses:	YES
Some Courses Online:	NO
Full Program Online:	NO
Distance Learning/Offsite:	NO
Executive Education:	NO
Overseas Study Abroad:	NO

Faculty

Full-Time Faculty:	8
Part-Time Faculty:	4
Faculty to Student Ratio:	1:20
Primary Teaching Methods:	

Case Study	Team Projects
Student Presentation	Lecture
Field Projects	Group Discussion

Faculty Who Consult Outside:	25-49%
Faculty Involvement:	
Top 5 Faculty Publications:	

Students

Total Enrollment:			100
Full-Time Enrollment:			100
Men:	50%	Women:	50%
Hispanic:	3%	African-American:	40%
Other Minorities:	10%	International:	2%
Average Age:	35	Age Range:	25-60
Work Full Time:			75-99%
Have HR Experience:			1-24%
Speak 2nd Language:			1-24%
Minimum Admission Requirements:			
UGPA:			2.5
GRE or GMAT Scores:			350 GMAT
Work Experience:			3 years
Other Considerations:			
Trade GMAT for GPA of 2.8 or higher			
Average Student Profile:			
UGPA:			3.0
GMAT Score:			410
Work Experience:			3 years

Program Resources

Students Required to Have Computers:			NO
Video Teleconferencing:			NO
Physical Library Facilities:			YES
Online Library Facilities:			YES
HRCI Certification Preparation:			YES
SHRM Student Chapter:			NO
URL:			
Fellowships:	NO	AMT:	
Scholarships:	NO	AMT:	
Assistantships:	NO	AMT:	
Eligibility:			N/A

Curriculum

Required Courses:
Accounting
Finance
Marketing
Management
HR Strategy
Production Operations Management
Business Strategy
Total Quality Management

Most Popular Elective Courses: N/A
Career Tracks/Concentrations:
  Management   Finance
  Nonprofit   Manufacturing
Internship Required: NO

Career Services
Career Services Offered: N/A
Summer Internship Placement Rate: N/A
Facilitate Placement: NO
Full-Time Placement Rate: N/A
Internship Placement Rate: N/A
Average Starting Salary (Full-Time Graduates): N/A
Average Sign-on Bonus: N/A
Companies Recruiting HR Master's Graduates: N/A

Contact Information
Trevecca Nazarene University
333 Murfeesboro Road
Nashville, TN 37210
www.Trevecca.edu

Administrative Contact
Jon Burch, Assistant Director
Telephone: (615) 248-1535
jburch@trevecca.edu

Faculty Contact
Dr. Mary Ann Meiners
Telephone: (615) 248-1612
mmeiners@trevecca.edu

Admission Deadlines
N/A
Online Application: YES

Troy State University, Fort Benning

Fort Benning, Georgia
Department of Business and Management

Degree
Master of Science in Human Resource Management (MSHRM)

University Overview
Troy State University, Fort Benning, Georgia, campus offers the working adult evening, weekend, and Internet courses for undergraduate and graduate degrees in Business and Management.

Program Description
The MSHRM degree is an operational, rather than an academic, degree designed to prepare graduates for HRM positions in the public or private sectors.

Degree Requirements
Total Credits Required: 30
Average Credits per Course: 3
Course Schedule: 5 terms per academic year
Total Courses Required: 10
HR/IR Courses Required: 8
Average Time for Completion: 2 years
Maximum Time Allowed for Completion: 8 years
Accepts Credits from Other Universities: YES
Total: 12 Hours

Tuition
In-state $4,350   (per year)
                   $145   (per credit hour)
Out-of-state $4,350   (per year)
                   $145   (per credit hour)

Program Delivery
Traditional Day Program: NO
Nontraditional Program: YES
  Evening Program: YES
  Weekend Program: YES
  Program Completed Evening/Weekend: YES
  Summer Courses: YES
  Some Courses Online: YES
  Full Program Online: NO
  Distance Learning/Offsite: YES
  Executive Education: YES
  Overseas Study Abroad: YES

Faculty
Full-Time Faculty: 3
Part-Time Faculty: 12
Faculty to Student Ratio: 1:20
Primary Teaching Methods:
  Lecture   Team Projects
  Student Presentation Group Discussion
Faculty Who Consult Outside: 1-24%
Faculty Involvement:
Top 5 Faculty Publications:

Students
Total Enrollment: 100
Full-Time Enrollment: 50
  Men: N/A   Women: N/A
  Hispanic: N/A   African-American: N/A
  Other Minorities: N/A International N/A:
  Average Age: N/A   Age Range: N/A
Work Full Time: 75-99%
Have HR Experience: 25-49%
Speak 2nd Language: 1-24%
Minimum Admission Requirements:
  UGPA: 2.5
  GRE Score: 850
  GMAT Score: 450
  Work Experience: NONE
  Combined
Other Considerations:
  Students not meeting GPA and/or GRE, GMAT or MAT minimums are admitted on a conditional status and are reviewed after completion of the first four courses.
  Average Student Profile:
  UGPA: N/A
  GRE/GMAT Score: N/A
  Work Experience: N/A

Program Resources
Students Required to Have Computers: NO
Video Teleconferencing: YES
Physical Library Facilities: YES
Online Library Facilities: YES
HRCI Certification Preparation: YES
  Encourages study groups
  Offer SHRM Learning System as teaching tool
  Offer practice exams
  Curriculum based on certification exam
  Preparation courses offered online
SHRM Student Chapter: YES
URL:

Fellowships:	NO	AMT:
Scholarships:	YES	AMT:
Assistantships:	NO	AMT:
Eligibility:		N/A

Curriculum

Required Courses:
- HR Strategy
- Recruitment/Retention
- Compensation/Benefits
- Employment Law
- Development/Training
- HR Measurement
- Performance Management
- Performance Management, Organizational
- Organizational Behavior

Most Popular Elective Courses:
- Labor Relations
- Business Ethics
- Leadership and Motivation
- Organizational Development and Change

Career Tracks/Concentrations:	N/A
Internship Required:	NO

Career Services

Career Services Offered:

Internships	SHRM Student Chapter

Summer Internship Placement Rate:	N/A
Facilitate Placement:	YES
Full-Time Placement Rate:	N/A
Internship Placement Rate:	N/A
Average Starting Salary (Full-Time Graduates):	N/A
Average Sign-on Bonus:	N/A
Companies Recruiting HR Master's Graduates:	N/A

Points of Excellence

The strengths of the TSU-Fort Benning's MSHRM program are in both its operational HR functional area content and the quality of its full- and part-time faculty, all of whom have terminal degrees in the appropriate area and most of whom are either professionally certified (SPHR) or working in the HR area of the course they are instructing.

Contact Information

Troy State University
P.O. Box 2456
Ft. Benning, GA 31995-2456
www.tsufb.edu

Administrative Contact
Ms. Felecia Kelly, Graduate Program Coordinator
Telephone: (706) 689-4744
kellyf@trojan.troyst.edu

Faculty Contact
Dr. Ron Robinson, SPHR, Associate Director for Business and Management Programs
Telephone: (706) 689-4744
robinson@trojan.troyst.edu

Admission Deadlines

Year-Round Admission

Online Application:	YES

Troy State University, Montgomery

Montgomery, Alabama
Division of Business

Degree
Master of Science in Human Resource Management (MSHRM)

University Overview
State-funded university with an enrollment of 3,500 students. Students typically attend school part time and are working adults.

Program Description
Course content design balanced toward SPHR certification.

Degree Requirements

Total Credits Required:	50
Average Credits per Course:	3
Course Schedule:	Semester
Total Courses Required:	10
HR/IR Courses Required:	9
Average Time for Completion:	1 ½ years
Maximum Time Allowed for Completion:	N/A
Accepts Credits from Other Universities:	YES
Total:	9 Hours (Semester)

Tuition

In-state	$2,480	(per year)
	$62	(per credit hour)
Out-of-state	$4,960	(per year)
	N/A	(per credit hour)

Program Delivery

Traditional Day Program:	NO
Nontraditional Program:	YES
Evening Program:	YES
Weekend Program:	YES
Summer Courses:	YES
Some Courses Online:	YES
Full Program Online:	NO
Distance Learning/Offsite:	YES
Executive Education:	YES*
Overseas Study Abroad:	YES

Master of Science in Management, every other weekend, one year, cohort graduation

Faculty

Full-Time Faculty:	4
Part-Time Faculty:	6
Faculty to Student Ratio:	1:20

Primary Teaching Methods:

Case Study	Team Projects
Experiential Learning	Lecture

Faculty Who Consult Outside:	25-49%

Faculty Involvement:
- Director of Student Relations, State of Alabama
- Student Chapter Advisor, SHRM

Top 5 Faculty Publications:
- *Simulation and Gaming*
- *Journal of Management Education*

Students

Total Enrollment:			75
Full-Time Enrollment:			49%
Men:	49%	Women:	51%
Hispanic:	0%	African-American:	43%

115

Other Minorities:	1%	International:	0%
Average Age:	34	Age Range:	23-58
Work Full Time:			75-99%
HR Experience:			1-24%
Speak 2nd Language:			1-24%
Minimum Admission Requirements:			
UGPA:			3.0 & GMAT
Other Considerations:			N/A
Average Student Profile:			
Work experience:			10 years

Program Resources

Students Required to Have Computers:	NO
Video Teleconferencing:	YES
Physical Library Facilities:	YES
Online Library Facilities:	YES
HRCI Certification Preparation:	YES

Links students to local SHRM chapter study groups

Offer our own workshops, taught by SPHR and PHR certified teachers

Offer practice exams

SHRM Student Chapter:	YES
Fellowships:	NO
Scholarships:	NO
Assistantships:	NO
Eligibility:	N/A

Curriculum

Required Courses:
HR Strategy
Compensation/Benefits
Employment Law
Management
Selection
Research Methods
Training & Development
Organizational Behavior

Most Popular Elective Courses:	N/A

Career Tracks/Concentrations:

Counseling	Information Systems
Management	

Internship Required:	NO

Career Services

Career Services Offered:

SHRM Student Chapter	Interview Training
Resume Services	Internships
Career Planning	Job Search Techniques

Summer Internship Placement Rate:	N/A
Full-Time Placement Rate:	N/A
Average Starting Salary (Full-Time Graduates):	N/A
Average Sign-on Bonus:	N/A
Companies Recruiting HR Master's Graduates:	40

Points of Excellence

Resources: The Human Resource Leadership Institute (HRLI) seeks to involve students and faculty in community and business projects. The student chapter of SHRM is closely tied with the professional chapter in Montgomery. Alumni and local HR practitioners are very supportive of the program as guest speakers. These relationships provide our students with many opportunities for consulting projects and internships. The student chapter of SHRM has won Superior Merit Awards consistently since its inception in 1996.

Contact Information

Troy State University
P.O. Drawer 4419
Montgomery, AL 36103-4419
www.tsum.edu

Charles V. Durham, Interim Dean, Division of Business
Telephone: (334) 241-9597   FAX: (334) 241-9734
Cdurham@tsum.edu

Dr. Don McDonald, SPHR, Graduate Faculty
Telephone: (334) 241-9725   FAX: (334) 241-9734
mcdonald@tsum.edu

Admission Deadlines

Online Application:	YES

Troy State University, Western Region

Davis-Monthan AFB, Arizona; Malmstrom AFB, Montana; Holloman AFB, New Mexico
University College

Degree
Master of Science in Human Resource Management (MSHRM)

University Overview
Troy State University is a public institution catering to military and civilian students. The University College offers flexible academic programs. Main campus is located in Troy, Alabama.

Program Description
The Master of Science in Human Resource Management is a professional program designed to offer graduates of diversified undergraduate programs an opportunity to obtain a proficiency in human resource management skills. This degree program is a professional master's program that requires an understanding of the accepted professional practices in the field of HRM.

Degree Requirements

Total Credits Required:	30
Average Credits per Course:	3
Course Schedule:	Semester
Total Courses Required:	10
HR/IR Courses Required:	9
Average Time for Completion:	1 year
Maximum Time Allowed for Completion:	8 years
Accepts Credits from Other Universities:	YES
Total:	12 Hours

Tuition

In-state	$6,600	(per year)
	$220	(per credit hour)
Out-of-state	$6,600	(per year)
	$220	(per credit hour)

Program Delivery

Traditional Day Program:	NO
Nontraditional Program:	YES
Evening Program:	YES
Weekend Program:	YES
Program Completed Evening/Weekend:	YES
Summer Courses:	YES
Some Courses Online:	YES
Full Program Online:	YES
Distance Learning/Offsite:	NO
Executive Education:	NO
Overseas Study Abroad:	NO

Faculty

Full-Time Faculty:	4
Part-Time Faculty:	12
Faculty to Student Ratio:	1:20

Primary Teaching Methods:

Case Study	Research
Student Presentations	Team Projects

Faculty Who Consult Outside:	100%

Faculty Involvement:
Society for Human Resource Management
New software development for personnel classification systems. Corporate university partnerships in the New Millennium.
Top 5 Faculty Publications:

Students

Total Enrollment:			30
Full-Time Enrollment:			10
Men:	40%	Women:	60%
Hispanic:	10%	African-American:	3%
Other Minorities:	13%	International:	0%
Average Age:	35	Age Range:	24-50
Work Full Time:			75-99%
Have HR Experience:			1-24%
Speak 2nd Language:			1-24%

Minimum Admission Requirements:

UGPA:	2.5
GRE Score:	850
GMAT Score:	450
Work Experience:	0

Other Considerations:

Average Student Profile:

UGPA:	3.0
GRE Score:	1000
GMAT Score:	500
Work Experience:	0

Program Resources

Students Required to Have Computers:		NO
Video Teleconferencing:		YES
Physical Library Facilities:		YES
Online Library Facilities:		YES
HRCI Certification Preparation:		NO
SHRM Student Chapter:		NO
URL:		
Fellowships:	NO	AMT:
Scholarships:	YES	AMT: $660
Assistantships:	NO	AMT:
Eligibility: Part-Time/Full-Time		

Curriculum

Required Courses:
HR Strategy
Employee Relations
Compensation/Benefits
Labor Relations
Training & Development
Research Techniques
Recruitment/Retention
Advance Concepts & Topics in Management
Employment Law
Organization Behavior
Management

Most Popular Elective Courses:
Organization Theory, Information Systems for HRM

Career Tracks/Concentrations:	N/A
Internship Required:	NO

Career Services

Career Services:

Resume Services	Letters of Recommendation

Summer Internship Placement Rate:	
Facilitate Placement:	YES
Full-Time Placement Rate:	N/A
Internship Placement Rate:	N/A
Average Starting Salary (Full-Time Graduates):	$30,000
Average Sign-on Bonus:	N/A
Companies Recruiting HR Master's Graduates:	N/A

Points of Excellence

Troy State University retains faculty who have both academic qualifications and extensive practical experience in the field of HRM. Faculty members excel in the areas of selection, recruitment and compensation management. Special projects are applied to each student's place of employment. One full-time faculty member received the 2001 HR Southwest Educator of the Year Award. Faculty are actively involved in SHRM and encourage students to join local SHRM chapters.

Contact Information

Troy State University
596 Fourth Street
Holloman AFB, NM 88330
tsuwr.troyst.edu

Peggy McCoy-Emerson, Site Director
Telephone: (505) 479-4410/0828
troy@zianet.com

Steve Werling, SPHR; HR Faculty
Telephone: (210) 697-8232
steve@werling.com

Admission Deadlines:

When student registers for class

Online Application:	NO

University of Albany

Albany, New York
School of Business

Degree

Master of Business Administration - Human Resources Information Systems (MBA/HRIS)

University Overview

Public university in the New York State University system with more than 16,000 students.

Program Description

Full-time traditional day program provides unique concentration in Human Resources Information Systems. Intensive program emphasizes team learning and practical experience. Each student completes a nine-month consulting engagement and is trained in the use of PeopleSoft.

Degree Requirements

Total Credits Required:	60
Average Credits per Course:	3
Course Schedule:	Semester
Total Courses Required:	20
HR/IR Courses Required:	8
Average Time for Completion:	2 years
Maximum Time Allowed for Completion:	6 years
Accepts Credits from Other Universities:	NO
Total:	N/A

Tuition

In-state	$4,550	(per year)
	$213	(per credit hour)
Out-of-state	$8,230	(per year)
	N/A	(per credit hour)

Program Delivery

Traditional Day Program:	YES
Nontraditional Program:	NO
Evening Program:	NO
Weekend Program:	NO
Summer Courses:	N/A
Some Courses Online:	NO
Full Program Online:	NO
Distance Learning/Offsite:	NO
Executive Education:	N/A
Overseas Study Abroad:	NO

Faculty

Full-Time Faculty:	9
Part-Time Faculty:	5
Faculty to Student Ratio:	1:10

Primary Teaching Methods:

Field Projects	Research
Lecture	Team Projects
Computer Simulations	

Faculty Who Consult Outside:	25-49%

Faculty Involvement:
Editorial Board, International Association for Human Resources
Information Management Journal

Top 5 Faculty Publications:
Journal of Business Venturing
Journal of Quality Management
Leadership Quarterly

Students

Total Enrollment:			20
Full-Time Enrollment:			100%
Men:	40%	Women:	60%
Hispanic:	15%	African-American:	10%
Other Minorities:	15%	International:	25%
Average Age:	26	Age Range:	22-40
Work Full Time:			1-24%
HR Experience:			25-49%
Speak 2nd Language:			25-49%

Minimum Admission Requirements:

GMAT Score:	580

Other Considerations:
Work experience
Individual review of whole student

Average Student Profile:

GMAT Score:	605
Work Experience:	2 years

Program Resources

Students Required to Have Computers:			N/A
Video Teleconferencing:			NO
Physical Library Facilities:			N/A
Online Library Facilities:			N/A
HRCI Certification Preparation:			NO
SHRM Student Chapter:			YES
Fellowships:	1	AMT:	$7,500
Scholarships:	4	AMT:	$6,550
Assistantships:	22	AMT:	$5,550
Eligibility:			Full-Time Enrollment

Curriculum

Required Courses:
Accounting
Finance
HR Strategy
Marketing
Compensation/Benefits
Development/Training
Recruitment/Retention
Management
HR Measurement
Business Functional Areas
Field Project
Business Statistics

Most Popular Elective Courses:
Information Technology
Mgmt. Information Systems

Career Tracks/Concentrations:	N/A
Internship Required:	YES

Career Services

Career Services Offered:

Mentoring	Field Trips
SHRM Student Chapter	Interview Training
Campus Interviews	Internships

Summer Internship Placement Rate:	100%
Full-Time Placement Rate:	100%
Average Starting Salary (Full-Time Graduates):	$72,000
Average Sign-on Bonus:	$10,000
Companies Recruiting HR Master's Graduates:	15

Points of Excellence

Curriculum: Required field projects in which class members act as consultants to well-established corporations and not-for-profit enterprises. These consulting engagements require deliverable products for the client organizations. Past projects have included a wide range of assignments and work products: HRIS needs analysis, HRIS implementation, employee and managerial training, legal compliance, HR process re-engineering, employee surveys, development of database applications (e.g., applicant tracking, COBRA compliance, benefits reviews), technology reviews, recruiting and selection process design, and other areas of human resource management.

Placement: Students are given a final exam in a simulation/role-play format and given feedback on both HRIS content knowledge and style. All student resumes can be accessed online from the department web page. Students typically receive multiple job offers upon graduation.

Contact Information

University of Albany
1400 Washington Ave.
Albany, NY 12222
www.albany.edu

Geraldine Mohyla, Secretary
Telephone: (518) 442-4966   FAX: (518) 442-4765
g.mohyla@albany.edu

Hal G. Gueutal, Professor
Telephone: (518) 442-4966   FAX: (518) 442-4765
HGG37@NYCAP.RR.COM

Admission Deadlines

Online Application:	YES

University of Baltimore

Baltimore, Maryland
Gordon College of Liberal Arts

Degree
Master of Science in Applied Psychology, Specialization in Industrial/Organizational Psychology (MS-I/O)

University Overview
State funded, with 4,500 students enrolled in upper-division undergraduate and graduate studies. The focus is professional.

Program Description
Students in this specialization acquire the foundation in the theories and methods of I/O psychology. They also develop skills to apply their knowledge in businesses, consulting firms, and local, state, and federal government agencies. Many elective courses are taken in the Business School.

Degree Requirements
Total Credits Required:	42
Average Credits per Course:	3
Course Schedule:	Semester
Total Courses Required:	14
HR/IR Courses Required:	10
Average Time for Completion:	2 ½ years
Maximum Time Allowed for Completion:	7 years
Accepts Credits from Other Universities:	YES
Total:	12 Hours

Tuition
In-state	$7,396	(per year)
	$420	(per credit hour)
Out-of-state	$10,708	(per year)
	N/A	(per credit hour)

Program Delivery
Traditional Day Program:	YES
Nontraditional Program:	YES
Evening Program:	YES
Weekend Program:	NO
Summer Courses:	YES
Some Courses Online:	NO
Full Program Online:	NO
Distance Learning/Offsite:	NO
Executive Education:	NO
Overseas Study Abroad:	NO

Faculty
Full-Time Faculty:	10
Part-Time Faculty:	6
Faculty to Student Ratio:	1:15

Primary Teaching Methods:
Lecture	Team Projects
Student Presentations	Group Discussion
Computer Simulation	

Faculty Who Consult Outside: 100%

Faculty Involvement:
Editorial Board, Applied Human Resource Management Research
Program Committee, Society for Industrial/Organizational Psychology

Top 5 Faculty Publications:
Journal of Business and Psychology
Applied HRM Research
The Flawless Consulting Companion and Field Book

The Fourteenth Mental Measurements Yearbook
International Personnel Management Assoc. News

Students
Total Enrollment:			67
Full-Time Enrollment:			52%
Men:	33%	Women:	67%
Hispanic:	3%	African-American:	14%
Other Minorities:	3%	International:	3%
Average Age:	33	Age Range:	22-55
Work Full Time:			N/A
HR Experience:			1-24%
Speak 2nd Language:			1-24%

Minimum Admission Requirements:
GRE, UGPA:	3.0 in Psychology

Other Considerations:
Conditional admission for low GPA or lack of psychology undergraduate degree and relevant work experience

Average Student Profile:
GRE Score:	500 per test (Q&V&A)
Work experience:	2-3 years

Program Resources
Students Required to Have Computers:			NO
Video Teleconferencing:			NO
Physical Library Facilities:			YES
Online Library Facilities:			YES
HRCI Certification Preparation:			NO
SHRM Student Chapter:			YES
Fellowships:			NO
Scholarships:			NO
Assistantships:	3	AMT:	$6,000
Eligibility:			All Students

Curriculum
Required Courses:
Organizational Psychology
Personnel Psychology
Job Analysis
Motivation & Leadership
Personnel Assessment
Practical Applications in I/O
Research Methods
Statistics

Most Popular Elective Courses:
Employment Law
Training & Development
Employee Selection
Work Groups in Organizations
Human Relations
Conflict Management
Internship in I/O Psych
Compensation

Career Tracks/Concentrations:
Counseling	Industrial/Organizational
Psychological Applications	Psychology

Internship Required: NO

Career Services
Career Services Offered:
Mentoring	Internships
SHRM Student Chapter	Career Center

Summer Internship Placement Rate:	N/A
Full-Time Placement Rate:	N/A
Average Starting Salary (Full-Time Graduates):	N/A
Average Sign-on Bonus:	N/A
Companies Recruiting HR Master's Graduates:	N/A

Points of Excellence

Resources: The Baltimore/Washington, DC, area offers exceptionally rich opportunities for internships and other forms of practical experience in public and private sector agencies, small and large businesses, human resource consulting firms, and other organizations. The program's faculty members are well connected in the area and work with students to find suitable placements.

Contact Information

Gordon College of Liberal Arts
University of Baltimore
1420 N. Charles St.
Baltimore, MD 21201-5779
www.ubalt.edu/dapqm

Paul M. Mastrangelo, Ph.D., Director of M.S. In Applied Psychology
Telephone: (410) 837-5310   FAX: (410) 837-5336
pmastrangelo@ubmail.ubalt.edu

Admission Deadlines

March for Fall admissions, December 1 for Spring admissions, and rolling deadlines as space permits
Online Application: YES

University of Central Florida

Orlando, Florida
College of Business Administration

Degree

Master of Science in Human Resource and Change Management (MSM/HR/CM)

University Overview

The University of Central Florida is a major metropolitan state research university whose mission is to deliver a comprehensive program of teaching, research, and service.

Program Description

New program launched in fall 2000. Program provides highly focused graduate study in the areas of managing change and human resources in contemporary organizations. It offers an alternative to those interested in pursuing graduate work in business, but who desire a program more focused on a career in management. Those with business background need only 30 credits. Otherwise, 42 credits are required.

Degree Requirements

Total Credits Required:	30-42
Average Credits per Course:	3
Course Schedule:	Semester
Total Courses Required:	10
HR/IR Courses Required:	10
Average Time for Completion:	1-2 Years
Maximum Time Allowed for Completion:	7 Years
Accepts Credits from Other Universities:	NO
Total:	N/A

Tuition

In-state	N/A	(per year)
	$162	(per credit hour)
Out-of-state	N/A	(per year)
	$569	(per credit hour)

Program Delivery

Traditional Day Program:	NO
Nontraditional Program:	YES
Evening Program:	YES
Weekend Program:	NO
Summer Courses:	YES
Some Courses Online:	NO
Full Program Online:	NO
Distance Learning/Offsite:	NO
Executive Education:	NO
Overseas Study Abroad:	NO

Faculty

Full-Time Faculty:	15
Part-Time Faculty:	5
Faculty to Student Ratio:	1:20

Primary Teaching Methods:

Case Study	Team Projects
Field Projects	Student Presentations
Computer Simulation	

Faculty Who Consult Outside:	1-24%
Faculty Involvement:	N/A

Top 5 Faculty Publications:
Journal of Applied Psychology
Academy of Management Journal
Academy of Management Review
Administrative Science
Strategic Management Journal

Students

Total Enrollment:			40
Full-Time Enrollment:			13%
Men:	50%	Women:	50%
Hispanic:	15-20%	African-American:	N/A
Other Minorities:	N/A	International:	N/A
Average Age:	29	Age Range:	22-58
Work Full Time:			75-99%
HR Experience:			25-49%
Speak 2nd Language:			1-24%

Minimum Admission Requirements:

GMAT Score:	500
GRE Score:	1000
Other Considerations:	N/A

Average Student Profile:

GMAT Score:	545
Work experience:	9 years

Program Resources

Students Required to Have Computers:			NO
Video Teleconferencing:			YES
Physical Library Facilities:			YES
Online Library Facilities:			YES
HRCI Certification Preparation:			Under Development
SHRM Student Chapter:			NO
Fellowships:	5	AMT:	$8,000
Scholarships:			NO
Assistantships:	5	AMT:	$4,000
Eligibility:			Full-Time Enrollment

Curriculum

Required Courses:
  HR Strategy
  International HR
  HR Measurement
  Business Functional Areas
  Change Management Statistics

Most Popular Elective Courses:
 Organizational Behavior
 Organizational Communication
Career Tracks/Concentrations: N/A
Internship Required: YES

Career Services
Career Services Offered:
 Resume Services   Campus Interviews
 Internships   Field Projects
Summer Internship Placement Rate: N/A
Full-Time Placement Rate: (Most students already employed)
Average Starting Salary (Full-Time Graduates): N/A
Average Sign-on Bonus: N/A
Companies Recruiting HR Master's Graduates: N/A

Points of Excellence
Curriculum: Program prepares graduates to participate in many different change initiatives and decisions involving employment and hiring, training and development, compensation, contract negotiation and administration, and other reorganization activities. Students complete a supervised field project that addresses a practical HR change issue faced by a real organization. Students identify a field site; plan, collect, and analyze project data; and make recommendations to that organization.

Contact Information
University of Central Florida
College of Business Graduate Programs
P.O. Box 161400
Orlando, FL 32816-1400
www.bus.ucf.edu

Ms. Judy Ryder, Graduate Business Advisor
Telephone: (407) 823-2364   FAX: (407) 823-6206
Judy.Ryder@bus.ucf.edu

Admission Deadlines
July 15 for Fall admissions
Online Application: YES

University of Cincinnati

Cincinnati, Ohio
College of Arts and Sciences,
Department of Economics

Degree
Master of Arts in Labor and Employment Relations (MALER)

University Overview
The University of Cincinnati is one of two flagship state universities in Ohio. A Research I Institution, it enrolls some 34,000 students. Cincinnati is a flourishing metropolitan area with a diversified economy and a population of over 2 million.

Program Description
For over 30 years, the Master of Arts Program in Labor and Employment Relations has been successful in helping students to establish or further professional careers in human resource management and labor relations.

Degree Requirements
Total Credits Required: 53
Average Credits per Course: 3-4
Course Schedule: Quarter
Total Courses Required: 15
HR/IR Courses Required: 15

Average Time for Completion: 1-2 years
Maximum Time Allowed for Completion: 7 years
Accepts Credits from Other Universities: NO
Total: N/A

Tuition
In State $9,096   (per year)
                  $228   (per credit hour)
Out-of-state $16,940   (per year)
                  $424   (per credit hour)

Program Delivery
Traditional Day Program: NO
Nontraditional Program: YES
 Evening Program: YES
 Weekend Program: YES
 Summer Courses: YES
 Some Courses Online: NO
 Full Program Online: NO
 Distance Learning/Offsite: NO
 Executive Education: NO
 Overseas Study Abroad: NO

Faculty
Full-Time Faculty: 4
Part-Time Faculty: 12
Faculty to Student Ratio: 1:10
Primary Teaching Methods:
 Case Study   Team Projects
 Student Presentations   Group Discussion
 Computer Simulations
Faculty Who Consult Outside: 1-24%
Faculty Involvement:
 Board Member, Human Resources Certification Institute
 Coordinator, International Industrial Relations Association Study Group on the Practice and Theory of Negotiation
 Member, SHRM College Relations Committee
 Member, University Council of Industrial Relations Programs
Top 5 Faculty Publications: N/A

Students
Total Enrollment: 76
Full-Time Enrollment: 22%
 Men: 28%   Women: 72%
 Hispanic: 3%   African-American: 20%
 Other Minorities: 3%   International: 3%
 Average Age: N/A   Age Range: N/A
Work Full Time: 50-74%
HR Experience: 75-99%
Speak 2nd Language: 1-24%
Minimum Admission Requirements:
 UGPA: 3.0
Other Considerations:
 Demonstration of ability to complete program
 Work experience
Average Student Profile: N/A

Program Resources
Students Required to Have Computers: NO
Video Teleconferencing: NO
Physical Library Facilities: YES
Online Library Facilities: YES
HRCI Certification Preparation: YES
 Preparation course offered for one credit
SHRM Student Chapter: YES
Fellowships: NO
Scholarships: Varies   AMT: $8,186 (in-state)
                                      $15,246 (out-of-state)

121

Assistantships:	Varies	AMT:	$16,282 (in-state)
			$22,165 (out-of-state)
Eligibility:			Full-Time Enrollment

Curriculum
Required Courses:
Human Resource Mgmt.
Compensation
Employment Law
HRIS
Labor Relations Law
Research Methods
Economics of HR
Collective Bargaining
Strategic HR Management
HR & Accounting
Most Popular Elective Courses:
Training & Development
Staffing
International HR
Negotiation
Motivation
TQM
Organizational Behavior
Staffing
Dispute Resolution
Public Sector Labor Relations
Health & Work
The Diverse Workforce
Career Tracks/Concentrations:

| Human Resource | Labor Relations |
| Management | |

Internship Required: NO

Career Services
Career Services Offered:

| SHRM Student Chapter | Internships |

Summer Internship Placement Rate:	N/A
Full-Time Placement Rate:	N/A
Average Starting Salary (Full-Time Graduates):	N/A
Average Sign-on Bonus:	N/A
Companies Recruiting HR Master's Graduates:	N/A

Points of Excellence
Curriculum: The faculty team includes both full-time members with PhDs in appropriate disciplines and adjunct faculty who practice professionally in their areas of teaching specialization. Most students already are pursuing careers in human resources and labor relations and bring a wealth of experience into the classroom. Emphasis on interactive and collaborative learning techniques, providing ample opportunity to share this richness of experience. Students and faculty learn from each other. Professional organizations and a large community of practicing professionals in human resources and labor relations provide additional valuable learning resources.

Contact Information
Department of Economics
University of Cincinnati
Cincinnati, OH 45221-0371
www.uc.edu

Geri Kirchner, Administrative Secretary
Graduate Programs
Telephone: (513) 556-2670   FAX: (513) 556-2669
geri.kirchner@uc.edu

Howard M. Leftwich, Ph.D.
Professor & Program Coordinator
Telephone: (513) 556-2615   FAX: (513) 556-2669
howard.leftwich@uc.edu

Admission Deadlines
Online Application: YES

University of Colorado at Denver

Denver, Colorado
Graduate School of Business Administration

Degree
Master of Science in Management (MSM)

University Overview
State university with approximately 11,000 students located in downtown Denver.

Program Description
The Master of Science in Management program is designed to prepare individuals for significant managerial responsibilities in the private and public sectors. The HR track provides students with advanced knowledge of state-of-the-art tools and techniques to recruit, hire, develop, and reward managerial and non-managerial employees.

Degree Requirements
Total Credits Required:	48
Average Credits per Course:	3
Course Schedule:	Semester
Total Courses Required:	16
HR/IR Courses Required:	7
Average Time for Completion:	3-4 years
Maximum Time Allowed for Completion:	5 years
Accepts Credits from Other Universities:	YES
Total:	9 Hours

Tuition
In-state	$4,428	(per semester)
	$246	(per credit hour)
Out-of-state	$15,066	(per semester)
	$837	(per credit hour)

Program Delivery
Traditional Day Program:	NO
Nontraditional Program:	YES
Evening Program:	YES
Weekend Program:	NO
Summer Courses:	YES
Some Courses Online:	YES
Full Program Online:	NO
Distance Learning/Offsite:	YES
Executive Education:	NO
Overseas Study Abroad:	NO

Faculty
Full-Time Faculty:	7
Part-Time Faculty:	4
Faculty to Student Ratio:	1:20

Primary Teaching Methods:

| Case Study | Student Presentations |
| Field Projects | Lecture |

Faculty Who Consult Outside: 75-99%

Faculty Involvement:
Program Chair, Iberoamerican Academy of Management
Executive Committee, HR Division of the Academy of Management
Representative at Large, Academy of Management
Numerous Board Memberships

Top 5 Faculty Publications:
Academy of Management Journal
Academy of Management Review
Academy of Management Executive
Personnel Psychology
Organizational Research Methods

Students

Total Enrollment:			45
Full-Time Enrollment:			17%
Men:	38%	Women:	62%
Hispanic:	0%	African-American:	7%
Other Minorities:	0%	International:	2%
Average Age:	30	Age Range:	N/A
Work Full Time:			50-74%
HR Experience:			75-99%
Speak 2nd Language:			1-24%
Minimum Admission Requirements:			N/A

Other Considerations:
UGPA, GMAT, work experience, essay, and recommendations

Average Student Profile:

GMAT Score:	540
Work experience:	4 years

Program Resources

Students Required to Have Computers:			NO
Video Teleconferencing:			NO
Physical Library Facilities:			YES
Online Library Facilities:			YES
HRCI Certification Preparation:			YES

Encourages student study groups
Links students to local SHRM chapter study groups

SHRM Student Chapter:			YES
URL:		carbon.cudenver.edu/~haguinis/shrm.html	
Fellowships:			NO
Scholarships:	10	AMT:	$1,100
Assistantships:	10	AMT:	$1,300/semester
Eligibility:			N/A

Curriculum

Required Courses:
Functional Areas
Accounting
Marketing
HR Measurement
Compensation/Benefits
Recruitment/Retention
Employment Law

Most Popular Elective Courses:
Organizational Change
Public Administration

Career Tracks/Concentrations:	N/A
Internship Required:	NO

Career Services

Career Services Offered:

Mentoring	Links with local SHRM chapter
SHRM Student Chapter	Campus Interviews
Resume Services	

Summer Internship Placement Rate:	N/A
Full-Time Placement Rate:	N/A
Average Starting Salary (Full-Time Graduates):	N/A

Average Sign-on Bonus:	N/A
Companies Recruiting HR Master's Graduates:	N/A

Points of Excellence

Students: Many students have backgrounds rich in business experience, which greatly enhance the educational process. Most students are working adults who maintain full-time employment and are exceptionally serious about their education. Although a high percentage attend evening classes, a significant number are also full-time students attending classes offered during the day. This rich mix of backgrounds, experience, and perspectives, when coupled with the strengths of excellent faculty, fosters stimulating classroom interaction and keen competition.

Contact Information

Graduate School of Business Administration
Campus Box 165
P.O. Box 173364
Denver, CO 80217-3364
www.cudenver.edu/public/business

Linda Olson, Director, Graduate Programs
Telephone: (303) 556-5875   FAX: (303) 556-5904
lolson@carbon.cudenver.edu

Herman Aguinis, Ph.D.
Director, MS in Management Program
Telephone: (303) 556-2512   FAX: (303) 556-5899
Herman.Aguinis@.cudenver.edu

Admission Deadlines

June 1 for Fall admissions

Online Application:	NO

University of Dallas

Irving, Texas
Graduate School of Management

Degree

Master of Business Administration with concentration in Human Resource Management (MBA)

University Overview

A small, private, Catholic university in Irving, Texas.

Program Description

Practice-oriented program targeted to working adults, allowing focus on HR fundamentals, organizational development, or international HR.

Degree Requirements

Total Credits Required:	49
Average Credits per Course:	3
Course Schedule:	Trimester
Total Courses Required:	16
HR/IR Courses Required:	5
Average Time for Completion:	2 ½ years
Maximum Time Allowed for Completion:	6 years
Accepts Credits from Other Universities:	YES
Total:	12 Hours

Tuition

In-state	N/A	(per year)
	$423	(per credit hour)
Out-of-state	N/A	(per year)
	$423	(per credit hour)

Program Delivery

Traditional Day Program:	NO
Nontraditional Program:	YES
Evening Program:	YES
Weekend Program:	YES
Program Completed Evening/Weekend:	YES
Summer Courses:	YES
Some Courses Online:	YES
Full Program Online:	YES
Distance Learning/Offsite:	YES
Executive Education:	YES
Overseas Study Abroad:	YES

Faculty

Full-Time Faculty:	5
Part-Time Faculty:	0
Faculty to Student Ratio:	1:10

Primary Teaching Methods:

Team Projects	Experiential Learning
Lecture	Field Projects
Student Presentation	

Faculty Who Consult Outside:	75-99%
Faculty Involvement:	

Top 5 Faculty Publications:
Proceeding of the Institute of Behavioral and Applied Management
Creating Performing Organizations
The Journal of Managerial Issues
Handbook of Work and Health Psychology

Students

Total Enrollment:			N/A
Full-Time Enrollment:			N/A
Men:	N/A	Women:	N/A
Hispanic:	N/A	African-American:	N/A
Other Minorities:	N/A	International:	N/A
Average Age:	33	Age Range:	22-75
Work Full Time:			75-99%
Have HR Experience:			1-24%
Speak 2nd Language:			25-49%

Minimum Admission Requirements:

UGPA:	Varies
GRE or GMAT Scores:	400
Work Experience:	5 years
Other Considerations:	YES

Average Student Profile:

UGPA:	3.1
GMAT Score:	550
Work Experience:	7 years

Program Resources

Students Required to Have Computers:	NO
Video Teleconferencing:	NO
Physical Library Facilities:	YES
Online Library Facilities:	YES
HRCI Certification Preparation:	YES
Encourage student study groups	
Link students to local SHRM chapter	
SHRM Student Chapter:	NO
URL:	

Fellowships:	NO	AMT:	
Scholarships:	NO	AMT:	
Assistantships:	YES	AMT:	$1,522
Eligibility:			Full-Time Enrollment

Curriculum

Required Courses:
Accounting
Marketing
Management
Data Analysis for Decision Making
Global Business
Economics and Competitive Advantage

Most Popular Elective Courses:
Training and Development
Managing Complex Organizations

Career Tracks/Concentrations:

General HR Management	Organizational Development
International HR Management	Strategic Leadership

Internship Required:	NO

Career Services

Career Services Offered:	N/A
Summer Internship Placement Rate:	N/A
Facilitate Placement:	YES
Full-Time Placement Rate:	N/A
Internship Placement Rate:	N/A
Average Starting Salary (Full-Time Graduates):	N/A
Average Sign-on Bonus:	N/A
Companies Recruiting HR Master's Graduates:	N/A

Points of Excellence

See our web site.

Contact Information

University of Dallas
Graduate School of Management
1845 E. Northgate Drive
Irving, TX 75062
gsm.udallas.edu

Administrative Contact
Sarah Stivison
Telephone: (972) 721-5174
sstiviso@gsm.udallas.edu

Faculty Contact
J. Lee Whittington
Telephone: (972) 721-5277
jlwhitt@gsm.udallas.edu

Brian Murray
Telephone: (972) 721-5277
bmurray@gsm.udallas.edu

Admission Deadlines

July 15 for Fall admissions, November 15 for Spring admissions, March 15 for Summer admissions

Online Application:	YES

University of Hawaii at Manoa

Honolulu, Hawaii
College of Business Administration, Management and Industrial Relations Department

Degree

Master of Human Resource Management

University Overview

The University of Hawaii at Manoa is a research university of international standing. It creates, refines, disseminates, and perpetuates human knowledge. It offers a comprehensive array of undergraduate, graduate, and professional degrees through the doctoral level.

Program Description
The Master of Human Resource Management program is an accelerated executive format for working professionals and specifically customized to equip human resource managers with the tools to effectively meet the challenges of an ever-changing business climate.

Degree Requirements
Total Credits Required:	30
Average Credits per Course:	3
Course Schedule:	Other
Total Courses Required:	10
HR/IR Courses Required:	10
Average Time for Completion:	1 ¾ years
Maximum Time Allowed for Completion:	1 ¾ years
Accepts Credits from Other Universities:	YES
Total:	N/A

Tuition
In-state	$14,000	(per year)
	N/A	(per credit hour)
Out-of-state	$14,000	(per year)
	N/A	(per credit hour)

Program Delivery
Traditional Day Program:	NO
Nontraditional Program:	YES
Evening Program:	YES
Weekend Program:	YES
Program Completed Evening/Weekend:	YES
Summer Courses:	YES
Some Courses Online:	NO
Full Program Online:	NO
Distance Learning/Offsite:	NO
Executive Education:	YES
Overseas Study Abroad:	N/A

Faculty
Full-Time Faculty:	12
Part-Time Faculty:	12
Faculty to Student Ratio:	1:10

Primary Teaching Methods:
Experiential Learning   Research
Student Presentation

Faculty Who Consult Outside:	50-74%

Faculty Involvement:
Board Member, NAMTAC
Top 5 Faculty Publications:

Students
Total Enrollment:			N/A
Full-Time Enrollment:			N/A
Men:	N/A	Women:	N/A
Hispanic:	N/A	African-American:	N/A
Other Minorities:	N/A	International:	N/A
Average Age:	N/A	Age Range:	N/A
Work Full Time:			N/A
Have HR Experience:			N/A
Speak 2nd Language:			N/A

Minimum Admission Requirements:
UGPA:	3.0
GRE or GMAT Scores:	500
Work Experience:	5 years

Average Student Profile:
UGPA:	N/A
GMAT Score:	N/A
Work Experience:	N/A

Program Resources
Students Required to Have Computers:	NO
Video Teleconferencing:	NO
Physical Library Facilities:	YES
Online Library Facilities:	YES
HRCI Certification Preparation:	YES

Link students to local SHRM chapter
Base curriculum on certification exam
SHRM Student Chapter:	YES
URL:	

Fellowships:	NO	AMT:	
Scholarships:	YES	AMT:	$7,000
Assistantships:	NO	AMT:	
Eligibility:			Full-Time Enrollment

Curriculum
Required Courses:
HR Strategy
International HR
Compensation/Benefits
Recruitment/Retention
Development/Training
Management
Employee Relations
Labor Relations
Organizational Behavior
Employment Law

Most Popular Elective Courses:	N/A
Career Tracks/Concentrations:	N/A
Internship Required:	YES

Career Services
Career Services Offered:
Campus Interview   Resume Services
Summer Internship Placement Rate:	N/A
Facilitate Placement:	YES
Full-Time Placement Rate:	N/A
Internship Placement Rate:	N/A
Average Starting Salary (Full-Time Graduates):	N/A
Average Sign-on Bonus:	N/A
Companies Recruiting HR Master's Graduates:	N/A

Points of Excellence
Summer program provides opportunity to attend international courses with world-class faculty who augment our regular full-time faculty. Each course team taught with a practitioner. Costs are all-inclusive (books, meals, materials, residency weekend).

Contact Information
Master of Human Resource Management Program, CBA
University of Hawaii at Manoa
2404 Maile Way #B201
Honolulu, HI 96822
www.cba.hawaii.edu/MHRM

Administrative Contact
Cecie Streitman
Telephone: (808) 956-3260
Cecie@cba.hawaii.edu

Faculty Contact
Dr. Elaine Bailey
Telephone: (808) 956-8731
Elaine@cba.hawaii.edu

Admission Deadlines
November 15, June 1
Online Applications: NO

University of Houston, Clear Lake

Houston, Texas
School of Business and Public Administration

Degree
Master of Arts in Human Resource Management (MAHRM)

University Overview
University of Houston – Clear Lake (UHCL) is an upper division and graduate school located adjacent to NASA's Johnson Space Flight Center between Houston and Galveston.

Program Description
Unique competency-based program to produce individuals that become strategic business partners with mastery in the functional areas of HRM as well as general business.

Degree Requirements
Total Credits Required:	42
Average Credits per Course:	3
Course Schedule:	Semester
Total Courses Required:	14
HR/IR Courses Required:	10
Average Time for Completion:	2 ½ years
Maximum Time Allowed for Completion:	5 years
Accepts Credits from Other Universities:	YES
Total:	12 Hours

Tuition
In-state	N/A	(per year)
	$217	(per credit hour)
Out-of-state	N/A	(per year)
	$352	(per credit hour)

Program Delivery
Traditional Day Program:	NO
Nontraditional Program:	YES
Evening Program:	YES
Weekend Program:	NO
Program Completed Evening/Weekend:	YES
Summer Courses:	YES
Some Courses Online:	YES
Full Program Online:	NO
Distance Learning/Offsite:	NO
Executive Education:	NO
Overseas Study Abroad:	NO

Faculty
Full-Time Faculty:	9
Part-Time Faculty:	4
Faculty to Student Ratio:	1:20

Primary Teaching Methods:
Case Study   Team Projects
Experiential Learning   Group Discussion

Faculty Who Consult Outside:	25-49%

Faculty Involvement:
Top 5 Faculty Publications:
Journal of Management Education
Human Resource Management Review
Journal of Vocational Behavior
Human Resource Development Quarterly
Journal of Organizational Change Management

Students
Total Enrollment:	52
Full-Time Enrollment:	10%

Men:	27%	Women:	73%
Hispanic:	12%	African-American:	8%
Other Minorities:	8%	International:	8%
Average Age:	33	Age Range:	24-54
Work Full Time:			75-99%
Have HR Experience:			50-74%
Speak 2nd Language:			1-24%

Minimum Admission Requirements:
UGPA:	N/A
GRE or GMAT Scores:	N/A
Work Experience:	N/A

Other Considerations:
Average Student Profile:
UGPA:	3.2
GMAT Score:	475
Work Experience:	3 years

Program Resources
Students Required to Have Computers:	NO
Video Teleconferencing:	YES
Physical Library Facilities:	YES
Online Library Facilities:	YES
HRCI Certification Preparation:	YES
Link to local SHRM chapter	
Base curriculum on certification exam	
SHRM Student Chapter:	YES
URL:	

Fellowships:	NO	AMT:	
Scholarships:	YES	AMT:	$1,500
Assistantships:	YES	AMT:	Varies
Eligibility:	Full-Time Enrollment (Assistantships)		

Curriculum
Required Courses:
Accounting
Recruitment/Retention
HR Strategy
Employment Law
International HR
Management
Compensation/Benefits
Business Functional Areas
Development/Training
HRIS
Group Processes
Ethics

Most Popular Elective Courses:
Life/Work Planning
Management of Technical Professionals
International Business
Stress Management
Future Studies

Career Tracks/Concentrations:
Instructional Technology   Organizational
Information Systems   Development/Change
Health and Safety

Internship Required:	NO

Career Services
Career Services Offered:
SHRM Student Chapter   Internships

Summer Internship Placement Rate:	N/A
Facilitate Placement:	NO
Full-Time Placement Rate:	5%
Internship Placement Rate:	N/A
Average Starting Salary (Full-Time Graduates):	N/A
Average Sign-on Bonus:	N/A
Companies Recruiting HR Master's Graduates:	N/A

Points of Excellence

The University of Houston - Clear Lake (UHCL) HRM degree is unique in several respects. First, we have a world-class faculty, all with PhDs from some of the most noted universities (UCLA, Tulane, Bowling Green, Oregon, University of Massachusetts). Many of our faculty have had considerable consulting experience or experience as HRM officers of major corporations. Second, the program was built around a competency-based HRM system. The focus is to produce high level change agents, not an entry-level HR generalist. The curricular emphasis is on general business, functional specialties, and strategic skill sets. Each student must demonstrate proficiency in 84 specific competency areas in five different competency clusters. The curriculum is built on the notion that HR must be a strategic component in the overall enterprise in order to have an impact upon the bottom line. A combination of cognitive, interpersonal, and quantitative skills are emphasized to this end.

Contact Information

University of Houston - Clear Lake
School of Business and Public Administration
2700 Bay Area Boulevard
Houston, TX 77058
www.cl.uh.edu

Administrative Contact
Dr. Joan Bruno
Telephone: (281) 283-3110
Bruno@cl.uh.edu

Faculty Contact
Kevin Wooten
Telephone: (281) 283-3237
wooten@cl.uh.edu

Admission Deadlines

June 1, October 1
Online Application: YES

University of Illinois, Urbana-Champaign

Champaign, Illinois
Institute of Labor and Industrial Relations

Degree

Master in Human Resources and Industrial Relations (MHRIR)

University Overview

One of the world's great research universities, originally one of 37 land grant institutions founded in 1867, with a current student population of over 55,000. Campus is 140 miles south of Chicago and 170 miles northeast of St. Louis. Program is member of GOALS consortium.

Program Description

Full-time traditional day program offers multidisciplinary approach to the study of all aspects of the employment relationship.

Degree Requirements

Total Credits Required:	48
Average Credits per Course:	4
Course Schedule:	Semester
Total Courses Required:	12
HR/IR Courses Required:	3
Average Time for Completion:	1 ½ years

Maximum Time Allowed for Completion:	3 years
Accepts Credits from Other Universities:	YES
Total:	N/A

Tuition

In-state	$2,121	(per semester)
	N/A	(per credit hour)
Out-of-state	$5,876	(per semester)
	N/A	(per credit hour)

Program Delivery

Traditional Day Program:	YES
Nontraditional Program:	NO
Evening Program:	NO
Weekend Program:	NO
Summer Courses:	N/A
Some Courses Online:	NO
Full Program Online:	NO
Distance Learning/Offsite:	NO
Executive Education:	N/A
Overseas Study Abroad:	NO

Faculty

Full-Time Faculty:	9
Part-Time Faculty:	11
Faculty to Student Ratio:	1:10

Primary Teaching Methods:

Case Study	Team Projects
Computer-Aided Instruction	Lecture
Student Presentation	Computer Simulation

Faculty Who Consult Outside:	1-24%

Faculty Involvement:
Editor, Academy of Management Journal
Member, Board of Directors for GOALS
Member, SHRM College Relations Committee

Top 5 Faculty Publications:
Journal of Applied Psychology
Personnel Psychology
Industrial and Labor Relations Review
Academy of Management Journal
American Economic Review

Students

Total Enrollment:			125
Full-Time Enrollment:			100%
Men:	31%	Women:	69%
Hispanic:	3%	African-American:	15%
Other Minorities:	6%	International:	9%
Average Age:	25	Age Range:	21-40
Work Full Time:			1-24%
HR Experience:			1-24%
Speak 2nd Language:			1-24%

Minimum Admission Requirements:

UGPA:	3.0 + GRE (V&Q)

Other Considerations:
Recommendations, personal statement, and work experience may compensate for lower scores.

Average Student Profile:

GRE Score:	110
UGPA:	3.5
Work experience:	1 year

Program Resources

Students Required to Have Computers:	N/A
Video Teleconferencing:	YES
Physical Library Facilities:	N/A
Online Library Facilities:	N/A
HRCI Certification Preparation:	NO
SHRM Student Chapter:	YES

Fellowships:	20	AMT:	$6,000 + tuition
Scholarships:	NO		
Assistantships:	12-15	AMT:	$5,596 + tuition
Eligibility:			Full-Time Enrollment

Curriculum

Required Courses:
- Employment Relation Systems
- Quantitative Methods
- Research Methods

Most Popular Elective Courses:
- Collective Bargaining
- International HR
- Compensation Systems
- HRIS
- HR Planning & Staffing
- HR Strategy
- Government Regulation
- Labor Law
- Organizational Behavior
- Labor Economics
- Training/Development
- I/O Psychology

Career Tracks/Concentrations:	N/A
Internship Required:	NO

Career Services

Career Services Offered:

Mentoring	Interview Training
Field Trips	Campus Interviews
Internships	SHRM Student Chapter
Resume Services	Corporate Information
Sessions	

Summer Internship Placement Rate:	100%
Full-Time Placement Rate:	90-100%
Average Starting Salary (Full-Time Graduates):	$58,000
Average Sign-on Bonus:	$7,050
Companies Recruiting HR Master's Graduates:	85

Points of Excellence

Curriculum: The University of Illinois, Urbana-Champaign has developed a comprehensive outcomes assessment program in which learning outcomes of graduate students are measured to ensure that participating programs meet the goals of the students. These measures include expectation surveys, exit interview surveys, focus groups, teaching effectiveness measures, and interviews with recruiters. This feedback is used to review curriculum and course design.

Resources: Program has a well-established financial support network in which individuals and organizations provide annual financial packages between $10,000 and $20,000 to qualified ILIR students based on competitive academic merit. University has the third largest library in the country.

Placement: Aggressive and personalized placement activities characterize the program. Web-based technology enables students to access interview schedules and job descriptions anywhere in the world.

Contact Information

Institute of Labor and Industrial Relations
504 E. Armory Ave.
Champaign, IL 61820
www.ilir.uiuc.edu

Becky Barker, Student Affairs Coordinator
Telephone: (217) 333-2381   FAX: (217) 244-9290
e-barker@uiuc.edu

Michael LeRoy, Chair, Admissions Committee
Telephone: (217) 244-4092   FAX: (217) 244-9290
m-leroy@uiuc.edu

Admission Deadlines
February 1 for Fall admissions

Online Application:	YES

University of Maryland

College Park, Maryland
Robert H. Smith School of Business

Degree
Master of Business Administration with Human Capital concentration (MBA-HC)

University Overview
The University of Maryland at College Park is the flagship campus of the University of Maryland and is located in the Washington, DC, metropolitan area. The campus benefits from its site within the thriving, high-tech Baltimore-Washington corridor, its access to a rich variety of cultural resources, and its proximity to major recreational areas, such as the Chesapeake Bay.

Program Description
Program emphasizes the use of strategic human resource management to provide competitive advantage in the new economy. Coursework stresses the importance of vertical alignment between business strategy and human resource programs, as well as horizontal alignment among the firm's various human resource programs, as determinants of firm performance.

Degree Requirements

Total Credits Required:	54
Average Credits per Course:	2-3
Course Schedule:	Semester
Total Courses Required:	14
HR/IR Courses Required:	4
Average Time for Completion:	1 ½ -2 years
Maximum Time Allowed for Completion:	3 years
Accepts Credits from Other Universities:	YES
Total:	N/A

Tuition

In-state	$10,798	(per year)
	N/A	(per credit hour)
Out-of-state	$15,424	(per year)
	N/A	(per credit hour)

Program Delivery

Traditional Day Program:	YES
Nontraditional Program:	YES
Evening Program:	YES
Weekend Program:	YES
Summer Courses:	N/A
Some Courses Online:	NO
Full Program Online:	NO
Distance Learning/Offsite:	YES
Executive Education:	N/A
Overseas Study Abroad:	YES

Faculty

Full-Time Faculty:	120
Part-Time Faculty:	45
Faculty to Student Ratio:	1:9
Primary Teaching Methods:	

Case Study	Experiential Learning
Field Projects	Team Projects
Student Presentations	Group Discussion
Lecture	Speakers
Distance Learning	Student Presentation

Faculty Who Consult Outside: 50-74%

Faculty Involvement:
   Fellows of Academy of Management
   Editorial Boards: *Journal of Applied Psychology, Human Resource Management Review, Journal of Organizational Behavior, Journal of Management,* and *Academy of Management Journal*
   Associate Editor, *Journal of Vocational Behavior*
   Executive committees of divisions of the Academy of Management

Top 5 Faculty Publications: See web site

Students

Total Enrollment:			1,100
Full-Time Enrollment:			470
Men:	63%	Women:	37%
Hispanic:	3%	African-American:	5.5%
Other Minorities:	9.5%	International:	38%
Average Age:	27	Age Range:	22-41
Work Full Time:			0%
HR Experience:			1-24%
Speak 2nd Language:			1-24%

Minimum Admission Requirements:

GMAT:	590 (normally)
UGPA:	3.0

Other Considerations:
   Professional work experience and leadership

Average Student Profile:

GMAT:	655
GPA:	3.35
Work experience:	5.4 years

Program Resources

Students Required to Have Computers:	N/A
Video Teleconferencing:	N/A
Physical Library Facilities:	N/A
Online Library Facilities:	N/A
HRCI Certification Preparation:	YES

   Methods: speakers, study groups; also preparatory classes available in local area

SHRM Student Chapter:			YES
Fellowships:	Varies	AMT:	$10,600 + tuition waivers
Scholarships:	Varies	AMT:	Varies
Assistantships:	Varies	AMT:	$5,300 + tuition waivers
Eligibility:			Full-Time Enrollment

Curriculum

Required Courses:
   Business Communications
   Managerial Economics/Public Policy
   Financial Accounting
   Data, Models, and Decisions
   Leadership and Teamwork
   Marketing Management
   Global Economic Environment
   Managing Human Capital
   Managerial Accounting
   Strategic Management
   Strategic Information Systems
   Supply Chain Logistics
   Operations Management

Most Popular Elective Courses:
   Executive Power and Negotiations
   Change Management
   Performance & Rewards Management
   Managing e-Commerce
   Strategic Human Resources
   Leadership, Consulting, and Team Skills
   Self and Organizational Development
   Teams: Actual and Virtual
   Implementing Strategy

Career Tracks/Concentrations:	N/A
Internship Required:	N/A

Career Services

Career Services Offered:	
Summer Internship Placement Rate:	75%
Full-Time Placement Rate:	95-100%
Average Starting Salary (Full-Time Graduates):	$59,700
Average Sign-on Bonus:	$7,300
Companies Recruiting HR Master's Graduates:	55

Points of Excellence

The curriculum in HR emphasizes the Strategic HR Change Agent Role. Specific course sections designed to develop and emphasize this role include Organizational Change Models.

Faculty: Distinguished faculty includes prolific scholars and award-winning teachers who consult with a variety of organizations on management issues. Four faculty members are Fellows of Academy of Management. Four serve on the board of leading professional journals. Many are involved in innovative consulting work that targets research with current HR issues.

Contact Information

Robert H. Smith School of Business
Master's Programs Office
University of Maryland
2308 Van Munching Hall
College Park, MD 20742
www.rhsmith.umd.edu

Sabrina White, Director of Admissions
Telephone: (301) 405-2278   FAX: (301) 314-9862
Mba_info@rhsmith.umd.edu

Admission Deadlines

May 1 for Fall admissions
Online Application: YES

University of Minnesota

Minneapolis, Minnesota
Carlson School of Management,
Industrial Relations Center

Degree

Master of Human Resources and Industrial Relations (MA-HRIR)

University Overview

A top-20 public university located in downtown Minneapolis with great access to internships, employment, and mentorship opportunities in HR.

Program Description

The Masters program has an HR generalist emphasis structured around six areas: staffing, training and development, organizational theory and behavior, compensation and benefits, labor market analysis, and labor relations. The second year of the program offers classes only in the evening so students may work at internships.

Degree Requirements

Total Credits Required:	48
Average Credits per Course:	2-4
Course Schedule:	Semester
Total Courses Required:	17
HR/IR Courses Required:	14
Average Time for Completion:	2 years
Maximum Time Allowed for Completion:	7 years
Accepts Credits from Other Universities:	YES
Total:	18 Hours

Tuition

In-state	$6,785	(per year)
	N/A	(per credit hour)
Out-of-state	$12,535	(per year)
	N/A	(per credit hour)

Program Delivery

Traditional Day Program:	YES
Nontraditional Program:	YES
Evening Program:	YES
Weekend Program:	NO
Summer Courses:	YES
Some Courses Online:	NO
Full Program Online:	NO
Distance Learning/Offsite:	NO
Executive Education:	NO
Overseas Study Abroad:	YES

Faculty

Full-Time Faculty:	18
Part-Time Faculty:	14
Faculty to Student Ratio:	1:10

Primary Teaching Methods:

Case Study	Team Projects
Lecture	Student Presentations
Field Projects	

Faculty Who Consult Outside: 1-24%

Faculty Involvement:
Society for Industrial and Organizational Psychology
Industrial Relations Research Association
International Industrial Relations Association
National Academy of Arbitrators
University and College Labor Education Association
Board of Directors, GOALS

Top 5 Faculty Publications:
Journal of Applied Psychology
Personnel Psychology
Journal of Human Relations
Industrial and Labor Relations Review
Journal of Economic Behavior & Organization

Students

Total Enrollment:			240
Full-Time Enrollment:			59%
Men:	35%	Women:	65%
Hispanic:	1%	African-American:	6%
Other Minorities:	5%	International:	15%
Average Age:	26	Age Range:	22-45
Work Full Time:			25-49%
HR Experience:			25-49%
Speak 2nd Language:			1-24%

Minimum Admission Requirements:

GRE Score:	450
GMAT Score:	450
UGPA:	3.0

Other Considerations:
Experience and recommendations
Average Student Profile:

GMAT Score:	580
or GRE Score:	500(V), 600(Q)
UGPA:	3.5

Program Resources

Students Required to Have Computers:	NO
Video Teleconferencing:	YES
Physical Library Facilities:	YES
Online Library Facilities:	YES
HRCI Certification Preparation:	NO
SHRM Student Chapter:	YES

Fellowships:	14	AMT:	$6,000
Scholarships:			NO
Assistantships:	8	AMT:	$5,000
Eligibility:			Full-Time Enrollment

Curriculum

Required Courses:
Staffing/Recruitment
Development/Training
Org. Behavior & Theory
Labor Market Analysis
Compensation/Benefits
Quantitative Methods
Labor Relations

Most Popular Elective Courses:
HRIS
International HR
Employment Law
Managing Diversity
Financial Accounting
Managerial Communication

Career Tracks/Concentrations:

Compensation and Benefits	HR Generalist
Labor Relations	Staffing, Training, and Development

Internship Required: YES

Career Services

Career Services Offered:

Mentoring	Field Trips
SHRM Student Chapter	Resume Services
Interview Training	Campus Interviews
Internships	Career Options Panels

Summer Internship Placement Rate:	95-100%
Full-Time Placement Rate:	95-100%
Average Starting Salary (Full-Time Graduates):	$62,400
Average Sign-on Bonus:	$6,000
Companies Recruiting HR Master's Graduates:	50

Points of Excellence

Curriculum: A recent innovation is the launch of a field project course in which teams of students help local organizations with HR problems. The program has also significantly increased the access to core MBA classes such as Financial Accounting and has developed an MBA-type managerial communications class focused on HR applications.

Placement: Minnesota has a strong alumni network. More than 2,000 successful alumni provide a network of HR professionals who provide support to the graduate program. One direct benefit is the student-alumni mentorship program in which students are paired with local alumni. Metropolitan location facilitates student access to local working professionals. Alumni around the country are instrumental in developing and maintaining strong corporate linkages which provide case studies and guest speakers for classes and employment opportunities for students.

Contact Information

3-300 Carlson School of Management
321 19th Ave. South
Minneapolis, MN 55455-0438
www.irc.csom.umn.edu

Robert Glunz, Department Administrator
Telephone: (612) 625-5563   FAX: (612) 624-8360
rglunz@csom.umn.edu

John W. Budd, Associate Professor & Director
Graduate Studies
Telephone: (612) 624-2500   FAX: (612) 624-8360
jbudd@csom.umn.edu

Admission Deadlines

June 15 for Fall admissions
Online Application: NO

University of New Haven

West Haven, Connecticut
College of Arts and Sciences,
Department of Psychology

Degree

Master of Arts in Industrial/Organizational Psychology (MA-I/O)

University Overview

Private comprehensive university based in southern New England. Prepares both traditional and returning students for successful careers in a global society.

Program Description

The study and practice of industrial and organizational psychology is directed toward enhancing the effectiveness and functioning of organizations by applying psychological principles to human work behavior. The primary goal of the program is to provide students with the knowledge and experience necessary to improve the satisfaction and productivity of people at work.

Degree Requirements

Total Credits Required:	48
Average Credits per Course:	3
Course Schedule:	Trimester
Total Courses Required:	14 + Internship or Thesis
Average Time for Completion:	1 ½ -2 years
Maximum Time Allowed for Completion:	5
Accepts Credits from Other Universities:	YES
Total:	15 Hours

Tuition

In-state	N/A	(per year)
	$390	(per credit hour)
Out-of-state	N/A	(per year)
	$390	(per credit hour)

Program Delivery

Traditional Day Program:	NO
Nontraditional Program:	YES
Evening Program:	YES
Weekend Program:	YES
Summer Courses:	YES
Some Courses Online:	NO
Full Program Online:	NO
Distance Learning/Offsite:	NO
Executive Education:	NO
Overseas Study Abroad:	YES

Faculty

Full-Time Faculty:		4
Part-Time Faculty:		3
Faculty to Student Ratio:		1:20
Primary Teaching Methods:		
Case Study	Team Projects	
Experiential Learning	Lecture	
Faculty Who Consult Outside:		N/A
Faculty Involvement:		N/A
Top 5 Faculty Publications:		N/A

Students

Total Enrollment:			80
Full-Time Enrollment:			67%
Men:	44%	Women:	56%
Hispanic:	2%	African-American:	4%
Other Minorities:	2%	International:	7%
Average Age:	30	Age Range:	22-60
Work Full Time:			25-49%
HR Experience:			N/A
Speak 2nd Language:			N/A
Minimum Admission Requirements:			
GRE and UGPA:			3.0
Other Considerations:			
Review of total achievement			
Average Student Profile:			
GRE Scores:			1100 (530V & 570Q)
Work experience:			5 years

Program Resources

Students Required to Have Computers:			NO
Video Teleconferencing:			NO
Physical Library Facilities:			YES
Online Library Facilities:			YES
HRCI Certification Preparation:			YES
Encourages student study groups			
Links students to local SHRM chapter study groups			
Offers the SHRM Learning System as a teaching tool			
Offers practice exams			
SHRM Student Chapter:			YES
Fellowships:	6	AMT:	$500
Scholarships:	3	AMT:	$500
Assistantships:	25	AMT:	$9,000
Eligibility:			Full-Time Enrollment

Curriculum

Required Courses:
  Industrial Relations
  Statistics
  Research Methods
  Organizational Behavior
  Industrial Psychology
  Assessment
  Motivation
  Seminar in I/O Psychology
Most Popular Elective Courses:
  International HR
  Compensation/Benefits
  Development/Training
  Recruitment/Retention
  Employment Law
  Management
  Conflict Management
  Leadership & Team Bldg.
  Organizational Change
  Performance Management

Career Tracks/Concentrations:
Industrial Psychology/   Organizational Psychology
Human Resources   Conflict Management
Internship Required: NO

Career Services
Career Services Offered:
Mentoring   Interview Training
Field Trips   Campus Interview
SHRM Student Chapter   Internships
Resume Services

Summer Internship Placement Rate:	100%
Full-Time Placement Rate:	75-100%
Average Starting Salary (Full-Time Graduates):	$58,500
Average Sign-on Bonus:	$2,000
Companies Recruiting HR Master's Graduates:	5

Points of Excellence
Curriculum: Students gain practical HRM and OD experience, which translates into increased marketability through project-based work.

Resources: The University of New Haven is affiliated with the Human Resource Association of Greater New Haven. It provides internship opportunities, mentoring, job shadowing, scholarships, speakers, and workshops. PHR certification study each year allows students to certify before entering the job market and allows those with prior HRM experience to enhance their knowledge of the field and increase their marketability at the same time.

Contact Information
University of New Haven
Department of Psychology
300 Orange Ave.
West Haven, CT 06516
www.newhaven.edu

Tara L'Heureux, Ph.D., Program Coordinator, I/O Psychology
Telephone: (203) 932-7341   FAX: (203) 932-7429
Lheureux@charger.newhaven.edu

Admission Deadlines
Online Application: YES

University of North Florida

Jacksonville, Florida
College of Business Administration

Degree
Master of Human Resource Management (MHRM)

University Overview
State-funded metropolitan university.

Program Description
Part-Time graduate program designed to provide a professional education to persons wishing to specialize in personnel management and industrial relations in business and industry.

Degree Requirements
Total Credits Required:	36
Average Credits per Course:	3
Course Schedule:	Semester
Total Courses Required:	12
HR/IR Courses Required:	8
Average Time for Completion:	2-3 years
Maximum Time Allowed for Completion:	7 years

Accepts Credits from Other Universities:	YES
Total:	N/A

Tuition
In-state	$6,000	(per year)
	$500	(per credit hour)
Out-of-state	$18,000	(per year)
	$1,500	(per credit hour)

Program Delivery
Traditional Day Program:	NO
Nontraditional Program:	YES
Evening Program:	YES
Weekend Program:	NO
Summer Courses:	N/A
Some Courses Online:	NO
Full Program Online:	NO
Distance Learning/Offsite:	NO
Executive Education:	N/A
Overseas Study Abroad:	NO

Faculty
Full-Time Faculty:	6
Part-Time Faculty:	3
Faculty to Student Ratio:	1:10

Primary Teaching Methods:
Experiential Learning   Research
Team Projects   Field Projects
Computer Simulation

Faculty Who Consult Outside:	25-49%

Faculty Involvement:
Director and Secretary Treasurer, SHRM Foundation Board
Vice Chair, Academy of International Business Southeast
Top 5 Faculty Publications:
Production and Inventory Management Journal
Employee Responsibilities and Rights Journal
Labor Law Journal
Journal of Labor Research
Management Information Systems Quarterly

Students
Total Enrollment:			30
Full-Time Enrollment:			0%
Men:	30%	Women:	70%
Hispanic:	10%	African-American:	7%
Other Minorities:	3%	International:	0%
Average Age:	31	Age Range:	N/A
Work Full Time:			75-99%
HR Experience:			75-99%
Speak 2nd Language:			1-24%

Minimum Admission Requirements:
GMAT & UGPA:	3.0
Other Considerations:	N/A

Average Student Profiles:
GMAT Score:	479

Program Resources
Students Required to Have Computers:		N/A
Video Teleconferencing:		NO
Physical Library Facilities:		N/A
Online Library Facilities:		N/A
HRCI Certification Preparation:		YES

Links students to local SHRM chapter study groups
SHRM Student Chapter:		YES
Fellowships:		NO
Scholarships:	2	AMT: $1,000
Assistantships:	2	AMT: $6,000
Eligibility:		Full-Time Enrollment

Curriculum

Required Courses:
> HR Strategy
> Compensation/Benefits
> Employment Law
> Management
> Employment Relations
> Labor Relations
> HR Measurement

Most Popular Elective Courses:
> Statistics
> Quantitative Management
> Economics
> Development/Training
> Health Administration
> Public Administration

Career Tracks/Concentrations:	N/A
Internship Required:	NO

Career Services

Career Services Offered:

Mentoring	SHRM Student Chapter
Resume Services	Interview Training
Internships	

Summer Internship Placement Rate:	N/A
Full-Time Placement Rate:	(all students employed full-time)
Average Starting Salary (Full-Time Graduates):	N/A
Average Sign-on Bonus:	N/A
Companies Recruiting HR Master's Graduates:	N/A

Points of Excellence

Curriculum: The major program orientation is toward business and industry, with a focus on the productive use of human resources in the pursuit of enterprise goals. A primary program theme is the interrelationship between quality of work life and the personal satisfaction, growth, and development of employees, as well as their productivity, efficiency, and concern with quality and creativity. Consequently, courses dealing with institutional, legal, and regulatory considerations focus principally on personnel and industrial relations systems, practices, laws, and regulations in business and industry. Personnel and industrial relations systems, practices, laws, and regulations found in nonprofit and public organizations may be covered for comparative purposes, particularly where practices developing in the nonprofit or public arena pertain to business and industry.

Contact Information

University of North Florida
4567 St. John's Bluff Rd.
Jacksonville, FL 32233
www.unf.edu/coba

Jeffrey E. Michelman, Ph.D.
Associate Dean & Director of Graduate Studies
Telephone: (904) 620-2590   FAX: (904) 620-2594
jmichelm@unf.edu

Cheryl Van Deusen, Ph.D., Assistant Professor
Telephone: (904) 620-2780   FAX: (904) 620-2594
cvandeus@unf.edu

Admission Deadlines

Online Application:	YES

University of Rhode Island

Kingston, Rhode Island
Schmidt Labor Research Center

Degree

Master of Science in Labor Relations and Human Resources (MSLRHR)

University Overview

The University of Rhode Island is a state-funded institution that enrolls about 10,000 undergraduates and 3,000 graduate students. The University's main campus is situated in a spacious rural setting in Kingston, 30 miles south of Providence.

Program Description

Specializations are available in either labor relations or human resources. Exceptional students who come into the program with a well-defined interest and proposed plan of study may choose to create their own specialization.

Degree Requirements

Total Credits Required:	39
Average Credits per Course:	3
Course Schedule:	Semester
Total Courses Required:	13
HR/IR Courses Required:	13
Average Time for Completion:	2-3 years
Maximum Time Allowed for Completion:	6 years
Accepts Credits from Other Universities:	YES
Total:	12 Hours

Tuition

In-state	$3,540	(per year)
	$197	(per credit hour)
Out-of-state	$5,310	(per year)
	N/A	(per credit hour)

Program Delivery

Traditional Day Program:	NO
Nontraditional Program:	YES
Evening Program:	YES
Weekend Program:	YES
Summer Courses:	YES
Some Courses Online:	NO
Full Program Online:	NO
Distance Learning/Offsite:	NO
Executive Education:	NO
Overseas Study Abroad:	NO

Faculty

Full-Time Faculty:	15
Part-Time Faculty:	5
Faculty to Student Ratio:	1:10

Primary Teaching Methods:

Case Study	Experiential Learning
Student Presentations	Group Discussion

Faculty Who Consult Outside:	25-49%

Faculty Involvement:
> Secretary/Treasurer, University Council of Industrial Relations and Human Resource Programs
> Member, Steering Committee of the National Academy of Social Insurance Study Panel on Workers' Compensation

Top 5 Faculty Publications:
> *Journal of Vocational Behavior*
> *Labor Law Journal*
> *Journal of Collective Negotiations in Public Sector*

133

Students

Total Enrollment:			24
Full-Time Enrollment:			34%
Men:	54%	Women:	46%
Hispanic:	4%	African-American:	8%
Other Minorities:	0%	International:	0%
Average Age:	35	Age Range:	22-52
Work Full Time:			75-99%
HR Experience:			50-74%
Speak 2nd Language:			1-24%

Minimum Admission Requirements:
  UGPA
Other Considerations:
  Relevant work experience
Average Student Profiles:
  Two-thirds have management or trade union experience

Program Resources

Students Required to Have Computers:		NO
Video Teleconferencing:		NO
Physical Library Facilities:		YES
Online Library Facilities:		YES
HRCI Certification Preparation:		NO
SHRM Student Chapter:		NO
Fellowships:		NO
Scholarships:		NO
Assistantships:	2	AMT:	$9,555
Eligibility:		Full-Time Enrollment

Curriculum

Required Courses:
  HR Strategy
  International HR
  Compensation
  Development/Training
  Recruitment/Retention
  Employment Law
  Employee Relations
  Labor Relations
Most Popular Elective Courses:
  Negotiation and ADR
  Org. Theory & Behavior
  Arbitration & Mediation
  Employee Benefit Programs
Career Tracks/Concentrations:
  Human Relations   Labor Relations
Internship Required: N/A

Career Services

Career Services Offered:
  Mentoring   Field Trips
  Resume Services   Interview Training
  Campus Interviews   Internships

Summer Internship Placement Rate:	N/A
Full-Time Placement Rate:	N/A
Average Starting Salary (Full-Time Graduates):	N/A
Average Sign-on Bonus:	N/A
Companies Recruiting HR Master's Graduates:	N/A

Points of Excellence

Curriculum: The curriculum focuses on the policies and practices of labor relations and human resources, the legal environment, and interpersonal skill requirements for the HR/IR professional. The typical internship program involves a special project jointly supervised by the employer and the Center Director, such as the design and implementation of an Affirmative Action plan or training program. The outcome is a report describing the plan and providing a rationale for the particulars.

Placement: Mentoring is provided through both faculty and alumni on an individual basis. URI placement services offer career planning and placement services, including resume preparation and training in interviewing skills. In addition, URI placement services promote graduates through job fairs and scheduled corporate on-campus interviews.

Faculty: Faculty have a wide range of interests and expertise with numerous publications in top human resource and industrial relations journals. Two LRC faculty have earned university-wide recognition for their teaching ability within the past five years. Because of the low student/faculty ratio, students receive personal attention from faculty.

Contact Information

Schmidt Labor Research Center
University of Rhode Island
36 Upper College Rd.
Hart House
Kingston, RI 02881
www.uri.edu/research/lrc

Terry Thomason, Director
Telephone: (401) 874-2239   FAX: (401) 874-2954
thomason@uri.edu

Admission Deadlines

July 15 for Fall admissions
Online Application: NO

University of St. Thomas

St. Paul, Minnesota
College of Business

Degree

Master of Business Administration in Human Resource Management (MBA/HRM)

University Overview

Largest private university in Minnesota, founded in 1885. Total student enrollment is 11,000, with approximately 3,200 in the Graduate School of Business. It is the fourth largest graduate business school in the United States.

Program Description

The MBA in Human Resource Management degree program provides training in all the aspects of human resource administration, ranging from the theoretical to the applied. In addition, it integrates the common foundations of MBA study, including such topics as finance, marketing, and decision making.

Degree Requirements

Total Credits Required:	45-53
Average Credits per Course:	3
Course Schedule:	Semester
Total Courses Required:	15-17
HR/IR Courses Required:	No limit
Average Time for Completion:	2 ½-4 ½ years
Maximum Time Allowed for Completion:	9
Accepts Credits from Other Universities:	YES
Total:	9 Hours

Tuition

In-state	N/A	(per year)
	$480	(per credit hour)
Out-of-state	N/A	(per year)
	$480	(per credit hour)

Program Delivery

Traditional Day Program:	YES
Nontraditional Program:	YES
Evening Program:	YES
Weekend Program:	YES
Summer Courses:	YES
Some Courses Online:	YES
Full Program Online:	NO
Distance Learning/Offsite:	YES
Executive Education:	NO
Overseas Study Abroad:	YES

Faculty

Full-Time Faculty:	8
Part-Time Faculty:	18
Faculty to Student Ratio:	1:10

Primary Teaching Methods:

Case Study	Team Projects
Experiential Learning	Group Discussion
Computer Simulations	

Faculty Who Consult Outside:	75-99%

Faculty Involvement:
Vice President Twin Cities HR Association
Society of IO Psychology
TCHRA Strategic Planning Committee

Top 5 Faculty Publications:
Human Resource Management

Students

Total Enrollment:			260
Full-Time Enrollment:			18%
Men:	25%	Women:	75%
Hispanic:	2%	African-American:	6%
Other Minorities:	8%	International:	15%
Average Age:	33	Age Range:	22-59
Work Full Time:			75-99%
HR Experience:			50-74%
Speak 2nd Language:			25-49%

Minimum Admission Requirements:

GMAT Score:	500
GRE Score:	1500
Work experience:	2 years
UGPA:	3.0

Other Considerations:
Work experience, UGPA

Average Student Profiles:

GMAT Score:	540
GRE Score:	1680
Work experience:	10 years
UGPA:	3.4

Program Resources

Students Required to Have Computers:	YES
Video Teleconferencing:	YES
Physical Library Facilities:	YES
Online Library Facilities:	YES
HRCI Certification Preparation:	YES

Encourages student study groups/links students with local SHRM chapters
Bases curriculum on the certification exam content

SHRM Student Chapter:			YES
Fellowships:	Varies	AMT:	Varies
Scholarships:	Varies	AMT:	Varies
Assistantships:	Varies	AMT:	Varies
Eligibility:			All Students

Curriculum

Required Courses:
Accounting
Finance
Marketing
HR Strategy
Compensation/Benefits
Recruitment/Retention
Employment Law
Business Functional Areas

Most Popular Elective Courses:
Management Training
Org. Intervention & Design
Performance Systems
Strategic Analysis
Arbitration
Mediation

Career Tracks/Concentrations:
Benefits, Compensation, HR Law, International HR, Organizational Development, Training

Internship Required:	NO

Career Services

Career Services Offered:

Mentoring	Field Trips
SHRM Student Chapter	Resume Services
Interview Training	Campus Interview
Internships	Placement Services

Summer Internship Placement Rate:	N/A
Full-Time Placement Rate:	100%
Average Starting Salary (Full-Time Graduates):	$54,000
Average Sign-on Bonus:	N/A
Companies Recruiting HR Master's Graduates:	35-40

Points of Excellence

Faculty: Highly committed and approachable, with years of practical real world experience. Very strong ties to the business and professional community allow the program to draw on a broad range of experts and placement for jobs and field research opportunities for students and to support faculty needs. Excellent group of student advisors. Upon entering program, each student is assigned an advisor who will work with him or her until graduation.

Curriculum: In-depth course and faculty assessment system monitors and evaluates classroom and program performance. This is supported by student, alumni, and administrative input. Each instructor is evaluated by their students at the midpoint and the end of each course. The instructors are required to write a response to their evaluations and their action plan to address any issues that might have been uncovered. Instructor education and development program focuses on classroom performance, distance learning technology, and case method approaches.

Contact Information

St. Thomas University
Graduate School of Business
1000 LaSalle Ave.
Minneapolis, MN 55403
www.gsb.stthomas.edu

Phil Schechter, SPHR, Director
Sharon Gibson, Asst. Professor
Telephone: (651) 962-4245, 4259   FAX: (651) 962-4710
pischechter@stthomas.edu
skgibson@stthomas.edu

Admission Deadlines

July 1 for Fall admissions

Online Application:	YES

University of Scranton

Scranton, Pennsylvania
Department of Health Administration and
Human Resources

Degree
Master of Science in Human Resources (MSHR)

University Overview
Private (Jesuit), coeducational, master's level institution. Approximately 4,800 students located in the beautiful Northeast Pennsylvania mountains, two hours from New York City and Philadelphia.

Program Description
The program contains three major specializations from which to choose. Organizational Leadership provides a broad academic preparation in general organization leadership and administration. Human Resources and Human Resources Development are more specialized and prepare the student for delineated professional roles in human resources administration. The specialization is shown in the student's transcript. Most students attend program part time.

Degree Requirements
Total Credits Required:	39
Average Credits per Course:	3
Course Schedule:	Semester
Total Courses Required:	13
HR/IR Courses Required:	13
Average Time for Completion:	1 ½-2 years
Maximum Time Allowed for Completion:	6 years
Accepts Credits from Other Universities:	YES
Total:	9 Hours

Tuition
In-state	N/A	(per year)
	$490	(per credit hour)
Out-of-state	N/A	(per year)
	$490	(per credit hour)

Program Delivery
Traditional Day Program:	NO
Nontraditional Program:	YES
Evening Program:	YES
Weekend Program:	NO
Summer Courses:	YES
Some Courses Online:	NO
Full Program Online:	NO
Distance Learning/Offsite:	NO
Executive Education:	NO
Overseas Study Abroad:	NO

Faculty
Full-Time Faculty:	2
Part-Time Faculty:	5
Faculty to Student Ratio:	1:20

Primary Teaching Methods:
Lecture	Case Study
Research	Team Projects
Computer Simulations	

Faculty Who Consult Outside:	N/A
Faculty Involvement:	N/A
Top 5 Faculty Publications:	N/A

Students
Total Enrollment:	70
Full-Time Enrollment:	15%

Men:	N/A	Women:	N/A
Hispanic:	N/A	African-American:	N/A
Other Minorities:	N/A	International:	N/A
Average Age:	35	Age Range:	22-55
Work Full Time:			75-99%
HR Experience:			75-99%
Speak 2nd Language:			1-24%

Minimum Admission Requirements:
  UGPA
Other Considerations:
  Can be accepted on probationary basis
Average Student Profiles:
Work experience:	8 years

Program Resources
Students Required to Have Computers:			NO
Video Teleconferencing:			YES
Physical Library Facilities:			YES
Online Library Facilities:			YES
HRCI Certification Preparation:			YES
Encourages student study groups			
Links students to local SHRM chapter study groups			
SHRM Student Chapter:			YES
Fellowships:			NO
Scholarships:			NO
Assistantships:	1	AMT:	Tuition + stipend
Eligibility:			N/A

Curriculum
Required Courses:
  HR Strategy
  International HR
  Compensation/Benefits
  Development/Training
  Recruitment/Retention
  Employment Law
  Management
  Labor Relations
  HR Measurement
  Organizational Leadership
Most Popular Elective Courses:
  EAP
  Health & Safety
  Organizational Change
  Control & Budget
  HR Planning
  Group Behavior
  Ethics
Career Tracks/Concentrations:
Human Resources	Human Resource Development
Organizational Leadership	

Internship Required:	NO

Career Services
Career Services Offered:
Mentoring	SHRM Student Chapter
Resume Services	Interview Training
Internships	

Summer Internship Placement Rate:	N/A
Full-Time Placement Rate:	N/A
Average Starting Salary (Full-Time Graduates):	N/A
Average Sign-on Bonus:	N/A
Companies Recruiting HR Master's Graduates:	N/A

Points of Excellence
Curriculum: The HR curriculum has three core courses. Two core courses, Organizational Leadership and Human Resources, provide foundational knowledge in organizational concepts, theories, and human resource practices and should be

taken in the first semester of study. The third core course, Professional Contribution, is a capstone course taken in the final semester before graduation. A specialization provides in-depth study in a particular area and encompasses five courses or 15 credits including one required course. The remaining 15 credits can be taken from other courses in the curriculum. For students with little work experience, an internship is recommended near the completion of coursework. Computer applications are integrated throughout the curriculum, so entering students are expected to have proficiency in word processing, spreadsheet, presentations, and database applications.

Contact Information

Dept. of Health Administration & Human Resources
University of Scranton
413 McGurrin Hall
Scranton, PA 18510
www.academic.uofs.edu/department/HAHR

Dr. William G. Wallick, Ph.D., CHE, SPHR
Telephone: (570) 941-4128   FAX: (570) 941-5882
wgw1@scranton.edu

Admission Deadlines

Online Application: NO

University of South Carolina

Columbia, South Carolina
Darla Moore School of Business

Degree
Master of Human Resources (MHR)

University Overview
The University of South Carolina is a state-funded institution with approximately 25,000 students.

Program Description
This full-time traditional day program offers broad exposure to HR strategy, business fundamentals, and international issues as well as functional areas of HR (e.g., selection, training, and labor relations).

Degree Requirements

Total Credits Required:	45-57
Average Credits per Course:	3
Course Schedule:	Semester
Total Courses Required:	13-17
HR/IR Courses Required:	10
Average Time for Completion:	1 ½ years
Maximum Time Allowed for Completion:	N/A
Accepts Credits from Other Universities:	YES
Total:	N/A

Tuition

In-state	$4,014	(per year)
	N/A	(per credit hour)
Out-of-state	$8,528	(per year)
	N/A	(per credit hour)

Program Delivery

Traditional Day Program:	YES
Nontraditional Program:	NO
Evening Program:	NO
Weekend Program:	NO
Summer Courses:	N/A
Some Courses Online:	NO
Full Program Online:	NO

Distance Learning/Offsite:	NO
Executive Education:	NO
Overseas Study Abroad:	NO

Faculty

Full-Time Faculty:	9
Part-Time Faculty:	0
Faculty to Student Ratio:	1:10

Primary Teaching Methods:

Lecture	Case Study
Team Projects	Student Presentations
Computer Simulations	

Faculty Who Consult Outside: 25-49%
Faculty Involvement:
    President, Industrial Relations Research Association (IRRA)
    Associate Editor, *Human Resource Management Journal*
    Member, Academic Partners Network
    Member, American Compensation Association
    Member, Board of Directors for The Industrial Relations Council on GOALS
Top 5 Faculty Publications:
    Personnel Psychology
    Industrial Relations
    Academy of Management Journal
    Human Resource Management Journal
    Journal of Applied Psychology

Students

Total Enrollment:			50
Full-Time Enrollment:			100%
Men:	34%	Women:	66%
Hispanic:	2%	African-American:	6%
Other Minorities:	8%	International:	12%
Average Age:	26	Age Range:	22-34
Work Full Time:			1-24%
HR Experience:			1-24%
Speak 2nd Language:			1-24%

Minimum Admission Requirements:
    GRE or GMAT & UGPA (no minimum specified)
Other Considerations:
    Work experience and recommendations
Average Student Profiles:

GMAT Score:	570
GRE Score:	600 all dimensions
Work experience:	2 years

Program Resources

Students Required to Have Computers:			NO
Video Teleconferencing:			NO
Physical Library Facilities:			YES
Online Library Facilities:			YES
HRCI Certification Preparation:			YES
Encourages student study groups			
Base curriculum upon certification exam content			
SHRM Student Chapter:			YES
Fellowships:	7	AMT:	$3,500 + reduced tuition and fees
Scholarships:			NO
Assistantships:	10	AMT:	$2,000 + reduced tuition and fees
Eligibility:			Full-Time Enrollment

Curriculum
Required Courses:
    Accounting
    Finance
    HR Strategy
    International HR
    Compensation/Benefits

Development/Training
Recruitment/Retention
Employment Law
Labor Relations
HR Measurement
Most Popular Elective Courses:
Work Teams
Managing Careers
Mergers & Acquisitions
Career Tracks/Concentrations: NO
Internship Required: YES

Career Services
Career Services Offered:
SHRM Student Chapter   Interview Training
Campus Interviews   Resume Services
Internships
Summer Internship Placement Rate: N/A
Full-Time Placement Rate: 95%
Average Starting Salary (Full-Time Graduates): $62,500
Average Sign-on Bonus: $1,000
Companies Recruiting HR Master's Graduates: 27

Points of Excellence
Faculty: The Distinguished Lecturer Series brings in over a dozen leading HR executives to provide guest lectures on the latest developments in HR. These lectures provide unique opportunities for our students to interact with leaders in the HR field. The Executive in Residence Program provides for a retired HR executive to serve on the MHR faculty and to mentor MHR students.

Curriculum: The University of South Carolina maintains strong relationships with corporate supporters through the HR Advisory Board. The board ensures that the curriculum reflects developments in the field and helps to provide internship placement opportunities and generous fellowship awards to our students.

Contact Information
Darla Moore School of Business
University of South Carolina
1705 College St.
Columbia, SC 29208
www.business.sc.edu/mhr

Dean Kress, Managing Director
Telephone: (803) 777-7015   FAX: (803) 777-6876
kress@moore.sc.edu

Brian Klaas, Ph.D., Academic Director
Telephone: (803) 777-4901   FAX: (803) 777-6876
klaasb@darla.badm.sc.edu

Admission Deadlines
July 15 for Fall admissions
Online Application: YES

University of Tennessee at Chattanooga

Chattanooga, Tennessee
Psychology Department

Degree
Master of Science in Psychology: Industrial/Organizational Specialty (MS)

University Overview
University of Tennessee at Chattanooga (UTC) is a public metropolitan university of about 8,000 students, of which about 1,300 are graduate students, located near the historic district of downtown Chattanooga.

Program Description
The program provides thorough coverage of industrial and organizational psychology and research methods for persons interested in immediate employment and those seeking the PhD degree.

Degree Requirements
Total Credits Required: 48
Average Credits per Course: 3
Course Schedule: Semester
Total Courses Required: 16
HR/IR Courses Required: 10
Average Time for Completion: 2 years
Maximum Time Allowed for Completion: 6 years
Accepts Credits from Other Universities: YES
Total: 6 Hours

Tuition
In-state	N/A	(per year)
	$175	(per credit hour)
Out-of-state	N/A	(per year)
	$275	(per credit hour)

Program Delivery
Traditional Day Program: NO
Nontraditional Program: YES
Evening Program: YES
Weekend Program: NO
Program Completed Evening/Weekend: YES
Summer Courses: YES
Some Courses Online: NO
Full Program Online: NO
Distance Learning/Offsite: NO
Executive Education: NO
Overseas Study Abroad: NO

Faculty
Full-Time Faculty: 4
Part-Time Faculty: 1
Faculty to Student Ratio: 1:10
Primary Teaching Methods:
Lecture   Research
Student Presentation   Team Projects
Faculty Who Consult Outside: 25-49%
Faculty Involvement:
Top 5 Faculty Publications:
American Journal of Surgery

Students
Total Enrollment:			30
Full-Time Enrollment:			25
Men:	43%	Women:	57%
Hispanic:	0%	African-American:	3%
Other Minorities:	0%	International:	0%
Average Age:	25	Age Range:	23-35
Work Full Time:			1-24%
Have HR Experience:			1-24%
Speak 2nd Language:			1-24%

Minimum Admission Requirements:
UGPA: 2.4
GRE Score: 450/test GRE
Work Experience: NONE

Other Considerations:
Average Student Profile:

UGPA:		3.4
GRE Score:		V:450, Q:550, A:630
Work Experience:		NONE

Program Resources

Students Required to Have Computers:			YES
Video Teleconferencing:			NO
Physical Library Facilities:			YES
Online Library Facilities:			YES
HRCI Certification Preparation:			NO
SHRM Student Chapter:			YES
URL:			
Fellowships:	YES	AMT:	$5,000
Scholarships:	NO	AMT:	
Assistantships:	YES	AMT:	$2,500/yr
Eligibility:			

Curriculum

Required Courses:
   Development/Training
   HR Measurement
   Organizational Psychology
   Groups/Teams
   Job Analysis
   Selection
   Organization Development
Most Popular Elective Courses:
   International Management
   EEO Management
Career Tracks/Concentrations:
   HR Generalist   PhD Preparation
Internship Required: YES

Career Services

Career Services Offered:
   Field Trips   SHRM Student Chapter
   Internships

Summer Internship Placement Rate:	N/A
Facilitate Placement:	YES
Full-Time Placement Rate:	100%
Internship Placement Rate:	N/A
Average Starting Salary (Full-Time Graduates):	$35,000
Average Sign-on Bonus:	N/A
Companies Recruiting HR Master's Graduates:	N/A

Points of Excellence

Strong methodological base and complete coverage of all areas important for MS degree in I/O Psychology. Emphasis in work experience is facilitated by department's good working relationship with local SHRM chapter and work organizations. University's recent emphasis on Metropolitan College will strengthen the MS program's ties to the local community.

Contact Information

University of Tennessee at Chattanooga
Psychology Department/2803
615 McCallie Avenue
Chattanooga, TN 37403
www.utc.edu/ioprog

Administrative Contact
Dr. David Pittenger, Head, Department of Psychology
Telephone: (423) 755-4264
David-pittenger@utc.edu

Faculty Contact
Dr. Michael Biderman
Telephone: (423) 755-4268
Michael-Biderman @utc.edu

Admission Deadlines
March 15
Online Application: YES

University of Texas at Arlington

Arlington, Texas
College of Business, Department of Management

Degree
Master of Science in Human Resource Management (MSHRM)

University Overview
The University of Texas at Arlington (UTA) offers one of few specialized Master's in Human Resources statewide. Located in the center of the Dallas/Fort Worth Metroplex.

Program Description
Provides courses in all aspects of human resource administration as well as common foundations of MBA study. Full- or part-time study.

Degree Requirements

Total Credits Required:	36-48
Average Credits per Course:	3
Course Schedule:	Semester
Total Courses Required:	16
HR/IR Courses Required:	6-8
Average Time for Completion:	Varies
Maximum Time Allowed for Completion:	6 years
Accepts Credits from Other Universities:	YES
Total:	9 Hours (Semester)

Tuition

In-state	$4,521	(per year)
	N/A	(per credit hour)
Out-of-state	$11,331	(per year)
	N/A	(per credit hour)

Program Delivery

Traditional Day Program:	NO
Nontraditional Program:	YES
Evening Program:	YES
Weekend Program:	YES
Summer Courses:	YES
Some Courses Online:	YES
Full Program Online:	NO
Distance Learning/Offsite:	NO
Executive Education:	NO
Overseas Study Abroad:	NO

Faculty

Full-Time Faculty:	14
Part-Time Faculty:	Varies
Faculty to Student Ratio:	N/A

Primary Teaching Methods:
   Case Study   Lecture
   Team Projects   Student Presentations

Faculty Who Consult Outside:	1-24%
Faculty Involvement:	N/A

Top 5 Faculty Publications:
Journal of Applied Psychology
Academy of Management Executive
Journal of Management
Journal of Organizational Behavior
Organizational Behavior and Human Decision Processes

Students

Total Enrollment:			20
Full-Time Enrollment:			30%
Men:	30%	Women:	70%
Hispanic:	5%	African-American:	10%
Other Minorities:	10%	International:	10%
Average Age:	28	Age Range:	24-45
Work Full Time:			50-74%
HR Experience:			75-99%
Speak 2nd Language:			25-49%

Minimum Admission Requirements:

GMAT Score:	30th percentile
Work Experience:	NONE

Other Considerations:
GMAT/UGPA compensatory formula

Average Student Profiles:

GMAT Score:	500
Work experience:	7 years
UGPA:	3.0

Program Resources

Students Required to Have Computers:	NO
Video Teleconferencing:	YES
Physical Library Facilities:	YES
Online Library Facilities:	YES
HRCI Certification Preparation:	YES

Coursework closely corresponds with exam content areas
Encourage student study groups
Link student to local SHRM chapter studay groups

SHRM Student Chapter:			YES
Fellowships:			YES
Scholarships:			YES
Assistantships:	Varies	AMT:	$9,000-$11,000
Eligibility:			Full-Time Enrollment

Curriculum

Required Courses:
Accounting
Finance
Marketing
HR Strategy
Compensation/Benefits
Development/Training
Recruitment/Retention
Performance Evaluation & Staffing
Management
Business Functional Areas

Most Popular Elective Courses:
Labor Relations
Organizational Behavior
Human Resource Law
Diversity in Organizations
Stress

Career Tracks/Concentrations:	N/A
Internship Required:	NO

Career Services

Career Services Offered:

Mentoring	SHRM Student Chapter
Resume Services	Field Trips
Internships	

Summer Internship Placement Rate:	N/A
Full-Time Placement Rate:	N/A
Average Starting Salary (Full-Time Graduates):	$45,000
Average Sign-on Bonus:	N/A
Companies Recruiting HR Master's Graduates:	N/A

Points of Excellence

Curriculum: Students are required to form teams. Each team must find a client for whom to do a consulting project. The team must then present the results to the client and their class. Some students have received job offers from their clients upon graduation.

Faculty: Use of diverse speakers in the HR field supplements the coursework. Because of the University of Texas at Arlington's unique location, the school has access to many large corporations. The HR Program strives to take advantage of these experts.

Contact Information

The University of Texas at Arlington
Management Department
Box 19467
Arlington, TX 76019-0467
www.management.uta.edu

Dr. Myrtle Bell
Telephone: (817) 272-3857   FAX: 817-272-3122
mpbell@uta.edu

Admission Deadlines

June 14 for Fall admissions

Online Application:	YES

University of West Florida

Pensacola, Florida
Department of Psychology

Degree
Master of Industrial/Organizational Psychology (MAI/O)

University Overview
Public university (state-funded) with approximately 8,000 students, located in Pensacola, Florida.

Program Description
Full-time traditional day program emphasizes personnel selection/appraisal, organizational change and development, and organizational psychology.

Degree Requirements

Total Credits Required:	42
Average Credits per Course:	3
Course Schedule:	Semester
Total Courses Required:	11
HR/IR Courses Required:	4
Average Time for Completion:	2-3 years
Maximum Time Allowed for Completion:	7 years
Accepts Credits from Other Universities:	N/A
Total:	N/A

Tuition

In-state	N/A	(per year)
	$156	(per credit hour)
Out-of-state	N/A	(per year)
	$535	(per credit hour)

Program Delivery

Traditional Day Program:	YES
Nontraditional Program:	NO
Evening Program:	NO
Weekend Program:	NO
Summer Courses:	YES
Some Courses Online:	NO
Full Program Online:	NO
Distance Learning/Offsite:	NO
Executive Education:	NO
Overseas Study Abroad:	NO

Faculty

Full-Time Faculty:	3
Part-Time Faculty:	0
Faculty to Student Ratio:	1:10

Primary Teaching Methods:
  Field Projects   Lecture
  Student Presentations   Group Discussion

Faculty Who Consult Outside: 1-24%
Faculty Involvement:
  Southeastern Psychological Association
  Executive Board of Chairs of Graduate Departments of Psychology (COGDOP)
  Member of Society for Industrial/Organizational Psychologists (SIOP)
  Member of SHRM
Top 5 Faculty Publications: N/A

Students

Total Enrollment:			29
Full-Time Enrollment:			67%
Men:	31%	Women:	69%
Hispanic:	3%	African-American:	10%
Other Minorities:	3%	International:	3%
Average Age:	N/A	Age Range:	N/A
Work Full Time:			1-24%
HR Experience:			1-24%
Speak 2nd Language:			1-24%

Minimum Admission Requirements:
  GRE Score: 1000 or UGPA: 3.0
Other Considerations:
  Letters of recommendation and intent, GPA, GRE
Average Student Profiles:
  GRE Score: 1070

Program Resources

Students Required to Have Computers:			NO
Video Teleconferencing:			NO
Physical Library Facilities:			YES
Online Library Facilities:			YES
HRCI Certification Preparation:			NO
SHRM Student Chapter:			YES
Fellowships:	2	AMT:	N/A
Scholarships:			NO
Assistantships:	6	AMT:	$2,875
Eligibility:			Full-Time Enrollment

Curriculum

Required Courses:
  Research Methods
  Statistics
  Organizational Development
  Personnel
  Selection/Appraisal
Most Popular Elective Courses:
  Social Psychology
  Legal Issues in I/O Psych

  Human Factors
  Training & Development
Career Tracks/Concentrations:
  Personnel   Organizational Development
  Human Factors
Internship Required: YES

Career Services

Career Services Offered:
  Field Trips   SHRM Student Chapter
  Resume Services   Internships

Summer Internship Placement Rate:	100%
Full-Time Placement Rate:	100%
Average Starting Salary (Full-Time Graduates):	N/A
Average Sign-on Bonus:	N/A
Companies Recruiting HR Master's Graduates:	N/A

Points of Excellence

Curriculum: In addition to traditional classroom formats, curriculum includes hands-on experience through internships, practicum, and class projects.

Contact Information

University of West Florida
Department of Psychology
11000 University Parkway
Pensacola, FL 32514
www.uwf.edu

Diana Robinson, Office Manager
Telephone: (850) 474-2363   FAX: (850) 857-6060
drobinso@uwf.edu

Steven Kass, Ph.D., Assistant Professor
Coordinator I/O Psychology Program
Telephone: (850) 474-2107   FAX: (850) 857-6060
skass@uwf.edu

Admission Deadlines

July 1 for Fall admissions
Online Application: YES

University of Wisconsin-IR

Madison, Wisconsin
Industrial Relations Research Institute

Degree

Master of Industrial Relations (MAIR)

University Overview

A state university with over 40,000 students located in Madison, Wisconsin.

Program Description

The Industrial Relations Research Institute is one of the oldest independent degree programs in industrial relations in the United States. This interdisciplinary program offers a master's and doctoral program in industrial relations. The majority of students in the master's program accept professional positions in human resource management with major U.S. corporations.

Degree Requirements

Total Credits Required:	30-39
Average Credits per Course:	2-4
Course Schedule:	Semester
Total Courses Required:	15
HR/IR Courses Required:	10
Average Time for Completion:	2 years

Maximum Time Allowed for Completion:	6 years
Accepts Credits from Other Universities:	YES
Total:	N/A

Tuition

In-state	$5,406	(per year)
	$300	(per credit hour)
Out-of-state	$17,110	(per year)
	N/A	(per credit hour)

Program Delivery

Traditional Day Program:	YES
Nontraditional Program:	NO
Evening Program:	NO
Weekend Program:	NO
Summer Courses:	N/A
Some Courses Online:	NO
Full Program Online:	NO
Distance Learning/Offsite:	NO
Executive Education:	N/A
Overseas Study Abroad:	NO

Faculty

Full-Time Faculty:	6
Part-Time Faculty:	0
Faculty to Student Ratio:	1:10

Primary Teaching Methods:

Case Study	Research
Student Presentation	Computer-Aided Instruction
Team Projects	Experiential Learning
Field Projects	Group Discussion

Faculty Who Consult Outside:	N/A
Faculty Involvement:	N/A
Top 5 Faculty Publications:	N/A

Students

Total Enrollment:			27
Full-Time Enrollment:			100%
Men:	51%	Women:	49%
Hispanic:	0%	African-American:	0%
Other Minorities:	4%	International:	59%
Average Age:	30	Age Range:	21-45
Work Full Time:			1-24%
HR Experience:			1-24%
Speak 2nd Language:			25-49%

Minimum Admission Requirements:
    GRE or GMAT and UGPA
Other Considerations:
    Letters of recommendation and work experience
    Conditional admittance on academic probation possible
Average Student Profile:

| GRE Score: | 1760 |

Program Resources

Students Required to Have Computers:			N/A
Video Teleconferencing:			YES
Physical Library Facilities:			N/A
Online Library Facilities:			N/A
HRCI Certification Preparation:			NO
SHRM Student Chapter:			YES
Fellowships:	3	AMT:	$12,500 + Tuition
Scholarships:	4-7	AMT:	$2,500
Assistantships:	2-3	AMT:	$6,785 + Tuition
Eligibility:			Full-Time Enrollment

Curriculum

Required Courses:
    Research Theory & Methods
    HR Strategy

International HR
Compensation/Benefits
Development/Training
Recruitment/Retention
Employment Law
Employee Relations
Labor Relations
HR Measurement
Most Popular Elective Courses:
    Management
    Unions & Collective Bargaining

| Career Tracks/Concentrations: | N/A |
| Internship Required: | NO |

Career Services

Career Development Opportunities/Placement Service:

Mentoring	Interview Training
Field Trips	Campus Interviews
SHRM Student Chapter	Internships
Resume Services	

Summer Internship Placement Rate:	100%
Full-Time Placement Rate:	95%
Average Starting Salary (Full-Time Graduates):	$50,000
Average Sign-on Bonus:	$5,000
Companies Recruiting HR Master's Graduates:	12

Points of Excellence

Students: Students come to the Institute with a variety of backgrounds and interests. Because the Institute is located in the College of Letters and Science, the Institute attracts a diverse student body including a substantial fraction of foreign students. While most students work for major U.S. corporations after graduation, a significant minority of graduates goes to work for trade unions. Students value this diversity and it greatly enhances the education experience of the program.

Curriculum: Students focus in one of four areas: Labor Markets and Employment Policy; Unions and Collective Bargaining; Human Resource Management; or International and Comparative Industrial Relations. In addition to core coursework, master's students take electives and complete either a thesis or tutorial project.

Contact Information

Industrial Relations Research Institute
University of Wisconsin-Madison
4226 Social Sciences
1180 Observatory Dr.
Madison, WI 53706-1393
polyglot.lss.wisc.edu/irri/irri.html

Ruth Robarts
Director of Student and Administrative Services
Telephone: (608) 262-9889   FAX: (608) 265-4591
rrobarts@facstaff.wisc.edu

Admission Deadlines

February 1 for Fall admissions
| Online Application: | YES |

University of Wisconsin-MBA

Madison, Wisconsin
Graduate School of Business, Management and Human Resources Department

Degree
Master of Business Administration with concentration in Human Resources Management (MBA-HRM)

University Overview
Public research university with over 40,000 students enrolled as undergraduates and in numerous graduate professional programs.

Program Description
The MBA program permits a concentration in management and human resources that includes the taking of specialized HR and organizational behavior courses, along with other required business courses. The degree permits the taking of some coursework outside the school in areas such as economics, industrial relations, law, sociology, and psychology. Business foundation courses are required in addition to credits.

Degree Requirements
Total Credits Required:	36
Average Credits per Course:	2-3
Course Schedule:	Semester
Total Courses Required:	15
HR/IR Courses Required:	6
Average Time for Completion:	2 years
Maximum Time Allowed for Completion:	6 years
Accepts Credits from Other Universities:	YES
Total:	N/A

Tuition
In-state	$6,524	(per year)
	N/A	(per credit hour)
Out-of-state	$18,282	(per year)
	N/A	(per credit hour)

Program Delivery
Traditional Day Program:	YES
Nontraditional Program:	NO
Evening Program:	NO
Weekend Program:	NO
Summer Courses:	N/A
Some Courses Online:	NO
Full Program Online:	NO
Distance Learning/Offsite:	NO
Executive Education:	N/A
Overseas Study Abroad:	NO

Faculty
Full-Time Faculty:	8
Part-Time Faculty:	0
Faculty to Student Ratio:	1:20

Primary Teaching Methods:
Experiential Learning   Team Projects
Field Projects   Lecture

Faculty Who Consult Outside:	1-24%

Faculty Involvement:
SHRM National Employment Committee
SHRM Foundation Board
Human Resources and Organizational Divisions of Academy of Management
See also web site
(wiscinfo.doit.wisc.edu/bschool/dept/mgmt.htm)
Top 5 Faculty Publications: See web site

Students
Total Enrollment:			39
Full-Time Enrollment:			100%
Men:	51%	Women:	49%
Hispanic:	5%	African-American:	3%
Other Minorities:	9%	International:	18%
Average Age:	26	Age Range:	N/A
Work Full Time:			1-24%
HR Experience:			1-24%
Speak 2nd Language:			25-49%

Minimum Admission Requirements:
GRE or GMAT and UGPA
Other Considerations:
Letters of recommendation and work experience
Conditional admittance on academic probation possible
Average Student Profiles:
GMAT Score:	600
Work Experience:	4 years

Program Resources
Students Required to Have Computers:			N/A
Video Teleconferencing:			YES
Physical Library Facilities:			N/A
Online Library Facilities:			N/A
HRCI Certification Preparation:			YES
SHRM Student Chapter:			YES
Fellowships:	YES	AMT:	$12,500 + tuition
Scholarships:	YES	AMT:	$2,500
Assistantships:	2-5	AMT:	$8,900 + tuition
Eligibility:			Full-Time Enrollment

Curriculum
Required Courses:
Research Theory & Methods
HR Strategy
International HR
Compensation/Benefits
Development/Training
Recruitment/Retention
Employment Law
Employee Relations
Labor Relations
HR Measurement
Most Popular Elective Courses:
Management
Unions & Collective Bargaining
Career Tracks/Concentrations:	N/A
Internship Required:	NO

Career Services
Career Services Offered:
Mentoring   Interview Training
Field Trips   Campus Interviews
SHRM Student Chapter   Internships
Resume Services

Summer Internship Placement Rate:	N/A
Full-Time Placement Rate:	N/A
Average Starting Salary (Full-Time Graduates):	N/A
Average Sign-on Bonus:	N/A
Companies Recruiting HR Master's Graduates:	N/A

Points of Excellence
Students: The programs allow students to access a great number of HR courses, both within and outside the school. Examples of courses include HR strategy and management, staffing, compensation, labor relations, adult learning, employment law, benefits, labor markets, organization theory, HR research methods, HR skills for managers, organizational behavior, performance management, and an HR seminar.

Placement: The school operates a large Career Services Office that provides a variety of informational, counseling, and job search programs for students and alumni.

Resources: The school and the MHR department are housed within Grainger Hall, a new state-of-the-art facility in the heart of the UW-Madison campus. The building features the latest in classroom technology and classroom layouts, student lounges, eating facilities, and a large library.

Contact Information

Industrial Relations Research Institute
University of Wisconsin-Madison
4226 Social Sciences
11800 Observatory Dr.
Madison, WI 53706-1393
polyglot.lss.wisc.edu/irri/irri.html

Donna Wallace
MHR Department Assistant
Telephone: (608) 263-3648   FAX: (608) 262-8773
dwallace@bus.wisc.edu

Donald Schwab
MHR Department Chair and Professor
Telephone: (608) 263-3463   FAX: (608) 262-8773
dschwab@bus.wisc.edu

Admission Deadlines

Online Application:	YES

University of Wisconsin, Milwaukee

Milwaukee, Wisconsin
School of Business Administration

Degree
Masters in Human Resources and Labor Relations (MHRLR)

University Overview
University of Wisconsin, Milwaukee (UWM), is a comprehensive research/public university. Located in urban Milwaukee, the university offers many of its programs in evenings and weekends to accommodate student needs. The university also uses the community for internships and research opportunities. The second largest university in the state, it has more than 24,000 students enrolled in a wide variety of undergraduate and graduate degrees including nearly 20 PhD programs.

Program Description
The MHRLR program offers students an interdisciplinary blend of courses and faculty in the areas of human resources and labor relations. The MHRLR program prepares students for careers as practitioners, and emphasizes a firm educational grounding in both liberal arts and business administration.

Degree Requirements

Total Credits Required:	36
Average Credits per Course:	3
Course Schedule:	Semester
Total Courses Required:	12
HR/IR Courses Required:	6
Average Time for Completion:	3 years
Maximum Time Allowed for Completion:	7 years
Accepts Credits from Other Universities:	YES
Total:	14 Hours

Tuition

In-state	N/A	(per year)
	$1,265	(per 3 credit hour course)
Out-of-state	N/A	(per year)
	$3,759	(per 3 credit hour course)

Program Delivery

Traditional Day Program:	NO
Nontraditional Program:	YES
Evening Program:	YES
Weekend Program:	NO
Program Completed Evening/Weekend:	YES
Summer Courses:	YES
Some Courses Online:	NO
Full Program Online:	NO
Distance Learning/Offsite:	NO
Executive Education:	NO
Overseas Study Abroad:	NO

Faculty

Full-Time Faculty:	6
Part-Time Faculty:	5
Faculty to Student Ratio:	1:20
Primary Teaching Methods:	

Lecture	Team Projects
Student Presentation	Group Discussion

Faculty Who Consult Outside:	N/A
Faculty Involvement:	
Top 5 Faculty Publications:	

Journal of Applied Psychology
Industrial & Labor Relations Review
Academy of Management Journal
Industrial Relations

Students

Total Enrollment:			53
Full-Time Enrollment:			20%
Men:	30%	Women:	70%
Hispanic:	4%	African-American:	10%
Other Minorities:	N/A	International:	13%
Average Age:	27	Age Range:	22-50
Work Full Time:			75-99%
Have HR Experience:			25-49%
Speak 2nd Language:			1-24%
Minimum Admission Requirements:			
UGPA:			2.75
GRE or GMAT Scores:			N/A
Work Experience:			N/A
Other Considerations:			NO
Average Student Profile:			
UGPA:			3.0
GMAT Score:			50th Percentile
Work Experience:			N/A

Program Resources

Students Required to Have Computers:			NO
Video Teleconferencing:			NO
Physical Library Facilities:			YES
Online Library Facilities:			YES
HRCI Certification Preparation:			NO
SHRM Student Chapter:			YES
URL:		www.uwm.edu/StudentOrg/SHRM/	
Fellowships:	YES	AMT:	N/A
Scholarships:	NO	AMT:	
Assistantships:	NO	AMT:	
Eligibility:			

Curriculum

Required Courses:
- HR Strategy
- Recruitment/Retention
- Employment Law
- Employee Relations
- Labor Relations
- Labor Economics
- Collective Bargaining

Most Popular Elective Courses:
- Compensation
- Managing Diversity
- Mediation and Negotiation
- Training and Development
- Benefits

Career Tracks/Concentrations:
Mediation and Negotiation	International Human Resource Management

Internship Required: NO

Career Services

Career Services Offered:
SHRM Student Chapter	Interview Training
Resume Service	Campus Interview
Internships	

Summer Internship Placement Rate:	N/A
Facilitate Placement:	NO
Full-Time Placement Rate:	N/A
Internship Placement Rate:	N/A
Average Starting Salary (Full-Time Graduates):	N/A
Average Sign-on Bonus:	N/A
Companies Recruiting HR Master's Graduates:	N/A

Points of Excellence

The program is designed for full-time and part-time students who seek careers in the private or public sectors, and with unions or management. Elective courses and options within the core requirements allow students to gain specialized knowledge needed to work in a variety of areas.

Contact Information

MHRLR Program
UWM Bolton Hall 842
P.O. Box 413
Milwaukee, WI 53201-0413
www.uwm.edu/Dept/MHRLR

Administrative & Faculty Contact
Susan Donohue
Telephone: (414) 229-4009
Suedono@uwm.edu

Admission Deadlines

Rolling admission policy, due date is two months prior to start of semester.
Online Application: YES

University of Wisconsin, Whitewater

Whitewater, Wisconsin
School of Business

Degree

Master of Business Administration with an emphasis in HR Management (MBA-HR)

University Overview

Regional comprehensive university that is part of the University of Wisconsin system, and located in southeastern Wisconsin. Nontraditonal program offers courses over the Internet anywhere in the world.

Program Description

New program began in 1998 and offers a MBA with an emphasis in human resource management.

Degree Requirements

Total Credits Required:	36
Average Credits per Course:	3
Course Schedule:	Semester
Total Courses Required:	14
HR/IR Courses Required:	3
Average Time for Completion:	2-4 years
Maximum Time Allowed for Completion:	7 years
Accepts Credits from Other Universities:	YES
Total:	N/A

Tuition

In-state	$4,378	(per year)
	$243	(per credit hour)
Out-of-state	$12,750	(per year)
	$708	(per credit hour)

Program Delivery

Traditional Day Program:	NO
Nontraditional Program:	YES
Evening Program:	YES
Weekend Program:	NO
Summer Courses:	N/A
Some Courses Online:	YES
Full Program Online:	NO
Distance Learning/Offsite:	YES
Executive Education:	N/A
Overseas Study Abroad:	YES

Faculty

Full-Time Faculty:	5
Part-Time Faculty:	0
Faculty to Student Ratio:	1:20

Primary Teaching Methods:
Computer-Aided Instruction	Case Study
Experiential Learning	Lecture
Student Presentations	

Faculty Who Consult Outside: 25-49%
Faculty Involvement:
- SHRM College Relations Committee
- IRRA Chair and Selection Committee
- Academy of Management Proceedings Editor and Placement Committee

Top 5 Faculty Publications:
- *Academy of Management Review*
- *Canadian Journal of Administrative Management*
- *Quality Resource Journal*
- *Human Resource Management Journal*
- *Health Care Manager*

Students

Total Enrollment:			20
Full-Time Enrollment:			25%
Men:	35%	Women:	65%
Hispanic:	5%	African-American:	5%
Other Minorities:	5%	International:	5%
Average Age:	30	Age Range:	23-39
Work Full Time:			50-74%
HR Experience:			25-49%

145

Speak 2nd language:		1-24%

Minimum Admission Requirements:
  GRE and UGPA

Other Considerations:		None

Average Student Profiles:

Work experience:		2 years

Program Resources

Students Required to Have Computers:			N/A
Video Teleconferencing:			NO
Physical Library Facilities:			N/A
Online Library Facilities:			N/A
HRCI Certification Preparation:			YES

  Links students to local SHRM chapter study groups
  Offers practice exams

SHRM Student Chapter:			YES
Fellowships:			NO
Scholarships:			NO
Assistantships:	2	AMT:	$5,800
Eligibility:		Full-Time Enrollment	

Curriculum

Required Courses:
  Accounting
  Finance
  Marketing
  Management
Most Popular Elective Courses:
  International Management
  HR Strategy
  Training & Development
  Compensation/Benefits

Career Tracks/Concentrations:		N/A
Internship Required:		NO

Career Services

Career Services Offered:

Mentoring	Field Trips
SHRM Student Chapter	Resume Services
Campus Interviews	Internships

Summer Internship Placement Rate:		N/A
Full-Time Placement Rate:		N/A
Average Starting Salary (Full-Time Graduates):		N/A
Average Sign-on Bonus:		N/A
Companies Recruiting HR Master's Graduates:		N/A

Points of Excellence

Curriculum: Courses emphasize the application of HR issues in the workplace. In the Training & Development course, distance learning methods require students to develop their own distance learning modules. Many students help develop actual organizational training programs and assist with research projects such as developing an evaluation for an organizational training program. Strong alumni base provides a source of expertise for use both in class and via the web.

Faculty: Mentoring and coaching is a strong part of the HR program at the graduate level. Faculty actively seek both internship and career opportunities for students. Students actively participate with faculty in a variety of SHRM activities such as attending professional meetings, serving on committees, and attending state and regional conferences. Faculty are able to use their years of organizational HR experience to assist students in career planning and job search.

Contact Information

Graduate School of Business
University of Wisconsin/Whitewater
800 W. Main St.
Whitewater, WI 53190
www.uww.edu/index4.html

Donald K. Zahn, Associate Dean of Business
Telephone: (262) 472-1945   FAX: (262-) 472-4863
zahnd@mail.uww.edu

Richard J. Wagner, Professor of Management
Telephone: (262) 472-5478   FAX: (262) 472-4863
wagnerr@uww.edu

Admission Deadlines

July 15 for Fall admissions

Online Application:	YES

Utah State University

Logan, Utah

Degree

Master of Social Science in Human Resource Management (MSSHRM)

University Overview

State-funded university with more than 20,000 students located in Logan, Utah.

Program Description

Master of Social Science in Human Resource Management. Satellite delivery to Utah State distance education sites on weekends with live instructors in Salt Lake City.

Degree Requirements

Total Credits Required:	36
Average Credits per Course:	3
Course Schedule:	Semester
Total Courses Required:	12
HR/IR Courses Required:	12
Average Time for Completion:	1-2 years
Maximum Time Allowed for Completion:	5 years
Accepts Credits from Other Universities:	YES
Total:	N/A

Tuition

In-state	$3,711	(per year)
	$249	(per credit hour)
Out-of-state	$11,913	(per year)
	N/A	(per credit hour)

Program Delivery

Traditional Day Program:	YES
Nontraditional Program:	YES
Evening Program:	YES
Weekend Program:	YES
Summer Courses:	N/A
Some Courses Online:	NO
Full Program Online:	NO
Distance Learning/Offsite:	YES
Executive Education:	N/A
Overseas Study Abroad:	NO

Faculty

Full-Time Faculty:	N/A
Part-Time Faculty:	N/A
Faculty to Student Ratio:	N/A

Primary Teaching Methods:
  Case Study   Team Projects
  Experiential Learning   Group Discussion
Faculty Who Consult Outside: 50-74%
Faculty Involvement:
  Governance Committee of Social Issues, Academy of Management
  President, Academy of Legal Studies in Business
Top 5 Faculty Publications:
  Academy of Management Journal
  Journal of Labor Economics
  Journal of Management Education
  Journal of Business Venturing

Students

Total Enrollment:			60
Full-Time Enrollment:			25%
Men:	56%	Women:	44%
Hispanic:	2%	African-American:	4%
Other Minorities:	17%	International:	35%
Average Age:	35	Age Range:	22-61
Work Full Time:			75-99%
HR Experience:			50-74%
Speak 2nd Language:			50-74%

Minimum Admission Requirements:
  GRE or GMAT: 40th Percentile
  UGPA: N/A
Other Considerations: None
Average Student Profiles: N/A

Program Resources

Students Required to Have Computers: N/A
Video Teleconferencing: NO
Physical Library Facilities: N/A
Online Library Facilities: N/A
HRCI Certification Preparation: YES
  Encourages student study groups
  Bases the curriculum on the certification exam
SHRM Student Chapter: YES
Fellowships: NO
Scholarships: NO
Assistantships: NO
Eligibility: N/A

Curriculum

Required Courses:
  HR Strategy
  Compensation/Benefits
  Development/Training
  Recruitment/Retention
  Employment Law
  Management
  Employee Relations
  Labor Relations
Most Popular Elective Courses:
  Labor Market Policy
  Stress Management
  International HR
  Business Communications
Career Tracks/Concentrations: N/A
Internship Required: YES

Career Services

Career Services Offered:
  Mentoring   Field Trips
  SHRM Student Chapter   Resume Services
Summer Internship Placement Rate: N/A
Full-Time Placement Rate: N/A

Average Starting Salary (Full-Time Graduates): N/A
Average Sign-on Bonus: N/A
Companies Recruiting HR Master's Graduates: N/A

Points of Excellence
Curriculum: Internship programs vary depending on the student. Many local companies use students for project-based work assignments. Internship projects range from 1-3 months and supervision is supplied by the company. The end product is often a report that the student delivers to the company and the class.

Contact Information
Utah State University
MHR Department
3555 University Blvd.
Logan, UT 84321-3555
www.usu.edu/~mhrdept/program/frprogram.html

Gaylen Chandler, Director
MSS/HRM Program
Telephone: (435) 797-2365   FAX: (435) 797-1061
Chandler@6202.usu.edu

Admission Deadlines
Online Application: NO

Vanderbilt University

Nashville, Tennessee
Owen Graduate School of Management

Degree
Master of Business Administration with a Human Resource focus (MBA-HR)

University Overview
Private university with about 10,000 students in Nashville, Tennessee.

Program Description
This full-time, traditional day MBA program with an HRM concentration provides students with a solid foundation in management. Students interested in HRM take six electives. These students are in high demand among recruiters because they have a stronger business foundation. About half of our HR students end up working for consulting firms, while the other half work in corporate HR departments.

Degree Requirements
Total Credits Required: 60
Average Credits per Course: 2
Course Schedule: 7-Week Terms
Total Courses Required: 25-30
HR/IR Courses Required: 6
Average Time for Completion: 2 years
Maximum Time Allowed for Completion: N/A
Accepts Credits from Other Universities: YES
Total: N/A

Tuition
In-state	$27,560	(per year)
	N/A	(per credit hour)
Out-of-state	$27,560	(per year)
	N/A	(per credit hour)

Program Delivery
Traditional Day Program: YES
Nontraditional Program: NO

Evening Program:	NO
Weekend Program:	NO
Summer Courses:	NO
Some Courses Online:	NO
Full Program Online:	NO
Distance Learning/Offsite:	NO
Executive Education:	YES*
Overseas Study Abroad:	YES

Not in HR

Faculty

Full-Time Faculty:	45
Part-Time Faculty:	16
Faculty to Student Ratio:	1:10

Primary Teaching Methods:

Case Study	Team Projects
Student Presentations	Lecture

Faculty Who Consult Outside: 1-24%

Faculty Involvement:
Board, International Association for Conflict Management
Chair, Conflict Management Division of Academy of Management
Editorial Boards of Academy of Management Review, Industrial and Labor Relations Review, *International Journal of Conflict Management, Journal of Personality and Social Psychology, and Organization Science*

Top 5 Faculty Publications:
Journal of Personality and Social Psychology
Harvard Business Review
Journal of Applied Psychology

Students

Total Enrollment:			439
Full-Time Enrollment:			100%
Men:	76%	Women:	24%
Hispanic:	1%	African-American:	3%
Other Minorities:	5%	International:	29%
Average Age:	26	Age Range:	21-34
Work Full Time:			0%
HR Experience:			1-24%
Speak 2nd Language:			25-49%

Minimum Admission Requirements:

GMAT Score:	600 and UGPA

Other Considerations:
Professional experience and leadership potential

Average Student Profiles:

GMAT Score:	645
Work experience:	4 ½ years
UGPA:	3.23

Program Resources

Students Required to Have Computers:			YES
Video Teleconferencing:			YES
Physical Library Facilities:			YES
Online Library Facilities:			YES
HRCI Certification Preparation:			NO
SHRM Student Chapter:			YES
Fellowships:	20-30	AMT:	$6,500
Scholarships:	150-175	AMT:	$7,000
Assistantships:	25	AMT:	$2,500
Eligibility:			Full-Time Enrollment

Curriculum

Required Courses:
Accounting
Finance
Marketing
Leading Teams and Organizations

Most Popular Elective Courses:
Compensation
Staffing
Labor Relations
Organizational Design
Change Management
Work Team Design
Innovation
EEOC Practicum

Career Tracks/Concentrations:	N/A
Internship Required:	YES

Career Services

Career Services Offered:

Mentoring	Field Trips
Resume Services	Interview Training
Campus Interviews	Internships

Summer Internship Placement Rate:	N/A
Full-Time Placement Rate:	90-100%
Average Starting Salary (Full-Time Graduates):	$82,405
Average Sign-on Bonus:	$21,085
Companies Recruiting HR Master's Graduates:	20-25

Points of Excellence

Curriculum: Main innovation is simply to have a solid HR program within an MBA program. Students come out with broad business skills and an ability to move from HR to other functional areas in companies. Outside HR, the first concentration is in electronic commerce, with a strong program in finance and services marketing. All students are required to have their own computer.

Placement: The Career Management Center provides a full range of services exclusively for MBA students and alumni. They offer a variety of skills development workshops and one-on-one counseling to help prepare candidates for lifelong career success. Various student groups also provide opportunities for interview skills development and interaction with business leaders and alumni in specific fields. Most interns are offered full-time jobs with companies they intern with.

Contact Information

Vanderbilt University
Owen Graduate School of Management
401 21st Ave. South
Nashville, TN 37203
mba.vanderbilt.edu/external

Todd Reale, Director, MBA Program and Admissions
Telephone: (615) 322-6469   FAX: (615) 343-1175
admissions@owen.vanderbilt.edu

Admission Deadlines

Online Application: YES

Villanova University

Villanova, Pennsylvania
Graduate Program in Human Resource Management (MS)

Degree

Master of Science in Human Resource Management (MSHRM)

University Overview

Private Roman Catholic university with about 10,000 students located near Philadelphia, Pennsylvania.

Program Description
Generalist preparation with emphasis on employment, training, and organizational development.

Degree Requirements
Total Credits Required:	30-36
Average Credits per Course:	3
Course Schedule:	Semester
Total Courses Required:	10-12
HR/IR Courses Required:	7
Average Time for Completion:	1 ½ -2 years
Maximum Time Allowed for Completion:	6 years
Accepts Credits from Other Universities:	YES
Total:	6 Hours

Tuition
In-state	N/A	(per year)
	$445	(per credit hour)
Out-of-state	N/A	(per year)
	$445	(per credit hour)

Program Delivery
Traditional Day Program:	NO
Nontraditional Program:	YES
Evening Program:	YES
Weekend Program:	NO
Summer Courses:	YES
Some Courses Online:	NO
Full Program Online:	NO
Distance Learning/Offsite:	YES
Executive Education:	Under Development
Overseas Study Abroad:	NO

Faculty
Full-Time Faculty:	2
Part-Time Faculty:	5
Faculty to Student Ratio:	1:10

Primary Teaching Methods:

Case Study	Research
Experiential Learning	Field Projects
Lecture	Team Projects
Student Presentations	Group Discussion

Faculty Who Consult Outside:	100%

Faculty Involvement:
SHRM Health & Safety Committee
President, EWMN

Top 5 Faculty Publications:	N/A

Students
Total Enrollment:			80
Full-Time Enrollment:			100%
Men:	15%	Women:	85%
Hispanic:	3%	African-American:	5%
Other Minorities:	3%	International:	4%
Average Age:	27	Age Range:	22-53
Work Full Time:			75-99%
HR Experience:			75-99%
Speak 2nd Language:			1-24%

Minimum Admission Requirements:

GRE Score:	1500 and UGPA: 3.4
Other Considerations:	None

Average Student Profiles:

GRE Score:	1800
Work experience:	5 years

Program Resources
Students Required to Have Computers:	YES
Video Teleconferencing:	YES
Physical Library Facilities:	YES
Online Library Facilities:	YES
HRCI Certification Preparation:	YES

Encourages student study groups
Links students to local SHRM student chapter study groups

SHRM Student Chapter:			YES
Fellowships:	1	AMT:	$9,000 + Tuition
Scholarships:	2	AMT:	tuition only
Assistantships:	2	AMT:	$9,000 + Tuition
Eligibility:			Full-Time Enrollment

Curriculum
Required Courses:
Finance
HR Strategy
International HR
Compensation/Benefits
Development/Training
Recruitment/Retention
Employee Relations
HR Measurement

Most Popular Elective Courses:
HRIS
Compensation
Organizational Psychology
Employment Law

Career Tracks/Concentrations:	General Track
Internship Required:	YES

Career Services
Career Services Offered:

Mentoring	Field Trips
SHRM Student Chapter	Resume Services
Interview Training	Campus Interviews
Internships	

Summer Internship Placement Rate:	100%
Full-Time Placement Rate:	100%
Average Starting Salary (Full-Time Graduates):	$51,000
Average Sign-on Bonus:	N/A
Companies Recruiting HR Master's Graduates:	10-15

Points of Excellence
Placement: Most innovative characteristic is the involvement of those who have graduated over the past two decades and serve in advisory roles to program development, as mentors, and as visiting guest speakers in our classes. Alumni attend graduate fairs to aid in recruiting new students and are actively involved in recruiting our graduates to their companies. Local HR professionals are also involved. Several area HR VPs and directors have actively mentored our students. Three large SHRM chapters have supported the program including providing scholarships.

Contact Information
Villanova University
Graduate Program in HRD
800 Lancaster Ave.
Villanova, PA 19085
www.gradhrd.villanova.edu

David F. Bush, Ph.D., Professor & Program Director
Telephone: (610) 519-4746   FAX: (610) 519-4269
david.bush@villanova.edu

Admission Deadlines
Online Application:	YES

Virginia Commonwealth University

Richmond, Virginia
School of Business

Degree
Master of Science in Business with a major in Human Resource Management and Industrial Relations (MSHRMIR)

University Overview
A public, state-funded university with more than 21,000 students in Richmond, Virginia.

Program Description
Nontraditional, broad-based program with courses in all major areas of HR.

Degree Requirements
Total Credits Required:	30
Average Credits per Course:	3
Course Schedule:	Semester
Total Courses Required:	10
HR/IR Courses Required:	10
Average Time for Completion:	2 years
Maximum Time Allowed for Completion:	5 years
Accepts Credits from Other Universities:	YES
Total:	N/A

Tuition
In-state	$2,056	(per year)
	$273	(per credit hour)
Out-of-state	$6,013	(per year)
	N/A	(per credit hour)

Program Delivery
Traditional Day Program:	NO
Nontraditional Program:	YES
Evening Program:	YES
Weekend Program:	NO
Summer Courses:	N/A
Some Courses Online:	NO
Full Program Online:	NO
Distance Learning/Offsite:	NO
Executive Education:	N/A
Overseas Study Abroad:	NO

Faculty
Full-Time Faculty:	6
Part-Time Faculty:	0
Faculty to Student Ratio:	1:12

Primary Teaching Methods:
Case Study	Research
Field Projects	Student Presentations
Lecture	Group Discussion

Faculty Who Consult Outside:	50-74%
Faculty Involvement:	N/A
Top 5 Faculty Publications:	N/A

Students
Total Enrollment:			30
Full-Time Enrollment:			100%
Men:	27%	Women:	73%
Hispanic:	0%	African-American:	8%
Other Minorities:	7%	International:	7%
Average Age:	28	Age Range:	N/A
Work Full Time:			75-99%
HR Experience:			25-49%

Speak 2nd Language:	1-24%

Minimum Admission Requirements:
GMAT Score:	540 and UGPA

Other Considerations:
Look at the total individual

Average Student Profiles:
GMAT Score:	540
Work experience:	6 years

Program Resources
Students Required to Have Computers:	N/A
Video Teleconferencing:	YES
Physical Library Facilities:	N/A
Online Library Facilities:	N/A
HRCI Certification Preparation:	YES

Encourages student study groups
Links students to local SHRM chapter study groups

SHRM Student Chapter:			YES
Fellowships:			NO
Scholarships:			NO
Assistantships:	2-7	AMT:	$8,800
Eligibility:			Full-Time Enrollment

Curriculum
Required Courses:
HR Strategy
International HR
Compensation/Benefits
Development/Training
Recruitment/Retention
Employment Law
Employee Relations
Labor Relations
Research Methodology

Most Popular Elective Courses:	N/A
Career Tracks/Concentrations:	N/A
Internship Required:	NO

Career Services
Career Services Offered:
SHRM Student Chapter	Resume Services
Internships	

Summer Internship Placement Rate:	N/A
Full-Time Placement Rate:	N/A
Average Starting Salary (Full-Time Graduates):	N/A
Average Sign-on Bonus:	N/A
Companies Recruiting HR Master's Graduates:	10-15

Points of Excellence
Curriculum: Program covers every major aspect of HRMIR. This eclectic approach prepares the practitioner and provides a better experienced candidate to employers as a result of the exposure. The students are well versed in the field upon leaving the program.

Contact Information
Virginia Commonwealth University
School of Business
Floyd & Harrison Streets
Richmond, VA 23284
www.vcu.edu

George R. Gray, Associate Professor HRMIR
Telephone: (804) 828-1732
ggray@atlas.vcu.edu

Admission Deadlines
Online Application:	NO

Washington University

St. Louis, Missouri
College of Arts and Sciences

Degree
Master of Arts in Human Resource Management (MAHRM)

University Overview
Washington University is a private institution with a student enrollment of approximately 10,000.

Program Description
The Masters of Arts in HRM program is dedicated to the development of knowledge and skills for those whose objective is to improve the utilization of human resources in today's dynamic organizations. Students work full-time.

Degree Requirements
Total Credits Required:	36
Average Credits per Course:	3
Course Schedule:	Semester
Total Courses Required:	12
HR/IR Courses Required:	4
Average Time for Completion:	2-2 ½ years
Maximum Time Allowed for Completion:	5 years
Accepts Credits from Other Universities:	YES
Total:	N/A

Tuition
In-state	N/A	(per year)
	$270	(per credit hour)
Out-of-state	N/A	(per year)
	$270	(per credit hour)

Program Delivery
Traditional Day Program:	NO
Nontraditional Program:	YES
Evening Program:	YES
Weekend Program:	NO
Summer Courses:	N/A
Some Courses Online:	NO
Full Program Online:	NO
Distance Learning/Offsite:	NO
Executive Education:	N/A
Overseas Study Abroad:	NO

Faculty
Full-Time Faculty:	2
Part-Time Faculty:	17
Faculty to Student Ratio:	N/A

Primary Teaching Methods:
Lecture	Case Studies
Experiential Learning	Group Discussion

Faculty Who Consult Outside:	75-99%
Faculty Involvement:	N/A
Top 5 Faculty Publications:	N/A

Students
Total Enrollment:			50
Full-Time Enrollment:			100%
Men:	40%	Women:	60%
Hispanic:	0%	African-American:	8%
Other Minorities:	0%	International:	0%
Average Age:	26	Age Range:	22-50
Work Full Time:			100%
HR Experience:			50-74%
Speak 2nd Language:			1-24%

Minimum Admission Requirements:
GMAT
Other Considerations:
Work experience, writing sample, and references
Average Student Profiles:
Work experience:	4 years

Program Resources
Students Required to Have Computers:	N/A
Video Teleconferencing:	NO
Physical Library Facilities:	N/A
Online Library Facilities:	N/A
HRCI Certification Preparation:	YES
Encourages student study groups	
SHRM Student Chapter:	YES
Fellowships:	NO
Scholarships:	NO
Assistantships:	NO
Eligibility:	N/A

Curriculum
Required Courses:
Organizations and HR
Org. Behavior & Administration
Principles of Economics
Managerial Accounting
Statistics & Survey Design
Applied Project
Most Popular Elective Courses:
Training & Development
HR Planning
Labor Law & Labor Relations
International HR
Compensation
Benefits
Motivation
Leadership
Affirmative Action & EEO
Org. Change & Development
Business Ethics
Employee Health Issues
Group Processes
Negotiation
Career Tracks/Concentrations:	N/A
Internship Required:	NO

Career Services
Career Services Offered:
SHRM Student Chapter
Summer Internship Placement Rate:	N/A
Full-Time Placement Rate:	N/A
Average Starting Salary (Full-Time Graduates):	N/A
Average Sign-on Bonus:	N/A
Companies Recruiting HR Master's Graduates:	N/A

Points of Excellence
Curriculum: HR professionals and alumni are asked on a regular basis to review curriculum and recommend changes. The required capstone course consists of a project conducted by the student in their place of employment. The course "test" is a presentation to senior management concerning the project and recommendations.

Contact Information
Washington University
Campus Box 1085
St. Louis, MO 63130
www.artsci.wustl.edu

Jane Smith, Associate Dean
Telephone: (314) 935-6727   FAX: (314) 362-3265
jsmith@artsci.wustl.edu

Ronald Gribbins, Program Director
Telephone: (314) 362-3271   FAX: (314) 362-3265
grib@artsci.wustl.edu

Admission Deadlines
January 15 for Fall admissions
Online Application: YES

Webster University, Ozarks Regional Campus

Springfield, Missouri

Degree
Master of Arts Human Resources (MAHR)
Master of Arts Human Resources Development (MAHRD)
Master of Business Administration in Human Resources Management (MBAHRM)
Master of Business Administration in Human Resources Development (MBAHRD)

University Overview
Webster University's Ozarks Regional Campus is a private university located in Springfield, Missouri. We offer master's programs in business with a focus on real-world application and lifetime adult learning.

Program Description
Programs at our campus focus on working professionals. Most of our students are either working to advance in their current careers or wish to change their career path. The adjunct faculty in this program teach classes with a real world perspective. All work in the field in which they teach and hold a minimum of a master's degree.

Degree Requirements
Total Credits Required:	36
Average Credits per Course:	3
Course Schedule:	9-week courses
Total Courses Required:	12
HR/IR Courses Required:	12
Average Time for Completion:	2 ¼ years
Maximum Time Allowed for Completion:	10 years
Accepts Credits from Other Universities:	YES
Total:	12 Hours for MA, 9 Hours for MBA

Tuition
In-state	N/A	(per year)
	$345	(per credit hour)
Out-of-state	N/A	(per year)
	$345	(per credit hour)

Program Delivery
Traditional Day Program:	NO
Nontraditional Program:	YES
Evening Program:	YES
Weekend Program:	NO
Program Completed Evening/Weekend:	YES
Summer Courses:	YES
Some Courses Online:	YES
Full Program Online:	YES
Distance Learning/Offsite:	NO
Executive Education:	NO
Overseas Study Abroad:	YES

Faculty
Full-Time Faculty:	0
Part-Time Faculty:	50
Faculty to Student Ratio:	1:10
Primary Teaching Methods:	

  Experiential Learning   Team Projects
  Group Discussion   Lecture

Faculty Who Consult Outside:	NONE
Faculty Involvement:	
Top 5 Faculty Publications:	

Students
Total Enrollment:			132
Full-Time Enrollment:			0
Men:	64%	Women:	36%
Hispanic:	N/A	African-American:	N/A
Other Minorities:	N/A	International:	NONE
Average Age:	37	Age Range:	25-59
Work Full Time:			75-99%
Have HR Experience:			75-99%
Speak 2nd Language:			N/A
Minimum Admission Requirements:			
UGPA:			NONE
GRE or GMAT Scores:			Not Required
Work Experience:			0
Other Considerations:			
Average Student Profile:			
UGPA:			N/A
GMAT Score:			N/A
Work Experience:			N/A

Program Resources
Students Required to Have Computers:		NO
Video Teleconferencing:		NO
Physical Library Facilities:		YES
Online Library Facilities:		YES
HRCI Certification Preparation:		YES
SHRM Student Chapter:		NO
URL:		
Fellowships:	NO	AMT:
Scholarships:	NO	AMT:
Assistantships:	NO	AMT:
Eligibility:		

Curriculum
Required Courses:
  Organizational Communications
  Recruitment/Retention
  HR Strategy
  Employment Law
  Compensation/Benefits
  Management
  Development/Training
  Employee Relations
  HR Measurement
  Business Functional Areas
  Organizational Development
Most Popular Elective Courses:
  Labor Relations
  Internet Management Applications
  Corporate Responsibility
  Ethics, Values, and Legal Issues in HRDV

Career Tracks/Concentrations:	NO
Internship Required:	NO

Career Services

Career Services Offered:

Field Trips	Interview Training
Resume Services	

Career Center (based at St. Louis Campus, can be accessed online)

Summer Internship Placement Rate:	N/A
Facilitate Placement:	YES
Full-Time Placement Rate:	N/A
Internship Placement Rate:	N/A
Average Starting Salary (Full-Time Graduates):	N/A
Average Sign-on Bonus:	N/A
Companies Recruiting HR Master's Graduates:	N/A

Points of Excellence

The HRD and HRM programs on our campus are unique in that all the instructors are currently working in the area that they teach. All have at least a master's degree and seven years of work experience. The HRD and HRM program classes have a mix of students from other degree programs. This allows opportunities to network and learn from people who work in different functional areas of a company.

Contact Information

Webster University Ozarks Regional Campus
321 W. Battlefield
Springfield, MO 65807
www.webster.edu/ozark

Administrative Contact
Laura Ward, PHR
Telephone: (417) 883-0200
lward@webster.edu

Faculty Contact
Gail Hinshaw, Faculty Coordinator
Telephone: (417) 883-0200

Admission Deadlines

Rolling admission

Online Application:	YES

Webster University

St. Louis, Missouri
School of Business and Technology

Degree

Masters in Human Resource Management (MAHRM)

University Overview

Webster University is a private university offering Undergraduate/Master's degrees in all functional areas and a Doctorate of Management (emphasis in Leader and Organizational Change) located in Saint Louis, Missouri.

Program Description

The MAHRM covers the body of knowledge described by SHRM. The audience is HRM professionals seeking either the PHR or SPHR.

Degree Requirements

Total Credits Required:	36
Average Credits per Course:	3
Course Schedule:	9 weeks per course
Total Courses Required:	12
HR/IR Courses Required:	8
Average Time for Completion:	2 ¼ years
Maximum Time Allowed for Completion:	No Limit

Accepts Credits from Other Universities:	YES
Total:	12 Hours

Tuition

In-state	N/A	(per year)
	$398	(per credit hour)
Out-of-state	N/A	(per year)
	$398	(per credit hour)

Program Delivery

Traditional Day Program:	NO
Nontraditional Program:	YES
Evening Program:	YES
Weekend Program:	NO
Program Completed Evening/Weekend:	YES
Summer Courses:	YES
Some Courses Online:	YES
Full Program Online:	NO
Distance Learning/Offsite:	NO
Executive Education:	YES
Overseas Study Abroad:	YES

Faculty

Full-Time Faculty:	17
Part-Time Faculty:	250
Faculty to Student Ratio:	1:20

Primary Teaching Methods:

Case Study	Experiential Learning
Student Presentation	Lecture

Faculty Who Consult Outside:	1-24%

Faculty Involvement:
Chairperson, Non-Profit Sector, Academy of Business Administration

Top 5 Faculty Publications:

Students

Total Enrollment:			250
Full-Time Enrollment:			0
Men:	40%	Women:	60%
Hispanic:	N/A	African-American:	20%
Other Minorities:	5%	International:	5%
Average Age:	27	Age Range:	23-40
Work Full Time:			75-99%
Have HR Experience:			75-99%
Speak 2nd Language:			1-24%

Minimum Admission Requirements:

UGPA:	2.0
GRE or GMAT Scores:	Not Required
Work Experience:	Not Required
Other Considerations:	

Average Student Profile:

UGPA:	2.7
GMAT Score:	N/A
Work Experience:	N/A

Program Resources

Students Required to Have Computers:	NO
Video Teleconferencing:	YES
Physical Library Facilities:	YES
Online Library Facilities:	YES
HRCI Certification Preparation:	YES
SHRM Student Chapter:	NO
URL:	

Fellowships:	NO	AMT:	
Scholarships:	NO	AMT:	
Assistantships:	NO	AMT:	
Eligibility:			N/A

Curriculum

Required Courses:
  HR Strategy
  Recruitment/Retention
  Compensation/Benefits
  Employment Law
  Development/Training
  Management
  Employee Relations
  Labor Relations
  HR Measurement
Most Popular Elective Courses:
  Principle Center Leadership
  7 Habits of Highly Effective People
  Negotiating Skills
  Career Development
Career Tracks/Concentrations:
  HRM, HRD
Internship Required: NO

Career Services

Career Services Offered:
  Resume Services   Interview Training
  Campus Interview
Summer Internship Placement Rate: N/A
Facilitate Placement: YES
Full-Time Placement Rate: N/A
Internship Placement Rate: N/A
Average Starting Salary (Full-Time Graduates):   N/A
Average Sign-on Bonus: N/A
Companies Recruiting HR Master's Graduates: N/A

Points of Excellence

Webster University offers a blend of theory and practical application, which comes from the full-time faculty working closely with the part-time faculty to ensure the students get exposure to both. Webster's nine-week course length works well for working professionals to enhance their HR knowledge. Students are able to participate in a variety of projects designed to allow them to apply course knowledge to real-world problems. With 70 campus locations around the world, Webster provides students with an enormous networking group of both current students and alumni.

Contact Information

Nicholas Di Marco
School of Business and Technology
Webster University
470 East Lockwood Avenue
Saint Louis, MO 63119
www.webster.edu

Administrative Contact
Thomas Nicoli
Telephone: (314) 968-7497
nickoltcj@webster.edu

Faculty Contact
Nicholas Di Marco
Telephone: (314) 968-7026
dimarcnj@webster.edu

Admission Deadlines

Year round
Online Application: NO

West Chester University

West Chester, Pennsylvania
College of Arts and Sciences,
Department of Psychology

Degree

Master of Arts Industrial/Organizational Psychology (MAIOP)

University Overview

West Chester University (WCU) is a public, regional comprehensive university located in West Chester, Pennsylvania. WCU is centered in a growing business environment stretching along the eastern corridor from Baltimore to Boston.

Program Description

The Industrial/Organizational program provides a comprehensive treatment of both industrial and organizational topics, and includes specialized courses in Human Performance Technology. The program is targeted to both newly graduated BA students and non-traditionals working in the field.

Degree Requirements

Total Credits Required: 36
Average Credits per Course: 3
Course Schedule: Semester
Total Courses Required: 12
HR/IR Courses Required: 12
Average Time for Completion: 2 years
Maximum Time Allowed for Completion: 6 years
Accepts Credits from Other Universities: YES
Total: 6 Hours

Tuition

In-state	$4,140	(per year)
	N/A	(per credit hour)
Out-of-state	$7,000	(per year)
	N/A	(per credit hour)

Program Delivery

Traditional Day Program: NO
Nontraditional Program: YES
  Evening Program: YES
  Weekend Program: NO
  Program Completed Evening/Weekend: YES
  Summer Courses: YES
  Some Courses Online: NO
  Full Program Online: NO
  Distance Learning/Offsite: NO
  Executive Education: NO
  Overseas Study Abroad: N/A

Faculty

Full-Time Faculty: 4
Part-Time Faculty: 2
Faculty to Student Ratio: 1:10
Primary Teaching Methods:
  Field Projects   Team Projects
  Student Presentation   Lecture
Faculty Who Consult Outside:
Faculty Involvement:
  Coordinator of Small Grants – Organizational Behavior Management Network, Association for Behavior Analysis, International
Top 5 Faculty Publications:
  Handbook of Organizational Performance
  Journal of Applied Psychology
  Teaching of Psychology

Students

Total Enrollment:			30
Full-Time Enrollment:			12
Men:	40%	Women:	60%
Hispanic:	0%	African-American:	7%
Other Minorities:	0%	International:	3%
Average Age:	25	Age Range:	22-30
Work Full Time:			25-49%
Have HR Experience:			1-24%
Speak 2nd Language:			1-24%

Minimum Admission Requirements:

UGPA:	3.0
GRE or GMAT Scores:	500 GRE
Work Experience:	NONE

Other Considerations:
Average Student Profile:

UGPA:	3.2
GMAT Score:	530 GRE
Work Experience:	NONE

Program Resources

Students Required to Have Computers:			NO
Video Teleconferencing:			NO
Physical Library Facilities:			YES
Online Library Facilities:			YES
HRCI Certification Preparation:			NO
SHRM Student Chapter:			NO
URL:			
Fellowships:	NO	AMT:	
Scholarships:	NO	AMT:	
Assistantships:	YES	AMT:	$2,500/yr to $5,000/yr
Eligibility:			N/A

Curriculum

Required Courses:
Industrial Psychology
Human Performance Analysis and Management
Organizational Psychology
Psychometrics
Statistical Analysis
Advanced Seminar in I/O
Most Popular Elective Courses:
Performance-Based Training
Consulting
Career Tracks/Concentrations:

Internship Required:	YES

Career Services

Career Services Offered:

Mentoring	Interview Training
Campus Interview	Resume Services
Internships	

Summer Internship Placement Rate:	N/A
Facilitate Placement:	YES
Full-Time Placement Rate:	N/A
Internship Placement Rate:	N/A
Average Starting Salary (Full-Time Graduates):	N/A
Average Sign-on Bonus:	N/A
Companies Recruiting HR Master's Graduates:	N/A

Points of Excellence

Many courses require hands-on projects in businesses, allowing students to gain experience in the field. Many internships come through alumni network.

Contact Information

Department of Psychology
West Chester University
West Chester, PA 19383

Administrative & Faculty Contact
Phillip K. Duncan
Telephone: (610) 436-2110
Pduncan@wcupa.edu

Admission Deadlines

March 15

Online Application:	YES

Western Kentucky University

Bowling Green, Kentucky
Psychology Department

Degree

Master of Arts – Psychology (Industrial/Organizational) (MA)

University Overview

Western Kentucky University (WKU), a state university located in Bowling Green, Kentucky, has 15,000+ students. WKU is among the best comprehensive universities in the nation.

Program Description

A two-year full-time program adhering to a scientist-practitioner model, emphasizing measurement, personnel selection, performance appraisal, and training. This allows a student to develop skills for business, government, consulting, or research.

Degree Requirements

Total Credits Required:	42
Average Credits per Course:	3
Course Schedule:	Semester
Total Courses Required:	14
HR/IR Courses Required:	N/A
Average Time for Completion:	2 years
Maximum Time Allowed for Completion:	5 years
Accepts Credits from Other Universities:	YES
Total:	6 Hours

Tuition

In-state	$3,044	(per year)
	N/A	(per credit hour)
Out-of-state	$3,044	(per year)
	N/A	(per credit hour)

Program Delivery

Traditional Day Program:	YES
Nontraditional Program:	NO
Evening Program:	NO
Weekend Program:	NO
Program Completed Evening/Weekend:	NO
Summer Courses:	NO
Some Courses Online:	NO
Full Program Online:	NO
Distance Learning/Offsite:	NO
Executive Education:	NO
Overseas Study Abroad:	NO

Faculty

Full-Time Faculty:	3
Part-Time Faculty:	6
Faculty to Student Ratio:	1:5

155

Primary Teaching Methods:

Research	Lecture
Student Presentation	Experiential Learning

Faculty Who Consult Outside: 50-74%
Faculty Involvement:
    Governing Council – International Society for Political Science
Top 5 Faculty Publications:
    Controversies and Approaches in Authoritarianism Research Today
    School Innovations
    Sport Marketing Quarterly
    Journal of Rehabilitation
    Journal of Offender Rehabilitation

Students

Total Enrollment:			18
Full-Time Enrollment:			18
Men:	44%	Women:	56%
Hispanic:	0%	African-American:	5%
Other Minorities:	5%	International:	0%
Average Age:	27	Age Range:	23-47
Work Full Time:			NONE
Have HR Experience:			1-24%
Speak 2nd Language:			1-24%

Minimum Admission Requirements:
UGPA:	3.0
GRE Scores:	500 (Both Quantitative and Verbal)
Work Experience:	NONE

Other Considerations:
Average Student Profile:
UGPA:	3.4
GRE Score:	1100 (Verbal and Quantitative)
Work Experience:	N/A

Program Resources

Students Required to Have Computers:		NO
Video Teleconferencing:		YES
Physical Library Facilities:		YES
Online Library Facilities:		YES
HRCI Certification Preparation:		NO
SHRM Student Chapter:		YES
URL:		
Fellowships:	NO	AMT:
Scholarships:	NO	AMT:
Assistantships:	YES	AMT: $5,600
Eligibility:		Full-Time Enrollment

Curriculum

Required Courses:
    Compensation/Benefits
    Employment Law
    Development/Training
    Management
    HR Measurement
    Test Development and Validation
    Criterions Development
    Research Methodology
    Organizational Psychology
    Job Analysis
    Statistical Packages for the Computer
Most Popular Elective Courses: NONE
Career Tracks/Concentrations:
    Organizational Consultant
    Human Resources Management
    Training Development & Evaluation
    Test Validation for Selection and Placement
Internship Required: YES

Career Services

Career Services Offered:	N/A
Summer Internship Placement Rate:	N/A
Facilitate Placement:	YES
Full-Time Placement Rate:	50%
Internship Placement Rate:	N/A
Average Starting Salary (Full-Time Graduates):	$47,000
Average Sign-on Bonus:	N/A
Companies Recruiting HR Master's Graduates:	N/A

Points of Excellence

The Industrial/Organizational Psychology program at Western Kentucky University (WKU) is based on the scientist-practitioner model and is designed to be similar to a doctoral program. Our students are expected to attend on a full-time basis. Consequently, we support all of our students with assistantships. We intentionally keep the number of students in the program low in order that faculty may work closely with them and involve them in research and consulting. WKU emphasizes quantitative skills in the personnel area (e.g., job analysis). The program also covers organization behavior and development.

Contact Information

Department of Psychology
Western Kentucky University
Bowling Green, KY 42101
edtech.tph.wky.edu/~psych/areas/io/

Faculty Contact
Dr. Betsy Shoenfelt
Telephone: (270) 745-4418
betsy.shoenfelt@wku.edu

Admission Deadlines

March 1
Online Application: NO

Western Maryland College

Westminster, Maryland
Graduate and Professional Studies

Degree
Master of Science in Human Resource Development (MSHRD)

University Overview
Western Maryland College, a private liberal arts institution, serves 3,500 graduate and undergraduate students on campuses located near Baltimore, Maryland, Washington, DC, and southeastern Pennsylvania.

Program Description
Competency-based program offered to small cohorts of working professionals. Students have the opportunity to work closely with scholars and professionals in HR.

Degree Requirements

Total Credits Required:	39
Average Credits per Course:	3
Course Schedule:	Other
Total Courses Required:	13
HR/IR Courses Required:	11
Average Time for Completion:	2 ½ years
Maximum Time Allowed for Completion:	6 years
Accepts Credits from Other Universities:	YES
Total:	9 Hours

Tuition

In-state	N/A	(per year)
	$240	(per credit hour)
Out-of-state	N/A	(per year)
	$240	(per credit hour)

Program Delivery

Traditional Day Program:	NO
Nontraditional Program:	YES
Evening Program:	YES
Weekend Program:	YES
Program Completed Evening/Weekend:	YES
Summer Courses:	YES
Some Courses Online:	NO
Full Program Online:	NO
Distance Learning/Offsite:	NO
Executive Education:	NO
Overseas Study Abroad:	NO

Faculty

Full-Time Faculty:	3
Part-Time Faculty:	5
Faculty to Student Ratio:	1:20

Primary Teaching Methods:
Case Study   Team Projects
Student Presentation   Field Projects

Faculty Who Consult Outside:	1-24%
Faculty Involvement:	
Top 5 Faculty Publications:	

Students

Total Enrollment:			43
Full-Time Enrollment:			43
Men:	33%	Women:	67%
Hispanic:	5%	African-American:	19%
Other Minorities:	5%	International:	7%
Average Age:	31	Age Range:	22-45
Work Full Time:			75-99%
Have HR Experience:			25-49%
Speak 2nd Language:			1-24%

Minimum Admission Requirements:

UGPA:	2.75
GRE or GMAT Scores:	N/A
Work Experience:	N/A

Other Considerations:
Average Student Profile:

UGPA:	3.1
GMAT Score:	N/A
Work Experience:	N/A

Program Resources

Students Required to Have Computers:	NO
Video Teleconferencing:	YES
Physical Library Facilities:	YES
Online Library Facilities:	YES
HRCI Certification Preparation:	NO
SHRM Student Chapter:	YES
URL:	

Fellowships:	NO	AMT:	
Scholarships:	NO	AMT:	
Assistantships:	YES	AMT:	$720
Eligibility:			Full-Time Enrollment

Curriculum

Required Courses:
HR Strategy
Employment Law
Development/Training
HR Measurement
Career Development
Organizational Change and Development
Cultural Diversity
Most Popular Elective Courses:
Selection and Recruitment
Conflict Resolution
Leadership and Executive Development

Career Tracks/Concentrations:	N/A
Internship Required:	YES

Career Services

Career Services Offered:
Resume Services   Interview Training
Internships

Summer Internship Placement Rate:	N/A
Facilitate Placement:	YES
Full-Time Placement Rate:	N/A
Internship Placement Rate:	N/A
Average Starting Salary (Full-Time Graduates):	N/A
Average Sign-on Bonus:	N/A
Companies Recruiting HR Master's Graduates:	N/A

Contact Information

Graduate and Professional Studies
Western Maryland College
2 College Hill
Westminster, MD 21157
www.wmdc.edu

Administrative Contact
Crystal Perry
Telephone: (410) 857-2513
Cperry@wmdc.edu

Faculty Contact
Sherri Lind Hughes
Telephone: (410) 857-2525
shughes@wmdc.edu

Admission Deadlines

Rolling admissions

Online Application:	YES

West Virginia University

Morgantown, West Virginia
College of Business

Degree

Master of Science in Human Resources and Industrial Relations (MSIR)

University Overview

West Virginia University (WVU) is a land grant university of 23,000 students located on the banks of the Monongahela River in Morgantown, West Virginia. Established in 1867, WVU is the state's major research, doctoral-degree-granting institution and one of only 88 Research I institutions recognized by the Carnegie Foundation. WVU is 75 miles south of Pittsburgh and three hours from Washington, DC.

Program Description

The program requires core courses in a wide array of HR/IR topics, including HR theory and strategy, benefits, compensation, labor relations, employment law, conflict management, and HR/IR strategy. Admission is competitive. The top 35-40 students in the applicant pool are admitted. Out-of-state students can matriculate at in-state tuition rates. Students without business undergraduate degrees are required to complete 6 hours in basic courses in accounting, economics, finance, marketing, and management.

Degree Requirements

Total Credits Required:	42-48
Average Credits per Course:	3
Course Schedule:	Semester
Total Courses Required:	14
HR/IR Courses Required:	14
Average Time for Completion:	13 months
Maximum Time Allowed for Completion:	7 years
Accepts Credits from Other Universities:	YES
Total:	N/A

Tuition

In-state	$1,850	(per year)
	$225	(per credit hour)
Out-of-state	$4,300	(per year)
	N/A	(per credit hour)

Program Delivery

Traditional Day Program:	YES
Nontraditional Program:	NO
Evening Program:	NO
Weekend Program:	NO
Summer Courses:	N/A
Some Courses Online:	YES
Full Program Online:	NO
Distance Learning/Offsite:	YES
Executive Education:	N/A
Overseas Study Abroad:	YES

Faculty

Full-Time Faculty:	10
Part-Time Faculty:	2
Faculty to Student Ratio:	1:10

Primary Teaching Methods:

Lecture	Team Projects
Experiential Learning	Student Presentations

Faculty Who Consult Outside: 50-74%

Faculty Involvement:
Board member, World Assoc. of Case Methods and Research
President, Graduate Opportunities for Advanced Level Studies

Top 5 Faculty Publications:
Journal of Organizational Development
Academy of Management Journal
Journal of Social Psychology
Journal of Business Ethics

Students

Total Enrollment:			50
Full-Time Enrollment:			100%
Men:	52%	Women:	48%
Hispanic:	4%	African-American:	10%
Other Minorities:	27%	International:	16%
Average Age:	25	Age Range:	22-38
Work Full Time:			25-49%
HR Experience:			1-24%
Speak 2nd Language:			1-24%

Minimum Admission Requirements:

GMAT/GRE Scores:	50th Percentile

Other Considerations:
Work experience, writing sample, and references

Average Student Profiles:

Work experience:	3 years
GMAT and GRE Scores:	over 50th percentile
UGPA:	3.5

Program Resources

Students Required to Have Computers:	N/A
Video Teleconferencing:	YES
Physical Library Facilities:	N/A
Online Library Facilities:	N/A
HRCI Certification Preparation:	YES
Encourages student study groups:	
SHRM Student Chapter:	YES
Fellowships:	NO
Scholarships:	NO
Assistantships:	NO
Eligibility:	N/A

Curriculum

Required Courses:
Accounting
Finance
Marketing
HR Strategy
Compensation/Benefits
Development/Training
Recruitment/Retention
Employment Law
Management
Employee Relations
Labor Relations
Business Functional Areas

Most Popular Elective Courses:

Interviewing	Leadership and Work
HRIS	Group Dynamics
Negotiation Strategy	

Career Tracks/Concentrations:	N/A
Internship Required:	NO

Career Services

Career Development Opportunities/Placement Service:

Mentoring, Field Trips	SHRM Student Chapter
Resume Services	Interview Training
Campus Interview	Internships

Summer Internship Placement Rate:	N/A
Full-Time Placement Rate:	N/A
Average Starting Salary (Full-Time Graduates):	$55,000
Average Sign-on Bonus:	$3,000
Companies Recruiting HR Master's Graduates:	27

Points of Excellence

Curriculum: The MSIR/HR curriculum is constantly being updated to meet the leadership/business expectations of the HR/IR professional. The curriculum is designed with input from an advisory board of prominent alumni. It benchmarks other leading IR/HR schools. As the field evolves, so does the curriculum with innovative courses in HRIS, conflict management, HR strategy, and international HR with a continuous emphasis on leadership in the HR/IR profession.

Faculty: The faculty is highly interdisciplinary with terminal degrees in HR, Management, Law, Economics, Business Administration, Information Systems, Public Administration, and Psychology. They are concerned about the quality of the MS HR/IR graduate and are excellent in the classroom. Teaching excellence is a priority. Faculty incorporate their research and consulting experience into the classroom and require pragmatic project work/presentations from the students. There is considerable experiential learning from mock arbitration to salary surveys to design and delivery of training packages.

Placement: The program makes extensive use of the alumni. An active Alumni Executive Board is utilized for program innovation, advice, and support in expertise and financial contribution.

Each Friday is set aside for workshops and seminars by visiting HR/IR professionals and academics. Topics might be as varied as leadership development in a particular company to lectures on the evolution of Chinese HR/IR. Each year an alumni-sponsored all-day workshop brings in state-of-the-art national consultants to present on the hot topic of the year. Alumni are also instrumental in graduate placement and in subsequent career moves via an extensive networking system.

Contact Information
Director of MSIR Program
West Virginia University
P.O. Box 6025
Morgantown, WV 26506
www.be.wvu.edu/grad/msir/index.htm

Dr. Randyl D. Elkin, Director of MSIR Program
Telephone: (304)293-7922   FAX: (304) 293-8905
elkin@be.wvu.edu

Admission Deadlines
Online Application: YES

Widener University

Chester, Pennsylvania
School of Business Administration

Degree
Master of Science in Human Resource Management (MSHRM)

University Overview
Comprehensive private institution with campuses located in Pennsylvania and Delaware serving educational needs of students through degree programs ranging from associate to doctoral level.

Program Description
The MSHR offers HR generalists and specialists the opportunity to prepare for changing roles in functional areas such as OD, compensation and benefits, legal aspects, and HR policy and strategy.

Degree Requirements
Total Credits Required:	33
Average Credits per Course:	3
Course Schedule:	Semester
Total Courses Required:	11
HR/IR Courses Required:	9
Average Time for Completion:	2-3 years
Maximum Time Allowed for Completion:	7 years
Accepts Credits from Other Universities:	YES
Total:	6 Hours

Tuition
In-state	N/A	(per year)
	$545	(per credit hour)
Out-of-state	N/A	(per year)
	$545	(per credit hour)

Program Delivery
Traditional Day Program:	NO
Nontraditional Program:	YES
Evening Program:	YES
Weekend Program:	YES
Summer Courses:	YES
Some Courses Online:	NO
Full Program Online:	NO

Distance Learning/Offsite:	NO
Executive Education:	NO
Overseas Study Abroad:	NO

Faculty
Full-Time Faculty:	4
Part-Time Faculty:	4
Faculty to Student Ratio:	1:20

Primary Teaching Methods:
Case Study	Student Presentations
Team Projects	Group Discussion

Faculty Who Consult Outside:	50%
Faculty Involvement:	N/A
Top 5 Faculty Publications:	N/A

Students
Total Enrollment:			49
Full-Time Enrollment:			8%
Men:	26%	Women:	74%
Hispanic:	N/A	African-American:	N/A
Other Minorities:	N/A	International:	N/A
Average Age:	31	Age Range:	23-60
Work Full Time:			75-99%
HR Experience:			75-99%
Speak 2nd Language:			1-24%

Minimum Admission Requirements:
GMAT Score:	450
UGPA:	2.5

Other Considerations:
Work experience

Average Student Profile:
GMAT Score:	508
Work experience:	5 years

Program Resources
Students Required to Have Computers:	NO
Video Teleconferencing:	NO
Physical Library Facilities:	YES
Online Library Facilities:	YES
HRCI Certification Preparation:	NO
SHRM Student Chapter:	YES
Fellowships:	NO
Scholarships:	NO
Assistantships:	YES
Eligibility:	N/A

Curriculum
Required Courses:
HR Strategy
Recruitment/Retention
Employment Law
Organization
HR Management
HR Measurement
Current HR Issues

Most Popular Elective Courses:
Organizational Development
Training & Development
Compensation
Consulting Skills
Effective Teamwork
Social, Ethical & Global Issues

Career Tracks/Concentrations:	N/A
Internship Required:	NO

Career Services
Career Services Offered:
Mentoring	Interview Training
SHRM Student Chapter	Campus Interviews

159

Internships	Resume Services	
Skills Assessment	Alumni Networking	
Summer Internship Placement Rate:		N/A
Full-Time Placement Rate:		N/A
Average Starting Salary (Full-Time Graduates):		N/A
Average Sign-on Bonus:		N/A
Companies Recruiting HR Master's Graduates:		N/A

Points of Excellence

Curriculum: Educational experiences, both applied and theoretical, are designed to help human resource professionals understand and facilitate the human factors in an environment that is increasingly becoming service- and information-oriented. A case study approach is used in the classroom with full-time faculty working in concert with industrial specialists.

Students are able to take advantage of the comprehensive nature of Widener University by selecting courses in other graduate programs including Health & Medical Services Administration, Information Systems, Clinical Psychology, and Education.

Contact Information

Widener University
One University Place
Chester, PA 19013-4615
www.widener.edu
Gradbus.advise@widener.edu

Lisa B. Bussom, Asst. Dean, Graduate Business Program
Telephone: (610) 499-4305   FAX: (610) 499-4615
lisa.b.bussom@widener.edu

Admission Deadlines

Online Application:	NO

Xavier University

Cincinnati, Ohio
Department of Psychology

Degree

Master of Arts Industrial/Organizational Psychology

University Overview

Xavier University is a private, Jesuit-run institution located in Cincinnati, Ohio.

Program Description

Industrial/Organizational Psychology program emphasizes both research and applied skill sets. A research-based thesis and applied internship are required for degree completion.

Degree Requirements

Total Credits Required:	43
Average Credits per Course:	3
Course Schedule:	Semester
Total Courses Required:	10
HR/IR Courses Required:	9
Average Time for Completion:	2 ½ years
Maximum Time Allowed for Completion:	6 years
Accepts Credits from Other Universities:	YES
Total:	6 Hours

Tuition

In-state	$9,353	(per year)
	$435	(per credit hour)
Out-of-state	$9,353	(per year)
	$435	(per credit hour)

Program Delivery

Traditional Day Program:	YES
Nontraditional Program:	YES
Evening Program:	YES
Weekend Program:	NO
Program Completed Evening/Weekend:	NO
Summer Courses:	YES
Some Courses Online:	NO
Full Program Online:	NO
Distance Learning/Offsite:	NO
Executive Education:	NO
Overseas Study Abroad:	NO

Faculty

Full-Time Faculty:		2
Part-Time Faculty:		2
Faculty to Student Ratio:		1:10
Primary Teaching Methods:		
Experiential Learning	Team Projects	
Student Presentation	Lecture	
Faculty Who Consult Outside:		75-99%
Faculty Involvement:		
Top 5 Faculty Publications:		

Journal of Occupational and Organizational Psychology

Students

Total Enrollment:			20
Full-Time Enrollment:			100%
Men:	40%	Women:	60%
Hispanic:	0%	African-American:	10%
Other Minorities:	0%	International:	0%
Average Age:	24	Age Range:	23-37
Work Full Time:			1-24%
Have HR Experience:			1-24%
Speak 2nd Language:			25-49%
Minimum Admission Requirements:			
UGPA:			2.8
GRE or GMAT Scores:		GRE 400 Verbal, 400 Quantitative	
Work Experience:			NONE
Other Considerations:			

Work experience can compensate for lower GRE and GPA scores.

Average Student Profile:		
UGPA:		3.4
GMAT Score:	GRE 550 Verbal, 550 Quantitative	
Work Experience:		N/A

Program Resources

Students Required to Have Computers:			NO
Video Teleconferencing:			NO
Physical Library Facilities:			YES
Online Library Facilities:			YES
HRCI Certification Preparation:			NO
SHRM Student Chapter:			NO
URL:			
Fellowships:	NO	AMT:	
Scholarships:	NO	AMT:	
Assistantships:	YES	AMT:	$3,800/semester
Eligibility:		Full-Time Enrollment	

Curriculum

Required Courses:
Recruitment/Retention
Employment Law
Employee Relations
HR Measurement
Performance Assessment
Leadership

Most Popular Elective Courses:
  Training & Development
  Small Business Consulting
Career Tracks/Concentrations:

Management Consulting	HR Generalist
Marketing Analyst	Benefits/Compensation Analyst

Internship Required: YES

Career Services

Career Services Offered:
  Internships
Summer Internship Placement Rate: N/A
Facilitate Placement: NO
Full-Time Placement Rate: N/A
Internship Placement Rate: N/A
Average Starting Salary (Full-Time Graduates): $39,000
Average Sign-on Bonus: N/A
Companies Recruiting HR Master's Graduates:

Accenture Consulting	Children's Hospital
Chiquita Brands Company	(Cincinnati)
Information Resources Inc.	William M. Mercer, Inc.
OKI Systems	

Points of Excellence

The program limits admission to 10 students per year in order to provide high quality training by allowing students to develop a close working relationship with the faculty.

Contact Information

Xavier University
3800 Victory Parkway
Cincinnati, OH 45207-6511
www.xu.edu/psychology_grad/io_home.html

Administrative & Faculty Contact
Mark S. Nagy
Telephone: (513) 745-1958
nagyms@xu.edu

Admission Deadlines

March 1
Online Application: NO

Appendix A

Additional Resources

Graduate Program Directories

Business Week Online B-Schools Page
Information on full-time, part-time and executive MBA programs.
http://www.businessweek.com/bschools/

GradSchools.com
A comprehensive online source of graduate school information.
www.gradschools.com

Industrial Relations Research Association (IRRA) list of degree programs in industrial &
labor relations (both graduate and undergraduate).
http://www.irra.uiuc.edu

The International Association for Human Resource Information Management (IHRIM)
list of HRM programs (both graduate and undergraduate.)
http://www.ihrim.org/edcenter/hrprog/index.cfm

Peterson's Guide to Colleges and Universities.
www.petersons.com

Society for Industrial and Organizational Psychology (SIOP) list of graduate programs in
I/O psychology.
www.siop.org

SHRM Resources

Awards & Scholarships for HR Students
www.shrm.org/students/ (Click on "Awards, Grants & Scholarships")

SHRM Certification Preparation Courses
http://www.shrm.org/learning/cu.htm

SHRM Home Page
www.shrm.org

SHRM Membership Information
www.shrm.org/join

SHRM Professional Chapters—Contact Information
http://www.shrm.org/chapters/

SHRM Student Chapters—Contact Information
http://www.shrm.org/shrm-schapters/

SHRM Student Membership Home Page
www.shrm.org/students

Appendix B

SHRM Membership Information

The Society for Human Resource Management (SHRM®) is the world's largest association devoted to human resource management. Representing more than 165,000 individual members, the Society serves the needs of HR professionals by providing the most essential and comprehensive set of resources available. As an influential voice, SHRM is committed to advancing the human resource profession to ensure that HR is an essential and effective partner in developing and executing organizational strategy. Founded in 1948, SHRM currently has more than 500 affiliated chapters within the United States and members in more than 120 countries. Visit SHRM Online at **www.shrm.org**.

Membership in SHRM will enhance your career in many ways and can help you to:

- **Build Knowledge of the HR profession**
  Knowledge increases your value as an HR professional. SHRM is dedicated to providing the resources that are essential to staying in the forefront of the HR profession and increasing the HR competencies of its members.

- **Earn Professional Recognition**
  Employers, professionals and academics recognize SHRM as the leading HR organization. By joining SHRM, members demonstrate their commitment to the profession and their own continuing professional development.

- **Establish a Career Network of Highly Respected HR Professionals**
  Whether members are looking for advice, new ideas or even a new job, opportunity abounds within SHRM. Network with other leaders in the profession at SHRM seminars, conferences and online forums. As a benefit of membership, you will be listed in the SHRM online Membership Directory, a virtual "who's who" of the human resource profession.

SHRM Resources

What's in it for ME?

Whether members are looking for advice, new ideas or even a new job, opportunity abounds within SHRM*. Network with other leaders in the profession at SHRM seminars, conferences and online forums.

- Member-only areas of **SHRM Online®**, the premier web site for up-to-the-minute industry news, research results, publications, HR trends & forecasting, White Papers, and more. Use search agents to locate hot-button issues and resources

- A first-rate resource for **HR Jobs**—whether you're looking to fill a position, or to find a new job for yourself anywhere in the world

- Personalized answers to all of your HR-related questions by certified HR professionals in the **SHRM Information Center**—your HR hotline for help

- **SHRM Tookits**, including Benefits, Compensation, Workplace Diversity, Visa, Internship, Employee Relations, Elder Care, Layoff, and more

- **SHRM Forms Database**, including competitive practices, sample forms and policies, mission statements, RFPs, and job descriptions

- 165,000 of your professional peers and network with them through **HR Talk**, an online bulletin board service

- Cutting-edge **industry research** sponsored by the SHRM Research Department & SHRM Foundation on topics such as Job Absence and Turnover, 2001 Benefits Survey, and the Performance Management Survey

- Enhanced career skills by attending **discounted professional development** at SHRM Conferences & Seminars

- The online **SHRM Networking Directory**—a virtual "who's who" in the human resource profession

- Insightful current and archived issues of **publications** such as HR Magazine®, HR News®, SHRM® Legal Report, Workplace Visions®, Managing Smart, and more

- Active involvement in influencing legislation at state and national levels through **HRVoice**, your voice in government

- Opportunity to join the SHRM Global Forum® or one or more of the Professional Emphasis Groups (PEG's). These specialized groups provide continued professional development and networking by targeted area of interest

Let SHRM Work for You!

SHRM members receive free and unlimited professional answers to HR-related questions regarding new regulations, policies and general HR questions through the SHRM Information Center. Additionally, the SHRM Information Center is home to one of the world's largest HR libraries featuring thousands of resources, including electronic referrals, texts, journals, magazines and other research materials.

Staffed by certified HR professionals, the Information Center Specialists answer more than 60,000 questions each year—via phone, fax and e-mail—on a wide variety of topics related human resource management. Contact the SHRM Information Center toll-free at (800) 283-7476, option 5 (U.S. Only) or (703) 548-3440, option 5 or at **infocen@shrm.org**. (Members must have their valid member ID when requesting information.)

For more information about SHRM products and services, please visit **www.shrm.org/join** or call (800) 283-7476 (U.S. only) or (703) 548-3440. To join SHRM, complete the membership application located in the back of this directory and return it to SHRM.

** SHRM also offers student membership to qualified college students. Student members receive a different package of member benefits. For detailed information on student membership, please visit **www.shrm.org/students**.*

Appendix C

SHRM Professional Chapters

"Chapter Number" is used to identify chapter affiliation on your membership application and in SHRM records. For contact information, visit www.shrm.org/chapters.

LOCATION/CHAPTER	CITY	CHAPTER NUMBER
ALABAMA		
Birmingham SHRM	Birmingham	72
Calhoun County SHRM	Anniston	299
Cullman Area-SHRM	Cullman	598
East Alabama SHRM	Auburn/Opelika	161
Gadsden-Etowah SHRM	Gadsden	375
Marshall County HR Management Association	Guntersville	535
Mobile SHRM	Mobile	176
North Alabama Chapter of SHRM	Huntsville	253
Northwest Alabama SHRM	Winfield	338
SHRM SELMA	Selma	607
SHRM-Montgomery	Montgomery	92
Tennessee Valley Chapter of SHRM	Decatur	159
Tuscaloosa HR Professionals	Tuscaloosa	477
Wiregrass Human Resource Management Association	Dothan	158
ALASKA		
Anchorage SHRM	Anchorage	200
Juneau-Douglas Chapter	Juneau	357
Mat-Su Valley Chapter	Palmer	533
Northern Alaska Chapter	Fairbanks	453
ARIZONA		
Central Arizona HR Management Association	Casa Grande	301
East Valley HR Association	Phoenix	85
Metro Phoenix HR Association	Phoenix	52
Northern Arizona HR Association	Flagstaff	374
SHRM of Greater Tucson	Tucson	181
ARKANSAS		
Arkansas HR Association	Little Rock	90
NE Arkansas SHRM	Jonesboro	262
NOARK HR Association	Fayetteville/Bentonville	148
North Central Arkansas SHRM	Searcy	487
SHRM of Western Arkansas	Ft. Smith	187

LOCATION/CHAPTER	CITY	CHAPTER NUMBER
South Arkansas HR Association	El Dorado	373
West Central AR SHRM	Hot Springs	467
BAHAMAS		
Bahamas HR Development Assn	New Providence/Freeport	562
BERMUDA		
Bermuda Human Resource Association	Hamilton	115
CALIFORNIA		
Bay Area HR Executives Council	San Jose	344
Central Coast HR Association	Monterey	393
Central Valley HR Management Association	Modesto	499
HR Association of Central California	Fresno	107
Kern County Chapter of SHRM	Bakersfield	117
Northern California HR Association	San Francisco/Bay Area	47
Prof. In HR Assoc (PIHRA)	Los Angeles	30
Sacramento Area Human Resource Association	Sacramento	114
San Diego SHRM	San Diego	130
San Joaquin HR Association	Stockton	184
Santa Barbara HR Management Association	Santa Barbara	461
COLORADO		
Boulder Area HR Association	Boulder	362
Colorado Human Resource Association	Denver	40
Colorado Springs SHRM	Colorado Springs	411
High Country HR Association	Vail	401
Northern Colorado HR Association	Loveland	267
Western Colorado HR Association	Grand Junction	237
CONNECTICUT		
HR Association of Central Connecticut	Greater Hartford Area	332
HR Association of Greater New Haven	New Haven	389
Northwest Connecticut HR Association	Torrington	616
SHRM Western Connecticut	Danbury	441
SHRM-HR Leadership Association of Eastern CT	New London	589
Southern Connecticut Chapter	Darien	133
DELAWARE		
Del Mar Va Human Resources Group	Millsboro	572
Delaware Chapter SHRM	Wilmington	206
DISTRICT OF COLUMBIA		
HRA of the National Capital Area	Arlington, Virginia	25
FLORIDA		
Big Bend SHRM	Tallahassee	409
Central Florida HR Association	Orlando	50
Charlotte County SHRM	Punta Gorda	488
Greater Miami SHRM	Miami	38
Greater Pensacola Chap. of SHRM	Pensacola	88
HR Association of Broward County	Ft. Lauderdale	98
HR Association of Collier County	Naples	476
HR Tampa	Tampa	74
HRM Association of Palm Beach County	West Palm Beach	80
HRMA of Martin County, Inc.	Stuart	478
HRMA of SW Florida	Fort Myers	235
Jacksonville SHRM	Jacksonville	11
Lake-Sumter SHRM	Leesburg	483

LOCATION/CHAPTER	CITY	CHAPTER NUMBER
Mid-Florida SHRM	Lakeland	151
North Central Florida SHRM	Gainesville	216
Ocala HR Management Association	Ocala	429
Panhandle Personnel Association	Panama City	437
Sarasota HR Association	Sarasota	139
SHRM - Volusia/Flagler Chapter	Daytona Beach	546
SHRM/Emerald Coast Chapter	Ft. Walton Beach	459
South Brevard SHRM	Southern Brevard County	309
Space Coast HR Association	Cape Canaveral	68
St. Lucie County HR Association	Ft. Pierce	442
Suncoast HR Management Association	Clearwater	238
Treasure Coast HRA	Vero Beach	388
GEORGIA		
Athens Area SHRM	Athens	37
Augusta-Aiken SHRM	Augusta	581
Central Georgia Chapter SHRM	Conyers/Covington	141
Foothills of Georgia	Gainesville	624
Golden Isles SHRM	Brunswick	474
Greater Henry County Chapter of SHRM	McDonough	622
HR Middle Georgia	Macon	154
Laurens County HR Association	Dublin	335
Magnolia Midlands - SHRM	Statesboro	588
Northwest Georgia SHRM	Dalton	157
Savannah Area SHRM	Savannah	112
SHRM - Columbus Area	Columbus	128
SHRM Augusta Area Chapter	Augusta	43
SHRM Greater Rome Chamber of Comm.	Rome	520
SHRM-Atlanta	Atlanta	70
South Georgia Chapter	Thomasville	140
Southern Crescent SHRM	Morrow	605
Southwest Georgia SHRM/Albany Chapter	Albany	623
West Georgia SHRM	LaGrange	239
GUAM		
SHRM Guam		372
HAWAII		
Hawaii Island Chapter-SHRM	Hilo	443
Kauai Chapter-SHRM	Lihue	465
Maui Chapter-SHRM	Waikiki/Kahului	468
SHRM-Hawaii Chapter	Honolulu	208
IDAHO		
Eastern Idaho Chapter	Pocatello	110
HR Association of Treasure Valley	Boise/Nampa/Caldwell	111
Snake River Chapter SHRM	Twin Falls	226
ILLINOIS		
Bloomington-Normal HR Council	McLean County	64
Central Illinois HR Group	Champaign	246
Central Illinois SHRM	Springfield	223
Chicagoland's HR Association	Cook County	529
Decatur Area SHRM Chapter	Decatur	555
DuPage SHRM	Naperville	316
EA Human Resource Council	Peoria	326
HR Association of Greater Oak Brook	Oak Brook/Dupage County	212
HRA of East Central Illinois	Mattoon/Charleston	448
Illinois Valley Personnel Association	Princeton	596

LOCATION/CHAPTER	CITY	CHAPTER NUMBER
Kankakee Area HR Manager's Association	Iroquois/Kankakee	399
Northern Illinois SHRM	Lake Cty./North Cook Cty.	328
Northwest HR Council	Arlington Hts./Des Plaines	193
ILLINOIS continued		
Quincy Area Chapter of SHRM	Quincy	491
Rock River HR Prof. Association	Dixon	493
Rockford Area SHRM	Rockford	182
SHRM-Southwest Chicago Suburbs	Romeoville/Joliet	619
Society of HR Professionals of Greater (SHRP) Chicago	Chicago	4
Stateline SHRM	Crystal Lake	532
INDIANA		
East Central Indiana HR Association	Muncie	425
Eastern Indiana HR Association	Richmond	494
Evansville-Area Personnel Association	Evansville	32
Howard County Human Resources Association	Kokomo	573
HR Association of Central Indiana	Indianapolis	99
Michiana Chapter of SHRM	South Bend	16
Northeast Indiana HRA	Fort Wayne	174
Northern IN HR Mgmt Assn	LaPorte/Michigan City	452
Northwest Indiana Chapter of SHRM	Gary/Merrillville	270
South Central IN Human Resources Assn	Bloomington	512
Southeast Indiana HR Association	Columbus	549
Tippecanoe Area Personnel Association	Lafayette	127
Wabash Valley HRA	Terre Haute	22
IOWA		
Cedar Valley SHRM	Waterloo/Cedar Falls	93
Central Iowa Chapter of SHRM	Des Moines	34
Cyclone Country SHRM	Ames	191
Eastern Iowa HR Association	Cedar Rapids	300
Gateway Human Resource Association	Clinton	579
Great River HR Association	Rock Island	484
Human Resource Association of North Iowa	Mason City	423
Mississippi Valley HR Association	Burlington	247
Mt. Pleasant Area HR Association	Mt. Pleasant	594
Siouxland Chapter of SHRM	Sioux City	211
Southeast Iowa Chapter	Oskaloosa	507
Southwestern Iowa Chapter of SHRM	Creston	567
Tri-State HR Association	Dubuque	490
KANSAS		
Central Kansas SHRM Chapter	Hutchinson	75
HRMA of Johnson County	Overland Park	515
Jayhawk Chapter of SHRM	Lawrence	486
Salina HR Management Association	Salina	241
Southeast Kansas HR Association	Independence	553
Topeka Chapter SHRM	Topeka	428
Wichita Chapter of SHRM	Wichita	36
KENTUCKY		
Central Kentucky SHRM	Danville	396
Gateway Regional Chapter	Moorehead	612
Louisville SHRM Inc.	Louisville	73
Northern Kentucky HR Association	Florence	548
Paducah Area Employee Relations Association	Paducah	536
SHRM - Owensboro	Owensboro	103
SHRM-Bluegrass Chapter	Lexington	365

LOCATION/CHAPTER	CITY	CHAPTER NUMBER
Southern Kentucky SHRM	Bowling Green	410
Tri-County SHRM	Lebanon	584
Western Kentucky SHRM	Hopkinsville	385
LOUISIANA		
Acadiana SHRM	Lafayette	331
Bayou SHRM	Houma/Morgan City/Thibodaux	558
Central Louisiana SHRM	Alexandria	367
Greater Baton Rouge SHRM	Baton Rouge	257
HR Association of North Central LA	Ruston	354
HRMA of the New Orleans Area	New Orleans	63
Imperial Calcasieu HR Management Association	Lake Charles	402
Northeast Louisiana SHRM	Monroe	207
Northshore Region HR Association	Mandeville	580
Northwest Louisiana SHRM	Shreveport	258
MAINE		
HR Association of Southern Maine	South Portland	220
Maine Society for Healthcare HR Admin.	Augusta	599
Northeast Society of HR Management	Presque Isle/Caribou	283
SHRM-MIDCOAST-Maine	Rockland	610
MARYLAND		
Annapolis SHRM	Annapolis	574
Chesapeake HR Association Inc.	Baltimore	156
Frederick County Personnel Association	Frederick	231
Howard County Human Resources Society	Columbia	617
Montgomery County SHRM	Rockville	480
MASSACHUSETTS		
HR Management Association of Central MA	Worcester	41
HRMA of Western New England	Springfield/Holyoke	364
Metrowest HR Management Association	Framingham	454
Northeast Human Resources Association	MA/NH/RI/ME	561
MICHIGAN		
Association for Human Resource Management	Grand Rapids	435
Cadillac Area HR Association	Cadillac	361
Genesee Area HR Association	Flint	249
Greater Ann Arbor SHRM	Ann Arbor	408
HR Association of Greater Detroit	Detroit	29
HR Association of SE Michigan	Adrian	601
HR Council of Southwestern MI	St. Joseph	67
HR Group of Grand Rapids	Grand Rapids	57
HR Management Association of Mid-Michigan	Lansing	20
Kalamazoo HR Management Association	Kalamazoo	116
Lakeshore HR Management Association	Holland/Zeeland	282
Mid Michigan Human Resource Assn	Alma	426
Northeast Michigan Personnel Association	Alpena	421
Shiawassee Valley HR Management Association	Shiawassee County	534
South Central HR Management Association	Jackson	528
Traverse Area HRA	Traverse City	280
Valley Society of HR Managers	Saginaw	222
WATER	Muskegon/Big Rapids	632
MINNESOTA		
Brainerd Area Human Resource Association	Brainerd	566
Central Minnesota SHRM	St. Cloud	195
Hiawatha Valley SHRM	Red Wing	552

LOCATION/CHAPTER	CITY	CHAPTER NUMBER
North Star SHRM	Becker	621
Northland HR Association	Duluth	471
Rochester Human Resources Association	Rochester	550
SHRM-Southwest MN Chapter	Marshall	629
MINNESOTA continued		
South Central SHRM	Owatonna	591
Southern MN Area HR Association	Mankato	245
Twin Cities Human Resources Assn	Minneapolis/St. Paul	6
Winona Chapter SHRM	Winona	177
MISSISSIPPI		
Capital Area HR Association	Jackson	143
Delta HR Management Association	Greenwood/Cleveland	508
East Central Mississippi HR Association	Meridian	613
Golden Triangle Human Resource Association	Columbus	418
Harrison Hancock Chapter of SHRM	Gulfport	400
North Central MS HRA	Batesville/Grenada	602
Northeast Mississippi HR Association	Tupelo	196
South Mississippi Chap. of SHRM	Hattiesburg	79
MISSOURI		
HR Association of Central Missouri	Columbia/Jefferson City	201
HR Association of Northwest Missouri	St. Joseph	255
HRMA of Greater Kansas City	Kansas City	5
HRMA of Greater St. Louis	St. Louis	13
HRMA of West Central Missouri	Warrensburg	525
SE Missouri Personnel Association	Sikeston	427
Springfield Area HRA	Springfield	26
Tri-State Human Resources Association (MO)	Joplin	513
MONTANA		
Big Sky Chapter of SHRM	Missoula	104
Continental Divide Chapter	Butte	414
Flathead Valley Chapter	Kalispell	539
Gallatin Valley HR Association	Gallahn	415
Helena Chapter SHRM	Helena	286
Lake County Chapter of SHRM	Polson	611
SHRM of Great Falls	Great Falls	341
Yellowstone Valley Chapter of SHRM	Billings	315
NEBRASKA		
Central Nebraska HR Management Association	Grand Island	578
Great Plains HR Management Association	North Platte	564
HR Association of the Midlands	Omaha	19
Lincoln HR Management Association	Lincoln	48
NEVADA		
Northern Nevada HR Association	Reno	123
Sierra Nevada HR Assn	Carson City	565
Southern Nevada HR Association	Las Vegas	94
Tri-State HRA (AZ)	Bullhead/Kingman/Laughlin	506
NEW HAMPSHIRE		
Greater Nashua Area HR Association	Nashua	360
HRA Greater Concord, NH	Concord	462
Manchester Area HR Association	Manchester	198
Seacoast Human Resource Association	Portsmouth	451

LOCATION/CHAPTER	CITY	CHAPTER NUMBER
NEW JERSEY		
HR Association of Southern NJ	Millville	260
Human Resource Management Association	Trenton	152
Jersey Shore Association for HR	Tinton Falls	240
Morris County Area SHRM Chapter	Madison	224
North Jersey-Rockland SHRM	Haisbrouck Heights	125
SHRM - Gateway Chapter, Inc.	Jersey City	575
SHRM of Central New Jersey, Inc.	Somerset	142
Southern Shore HRMA of NJ	Atlantic City/Cape May	517
Sussex Warren HR Management Association	Newten	604
Tri-State HR Management Association	Cherry Hill	413
NEW MEXICO		
Four Corners HR Association	Farmington	523
HR Management Association of New Mexico	Albuquerque	66
Northern New Mexico HR Association	Santa Fe	455
Southeastern New Mexico HRA	Roswell	538
Southern New Mexico SHRM	Las Cruces	322
NEW YORK		
Capital Region HR Association	Albany	105
Central New York SHRM, Inc.	Syracuse	162
Champlain Valley HR Association	Plattsburgh	630
Genesee Valley Chapter SHRM	Rochester	395
HR Association of the Twin Tiers	Elmira/Horseheads	412
Human Resources Association of NY	New York City	1
Mid-Hudson HR Association	Poughkeepsie	524
Mid-Hudson Valley Chapter	Middletown/Newburgh	317
Mohawk Valley SHRM	Greater Utica	221
Niagara Frontier Chapter	Buffalo	232
North Country Human Resource Association	Jefferson/Lewis Counties	559
SHRM of Tompkins County	Ithaca	312
SHRM-Long Island Chapter Inc.	Long Island	213
Southern Tier Association for HR	Binghamton	343
St. Lawrence Valley HR Management Association	Potsdam	568
Westchester HR Management Association	White Plains	58
NORTH CAROLINA		
Central Carolina Personnel Association	Sanford	416
Charlotte Area Personnel Association	Charlotte	65
Fayetteville Area SHRM	Fayetteville	522
Golden East HR Management Association	Rocky Mount	626
HR Management Association of Greensboro	Greensboro	120
Iredell County Personnel Association	Statesville	210
Lower Cape Fear Personnel Association	Wilmington	101
North Carolina Coastal SHRM	Greenville	551
Raleigh/Wake HR Management Association	Raleigh	132
Rowan County HR Association	Salisbury	510
The Alamance County HR Association	Burlington	627
Triangle SHRM	Durham	76
Western North Carolina HR Association	Asheville	570
Winston-Salem SHRM	Winston Salem	86
NORTH DAKOTA		
Agassiz Valley Human Resource Association	Fargo	586
Central Dakota HR Association	Bismarck	250
Fargo-Moorhead HR Association	Fargo/Moorhead	259
Minot HR Association	Minot City	248
NE Dakota Area HR Association of SHRM	Grand Forks	276

LOCATION/CHAPTER	CITY	CHAPTER NUMBER
Southwest Area Human Resource Association	Dickinson	571
NORTHERN MARIANAS ISLANDS		
SHRM - Northern Marianas Chapter	Saipan	543
OHIO		
Akron Area Chapter of SHRM	Akron/Canton	9
Butler County SHRM	Hamilton/Fairfield/Oxford	3
Cleveland SHRM	Cleveland	44
Findlay Area HRA	Findlay	383
Greater Cincinnati HR Association	Cincinnati	8
Greater Lorain County Chap. SHRM	Lorain Cty	470
HRA of Central Ohio	Columbus	14
HRA of Southwestern Ohio	Wilmington	620
Lake/Geauga Area Chapter SHRM	Mentor/Willoughby	172
Lancaster Area SHRM	Fairfield County	391
Lima SHRM	Lima	18
Miami Valley HR Association	Dayton	194
Muskingum Valley HRMA	Muskingum	171
North Central Ohio PA of SHRM	Mansfield/Richland	87
Portage County HR Association	Kent	89
River Bend SHRM	Gallipolis/Pt. Pleasant WV	118
Sandusky County HR Management Association	Fremont	311
SHRM - Western Reserve Chapter	Niles	545
SHRM-Ashtabula Chapter	Ashtabula Cty	325
Southwestern Ohio SHRM	Wilmington	618
Springfield HR Management Association	Springfield	358
Steel Valley Human Resources Association	Weirton	31
The Toledo Area HR Association Inc.	Toledo	160
Tuscora Chapter of SHRM	New Philadelphia	597
Wayne Area HR Association	Wooster	108
OKLAHOMA		
Enid Chapter SHRM	Enid	289
Muskogee Area HR Association	Muskogee	273
Oklahoma City HR Society	Oklahoma City	129
SHRM-Woodward	Woodward	615
Southern Oklahoma HR Association	Duncan	631
Stillwater Area HR Association	Stillwater	554
Tulsa Area HR Association	Tulsa	175
OREGON		
Central Oregon Chapter	Bend	310
Columbia Gorge Chapter	Hood River	501
Klamath Basin Chapter of SHRM	Klamath Falls	569
Lane County HR Association	Eugene/ Springfield	168
Mid-Williamette Chapter	Corvallis	202
Portland HRMA	Portland	136
Rogue Valley Chapter	Medford	234
Salem Chapter	Salem	165
PENNSYLVANIA		
Berks County Chapter	West Reading	179
Butler Human Resources Association	Butler/Ceanberry	384
Cambria/Somerset HR Association	Johnstown/Somerset	329
Capital Area SHRM	Harrisburg	503
Chester County HR Association	Exton	614
Cumberland Valley Chapter of SHRM	Greencastle PA/Hagerstown	204
Greater Valley Forge HRA Inc.	King of Prussia/Malvern	405

LOCATION/CHAPTER	CITY	CHAPTER NUMBER
Greater Pottstown Area HR Association	Pottstown	469
Hanover Area Human Resource Association	Hanover	254
Harrisburg Area SHRM	Harrisburg	55
HR Association of Centre County	Bellefonte/State College	265
HR Mgmt Assn of North Central PA	DuBois	485
HR Management Association of Blair Cnty.	Altoona	21
HR Management Association of Northwest PA	Erie	35
Indiana County Area SHRM	Indiana	593
Lancaster County Association for HR	Lancaster	457
Lebanon Area Personnel Association	Lebanon	366
Lehigh Valley Chapter of SHRM	Bethlehem	150
Northeast PA Chapter (NEPA-SHRM)	Scranton/Pittson	519
Pittsburgh Human Resources Association	Pittsburgh	155
Schuylkill County SHRM	Schuylkill Haven	353
SHRM-Philadelphia Regional Chapter	Philadelphia	2
Southeastern PA SHRM Chapter	NE Phila. Bucks Co & Mont County	498
Susquehanna HR Management Association	Bloomsburg/Danville	131
West Branch HR Society	Williamsport	284
Westmoreland Human Resources Association	Greensburg	563
York Society for HR Management	York	444

PUERTO RICO

Puerto Rico-SHRM	San Juan	95

RHODE ISLAND

HR Management Association of Rhode Island	Providence	403
Southern RI HR Council	West Warwick	380

SOUTH CAROLINA

Anderson Area SHRM	Anderson	368
Coastal Organization of HR	Myrtle Beach	422
Columbia SHRM	Columbia	7
Greenville Area Personnel Association	Greenville	49
Midlands SHRM	Orangeburg	371
Oconee-Pickens Personnel Association	Seneca	173
Piedmont HR Management Association	Greenwood	349
Rock Hill Area Chapter of SHRM	Rock Hill	178
SHRM Pee Dee Chapter	Florence	576
Spartanburg HR Association	Spartanburg	77
Sumter Area Personnel Association	Sumter	458
Tri-County HR Management Association	Charleston	97

SOUTH DAKOTA

Aberdeen Human Resources Association	Aberdeen	496
Black Hills SHRM	Rapid City	336
Mitchell Area HR Association	Mitchell	544
Northeast South Dakota SHRM	Watertown	511
Sioux Empire SHRM	Sioux Falls	217
Southeast South Dakota SHRM	Yankton	595

TENNESSEE

Chattanooga HR Association	Chattanooga	387
Clarksville Area Chapter-SHRM	Clarksville	608
Highland Rim HR Management Association	Tullahoma/Lynchburg	285
Middle Tennessee SHRM	Nashville	83
Northeast Tennessee SHRM	Bristol	190
SHRM-Memphis Chapter	Memphis	134
South Central Tennessee Personnel Association	Mt. Pleasant	382
Stones River SHRM	Murfreesboro	541

LOCATION/CHAPTER	CITY	CHAPTER NUMBER
Tennessee Valley HR Association	Knoxville	347
Upper Cumberland SHRM	Cookeville	214
Volunteer Chapter SHRM	Dyersburg	272
TEXAS		
Austin HR Management Association, Inc.	Austin	244
Bay Area HR Management Association	Clear Lake	542
Big Country SHRM	Abilene	333
Brazos Valley HR Association	Bryan/College Station	330
Central Texas HR Management Assn	Temple	298
Concho Valley SHRM	San Angelo	230
Corpus Christi HR Management Association	Corpus Christi	185
Corsicana, Texas Chapter	Corsicana	582
Crosstimbers HR Management Association	Stephenville	439
Dallas HR Management Association, Inc.	Dallas	61
East Texas Human Resource Association	Longview	269
El Paso Society HRM	El Paso	292
Fort Worth HR Management Association	Ft. Worth	81
Houston HR Management Association	Houston	96
HR Prof. of the Permian Basin	Midland	319
Laredo Assn for HR Management	Laredo	433
Lower Valley Chapter SHRM	Brownsville/Harling	313
Lubbock Chapter of SHRM	Lubbock	186
Mid-Cities HR Association	Arlington	308
Mid-Tex Human Resource Management Association	Brownwood	609
Montgomery Cty. SHRM	The Woodlands	592
North Central Texas HR Association	Wichita Falls	271
North Texas HRMA	Denton	147
Panhandle HR Association	Amarillo	279
Pineywoods Chapter of SHRM	Nachadoches/Lufkin	603
Red River Valley HR Association	Paris	518
San Antonio HR Management Association	San Antonio	137
SHRM Heart of Texas Chapter	Waco	419
SHRM-Rio Grande Valley	Mc Allen	390
Southeast Texas HR Association	Beaumont	251
Texoma HR Management Association	Sherman and Denison	531
Tri-State SHRM Chapter	Texarkana	583
Williamson County HR Management Association, Inc.	Georgetown	577
UTAH		
Bridgerland SHRM	Logan	302
Color Country HR Association	St. George	479
HR Association of Central Utah	Provo	291
Northern Utah Chapter-SHRM	Ogden	218
Salt Lake SHRM	Salt Lake City	59
VERMONT		
Greater Rutland Area Personnel Executives	Rutland	502
Upper Valley HR Association	Lebanon/New Hampshire	606
Vermont Personnel Association	Burlington	119
VIRGINIA		
Charlottesville HR Association	Charlottesville	24
Dulles SHRM	Sterling	466
Fredericksburg Regional SHRM	Fredericksburg	417
Hampton Roads SHRM	Norfolk/Hampton	102
Leesburg/Greater Loudoun Chapter	Leesburg	537
New River Valley SHRM	Christiansburg	277
Northern Virginia SHRM	Arlington	324

LOCATION/CHAPTER	CITY	CHAPTER NUMBER
Richmond HR Management Association	Richmond	17
Roanoke Valley SHRM	Roanoke	82
Shenandoah Valley SHRM	Harrisonburg/Staunton	126
Southside Virginia SHRM	Danville	587
Southwest Virginia Personnel Association	Big Stone Gap	430
The SHRM of Central Virginia	Lynchburg	146
Twin County Virginia SHRM	Galax	590
Winchester Area SHRM	Winchester	446
VIRGIN ISLANDS		
The HR Association of St. Croix	St. Croix	625
Virgin Islands HR Mgmt Assoc.	St. Thomas/St. John	509
WASHINGTON		
Apple Valley HR Association	Wenatchee	540
Blue Mountain Chapter	Walla Walla	163
Columbia Basin Chapter	Richland	10
Lake Washington HR Association	Bellevue	320
Mt Baker Chapter of NHRMA & SHRM	Bellingham-Whatcom	209
Seattle Chapter	Seattle	100
SHRM Greater Grant County Chapter	Moses Lake	169
Skagit-Island HR Management Association	Sedro Woolley	492
Snohomish County Chapter NW HRMA	Everett	180
South King County Chapter	Federal Way/Auburn/Kent	434
South Puget Sound Chapter	Tacoma	167
Southwest Washington HR Mgmt Assn	Vancouver	585
Spokane Chapter	Spokane	166
West Sound HR Management Association	Bremerton	229
Yakima Valley Chapter	Yakima	261
WEST VIRGINIA		
Appalachian Chapter of the Virginias	Bluefield	481
Beckley Chapter of SHRM	Beckley	628
Mid Ohio Valley Chapter SHRM	Parkersburg	227
North Central West Virginia	Fairmont	475
SHRM Charleston Chapter	Charleston	323
Tri-State Chapter SHRM	Huntington	420
Upper Ohio Valley SHRM	Wheeling	560
WISCONSIN		
Blackhawk Human Resource Association	NC Wisconsin/NC Winn	71
Central Wisconsin SHRM	Wausau	138
Chippewa Valley SHRM	West Central WI	243
Fond du Lac Area HR Assn	Fond du Lac	495
Fox Valley Chapter-SHRM	WI Fox River Valley	78
Greater Madison Area SHRM, Inc.	Madison	53
Green Bay Area Chapter of SHRM	Green Bay	504
HRMA of Southeastern Wisconsin, Inc.	Milwaukee	15
Jefferson County HR Management Association	Jefferson County	557
La Crosse Area SHRM	La Crosse	288
Lakeshore Area HR Association	Manitowoc	505
Sheboygan Area Chapter-SHRM	Sheboygan	233
Stevens Point Area HR Association	Stevens Point	497
WYOMING		
Big Horn Mountain Chapter	Sheridan	431
Energy Capital Chapter of SHRM	Casper	340
Frontier Chapter	Cheyenne	295
Powder River Basin SHRM	Twin Falls	432

Appendix D

Society for Human Resource Management Student Chapters

Following is a list of colleges and universities with SHRM student chapters. Universities noted with an asterisk (*) have degree programs included in this directory. For chapter contact information and the most updated chapter list, visit www.shrm.org/students/chapters. "Chapter Number" is used to identify chapter affiliation on your membership application and in SHRM records.

STATE/UNIVERSITY	CHAPTER #
ALABAMA	
Auburn University - Auburn	#5005
Auburn University - Montgomery	#5059
Jacksonville State University	#5305
North Alabama Student Chapter	#5038
Troy State University - Dothan	#5110
Troy State University - Montgomery*	#5227
University of Alabama - Birmingham	#5344
University of North Alabama	#5314
University of South Alabama	#5121
ALASKA	
Alaska Pacific/Anchorage SHRM	#5269
ARIZONA	
Arizona State University	#5049
Arizona State University - West	#5024
Ottawa University - Phoenix	#5116
University of Arizona	#5215
ARKANSAS	
Arkansas State University	#5155
Harding University	#5032
University of Arkansas - Fayetteville	#5288
University of Arkansas - Little Rock	#5089
CALIFORNIA	
California Polytechnic State University - San Luis Obispo	#5168
California State University, Bakersfield	#5012
California State University, Chico	#5403
California State University, Fresno*	#5251
California State University, Hayward*	#5281
California State University, Long Beach*	#5234
California State University, Sacramento	#5092
Monterey Institute of International Studies*	#5282
Point Loma Nazarene University	#5470
San Francisco State University*	#5219
San Jose State University	#5062
Sonoma State University	#5122
COLORADO	
Colorado State University - Denver Center*	#5445
Colorado Technical University	#5474
Mesa State College	#5430
Metropolitan State College	#5322
University of Colorado - Boulder	#5043
University of Colorado - Colorado Springs	#5361
University of Colorado - Denver*	#5211
University of Southern Colorado	#5034
CONNECTICUT	
University of Connecticut	#5451
University of New Haven*	#5360
DELAWARE	
Wilmington College	#5237

STATE/UNIVERSITY	CHAPTER #
DISTRICT OF COLUMBIA	
Catholic University of America	#5240
George Washington University	#5073
FLORIDA	
Barry University	#5466
Florida Atlantic University - Davie	#5468
Florida Atlantic University	#5018
Florida Gulf Coast University	#5425
Florida Metropolitan University	#5284
Florida State University	#5259
Jacksonville University	#5102
National-Louis University –Tampa*	#493326
Nova Southeastern University*	#5006
Rollins College*	#5176
Saint Leo College - Tampa	#5394
St. Thomas University	#5144
Stetson University	#5301
University of Florida	#5253
University of Miami	#5383
University of North Florida*	#5098
University of West Florida*	#5180
Webster University	#5256
GEORGIA	
Georgia Southern University	#5187
Georgia State University*	#5046
Kennesaw State University*	#5338
Oglethorpe University	#5290
State University of West Georgia	#5029
Troy State University - Georgia Region	#5008
University of Georgia	#5021
Valdosta State University	#5469
GUAM	
University of Guam	#5356
HAWAII	
Hawaii Pacific University*	#5135
University of Hawaii*	#5061
IDAHO	
Boise State University	#5123
University of Idaho	#5053
ILLINOIS	
Benedictine University	#5379
Bradley University	#473262
DePaul University*	#5097
Eastern Illinois University	#5213
Elmhurst College	#5472
Illinois State University	#5162
Loyola University Chicago*	#5246
Northern Illinois University	#5124
Roosevelt University*	#5261
Southern Illinois University	#5131
Trinity College	#5171
University of Illinois*	#5132
University of Illinois - Chicago	#5308
Western Illinois University	#5077

STATE/UNIVERSITY	CHAPTER #
INDIANA	
Ball State University	#5081
Indiana Institute of Technology*	#5192
Indiana University - South Bend	#5311
Indiana University Northwest	#5318
Indiana/Purdue University - Ft. Wayne	#5167
Indiana/Purdue University - Indianapolis	#5404
Kentuckiana Student SHRM	#5247
Purdue University*	#5297
Purdue University Calumet	#5221
Purdue University North Central	#5307
St. Mary's College	#5320
University of Evansville	#5103
University of Notre Dame	#5173
University of Southern Indiana	#5093
Valparaiso University	#5310
IOWA	
Briar Cliff College	#5478
Buena Vista University	#5420
Drake University	#5387
Iowa State University*	#5040
Loras College	#5161
University of Iowa	#5107
University of Northern Iowa	#5244
KANSAS	
Kansas State University	#5148
South Central Kansas Student Chapter	#5461
University of Kansas	#5271
Wichita State University	#5022
KENTUCKY	
Murray State University	#5446
Western Kentucky University*	#5326
LOUISIANA	
Louisiana State University - Shreveport	#5335
Louisiana State University	#5300
Louisiana Tech University	#5125
McNeese State University	#5393
Nicholls State University	#5431
Southeastern Louisiana University	#5479
University of Louisiana - Monroe	#461888
University of New Orleans	#5390
MAINE	
University of Maine - Presque Isle	#5452
MARYLAND	
Loyola College in Maryland	#5372
Salisbury State University	#5457
Towson University*	#5051
University of Baltimore*	#5191
University of Maryland*	#5225
University of Maryland - Baltimore County	#5373
Western Maryland College*	#5459

STATE/UNIVERSITY	CHAPTER #
MASSACHUSETTS	
Bentley College	#5415
Northeastern University	#5163
Springfield College	#5197
University of Massachusetts - Amherst	#5294
MICHIGAN	
Central Michigan University	#5086
Davenport University	#5435
Eastern Michigan University*	#5041
Ferris State University	#5328
Grand Valley State University	#5119
Lawrence Tech University	#5233
Marygrove College*	#5302
Michigan State University*	#5094
Oakland University	#5378
University of Michigan - Dearborn	#5064
University of Michigan - Flint	#5453
Western Michigan University	#5364
MINNESOTA	
St. Cloud State University	#5388
University of Minnesota*	#5026
University of Minnesota - Duluth	#5262
University of St. Thomas*	#5255
Winona State University	#5362
MISSISSIPPI	
Mississippi State University	#5382
University of Mississippi	#5115
University of Southern Mississippi	#5471
MISSOURI	
Northwest Missouri State University	#5184
Southeast Missouri State University	#5209
Southwest Missouri State University*	#5149
St. Louis University	#5126
University of Missouri - Columbia	#5140
Washington University*	#5220
Webster University - St. Louis	#5487
MONTANA	
Montana State University - Bozeman	#5482
NEBRASKA	
Bellevue University	#5265
Creighton University	#5331
University of Nebraska - Lincoln	#5070
University of Nebraska - Omaha	#5141
University of Nebraska - Kearney	#5025
Wayne State College	#5264

STATE/UNIVERSITY	CHAPTER #
NEVADA	
University of Nevada - Las Vegas	#5273
University of Nevada - Reno	#480118
NEW JERSEY	
College of St. Elizabeth	#5045
Fairleigh Dickinson University*	#5334
Rider University	#5198
Rowan University	#5076
Rutgers University* - Graduate Chapter	#5154
Rutgers University	#5157
The College of New Jersey	#5223
NEW MEXICO	
Eastern New Mexico University	#5235
New Mexico State University	#5319
Southern Illinois University at Kirtland AFB	#5491
University of New Mexico	#5137
NEW YORK	
Adelphi University	#5476
Alfred University	#5258
Baruch College*	#5002
Binghamton University	#5341
Buffalo State College	#5158
Canisius College	#5392
Clarkson University	#5464
College of St. Rose	#5031
Columbia University Teachers College	#5007
Cornell University*	#5030
Le Moyne College	#5175
Long Island University*	#5295
New School University*	#5377
New York Institute of Technology*	#5460
New York University	#5357
Niagara University	#5268
Pace University - Pleasantville	#5366
Polytechnic University*	#5358
Rensselaer Polytechnic Inst.	#5397
NEW YORK continued	
St. Joseph's College*	#465362
St. Joseph's College - Brooklyn	#5449
SUNY - Albany	#5381
SUNY - Brockport	#5321
SUNY - Buffalo	#5091
SUNY - Geneseo	#5242
SUNY - Old Westbury	#5456
SUNY - Oswego	#5210
SUNY - Stonybrook	#5440
SUNY Institute of Technology	#5407
Syracuse University	#5090
Utica College	#5065
NORTH CAROLINA	
Appalachian State University*	#5111
Livingstone College	#5448
Meredith College	#5177
North Carolina State University	#5100

STATE/UNIVERSITY	CHAPTER #
Peace College	#5336
University of North Carolina - Charlotte	#5042
University of North Carolina - Greensboro	#5150
NORTH DAKOTA	
Minot State University	#5205
Tri-College SHRA (North Dakota)	#5417
OHIO	
Ashland University	#5462
Baldwin Wallace College	#5248
Bowling Green State University*	#5188
Capital University	#5376
Case Western Reserve University*	#5166
Cedarville College	#5350
Cleveland State University*	#5113
David N. Myers College	#5296
Franklin University	#5101
John Carroll University*	#5332
Kent State University	#5238
Marietta College	#5214
Miami Jacobs College	#5345
Miami University	#5202
Ohio State University*	#5142
Ohio University	#5186
Tiffin University	#5477
University of Akron	#5035
University of Cincinnati*	#5050
University of Findlay	#5133
University of Toledo	#5245
Wright State University	#5204
Youngstown State University	#5153
OKLAHOMA	
Northeastern Oklahoma State University	#5057
Oklahoma State University	#5114
Oral Roberts University	#5069
University of Central Oklahoma	#5232
University of Oklahoma - Offutt, NE	#502598
University of Tulsa	#5306
OREGON	
Portland State University	#5243
Southern Oregon University	#5222
University of Oregon	#5015
Willamette University - Atkinson	#5414
PENNSYLVANIA	
Albright College	#5312
Alvernia College	#5169
Bloomsburg University	#5044
Clarion University of Pennsylvania	#5352
Drexel University	#5052
Geneva College	#5010
Indiana University of Pennsylvania	#5181
Indiana University of Pennsylvania* - Graduate Chapter	#5182
Keystone College	#5439
King's College	#5239

STATE/UNIVERSITY	CHAPTER #
La Roche College*	#5347
Messiah College	#5285
Moravian College	#5134
Muhlenberg College	#5348
Pennsylvania State University*	#5413
Robert Morris College - Moon Township	#5066
Seton Hill College	#5434
Shippensburg University	#5454
Slippery Rock University	#5267
Saint Francis University*	#5298
Temple University - Philadelphia	#5118
University of Pittsburgh	#5483
University of Scranton*	#5037
Villanova University*	#5323
Widener University*	#5048
York College of Pennsylvania	#5374

PUERTO RICO

American University of Puerto Rico	#5481
Caribbean Center for Advanced Studies	#5349
Catholic University of Puerto Rico	#5096
Interamerican University - Arecibo	#5217
InterAmerican University of PR - Ponce	#5367
University of Puerto Rico - Bayamon	#5152
University of Puerto Rico - Aguadilla	#5437
University of Puerto Rico - Humacao	#5399
University of Puerto Rico - Mayaguez	#5333
University of Puerto Rico - Ponce	#5229
University of Puerto Rico - Rio Piedras	#5129
University of The Sacred Heart	#5013

RHODE ISLAND

Bryant College	#5412

SOUTH CAROLINA

Clemson University	#5075
College of Charleston	#480820
Saint Leo College - Shaw Campus	#5218
University of South Carolina*	#5117
University of South Carolina - Spartanburg	#5241
Winthrop College	#5074

SOUTH DAKOTA

Black Hills State University	#5231
Presentation College	#5486
University of South Dakota	#5283

TENNESSEE

Crichton College	#5450
East Tennessee State University	#5068
Freed-Hardeman University	#5429
Middle Tenn. State University - MBA	#5385
Middle Tennessee State University*	#5009
Tennessee State University	#5179
University of Memphis	#5185
University of Tennessee - Chattanooga*	#5280
University of Tennessee - Martin	#5279
Vanderbilt University*	#5343

STATE/UNIVERSITY	CHAPTER #
TEXAS	
Abilene Christian University	#5033
Baylor University	#5189
Houston Baptist University*	#5292
Lamar University	#5004
North Central Texas Student Chapter	#462104
Our Lady of the Lake University	#5353
St. Edward's University*	#5339
St. Mary's University	#5020
Southern Methodist University	#5400
Southwest Texas State University*	#5355
Tarleton State University - Central Texas	#5395
Tarleton State University*	#5329
Texas A & M University*	#5054
Texas A&M University - Corpus Christi	#5401
Texas A&M University - Commerce	#5165
Texas Christian University	#5139
Texas Women's University	#5287
University of Houston - Central Campus	#5455
University of Houston - University Park	#5011
University of Houston - Clear Lake*	#5146
University of North Texas	#5017
University of Texas - Arlington*	#5293
University of Texas - Austin (Graduate)	#5120
University of Texas - Austin (Undergraduate)	#5178
University of Texas - El Paso	#5365
University of Texas - Pan American	#5228
University of Texas - San Antonio	#5151
University of The Incarnate Word	#5428

UTAH

Brigham Young University*	#5023
Southern Utah University	#5475
University of Utah	#5028
Utah State University*	#5172
Utah Valley State College	#5484
Weber State University	#5391
Westminster College	#5108

VIRGINIA

George Mason University	#5375
James Madison University	#5303
Marymount University*	#5402
National-Louis University - McLean*	#5467
Old Dominion University	#5224
Radford University*	#5315
Roanoke Valley Student Chapter	#5299
Saint Leo College - Ft. Lee	#5203
Saint Leo College - Hampton Roads	#5354
Saint Leo College - Peninsula Chapter	#461883
Shenandoah University	#5423
Strayer University (VA Campus)	#5001
Troy State University - VA Region	#5080
University of Richmond	#5463
Virginia Commonwealth University*	#5027
Virginia Tech University	#5105

STATE/UNIVERSITY	CHAPTER #
WASHINGTON	
Central Washington University	#5201
Eastern Washington University	#5277
Gonzaga University	#5444
Pacific Lutheran University	#5313
University of Washington	#5104
Washington State University - Vancouver	#462157
Washington State University	#5072
Western Washington University	#5039
WEST VIRGINIA	
West Virginia Institute of Technology	#5060
West Virginia University*	#5127
WISCONSIN	
Marquette University*	#5236
Silver Lake College	#5485
University of Wisconsin - Eau Claire	#5250
University of Wisconsin - Green Bay	#5380
University of Wisconsin - La Crosse	#5266
University of Wisconsin - Madison*	#5164
University of Wisconsin - Milwaukee*	#5071
University of Wisconsin - Oshkosh	#5130
University of Wisconsin - Platteville	#5276
University of Wisconsin - Stevens Point	#5363
University of Wisconsin - Stout	#5418
University of Wisconsin - Whitewater*	#5249
Western Wisconsin Technical College	#5199

* Profiled in this directory.

Appendix E

How the SHRM Foundation Benefits You

The SHRM Foundation is a 501(c)(3) non-profit organizational affiliate of the Society for Human Resource Management (SHRM). Founded in 1966, the Foundation funds research, publications and a wide range of educational initiatives to advance the profession and enhance the effectiveness of HR professionals. With assets of more than $6 million, the SHRM Foundation serves as a catalyst for leading edge research. A volunteer board of leading academics and HR leaders governs the Foundation and contributions to the SHRM Foundation are tax-deductible.

Strategic Program Focus

Support Leading Edge Research

To help shape its research agenda, the Foundation keeps in close contact with top HR executives and top scholars. The Foundation has budgeted $300,000 for grants in 2002. Since 1998, 27 Foundation-funded projects have been completed and 78% of those have resulted in publications, presentations, or other significant impact. The SHRM Foundation is a co-sponsor of the prestigious $100,000 Michael R. Losey Human Resource Research Award.

Following is a list of 2002 SHRM Foundation research priorities and a sample of currently funded projects in each area:

HR Measurement:
- HRM and The Bottom Line: Does Industry Matter?
- Workplace Diversity and Corporate Performance

Global HR
- Global Ethical Dilemmas
- Women Expatriates

Technology:
- Influence of Information Technology on HR
- Recruiting in the 21st Century: Effect of Internet

Changing Role of HR Professional
- Changing Nature of the Employment Relationship

Presidential Initiatives:
- Making ERPs Work: The Strategic Importance of People
- HR Heroes: Profiles of Strategic Business Leaders

To maximize resources and impact, the SHRM Foundation often partners with companies and non-profit organizations on major research projects. For example, the groundbreaking book, *Making Mergers Work: The Strategic Importance of People,* was created in partnership with consulting firm Towers Perrin. *Financial Executive* magazine called the book "meaty, deep, and probing…. a valuable addition to the merger literature." The SHRM Foundation is now partnering with the Gallup Organization on a major research initiative to learn more about strategic HR leaders in a cross section of organizations.

Enhance HR Competencies

The Foundation conducts an annual Thought Leaders retreat to identify cutting edge issues shaping the future of the profession. It also creates materials and resources to assist HR professionals to better understand the personal and organizational impact of these issues. Through its sponsorship of the Masters Series at the SHRM Annual Conference, the Foundation brings together HR practitioners and leading thinkers in human resource management to explore provocative issues and share leadership insights.

Programs that enhance HR competencies:
- $250,000 grant to SHRM Information Center for technology and white papers
- Educational and certification scholarships for SHRM members
- Practical research and information
- Sponsorship of HR Surveys and Innovative Practices Award
- HR Challenges Ahead video and discussion guide

Bridge the Academic and HR Practitioner Communities

The updated 2nd edition of *Graduate Programs in Human Resource Management* provides a valuable tool for students and professionals seeking a degree program, recruiters looking for HR graduates and university officials interested in benchmarking their HR programs. To build bridges with the academic community, the Foundation works closely with the Academy of Management (AOM) and the Society for Industrial & Organizational Psychology (SIOP).

Academic/Practitioner Programs:
- Major sponsor of collegiate HR Games competition
- Major sponsor of HR/IR Conference on Innovative Teaching
- Student Scholarship program
- SHRM Chapter Advisor of the Year Award

For More Information

For more information on SHRM Foundation funding and projects, please visit the SHRM Foundation home page at www.shrm.org/foundation, or contact executive director Marty Walsh at (703) 535-6019 or mwalsh@shrm.org.

Appendix F

Send In Your Feedback

Has this directory been helpful to you? Would you like some additional information to be included in the next edition? Send in your ideas. To help us continually improve this product, please take a moment to complete this form and fax it back to the SHRM Foundation at (703) 535-6473. You can also e-mail your feedback to **bmcfarland@shrm.org**. *We want to hear from you!*

I am ❏ An HR practitioner seeking a grad program ❏ A recruiter
      ❏ A college student   ❏ A professor
      ❏ A university administrator   ❏ Other: _____

NOT HELPFUL   **VERY HELPFUL**

How helpful was this directory to you? (circle one)   1   2   3   4   5

Why? _____

_____

What information was missing from this book that should be included in future editions?

_____

_____

What did you like best about this directory? _____

_____

_____

What would you like to change about this directory? _____

_____

Do you know of a U.S. college or university with an HR-related master's program not included in this publication? If so, please let us know and we will invite them to submit a profile for the next edition. (Attach additional pages if needed.)

College/University: _____

Degree program: _____ State: _____ Web URL: _____

Contact Name: _____

Contact Phone or E-mail: _____

Your Name: _____ E-mail or Phone: _____

(Optional)

Thanks for your Feedback!

Alphabetical by College/University

Traditional Full-Time Programs

Evening or Weekend Programs

Programs that offer all or some courses Online

Programs that offer Distance Learning

Programs that provide HRCI Certification Preparation

JOIN SHRM TODAY! Membership Application

www.shrm.org
preferred method

FAX
(703) 535-6490

(800) 283-7476 *U.S. only*
(703) 548-3440
International access
TDD: (703) 548-6999

Society for Human Resource Management
P.O. Box 79482
Baltimore, MD 21279-0482, USA

MEMBERSHIP CATEGORIES

SHRM is an individual membership organization; it has no corporate or institutional memberships.

Please check one of the following three categories:

☐ **PROFESSIONAL MEMBER**
Individuals engaged in human resource management with at least three years of experience at the exempt level; or any individual certified by the Human Resource Certification Institute; or any faculty member with three or more years experience holding at least assistant professorial rank in HR; or full-time consultants with at least three years experience as an HR practitioner; or full-time attorneys with at least three years experience in counseling and advising clients on matters relating to the HR profession. Professional Members have voting rights and may hold office in the Society.

☐ **GENERAL MEMBER**
Individuals engaged in human resource management at the exempt level, but do not meet the requirements for Professional Member. General Members have voting rights, but may not hold office in the Society.

☐ **ASSOCIATE MEMBER**
Individuals in non-exempt human resource management positions as well as those who do not meet any of the foregoing categories, but have a bonafide interest in human resource management. Associate Members do not have voting rights and may not hold office in the Society.

*Full or part-time students are eligible for student membership rates. For more information, visit www.shrm.org/students.

*Individuals residing outside the United States qualify for the Online-only SHRM Global Forum. For more information, e-mail forum@shrm.org.

Additional Membership Opportunities

NOTE: Additional Membership Opportunities are available to SHRM Members. SHRM Student Members are eligible only to join the SHRM Global Forum.

☐ SHRM Global Forum®
The SHRM Global Forum provides information resources, networking and professional development opportunities for the global HR professional. **www.shrmglobal.org**

Professional Emphasis Groups (PEGs)
For continued professional development and networking by special interest.

☐ Media Human Resources Association® (MHRA)
MHRA serves human resource professionals within the print, broadcast and communications industry. **www.shrm.org/mhra**

☐ HR Technology X-Change™ (HRTX)
HRTX is designed for HR professionals interested in the strategic use of technology in the management of HR. **www.shrm.org/hrtx**

☐ SHRM Consultants Forum®
The SHRM Consultants Forum® serves to assist and encourage its members to advance their knowledge, skill and competency in the field of human resource management consulting. **www.shrm.org/consultants**

☐ Employment Management Association™ (EMA)
EMA provides employment-related programs, services and networking opportunities to individuals with employment accountabilities. **www.shrm.org/ema**

☐ SHRM High-Tech Net®
The SHRM High-Tech Net® provides networking and professional development opportunities to those involved in human resources in high-tech companies. **www.shrm.org/technet**

MEMBERSHIP DUES

IN ADDITION TO CHECKING 1 YEAR NATIONAL, please check all OTHER additional membership opportunities and calculate total. For example: 1 year National ($160) PLUS 1 year SHRM Global Forum ($95) would give an annual membership fee and total amount due SHRM of $255.

***NOTE:** SHRM membership is non-refundable and non-transferrable.*

***NOTE:** SHRM Global Forum and PEG membership expiration dates must coincide with SHRM National.*

Special First Year Offer!

☐ **1 Year National** . . . . ~~$160~~ **$145**
  ☐ 1 Year *SHRM Global Forum $95
  ☐ 1 Year SHRM High-Tech Net $100
  ☐ 1 Year MHRA $110
  ☐ 1 Year SHRM Consultants Forum $140
  ☐ 1 Year EMA. $75
  ☐ 1 Year HRTX $75

Total Amount Due to SHRM $ _____

Please Indicate Method of Payment
Allow 4-6 weeks for application processing if mailed. Immediate membership available via internet at www.shrm.org.

☐ Payment Enclosed. (US $/US bank only)

☐ Charge My: ☐ Visa ☐ MasterCard ☐ American Express
I authorize SHRM to charge my credit card $ _____

Credit Card #: _____

Daytime Phone #: _____

Name as it appears on credit card bill: _____

Expiration Date: _____

Signature: _____

☐ Bill Me $ _____. I understand my membership will not start until SHRM receives and processes my payment.

☐ SHRM only accepts P.O.s from government agencies.
P.O. Number: _____

SHRM annual dues are not deductible as charitable contributions for federal income tax purposes, but may be deductible as ordinary and necessary business expenses except that, under IRC section 162(e), 6.3% of the SHRM annual dues are not deductible. Additional dues categories of the SHRM Global Forum, MHRA, HRTX, SHRM Consultants Forum, EMA and SHRM High-Tech Net may be fully deductible, if considered as an ordinary and necessary business expense.

I hereby apply for membership in the Society for Human Resource Management and agree to pay the current applicable membership dues (of which $30 is applied towards HR Magazine and $25 for HRNews). I will abide by the SHRM Code of Ethical and Professional Standards in Human Resource Management. (Members may review the Code at www.shrm.org/ethics)

Signature _____ Date _____

Questions? (800) 283-7476 • (703) 548-3440 • TDD: (703) 548-6999 • E-mail: shrm@shrm.org

SOCIETY FOR HUMAN RESOURCE MANAGEMENT
MEMBERSHIP APPLICATION

DEMOGRAPHIC INFORMATION

Please complete the following: (This information assists us in analyzing the demographics of our membership and helps us to design new programming and other initiatives)

Gender: ☐ (Optional)
F   Female
M   Male

Birth Date: (Optional)
__ __/__ __/__ __
Month   Day   Year

Race/Ethnic Identification: ☐ (Optional)
0   Multi-cultural
1   American Indian/Alaskan Native
2   Asian/Pacific Islander
3   Black
4   Hispanic
5   White
6   Other: _____

Education: ☐
1   High School
2   Some College
3   Bachelor's Degree
4   Some College Beyond Bachelor's
5   Master's Degree
6   MBA
7   Doctorate

Company Size: ☐
1   Less than 100
2   100–499
3   500–999
4   1000–2499
5   2500–4999
6   5000–9999
7   10000–24999
8   25000 and over

Unit Level in Organization: ☐
1   Plant
2   Region
3   Division
4   Group
5   Subsidiary
6   Corporate
7   Other: _____

Department Size: ☐
0   Less than 5
1   5–9
2   10–24
3   25–49
4   50–99
5   100 and over

Title: ☐☐
(Mark the title that most closely describes your own)
13   President, CEO, Chairman, Partner, Principal
15   Vice President, Human Resources, Personnel or other Vice Presidents
17   Assistant /Associate Vice President, Human Resources, Personnel or other Assistant/Associate Vice Presidents

(continued)

20   Director, Human Resources, Personnel or other Directors
25   Assistant/Associate Director, Human Resources, Personnel or other Assistant/Associate Directors
30   Manager, Human Resources, Personnel, HR Generalist, or other Managers
35   Supervisor
40   Specialist
45   Administrator
47   Representative
50   Legal Counsel
55   Academician
60   Librarian
65   Consultant
99   Other: _____
_____

Function: ☐☐
50   HR Generalist
51   Employment/Recruitment
52   Benefits
53   Compensation
54   Labor/Industrial Relations
55   Training/Development
56   Organizational Development
57   Legal
58   Health/Safety/Security
59   Employee Assistance Programs
60   Employee Relations
61   Communications
62   EEO/Affirmative Action
63   HRIS
64   Research
65   Consultant
66   Administrative
67   International HRM
68   Diversity
99   Other: _____
_____

Business & Industry Code: ☐☐
70   Agriculture, Forestry, Fishing
71   Manufacturing (Non-Durable Goods)
72   Manufacturing (Durable Goods)
73   Transportation
74   Utilities
75   Wholesale/Retail Trade
76   Finance
77   Insurance
78   Services (Profit)
79   Services (Nonprofit)
80   Health
84   Real Estate
90   Educational Services
91   Government
92   Construction & Mining
93   Oil & Gas
95   Library—Corporate/Public/ Academic
96   Newspaper Publishing and Broadcasting
97   Independent Consultant
98   High-Tech
99   Other: _____
_____

MEMBER INFORMATION

Last Name _____   First Name _____   Middle Initial _____

Jr., Sr., Ph.D., etc. _____   SS# _____
(US Only--For Internal Purposes)

Certifications: ☐ PHR   ☐ SPHR   ☐ Other _____

Title _____

Company Name _____

Company Address _____

City _____   State/Province _____

Zip/Postal Code _____   Country _____

Phone # _____

Fax # _____

E-mail Address _____

Home Address _____

City _____   State/Province _____

Zip/Postal Code _____   Country _____

Phone # _____   Home e-mail: _____

Send Mail to: ☐ Home   ☐ Company

☐ Our member list is available to HR-related organizations. By checking this box, we will remove your name from this list.

☐ SHRM does not engage in the practice of selling members' e-mail addresses to any outside organizations. By checking here you will not receive any content-based or informational e-mails from and about SHRM as part of your membership.

Please indicate your SHRM chapter name/city & state OR number:

_____

CONVENIENT WAYS TO JOIN!

www.shrm.org (preferred method)

FAX to (703) 535-6490

(703) 548-3440 • 1-800-283-7476 • TDD: (703) 548-6999

Society for Human Resource Management
P.O. Box 79482,
Baltimore, MD 21279-0482, USA

For SHRM Headquarters Use Only

Date Entered: _____   Entered By: _____

ID #: _____

Date Pmt. rec'd. _____   Amt. _____

Co. Ck. _____   Pers. Ck. _____

Chapter Ck. _____

Source Code: EXT001